For Lo

We've come a long way from El Centro.

Best wishes,

Chuck

# Whirlwind and Storm

## A Connecticut Cavalry Officer in the Civil War and Reconstruction

**Charles E. Farnsworth**

OPEN BOOK
EDITIONS
A Berrett–Koehler Partner

# WHIRLWIND AND STORM
## A CONNECTICUT CAVALRY OFFICER IN THE CIVIL WAR AND RECONSTRUCTION

iUniverse books may be ordered through booksellers or by contacting:

iUniverse
1663 Liberty Drive
Bloomington, IN 47403
www.iuniverse.com
1-800-Authors (1-800-288-4677)

Because of the dynamic nature of the Internet, any web addresses or links contained in this book may have changed since publication and may no longer be valid. The views expressed in this work are solely those of the author and do not necessarily reflect the views of the publisher, and the publisher hereby disclaims any responsibility for them.

Cover design by Sam Farnsworth and James Gillispie.
Author photo by Mark Serr Photography.

Any people depicted in stock imagery provided by Thinkstock are models, and such images are being used for illustrative purposes only.
Certain stock imagery © Thinkstock.

ISBN: 978-1-4917-1963-3 (sc)
ISBN: 978-1-4917-1962-6 (hc)
ISBN: 978-1-4917-1964-0 (e)

Library of Congress Control Number: 2014900864

Printed in the United States of America.

iUniverse rev. date: 2/26/2014

*The Lord hath his way In the whirlwind and in the storm.*
-Epitaph on gravestone of Charles Farnsworth

Dedicated to the descendants of Lieutenant Colonel Charles Farnsworth, First Connecticut Cavalry Volunteers.

# Contents

# Illustrations

# Author's Note

The Civil War heroics of Lieutenant Colonel Charles Farnsworth are legendary in our family. We grew up with stories of the cavalry officer who took charge of his company of Connecticut horse soldiers and hunted down rebel irregulars, got shot, got captured, suffered for the Union cause. But it wasn't until the summer of 2000 during a show-and-tell dinner at a family reunion that I began wondering about his life.

Among photos and documents on display at a side table were a note from Abraham Lincoln and a later letter reporting the colonel's unexpected death. I thought both the note and the letter raised questions about the man and what had happened to him. What was his connection to the President? What really happened on the day he died? Was there more to his story than the legend? Well, my cousins told me, maybe so; they knew of a cardboard box of documents which included the colonel's diary and more than 135 of his letters, tied neatly in red ribbon. Rarely opened, they had been safely guarded by the family for more than 130 years. I decided to take a deeper, and then a broader look at my great grandfather's life. What I found proved far more intriguing than the family legend.

From 1860 to 1867, "Charlie," as he was universally known, wrote lively, opinionated letters to his family, initially about a gold rush as a youth, and then more extensively about fighting for the Union, his criticism of war leadership, his unbridled ambition for promotion, his harrowing eight months as a prisoner of war in Virginia, and his two years of early Reconstruction in Georgia. For a time, he also kept a small diary, loaded with terse but revealing notes about war and prison, and his plans for the future. In the diary, he encoded comments about romances with several women, especially of secret trysts with his future wife Harriet during a time he was engaged to another woman.

Although buffeted as a young adult by the abolition politics of the late 1850s, Charlie seemed slow to sense the impending crisis. Rejecting both the comfortable social life and political turbulence of his Norwich hometown, he decided to seek adventure and challenge at an early age. Barely out of secondary school, he moved to Chicago and got into the cast-iron stove business. A couple of years later, he joined the Pikes Peak gold rush of 1859. As 11 southern states seceded from the Union in early 1861, Charlie, back in Norwich, was undecided about his future. It was not until six months after the Civil War broke out that he decided to answer the call of his state and country, becoming a founding officer of the First Connecticut Cavalry Volunteers.

As an experienced horseman, the action and opportunities of the cavalry suited Charlie just fine. He undoubtedly thought it more glamorous—and less dangerous—than the infantry. But as bad luck would have it, riding out on horse patrols, he was nearly killed by a bushwhacker's musketshot to his chest, and later was captured and imprisoned by the Confederacy. Through it all, Charlie fought and suffered for the causes of abolition and union, sometimes pushing to the limit of the law in doing so. But he was also intent on gaining rank and position. Knowing that he was admired by senior officers, he kept a keen eye cocked for any chance to advance personally. He did not hesitate to pull political strings.

Leaving the army after two and a half years, Charlie used his family's connections with President Lincoln to become one of the first northern civilians allowed into Reconstruction Georgia. He made quick money as a commodities broker and then, seeking greater challenge and adventure in spite of his lack of farming experience, leased a run-down rice plantation, taking his young wife Harriet along into the remote and noxious lower Ogeechee River area.

Charlie could be brash, opinionated, proud, impulsive, and demanding. But he was highly-disciplined, perceptive, purposeful, and dependable. He preferred the outdoor rugged life, but thrived on romance and moved comfortably in the world of polite society. He expressed himself eloquently in his letters, but was not bookish. More than anything, he wanted adventure and personal success, and these goals sometimes outstripped prudent judgment. Men admired, trusted, and followed him. Women were attracted to him. He tried hard at every turn to join personal goals with the great causes of his time. Without trying to act idealistically, he usually did so.

It has been exhilarating but disconcerting, my plunge down the rabbit-hole of time, into Charlie's years in Norwich, the Shenandoah Valley,

Baltimore, a Richmond prison, and post-war Savannah. Like taking a vacation and meeting a man previously known only by his reputation. The Charlie I have come to know, and have described here, differs from the family legend, but is far more interesting.

I have tried to be fair and impartial in my views of this paternal great-grandfather; after all, a great-great-grandfather on my mother's side was Jefferson Davis.

Beyond Charlie's correspondence, I have resorted to official military records, Connecticut census and court records, newspapers, histories of the time, photographs and visits to sites where Charlie lived and fought, to fill out the picture of his life. Along the way, local historians and authors have generously helped me with their time and sources. This short biography is the product of that effort. Charlie's transcribed papers, annotated with my comments, appear in the appendix

Charlie was the pride (and worry) of his family, the one who struck out on his own at an early age, relentlessly seeking excitement and achievement. Caution was not his usual concern. But an over-weaning ambition can lead to heedlessness, and end in destruction. Such was the arc of his life.

# Chapter I

## Norwich and the Early Years

Charles Farnsworth was born in 1836 in Norwich, Connecticut, a small but prosperous New England port and industrial center with a population of 14,000. By the mid-1850s, shipping, shipbuilding, and manufacturing had made it one of the richest towns in Connecticut. It was estimated that Norwich led the state in the number of millionaires and had more millionaires per square mile than any city in America.[1]

C. B. Rogers & Co. was a major producer of wood-working machinery. The Falls Mill and the Shetucket Company were important cotton textile manufacturers, and the Yantic Mill, Uncas Mill, and A. P. Sturtevant Mill turned out large quantities of woolen products. Industries ran on hydraulic power, which had been harnessed at nearby Yantic Falls since the 1660s. The Bacon Manufacturing Company, Mowry Company, and Norwich Arms Company turned out tens of thousands of pistols, muskets, and rifles for the Union during the Civil War. Norwich was probably second only to Springfield, Massachusetts as a Northern armory. After the war, the Norwich arms companies collapsed.

Norwich harbor, nestled in a backwater where the Shetucket and Yantic Rivers flow together to form the Thames, served freight and passenger steamers bound for New York, Philadelphia, Boston, and even the West Indies. Livestock, lumber, furniture, saddles, and textiles were major exports. The Norwich & Worchester Railroad brought goods to the harbor from northern Connecticut and Massachusetts. Norwich had been a center of shipbuilding since colonial times, turning out schooners, whaling vessels, and, in the 1800s, coastal steamers—three of which were converted into gunships for the US navy during the Civil War.[2]

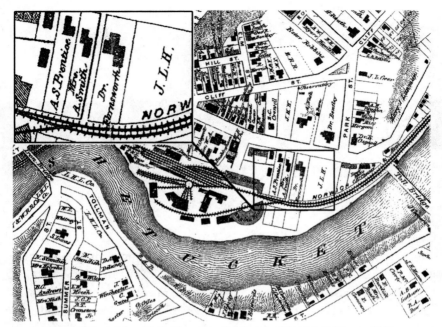

Central Norwich and the Farnsworth home on East Main Street, 1868.

Norwich was also a haven for the Underground Railroad, helping escaped slaves to get to Canada. Like Connecticut as a whole, Norwich rejected the Whig Party's half-measures toward abolition in 1856, voting solidly in the presidential election for Republican John C. Fremont, who nevertheless lost to Democrat James Buchanan. In 1858, Republican William A. Buckingham, the mayor of Norwich and a friend of Charlie's family, was elected governor of Connecticut on an anti-slavery platform. Two years later, he faced a strong challenge from Democrat Thomas Seymour, who argued that acceptance of southern slavery was constitutionally required. Abraham Lincoln, himself a candidate for high office, responded to Buckingham's call for support by campaigning in Norwich and four other Connecticut towns. Additional support for Buckingham—and the cause of abolition— was stirred up by the young "Wide-Awakes" with their dramatic evening torchlight parades. Still, Buckingham won by only 541 votes of more than 88,000 cast.[3] He never forgot Lincoln's helping hand, becoming one of the President's most reliable political supporters during the Civil War.

Charlie grew up in Norwich except for the six years (1845-50) that the family spent in Buffalo, New York, where is father helped found the anti-slavery Free Soil Party. On returning to Norwich, the family moved into an elegant home on East Main Street. After local elementary schooling, Charlie may have boarded at Monson Academy in Monson, Massachusetts. Testifying years later during an inquiry about Confederate prison conditions, Charlie referred to fellow officer William G. Ely, who did attend Monson, as a "schoolmate."[4] Unfortunately, Monson Academy records do not exist for the 1850s. There is no evidence Charlie attended college.

The Farnsworth family's Greek Revival home at 341 E. Main
St., Norwich, c. 1870. (Courtesy, Faith Jennings.)

In 1856, when he was only twenty, Charlie went off to Chicago, got into the iron foundry business, and was listed as a manufacturer of cast-iron stoves in the city directory for three years under the partnership name Johnston, Farnsworth & Co.[5] Charlie left the firm in 1859 for unknown reasons, although five years later he was forced to explain to his fiancée

3

what something he called "the Chicago affair" was all about.[6] In any case, Charlie went off to Denver in 1859, probably by train and then stagecoach, and observed firsthand the second year of the Pikes Peak gold rush. He seems not to have done any actual prospecting on that trip.

Returning to Chicago for the winter, Charlie went back to the Rockies in the spring of 1860 to try his hand at the actual enterprise of digging for gold. Perhaps feeling a bit chagrined about catching gold fever, he asked his brother Fred not to reveal his whereabouts to his parents. "If asked," he wrote, "say I am travelling, selling goods, and that I am not in Chicago much."[7] In the early spring of 1860, Charlie crossed the seven hundred miles from St. Joseph, Missouri, to Denver on a mule in the company of a family traveling in a mule-drawn wagon. It took them about three weeks.[8]

Covered wagon train near St. Joseph, Missouri, heading west, by unknown artist, c. 1859. Charlie would have crossed Nebraska to the Pikes Peak gold rush in a similar train (courtesy Atchison Historical Museum).

Charlie and two other prospectors then promptly hiked forty miles out of Denver into the Rockies, to "Mountain City," a settlement near present-day Central City, where they rented a cabin. A few days later, while looking at "quartz claims" about fifteen miles from the cabin, the men got trapped in a four-foot snow storm. They survived the night with nothing more than their overcoats and a campfire. After beating a hasty retreat from the spring storms back to Denver, Charlie thought about waiting until summer to go deeper into the mountains. But he also began to cast his eye about for real estate and other business opportunities in Denver itself.[9]

Whether he stayed longer in Denver is unknown. In the spring of 1861, after Abraham Lincoln had been elected and eleven states had seceded from the Union, Charlie was back in Norwich. The town and state were standing firmly with the new president, recognizing the bond he had cemented by his energetic campaigning for Buckingham a year earlier. Charlie's first response to the nation's political crisis was to try to get into the war supply business. He may have initially shied away from enlisting for combat because of the pessimistic tone of a letter he received from a friend, Captain E. K. Abbott, who was headed into the disastrous battle of First Manassas, July 1861.[10] (Abbott survived.) Instead, Charlie got letters of introduction from Governor Buckingham to promote a field tent to neighboring governors who were also raising armies.[11] The enterprise proved either unsuccessful or unsatisfying, however, and Charlie volunteered for military duty as an officer in mid-October 1861.

On both his paternal and maternal sides, Charlie descended from several generations of patriots and leaders. One grandfather, Amos Farnsworth, was a twenty-one year old farmer in Groton, Massachusetts, when he answered the call for American independence in April 1775 and marched off with his fellow minutemen to Concord just after the "shot heard 'round the world" was fired. The British had left before Amos and the others arrived, so they pushed on to Lexington, and then to Cambridge, from where they prepared a siege of the British position on what was erroneously called Bunker Hill. In an overwhelming counterattack by the British, Amos was shot in the forearm and back, but escaped and recovered. In 1776, he was sent west to defend Fort Ticonderoga, where he served as major of artillery.[12] (Amos's father, also named Amos, drowned while crossing the Lancaster River in Massachusetts in late 1775; taken together, the gunshot wound and the drowning might be seen as an eerie foreshadowing of Charlie's life.)

Charlie's father Ralph was a prominent doctor in Norwich for more than forty years, his practice renowned as "one of the best of any physician in Connecticut."[13] Ralph had risen from a modest farm family in Groton, Massachusetts, to finish seventh in the Harvard College class of 1821, a class that included Ralph Waldo Emerson. Ralph Farnsworth went on to earn a master's degree in 1825 and a medical degree in 1826, both at Dartmouth College. Two years later, he married Eunice Williams Billings, the twenty-four year old daughter of two prominent New London families, brought her up the Thames River to Norwich, and began his medical practice. For a year or so, he also taught chemistry at a local girls' school. In the 1830s, Ralph got caught up in the fervor of Connecticut's growing anti-slavery movement, and became a sponsor of the 1838 Connecticut Anti-Slavery Convention. But he also continued to enhance his reputation as a physician, getting himself appointed a public health officer in Norwich.[14]

In June 1845 Ralph moved his wife and three sons to Buffalo, New York.[15] His reasons are unclear, but probably included his disappointment that pro-slavery factions in Norwich had rioted earlier that year when abolitionist Henry B. Stanton was scheduled to speak at the town hall. The Second Congregational Church, to which the family belonged, had many free black members and had taken a strong abolitionist position. Determined to forge an effective political opposition to slavery, Ralph helped establish the Free Soil Party in Buffalo and served on its founding convention's select committee on delegates in 1848. Perhaps finding it too difficult to start a temporary medical practice with these political responsibilities, Ralph turned to commerce to support his family. He took a job at the G. S. Hazard grain-trading company, but still found time to serve as a vice-president of Buffalo's Association for the Relief of the Poor.[16] Upon returning to Norwich in 1850, Ralph re-established his medical practice while continuing to agitate for abolition, eventually through what emerged as the Republican Party, a movement that soon enjoyed wide support in Norwich.

When the Civil War broke out and Connecticut was given a quota for soldiers, Ralph was a harsh medical examiner of young men who were seeking to avoid service. In one instance, Ralph reportedly horse-whipped a malingerer, who thereupon quickly regained the use of his faked crippled leg.[17] Years later, the Norwich Medical Society remembered Ralph as "a man with the roughest kind of an exterior and the kindest kind of heart; a man of keen perception and ripe judgment; a man in advance of his time."[18]

Ralph provided his family with a comfortable living, but was not among the forty-six men listed by the Norwich assessor's office in 1865 as having annual income over $5,000. In the 1870 census, Ralph's personal assets were valued at $25,000 and his real estate at $8,000. Some of this came from his wife's family, and the money had enabled the couple to buy one of the finest homes in Norwich, at 341 East Main Street, a short distance from the governor's home.[19] In the 1840 census, the family listed three "free colored" domestic servants; in 1850, they had two servants, one Irish and one Negro; by 1860, the three servants listed were all from Ireland.[20] It would seem that Norwich's abolitionist fervor was making Ralph increasingly less comfortable with having even free black servants in the home.

Ralph's wife, the former Eunice Williams Billing, gave birth to nine children, Charlie coming in the middle. Only two others, Coddington Billings and Frederick, survived to adulthood. Charlie was the only one to serve during the Civil War; Billings, as he was known, was working in business and Fred was in college. Six other siblings—Walter, William, Isabella, Noyes, George, and Elizabeth—died before the war and before reaching age six. They are buried beneath a heartbreaking row of inscribed little gravestones at Yantic Cemetery in Norwich. A typical epitaph reads:

> Shed not for him the bitter tear,
> Nor give thyself to vain regret;
> 'Tis but the casket that lies here,
> The Gem that filled it sparkles yet.

Charlie's ambition to strike it rich through risky ventures—both before and after the war—was influenced by the family legacy of his mother, Eunice Williams Billings. Both the Williams and Billings families had prospered financially in ship-building, shipping, whaling, and other industries at New London and nearby Stonington. Eunice's father, Coddington Billings, a successful businessman and lawyer, became mayor and later a judge in New London. Her mother, the former Eunice Williams, by one account related years later, was thrifty but fun-loving. She reportedly bargained for almost anything at auctions, but would buy only if the price was right. She once brought home a coffin which, she told her husband, "will surely come in handy...and will do for either of us."[21] Unfortunately, it was used all too soon; she died a few years later when her daughter Eunice was only thirteen. The young Eunice was left desperately dependent for the approval of her father, as her long, apologetic, plaintive letters from Jamaica Plain Seminary, a boarding school in Massachusetts, pitifully reveal.[22] As an adult, Charlie's mother became a strong supporter and outspoken voice within Norwich's Second Congregational Church, donating a silver christening vase in 1845 after the former building had burned to the ground. One Sunday, upon hearing a patriotic, pro-Union sermon, Eunice, "a lady of dignity, arose in her seat in the rear of the gallery of the church, and shouted out 'Well done, good and faithful servant.'"[23]

The young Eunice's brothers, Noyes and William Williams Billings, grew up to carry on the Williams-Billings shipping and whaling businesses. Noyes became the mayor of New London (as had his father before him), and later was elected lieutenant governor of Connecticut as a Democrat.[24] Noyes provided $3,610 in 1833 for Ralph and Eunice to purchase their first home, near the Norwich ship harbor at 62-66 Main Street. Probably to protect the Billings family interests, the deed was taken in Eunice's name alone.[25] Ralph and Eunice sold the home in 1845 and moved to Buffalo, New York, but returned to Norwich in 1850, purchasing a Greek Revival-style house with a wrap-around porch at 341 E. Main Street, just down the way from the home of Norwich mayor, and the state's future governor, William Buckingham, for whom Ralph would become personal physician.[26]

The Billings brothers allowed brother-in-law Ralph to buy into their whaling business, to the latter's considerable profit. In return, Ralph apparently provided medical services to the company's seamen.[27] While the company continued its shipping business, whaling operations were shut down in 1851. It had been a dangerous enterprise: the Smithsonian Museum owns a painting based on a sketch by whaleman Cornelius Hulsart, who lost an arm as a member of the crew of the Billings's ship *Superior* while trying to subdue an enraged whale that they had harpooned.[28]

Conscious of his grandfather's valiant service in the Revolutionary War and his father's role in founding the Free Soil Party, Charlie, twenty-five years old in late 1861, probably felt pressure to serve the Union cause. Many of his Norwich friends were volunteering, and the college-educated Protestant elite of the time (which would include Charlie's family, even if he himself eschewed college) felt a duty to improve the world, in this case by shaping the South in the image of the North. To respond to the Union cause would show "character"—confidence and selflessness—which was highly prized.[29] For Charlie, however, joining the cavalry may have been just another of the exciting adventures that he was repeatedly drawn to.

"Capturing a Sperm Whale," 1835, by Cornelius Hulsurt, a crew member of the *Superior*, a whaler owned by the Billings family. Hulsurt lost an arm in the struggle to land the whale (courtesy Smithsonian American Art Museum).

# Chapter II

## Into the Whirlwind

When Lincoln was elected in November 1860, Charlie was twenty-four years old, unemployed, and living in his parents' stately home on East Main Street in Norwich. He had tried the iron foundry business in Chicago and had prospected for gold in the Rocky Mountains—both without success. He had not attended college. Nor had he gotten caught up in the struggle for abolition, as his father and many New Englanders had. On the contrary, Charlie apparently was enjoying Norwich social life as a young man without serious concerns.[30]

After war broke out in April 1861, Charlie contemplated a business of selling tents to the army and got letters of recommendation from two governors for that purpose. The project didn't get far, however, and in October Charlie volunteered for military duty. An accomplished horseman, Charlie was commissioned by Governor Buckingham as a lieutenant in the newly-formed First Battalion Connecticut Cavalry Volunteers in late 1861, assigned to duty as the battalion's adjutant, and ordered for training at Meriden, Connecticut, thirty-five miles west of Norwich.[31]

Governor Buckingham himself had come to politics and the cause of abolition in mid-life after a successful career as a businessman known for his keen financial sense and strict scruples. He had been elected mayor of Norwich four times between 1849 and 1857. Instrumental in forming the Connecticut Republican Party in 1856 (on the platform of "free soil, free labor, free speech, and free men"), he was elected governor in 1858. When Buckingham ran for re-election in 1860, Abraham Lincoln helped him defeat his Democratic opponent by giving five speeches in the state—one of them in Norwich. In return, Buckingham became one of Lincoln's most dependable allies throughout the war, enthusiastically supporting the president's limited suspension of the writ of habeas corpus and his issuance of the Emancipation Proclamation. The son of a farmer, Buckingham did not attend college, but had made a name for himself earlier as an honest and successful merchant in Norwich.[32]

Buckingham was a close friend of Charlie's parents. Both families belonged to Norwich's Second Congregational Church. It would be Charlie's good fortune to have such a staunch friend on his side during and after the war. The family enjoyed many dinners with the governor, but had to do without their usual wine; Buckingham was also president of Connecticut's Temperance Union.[33]

Upon reporting for cavalry training in Meriden, Charlie was faced with the task of selecting a good horse for himself. Within days, his uncle Walter Farnsworth was recommending a horse for him to buy, but Charlie thought he would do just as well if he picked a free one from the battalion's herd of three hundred.[34] Rising quickly in rank and leaving the softer life of an adjutant behind, Charlie, as a captain, took command of the battalion's Company B.[35] Although he was provided with a free horse, Charlie had to pay for his own sidearm and ammunition.[36]

The federal government had ordered the Northern states to equip their own troops, but Connecticut, like other states, was financially ill-prepared to do so. In the crisis, Governor Buckingham borrowed $50,000 against his own property, and donated the funds to help equip Connecticut's early regiments.[37] States also were required to raise troops in proportion to their population, but here Connecticut had little trouble, always meeting its quota, with or without the threat of a draft and with or without bonuses or the option of hiring a substitute.[38] The state's major contribution to the war effort was due in large part to the patriotic and energetic efforts of Buckingham.

Charlie's battalion trained in fair weather and snowstorms at Meriden for four months, the fine horses issued to them being quartered better than the men who rode them, according to one officer.[39] Charlie and the other 345 members of the battalion, commanded by Major Judson M. Lyon (whom Charlie would come to loath), were then ordered to Wheeling, Virginia.[40] Departing February 20, the battalion rode to New Haven, took a boat to Perth Amboy, New Jersey, boarded a train for Pittsburgh, and then took a frigid boat-ride down the Ohio River to Wheeling, arriving February 24.[41] Before Charlie left, his brethren at the Meriden Masonic Lodge No. 77 awarded him the honor of "Sublime Degree of Master Mason," with their highest regards.[42]

Charlie as a Lieutenant, November 1861 (unknown photographer).

Charlie as a Captain, May 1862 (photograph by W. H. Jennings, Norwich).

Charlie quickly exhibited his enthusiasm for rigorous training, especially for the traditional open-field cavalry charges he dreamed of—but would ultimately never see. At Wheeling, he drove his Company B across muddy terrain so heedlessly that several horses and men were injured. The troops recovered; the horses had to be destroyed.[43] Such hard experience would soon teach Union cavalrymen to take better care of their mounts, and higher command later issued orders that prohibited riding at faster than a walk except while in combat, even requiring the cavalrymen to dismount and walk beside their horses periodically.[44]

But it was not all training and no play during the battalion's months in Meriden. Charlie met, courted, and became engaged to be married to Georgia Ann Parker, the 24-year old daughter of one of Meriden's well-established families.[45] Her father Edmund was a successful silversmith and hardware manufacturer, but, unlike the Farnsworth family, was not an abolitionist. He and his brothers were outspoken Democrats, at least until Lincoln's election. Secession by several southern states changed the stance of Georgia's uncle Charles, who joined the Unionist cause and took charge of raising troops for Meriden's first infantry regiment. His leadership later got him elected mayor of the town.[46] Georgia's father Edmund, however, apparently never got aboard the Unionist bandwagon, and may have become a member of the Peace Democrats, who argued that Washington had no right to militarily resist the southern states' right to secede. While political differences did not keep Charlie and Georgia from falling for each other, some friction between their families over politics probably lingered.

## The Bushwhacker Scourge

After another month of training, the First Connecticut troopers and their mounts traveled by the Baltimore & Ohio Railway to Winchester in the Shenandoah Valley of Virginia, and then rode the final thirty miles to Camp Durfee in Moorefield, reporting for duty with General John C. Fremont's Mountain Department about March 29. The battalion was promptly assigned the task of subduing the many non-uniformed Confederate irregulars who had been raiding and harassing nearby encampments of infantry regiments. A day after he arrived, Charlie headed out on his first mounted patrol in search of the so-called "bushwhackers," who were hard to identify because they tended to meld back into the local farming populace after their raids. On April 3rd, his fourth or fifth day of scouting, Charlie's twelve-man patrol was ambushed by fourteen bushwhackers concealed on a hill above a rocky ravine about seven miles along a road from Moorefield toward Strasburg. According to one member of the battalion, Charlie had mistakenly led his men out of camp along a wrong route, and was reversing course when the attack came.[47] But it probably didn't matter; the patrol could have been ambushed anywhere in the Shenandoah.

Road from Moorefield to Strasburg, Virginia, along which Charlie was ambushed in April 1862 (photograph by author, September 2010).

In the attack, Charlie was shot through his left arm and chest by at least one musket ball. Although bleeding profusely and doubtlessly in great pain, he valiantly led his patrol in a counterattack, "driving with his few men the rebel cowards from their position."[48] Battalion bugler Herman Voltz was also severely wounded in the attack. Both he and Charlie were brought back to Camp Durfee for emergency treatment at a field hospital.

The number of shots and the exact location of Charlie's wounds have been somewhat unclear from the outset. Charlie initially wrote that a single shot had pierced his left ribs and lung, without mentioning any wound to his left arm—probably because the wound to his chest was so much more serious.[49] A member of the battalion, acting as newspaper correspondent, also reported one shot, "the ball having entered the thick of his arm, on the inside, passing through into his side, following a rib around, and coming out his back."[50] Five years later, however, a Norwich surgeon concluded that one shot had entered the left side of Charlie's chest, exiting near the spine, and a second shot had struck his left arm.[51] The earlier reports of a single musket ball probably were more accurate; the Norwich surgeon may have made unjustifiable assumptions later from the observable scars. In any case, it was an odd coincidence that Charlie suffered nearly the same gunshot wounds as his Revolutionary War grandfather Amos had—and would similarly recover.

Charlie was lucky to have a doctor in the family, and one who had political connections. Informed of his son's potentially fatal injuries, his father Dr. Ralph, along with his brother Billings, got letters of introduction from Governor Buckingham and rushed down to Moorefield to take care of Charlie.[52] The army gave Charlie a sixty-day leave, and he went home with his father to Norwich to recuperate.[53] Billings stayed on awhile at Moorefield, riding out on long scouting patrols with his brother's troops.[54]

The motivations of the Confederate bushwhackers are unclear. The lower Shenandoah Valley was intensely contested during the Civil War, with its major town of Winchester, Virginia, changing hands many times.[55] Perhaps residents were simply defending their lands from the depredations of Union troops, who, because of transportation bottlenecks, were "living off the country to a large extent," actions that reportedly "had induced a troublesome guerilla warfare."[56] The cavalry battalion's quartermaster, however, thought that the bushwhackers had been "commissioned by the Governor of Virginia to shoot us down from behind rocks and trees."[57]

Whatever their motives, Confederate guerrillas were a growing problem in the Shenandoah Valley until General Robert H. Milroy fought back with Union guerrillas of his own.[58] The North debated how to handle bushwhackers and other irregular forces until Lincoln issued General Order No. 100 in April 1863. Paragraph 82 reaffirmed the principle who combatants who concealed themselves among the citizenry, who fought out of uniform, and who were not part of a recognized hostile army were not covered by any traditional rules of war and "shall be treated summarily as highway robbers or pirates."[59] The Confederate Congress, anticipating this risk to its irregular forces, enacted the Partisan Ranger Act in early 1862, theoretically putting the guerrillas into uniform and placing them under regular command, in an effort to obtain the protections of the laws of war. But in practice the bands remained rag-tag, beyond central control, and the North paid no attention to the Confederate law.[60] Charlie continued to treat bushwhackers as little more than pirates, and would soon mete out a vindictive punishment far beyond what even paragraph 82 permitted.

Recovering from his injuries faster than expected, his wounds "scabbed over and dry as a bone," Charlie headed back to his Company B before his sixty-day leave expired.[61] He left for duty on May 26, traveling via New York, Baltimore, Harpers Ferry, and Winchester, but didn't catch up with his troops until about June 10. While stranded in Winchester, Charlie saw his cousin Mary Meredith (probably on his mother's side) and her husband Harry, both of whom had been arrested as northern sympathizers during an earlier Confederate occupation of the town.[62] Charlie had a hard time figuring out where in the Shenandoah his battalion was, but the two-week delay also resulted from losing track of his baggage and of his personal servant "Deny" (or Denny), one of the many slaves who had been declared free after they had escaped to Northern lines and then had been put to work for the Union cause. When a rumor circulated in Norwich that Denny "had run off," Charlie assured his family that was not the case, and that Denny was waiting for him in Strasburg.[63]

Former slaves like Denny were deemed by the North to be "contrabands of war," similar to other property taken from the South, which the North was free to use as it wished in the war. The tactic was conceived in May 1861 when three slaves who had been working on Confederate fortifications escaped across the mouth of the James River to Fort Monroe, located on a spit of land in the Hampton Roads area of Virginia. The fort commander, General Benjamin Butler, refused to return the three men and declared them to be contrabands of war—comparable to seized weapons, supplies, and horses—and treated them as freedmen.[64]

## Pursuing Jackson in the Shenandoah Valley

Charlie finally caught up with his battalion just after the bitter battles on June 8 and 9 at Cross Keys and Port Republic, two villages near the south fork of the Shenandoah River and about two-thirds the way up the valley. He was promptly made commander of the company serving as General Fremont's bodyguard.[65] The assignment would be short-lived, however; within weeks, Fremont resigned, humiliated that his corps had been put under the Army of Virginia, commanded by General John Pope, whom Fremont considered his junior.[66] Regardless of their assignment, Charlie's troops exalted in his return; Quartermaster Sergeant Weston Ferris wrote

"Captain Farnsworth arrived with us in Port Republic.
He was welcomed back to his command by his men most heartily.
He is looking well, only several shades lighter than the most of us;
but this Virginia climate will soon put the color on for him,
as he is not one of your parlor soldiers, but quarters with his men."[67]

Given the severe nature of his wounds, Charlie had been lucky to survive and be able to resume the rigorous duties of a cavalryman. His chest injury would plague him in the future, however.

At Port Republic, Charlie recoiled upon viewing the battlefield carnage, which was probably the first mass suffering he'd seen in the war. "Some 150 of our men dead upon the field and over 500 rebels, and the number of wounded I have no knowledge," he wrote, referring to infantry losses.[68] He added that he was disgusted with the leadership of General Fremont, whose disorderly troops were plundering civilians, and who had allowed the Confederates under General Thomas ("Stonewall") Jackson to succeed with their diversionary maneuvers in the valley. Charlie's estimate of 150 Union deaths was low, but his opinion of Fremont is shared by modern historians.[69]

No longer serving as General Fremont's bodyguard, Charlie and his men withdrew from Cross Keys sixty miles north to Strasburg with General Schenck's brigade. Back on reconnaissance duty, he scouted for several days as far as eighteen miles from camp in search of bushwhackers but found none. He then led a twenty-five-man patrol to clear the forty-mile Moorefield-Strasburg road of guerrillas.[70] Along the way they captured a suspected thief with a wagon hidden in the woods "loaded with plunder," and delivered the man to authorities in Winchester. A few days after that, Charlie passed over "the very spot" where he had been so grievously wounded in April, and some bushwhackers struck again. No soldiers were hit, but one horse was killed and three were wounded. In response, Charlie boasted that he had "burned every house within four miles and so reported."[71] His reaction vastly exceeded any legal authority to inflict reprisals, and it is a wonder that he was not court-martialed. General Pope, frustrated and angered by the continuing bushwhacker menace in the Shenandoah, had issued orders earlier that allowed Union forces to seize necessary civilian property without compensation and to execute captured guerrillas—measures that would be codified later in the Union's ultimate interpretation of the law of war, General Order No. 100.[72] But torching

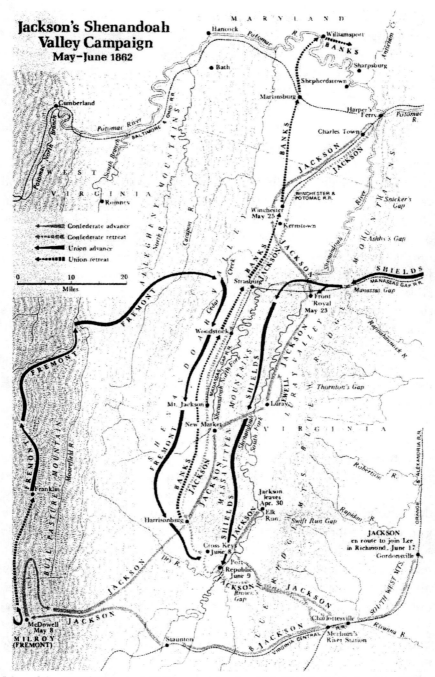

Map of the 1862 Shenandoah Valley campaign in which Charlie fought (reprinted from *Battle Cry of Freedom,* by James McPherson, permission from Oxford University Press).

20

the homes of civilians, at least some of whom were probably innocent of bushwhacking, violated this order as well as a specific prohibition issued a week earlier by General Nathaniel P. Banks, commander of the Shenandoah forces. General Fremont had executed two soldiers for mere pillaging and robbery.[73] Charlie was lucky that his commander, General Schenck, greatly admired Charlie for his initiative, previously calling him a "trump,"[74] a popular compliment of the time that meant "a dependable and exemplary person." Or perhaps Schenck turned a blind eye because he understood Charlie's need to avenge his wounds.

Charlie's harsh retribution may have had the effect of suppressing the irregulars. A mid-July patrol "received fire from some 15 bushwhackers," but suffered no casualties, and a later two-day mission was merely "a very pleasant trip" that "did not find any rebels to have a brush with."[75] At the time, Charlie didn't say whether the long days on horseback were made painful by his chest wounds, although that would eventually be his complaint. Bugler Voltz, shot in the leg during the April ambush, remained disabled throughout the summer, but ultimately returned to duty, re-enlisted, and rose to become bugler for the entire regiment.[76]

Charlie sent home two prizes he had captured in the 1862 Shenandoah Valley campaign: a surgeon's dress sword, which he had taken from a lieutenant colonel of the Louisiana Tigers, and a carbine that he had seized from a bushwhacker near Moorefield.[77]

## Challenging Authority with a Near-Mutiny

In July, Charlie began complaining about Union military organization and leadership. Ordered to ride southeast twenty miles out of the Shenandoah Valley toward Sperryville, he assumed that an attack on Richmond was being planned that would yield glory for his whole battalion. He thus became upset when the battalion was split up, and his Company B was assigned to a brigade commanded by a German immigrant, Major General Franz Sigel. Because it was composed mostly of German-Americans from Pennsylvania, Charlie at first disdained it as "a cursed Dutch brigade," but in time he would come to greatly admire Sigel. What bothered Charlie even more than mingling with the "Dutch" was what he deemed the "cowardly, ignorant, and disgraceful" leadership of his own battalion commander, Major Judson Lyon. Charlie charged that Lyon had run away from a clash in the woods with Confederates, defrauded the government through excessive expense charges for his horses and servants, planned an artillery barrage upon suspected bushwhackers (disregarding the probable damage to civilians), reneged on his mess bill, and had engaged in "improper actions with slaves."[78]

Charlie went so far as to threaten to "come home" unless either he was transferred or Major Lyon was removed.[79] But the threat was probably mere bluster. Having been commissioned by the governor and ordered to serve under the Federal War Department, Charlie was not free to come and go as he pleased.[80] Based on his family's connections with Governor Buckingham, however, Charlie may have assumed that his resignation, if offered, would be accepted. In any case, Charlie soon reconsidered, realizing that he would disgrace himself if he abandoned his troops. Instead, he put his energy behind creating a second battalion so that the First Connecticut could become a *regiment*.[81] A regiment, he thought, would gain respect and glory for itself; troops would no longer be detailed to other units. More importantly, creating a regiment would open up a promotion for himself to major or even to lieutenant colonel. Charlie was ready and eager to come home to recruit the five hundred or so cavalrymen a new battalion would require.

Meanwhile, the pressure on Major Lyon to resign increased. From above, Governor Buckingham asked him to come home. Seventeen court-martial charges were filed against him, alleging cowardice, fraud, and tyrannical and ungentlemanly conduct. From below, enlisted men signed a petition asking for a new commanding officer, and most of the officers backed them up. A few of the officers wavered—"crawfished," in Charlie's view.[82] The major himself, desperately trying to assess his predicament, was caught opening another officer's mail. Lyon then verbally tendered his resignation, buying himself time to negotiate for a "testimonial of esteem." General Schenck then issued the ultimatum that unless a resignation was submitted in writing "before sunset," Lyon would be tried by court-martial for the various charges. Lyon quickly obtained a medical certificate declaring that he was "unfit for service." His resignation was accepted, and he was dismissed for medical reasons in mid-August, just a month after his troops began their protest.

Charlie's friend Captain William S. Fish of Company A was promoted to major and given command of the battalion. Charlie did not seem jealous of his friend's success, being more interested in the project of enlarging the battalion to a regiment once Lyon was gone. Showing their disdain for Lyon, the battalion's officers denied him his requested "testimonial of esteem," and instead suggested that his court-martial charges be sent to him "bound in calf [leather]."[83] What could have been considered a mutiny by subordinate officers and men ended instead with a humiliating send-off of their commander.

Before the war, Judson Lyon had been a well-off lawyer and educator in Woodstock, Connecticut, so dubious of the abolition movement that he reportedly at one point joined the pro-slavery faction of the Know-Nothing Party. After his humiliating resignation from the First Connecticut Cavalry he returned home, where he probably was not well-received. He moved to Putnam five years later, re-established a law practice, and, in a major change of politics, became active in the Republican Party. He died in 1887.[84]

## The Bitter Taste of Battle

Although Charlie's month at Sperryville seemed taken up mostly with getting rid of Major Lyon, he did patrol the country-side enough to understand one dilemma confronting the local citizenry. Those who remained in the embattled area—mostly the elderly—had been convinced by the Richmond government that the principle of 1776-type independence was at stake in the conflict, *not* the institution of slavery. Charlie thought it a bit unfair to force these confused townspeople to take the required oath of loyalty to the Union, especially because they would have to take a similar oath of loyalty to the Confederacy if Southern forces re-entered the town.[85]

In early August, Charlie's Company B, still serving in General Sigel's brigade, advanced twenty-five miles south, where Charlie expected "some big fighting." But they got to the town of Cedar Mountain just as the Confederate forces were withdrawing from a fierce battle there. As at Port Republic, Charlie saw at Cedar Mountain the appalling aftermath of Civil War infantry combat. He accurately estimated that the Union had suffered some three thousand killed and wounded. Nonetheless, Charlie seemed excited that his brigade would now pursue the Confederates to Gordonsville, an important rail junction for Richmond.[86] His hopes were soon dashed, however; they would not march toward the Confederate capital, at least not yet.

Sensing that Confederate forces were about to strike in eastern Virginia, General John Pope, commander of the Union's Army of Virginia, ordered Sigel's brigade in late August to move from Cedar Mountain fifty miles north toward Washington. There, at Manassas/Bull Run, on the same field where the two sides had fought in 1861, Pope's army of sixty thousand would collide with the fifty-five thousand of Generals Stonewall Jackson and James Longstreet in a battle lasting two days.[87] Some elements of the First Connecticut stood in the rear to prevent "straggling," that is, deserting.[88] Others, like Charlie's Company B, engaged in "guarding [wagon] trains, scouting, and fighting." Charlie got off some shots in the first day's battle, and was proud of the success of his commander, General Sigel. But the second day's disaster—when Pope's forces were thrown into a panicked retreat by Longstreet's artillery barrages on their flank—resulted from cowardice, incompetence, and perhaps even treason, Charlie thought:[89]

> The stampede was a sight which pages could not tell…The fighting, instead of being all day, lasted about one hour, and during that time 75,000 [sic] of our men broke ranks and ran like <u>cowards</u>, which they were. It was now that the discipline of McClellan's and Burnside's troops told, and they held the enemy back, and saved the capital. Our men [illegible] did not stop running until the Potomac was reached. Whether there was a traitor in command or not I know not. But I do know the only capable man (in my opinion) that I have seen yet is the Dutchman.[90]

These were strong words for a mere captain of the cavalry, but it was neither the first nor last time Charlie would express harsh criticism of his superiors, always exempting "the Dutchman" General Sigel and a few others. Charlie escaped the Second Manassas debacle unscathed, although a Confederate shot had grazed the heel of his boot as he lay prone, "shooting at rebel skirmishers." And fragments of an exploding artillery shell had struck the curb bit of his horse, wounding the horse's mouth, and giving Charlie "a strong aversion" to cannon fire.[91]

## Defending the Capital

Retreating with the rest of Pope's army from Manassas to the outskirts of Washington, Charlie encamped at Georgetown with his company. He felt "tired and disheartened" by the defeat, and he was worried that his servant Denny, stricken with typhoid fever, might die. He felt relieved three weeks later when Denny's condition improved.[92] Throughout a long period of garrison duty in and around Washington that was beginning for him, Charlie was concerned that the cavalry in general might be falling into disfavor with Union commanders, and he felt an urgency to quickly double the size of his battalion in order to be promoted to lieutenant colonel.[93] Although command and prestige, rather than money, were his goals, such a promotion would have given him a nice raise—from $141 a month as a captain to $189 as a lieutenant colonel.[94]

Charlie and his friend Major Fish met with Generals Schenck and Sigel—*and* with Secretary of War Edwin Stanton himself—to argue for another battalion, one that Charlie would personally raise the troops for. In the end, Stanton sent a letter to Governor Buckingham authorizing a second cavalry battalion, but denied Charlie's request to go home to recruit for it.[95] Charlie quickly realized, however, that as soon as the new unit was authorized, he as its commanding officer would be free to recruit at will. Rather surprisingly, and obviously counterproductively, Charlie continued his rant about "treason at the table of the President's advisors"—an insubordination that Stanton would have punished if he had heard of it. In part, Charlie was over-reacting to promotion policies that he deemed unfair to "veteran" soldiers like himself.[96]

His older brother Billings visited Charlie at the Georgetown encampment in early September, taking the opportunity to inspect one of the horses that Charlie wanted to send home. This was the second time in five months that Billings had come from Norwich to see his brother the soldier. When the two disagreed on the horse's merits, Charlie bristled with sarcasm about his civilian brother's presumption of "superior judgment in regard to the animal." After Billings left a week later, Charlie, ignoring his brother's opinions, shipped the horse and one other home by rail. These were probably two of the many horses, captured or procured, that had been ruined for further military duty by the traumas of Second Manassas.[97]

Largely dismounted because of the loss of so many horses, the First Connecticut had been assigned in early September to defensive duties in Georgetown A few weeks later, the battalion was transferred to nearby Tenallytown, and then in late October to the Kalorama district of Washington. Charlie was unhappy with these defensive assignments. In an unseemly moment of petulance, he considered using his gunshot injuries as an excuse to get a medical discharge—unless he could get a second battalion authorized, with an accompanying promotion for himself.[98]

On September 17, 1862, the armies of Generals George B. McClellan and Robert E. Lee collided at Antietam Creek, Maryland; twenty-three thousand soldiers were killed or severely wounded in the largest single-day losses of the war. Lee withdrew from the battlefield two days later, and McClellan barely pursued him.[99] Lincoln and others sharply criticized McClellan's inaction, but in Washington, Charlie was quick to approve. He thought that McClellan was wise to move cautiously with his battle-weary "mob," and that such restraint gave "every soldier a feeling of security" under the general. Charlie nonetheless praised the president: "The news though not as good as we could wish, shows that a master hand moves the sinew of the nation, and a head equaled to the task conceives the great plans."[100] Six weeks later Charlie was completely on Lincoln's side, fully backing the decision to remove McClellan from command of the army because he had allowed Lee to escape from Antietam.[101] Charlie wanted Lincoln to act boldly to bring the war to a victorious end. Washington politics was undercutting the Northern strategy, he believed, and if the president could not move more decisively, then perhaps only a coup that installed a military dictator like General Joseph Hooker or General Philip Kearny could save the Union. For a second time, Charlie recklessly exclaimed to his family that there were traitors in the administration:

> And to my mind, treason lurks from the White House through all departments. Oh for a leader even if he wears a crown, and so say thousands. And should such a man spring up, the army will sustain him and place him in a large White building on Pennsylvania Avenue, Washington, D. C. It is so, however strange it may seem. And if it will bring war to a close and vindicate the North, why I say let it come.[102]

Throughout the war, Charlie's moods would swing from condemnation of Lincoln to an understanding and acceptance of his leadership. Luckily, Charlie never got into trouble for throwing around allegations of treason and traitorous actions.

Charlie was not one to accept the inactivity of garrison life very well. He yearned for action: to be sent into Virginia, or to Texas with General Fremont (despite his earlier criticism of the general), or to New Orleans with General Banks. He dreaded the thought of the rumored provost duty in Baltimore under General Schenck, who was still nearly incapacitated with pain and "nervousness" from arm wounds suffered at Second Manassas.[103] None of Charlie's hopes would be fulfilled in the fall of 1862. A different company was sent (with all of the battalion's horses) to provide security for General Sigel's headquarters in Fairfax, Virginia; General Fremont resigned long before his Texas expedition could take form; and General Banks did not call for the services of Charlie's cavalry. Nor was provost duty yet ordered. Charlie remained encamped in Washington throughout October and into November.[104]

Stuck in the capital with little to do, Charlie decided at least to live more comfortably than he had in the field. He asked his parents to send some food delicacies (including some Thanksgiving pies), along with his favorite overcoat. Special treats like grapes, ginger bread, and pumpkin pies soon arrived, along with books and newspapers, which he passed along to his troops after reading. Even the governor's wife, Mrs. Buckingham, despite her poor health, sent a "bundle." Having more than he needed, Charlie passed the gift along to General Schenck. Still anticipating a return to the field, Charlie ordered a steel-framed saddle-mounted valise that was designed to hold up in the rough riding of cavalry campaigns.[105]

## Scouting toward Fredericksburg

Charlie finally got some of the action he wanted in mid-November. The battalion, still under the command of Major Fish, was ordered on foot into what Charlie sarcastically called the "sacred ground" of Virginia. There, horses would be provided and the cavalry would scout for the Ninth New York Infantry Regiment, commanded by Colonel John Beardsley. Although Charlie thought he would have "some fun" on the mission, he grumbled about the regimental commander, for whom he had provided screening cover during the regiment's disorderly retreat from Second Manassas. The chaos, he thought, was the fault of Beardsley, whom he considered "a fool, a miserable officer."[106]

With fresh mounts, the First Connecticut scouted fifty miles into Virginia, along what is now Highway 1. Charlie again thought they might be headed for Richmond, "the damned city," as he called it. But the battalion advanced only to Falmouth, near Fredericksburg, arriving just a day or so after General Ambrose Burnside's army had failed in its attack across the Rappahannock River under withering Confederate gunfire.[107] A few weeks later, Major Fish was ordered to Baltimore to become provost marshal, and Charlie finally got the authority he coveted, as acting commander of the First Connecticut Cavalry. Assigned to a brigade under Colonel Louis Palma di Cesnola, a Sardinian count who had immigrated to America, the battalion scouted thirty miles west to Culpepper, but found no rebels north of the Rappahannock River. In a skirmish with rebels south of the river, however, four horses were killed by rifle fire, although no men were lost.[108]

Mounted Union cavalry officer, c. 1862. With his saber, kepi, and riding boots, Charlie would have looked like this (courtesy Library of Congress).

Ordered to withdraw from the Rappahannock, Charlie as acting commanding officer rode at the head of his three hundred cavalrymen ten miles north to Stafford Courthouse (just south of today's Quantico Marine Corps Reservation), where he ordered a temporary camp to be set up. His mind wandered far beyond the battalion's immediate concerns. Charlie now worried that the Union's recent defeat at Fredericksburg and the winter's status quo would undermine Union morale and cause "a clamor for peace from the North," resulting in a settlement in which "the South will dictate the terms."[109] A dictator was definitely needed, and General McClellan was his choice, even though a month earlier he had thought Lincoln was justified in firing the general. The North ought to be ruled with an iron hand like the South, Charlie mused. These were curious comments, given that the South was suffering far more from the lack of centralized authority than the North. Moreover, far from demonstrating dictatorial tendencies, McClellan would leave the army in 1864 to run for president on the Democratic "peace platform."

Despite the disaster at Fredericksburg, Charlie admired General Burnside for his determined efforts to attack across the Rappahannock River, and "rejoice[d] that we have a man that is not afraid to sacrifice life to gain a point." Overall, Charlie thought, "We are too much given to trying to save life. Soldiers are enlisted to be killed, if necessary, and war cannot be reaped unless we are men."[110] Few—then or now—would lend such support for Burnside; in his stubborn, futile attempts to take Fredericksburg, he had lost thirteen thousand troops, killed or wounded.[111]

Encamped at Stafford in early January 1863, Charlie reported having "gay times here scouting," with "several severe skirmishes," in one of which Corporal Michael Carver of Norwich was shot in the head while trying to capture two Confederate soldiers hidden in a nearby house. Surprisingly, this was only the first Connecticut cavalryman to be killed in action. A board of the battalion's officers authorized Carver's brother to burn down the offending house in retribution.[112]

While serving as acting battalion commander at the Stafford camp, Charlie wrote several long letters home, expressing his expectation of a promotion to match his new duties, anticipating a reassignment to Baltimore, and suggesting a new strategy on how the North could win the war. He was enjoying being in charge, and no longer yearned to come home to recruit for the newly-authorized second battalion.[113] Charlie's new strategic idea resembled the earlier Anaconda Plan of General Winfield Scott, with a bit of the later strategy of General William T. Sherman added: ignore Richmond for now, blockade and invade the Southern ports, liberate and enlist the slaves (putting "a full million men in the field"), destroy the productive capacities of the Confederacy. All of this, he thought, would surely "crush the rebellion in six months," as he expressed in the vernacular of the time:[114]

> The true conduct of the war now…5 large expeditions sent south—Charleston, Mobil, New Orleans, North Carolina, & then into Georgia—push into the cotton states, set the niggers free, arm them, and make them fight, thus keep our numbers on the increase and not recruit at home…

Officers put in command of nigger regiments. Those that
don't want to, send home. Push through the cotton states,
getting away the producing power [of] <u>slaves</u> and destroy
the producing country...We have the men and by the aid
of nigger regiments we could have a full million men in
the field. The present mode won't work, and the other will
crush the rebellion in six months.[115]

To accomplish his strategy, Charlie again recommended "a reign of
military power for the next year," this time with Secretary of State William H.
Seward and Secretary of War Stanton (whom he had met with three months
earlier) being replaced by Generals Butler and Banks.[116] These were curious
choices: Butler had just been removed from his New Orleans command for
alleged financial improprieties, and Banks had been defeated by Stonewall
Jackson in the Shenandoah Valley campaign the previous summer.

Lincoln, coincidentally, shared one of Charlie's ideas and put it into
action: the War Department began to form regiments of slaves freed by the
Emancipation Proclamation of January 1, 1863. From the Confederacy's
viewpoint, however, turning these slaves against their masters constituted
an act of insurrection, and justified the summary execution of black
soldiers, along with their white commanders, whenever captured on the
battlefield.[117] This high-level disagreement over a rule of war would later
impact Charlie quite directly.

Charlie continued to hold his commanding officer, Major Fish, in the
highest regard and assumed that he would benefit from Fish's promotion
to provost marshal general of Baltimore. Fish was "a great manager,
indefatigable in pushing any thing through he attempts. He is very Brassy
and it counts always. Again he is very smart and long headed."[118] Fish was
selfish, but Charlie considered that a virtue, cautioning his brother Fred in
a letter that "Brass and selfishness is said to get along. Your open hearted
free handed man never gets along. You must cultivate a little of both. I
don't mean for you to be a low gravelly man, but close mouth and look out
for #1."[119] Charlie was sure that Fish reciprocated this esteem:

[H]e knows I am the only one on whom he can depend...
And I don't think he will throw me off for any one
else; I know he won't for any one here. Blakeslee is very
underhanded and sly, and has tried several times to euchre

him. And Niles he does not like. Marcy he is well disposed
to but being the junior Capt he has but little chance of a
Majority unless we get a Regiment.[120]

Not only was Captain Blakeslee "underhanded and sly," Charlie thought,
but even worse, "unreliable."[121] Fourteen years after the war, Blakeslee, as
a brevet brigadier general and ordained minister, wrote the official history
of the First Connecticut Cavalry, paying several compliments to Charlie's
courage and energy—without having access to Charlie's letters, of course.
One wonders if Blakeslee would have praised Charlie so highly if he had
known what Charlie had written so disparagingly about him.

Charlie became more eager for independent garrison duty in Baltimore
as he grew disgruntled with the discriminatory preferences of his German-
American corps commander, Franz Sigel. Although he admired Sigel's
strong leadership, he felt unappreciated, complaining that

> [i]t is very unpleasant being in this Corps; it is all Dutch
> and no one but them stand any chance...They are a very
> poor set, no understanding of our ways or customs, and
> then put on airs because of their rank. We are always
> fighting. An American does any thing and they ignore it.
> A Dutch man moves and he is a big man.[122]

Charlie clearly failed to appreciate Sigel's unique ability to recruit
German immigrants—many of whom spoke almost no English—and to
shape them into a fighting infantry corps for the Union cause. Nevertheless,
for unspecified reasons, Sigel was relieved of his command in February
1863.[123]

The frustrating struggle for promotion and recognition was not
Charlie's only problem. Back home, some misunderstanding with his
fiancée Georgia Parker had erupted, and she had gone to see Charlie's
mother, Eunice. Of the visit to Norwich, Charlie wrote, "[I] trust that a
nearer acquaintance will not be unfavorable."[124] But his ardor for Georgia
was cooling. He tried to reassure his mother, who must have sensed some
weakening of the engagement, by declaring "if it lays with me alone there
will never be any break. Still I sometimes think I hardly deserve so fine a
wife."[125] He later confessed that he unfortunately was past the point where
he could write a "heavy love letter."[126] Charlie argued for a pragmatic

approach to marriage—advice he would later ignore—in a letter to his brother Fred at Yale:

> Every thing is lovely in Norwich and progressing finely. I should not wonder if it was a game but it is the queerest one I was ever engaged in. Still after the easy ones of the past, it is refreshing to find a strong and real woman, not carried away by any thing. It is the real wife one wants, not the sentimental school girl.[127]

## Keeping Order in Baltimore

In mid-January 1863, Charlie received orders to lead his battalion north to Baltimore, where he would assume duties as provost guard commander under Provost Marshal Fish. The Union had worried about being back-stabbed by secessionist elements in Baltimore ever since Lincoln, to avoid a suspected assassination plot, had been forced to slip through town at night in an unmarked carriage on his way to Washington in February 1861. Anxiety grew in 1862 after the South's victory at Second Manassas, when the Maryland legislature met to consider secession. (After the arrest of nearly fifty secessionists, the measure was not brought to a vote.) To establish the discipline necessary to convert his hard-riding cavalrymen into a thoughtful peace-keeping police force, Charlie began to issue written daily orders—even while on the march north. He signed General Order No. 1 while encamped at Dumphries, Virginia, about twelve miles north of Stafford: Horses were to be fed grain and hay twice daily, and ridden bareback to be watered twice a day, with "no excuses," one section read.[128]

Baltimore citizens were startled by the grimy look of Charlie's campaign-weary cavalrymen when they arrived in late January. "The fact of our coming from the front rather created a reputation of something grand. But a dirtier, poor[er], ravenous set never tread the city than we were when we came in. It took people down."[129] Now officially designated a regiment (although still of only battalion strength) the First Connecticut replaced the Thirteenth Pennsylvania Cavalry at Camp Chesebrough, a run-down site greatly in need of repair. Charlie undertook a complete overhaul of the camp, eventually turning it into a model garrison. Known before the war as the Mount Clare Mansion, the entire estate had recently been renamed in honor of the adjutant of the Eleventh Maryland Infantry, Lieutenant Colonel William G. Chesebrough.[130] A Baltimore & Ohio Railroad repair shop was located nearby, and one of the guard's duties undoubtedly was to protect the facility. (Abandoned after the war, the camp was later converted into Carroll Park in southwest Baltimore. The original mansion atop the hill is still there.[131])

Charlie's official title was commander of the provost guard & battalion, under Major Fish, the provost marshal general of Baltimore. Concerned with the allures of Baltimore as well as its subversive Confederate sentiments, Charlie strictly limited the number of his men allowed to visit the city during the day (five), and during the evening (four).[132] The provost guard's main task was to keep order among a restive citizenry, and it earned a reputation for suppressing secessionist activities. Any music with lyrics that might convey military secrets was banned. Especially suppressed was the recently written "Maryland, My Maryland," which had been put to music by Jenny and Hettie Cary, members of the notorious "Monument Street Girls," upper-class Baltimore women who sided with the South. Some of the hymn's lyrics were indeed subversive, at least in war-time:

From the gloomy bastille,
And Lincoln's big heel,
All iron-clad, lifted to rend us.
From Seward's soft speech
And the Cameron leech,
We pray thee, good Lord, to defend us.

Photographs of rebel soldiers or local fortifications were banned, newspapers were shut down, and membership in disloyal organizations was prohibited.[133]

The provost guard and local police filled Baltimore jails and the prison at nearby Fort McHenry with violators of these military orders.[134] Other arrests were made for the more serious crimes of spying and conspiracy to aid the South by running volunteers and goods through the Union blockade.[135] In the end, only one person was executed in Baltimore during the military occupation, and he had been convicted of bushwhacking and spying in *Virginia*.[136] In a zealous exhibition of his powers, General Schenck went so far as to order the arrest of anyone considered disloyal who tried to vote in the state elections of November 1863.[137] By that time, however, Charlie had been ordered away from Baltimore and had no hand in Schenck's dirty business—nor in an extortion scheme that Major Fish was later convicted of.

Baltimore, like Maryland itself, was politically divided over secession and the war. The state legislature kept the state in the Union by declaring that it had no constitutional authority to vote on the question of secession.[138] There were about as many free blacks as slaves in the state, but the slaves, unlike the practice of the South, often worked alongside whites in shipyards, workshops, and factories.[139]Lincoln himself was not popular in Maryland; he had run a distant fourth in the 1860 presidential election, garnering only 2 percent of the vote. Baltimore had been a headache for the Union since February 1861 after threats on Lincoln's life had forced him to sneak through the city in the dark of night en route to the capital. Concerns were heightened in April 1861 when a mob blocked the passage of Massachusetts troops on their way to protect Washington. Four soldiers and twelve civilians were killed in the following melee, known as the "Pratt Street riot"—the first combat deaths of the war. In response, Lincoln devised a railroad route around the city for future Northern troops, and gave them additional protection by ordering the suspension of the writ of habeas corpus along the route, although not within the city of Baltimore itself. The famous writ was generally available in Baltimore until late June 1863 when, fearing an invasion, General Schenck imposed martial law throughout the state.[140]

Charlie was quick to initiate an ambitious project of converting broken-down Camp Chesebrough into a "camp not equaled any where."[141] Horse barns, a hospital, a chapel, and a row of three-room cottages with kitchens for the officers were designed and built. The camp roads were paved with brick and troop barracks were repaired. Improved landscaping enhanced appearances.[142] The construction work provided the additional benefit of keeping the cavalrymen busy. For those "wild" soldiers who could not adapt to garrison life, Charlie imposed harsh punishment to make an example of them: "I sent one man to work on stone work for the government with ball & chain for a week, for disobeying an order." Charlie thought that soldiers despised the fearful, "mild" leader who sought popularity but loved the tough ones like him.[143]

In addition to supervising the extensive construction project, Charlie issued explicit rules for garrison life at Camp Chesebrough. In General Order No. 6, he laid down precise directions for arranging and numbering the soldiers' bunks in their barracks. He had shown this penchant for orderliness before, requiring his troopers to blast out tree stumps so that their tents could be aligned, even while on the march in late November

1862.[144] General Order No. 7 established a detailed procedure for morning muster at Chesebrough, repeated the rules for feeding and watering horses, and demanded that "[e]very soldier is expected to willingly and cheerfully perform all duty..." Another order incorporated a popular local tavern within the camp's borders so that his men had ready access to refreshments, but at the same time warning that any man leaving camp without a pass "will be severely punished."[145] Charlie wasn't a martinet by nature, but he did believe that all essential rules should be clearly stated and strictly enforced.

Camp Chesebrough, Baltimore, showing the structures that Charlie built or re-built in 1863 (courtesy, Maryland Historical Society, Baltimore, Robert G. Merrick Collection).

In early March, the First Connecticut finally got its long-sought regimental authority, even though the unit was still of battalion size. Now, as acting *regimental* commander, Charlie conducted an inspection of the unit's horses. In a March 9 report, he listed eighty-eight of the regiment's horses as unfit for service, described their condition, and made recommendations for their "disposition." Sadly, he had to "condemn" seventy-nine, releasing them to the army's quartermaster.[146]

Settling into the garrison life of a "gentleman soldier," as he called it, Charlie asked his mother to send him such fineries as handkerchiefs, towels, linen napkins, white shirts with studs and buttons, sheets, pillow cases, and carpeting for his cabin. He paid $100 to a local tailor for two suits, $150 for new boots and "horse trimmings," and made plans to buy a buggy for getting around town more stylishly. All in all, Charlie was happy to be safely in the rear echelon and out of the line of fire. "We are wholey indebted to [Major Fish] for our good place now, and I think we shall remain here for the war," he wrote, hopefully.[147] But such hopes would be dashed soon enough.

Charlie was also enjoying his duty of dabbling in Baltimore's Unionist social scene, which included attending operas, teas, balls, parties, and the weekly Union assemblies with their patriotic lectures, as well as calling at the homes of the well-connected. He had anticipated such a respite from the war at least two months earlier, clipping from a Baltimore newspaper's classified section under *Social Parties* the announcement of four dances, including one that would celebrate "The Glorious Flag of Our Union." On several occasions he saw his cousin Mary and her husband Harry Meredith, who had a home in Baltimore, as well as one in Winchester, Virginia.[148] He dropped in on troublesome "secesh" parties, finding them more curious than threatening. Some young Baltimore women claimed they would boycott any such gatherings altogether if they thought officers like Charlie might drop in:

> Sister and I do not make an appearance when Yanks are in
> the House, entertaining no sympathy for them.[149]

Overall, Charlie was having "lots of fun here...[with] the prospect of much amusement for the spring," and he worried only that the coming Lental season might limit the frivolities.[150]

As if to complete Charlie's new life as a gentleman soldier, Denny, his "contraband" servant, returned after spending four months recovering from typhoid fever. "He said I saved his life last summer and I was the only man he would have come back to. He is a fine fellow & [I] think dearest of us all," Charlie announced.[151] Having now seen the war's terrible bloodletting, Charlie earnestly admonished his brother Fred, age twenty and an ambivalent student at Yale, to "once and for all stop talking about the army. Don't even think of it. You are ten times better off out of it, and once in it, there is no let up. If the family cannot afford the expense, why, quit [college], but don't try the army."[152] Charlie sensed that his younger brother was simply not up to the rigors of military life.

In mid-March Charlie was struck a severe emotional blow. His good friend and cabin-mate, Captain Albert H. Niles, died of typhoid fever. The death was particularly shocking because Niles had seemed to be recovering from the illness. Now he was gone. Charlie tried to assuage his grief with a long, cold hike in the snow:

> The sudden death of Capt. Niles has made me feel unusual bad. He was one of our (Atwater & me) mess, we three having been together for some time. He was a very gentlemanly and friendly officer. His seat is now vacant, but I feel that he has entered upon better quarters in the mansions above. He died very suddenly indeed. He was buried with Military honors yesterday. I walked through the snow over five miles, and taken all the circumstances in consideration am not so well for it.[153]

Then, with a general order, Charlie provided prayerful comfort to the regiment's soldiers:

> It having pleased God to remove from our midst Capt. A. H. Niles, we bow in reverence before him, feeling that our Brother in arms who during the past year has been actually engaged in the putting down of the rebellion, and though he has passed unharmed through many a conflict, in yielding to the last Conqueror, has enlisted in the army of the great Captain of our salvation and entered upon quarters not made by hands, but eternal in the heavens.[154]

In March, Charlie was promoted to major, the minimum rank appropriate for a regimental commander. A month later, however, the War Department, probably aware that the First Connecticut was still only of battalion strength, reduced Charlie back to captain.[155] With typical brashness, Charlie continued to consider himself a major, and made no mention to his family of the War Department's retraction. Disputes over his proper rank would plague Charlie and his legacy into the future.

Charlie as a Major, April 1863 (photograph by W. H. Jennings, Norwich).

Believing that local subversion no longer posed a threat and that "the immediate fear of revolution is past," in April Charlie invited his mother and brother Fred to visit Baltimore. His mother declined, preferring to call on Georgia Parker's family in Meriden, perhaps feeling that she could serve Charlie better by strengthening ties between their own staunchly Republican family and Georgia's, aligned with the Peace Democrats. Charlie encouraged her plans: "You will find them real pleasant people, and will have a good time." He worried, though, that the toothaches his mother had been suffering would interfere with her enjoyment of the trip.[156]

Fred, on the other hand, accepted Charlie's invitation to Camp Chesebrough, arriving in late April, but apparently did not enjoy himself. Even worse, he annoyed Charlie with a variety of complaints and quibbles. Fred reportedly got upset when he realized that he hadn't brought suitable dress attire for the ball they attended, whined that he had gotten too tired from tagging along with Charlie on his daily duties, and even quarreled over the qualities of a horse, calling it a "cow." Nonetheless, Charlie said he was glad his younger brother had come, and happily covered the travel expenses. But he also added that Fred needed to curb his peevishness, should not be "so overexpectant, and [should] be contented with life as it comes." He described his own approach to life: "I have learned by some very bitter pills, but I took them, and at the present time there is not a person who takes things as they come more than I do." He predicted that "Fred will have many a rough corner rounded before he [takes things as they come]."[157] Charlie tended to follow his own advice and this attitude would serve him well in the months to come.

Like many in his regiment, Charlie was granted leave to go home for Connecticut's elections on April 1. Absentee voting was prohibited by the state's constitution until August 1864, and Connecticut's Peace Democrats had been opposed to allowing soldiers in the field to vote, fearing that most were Republicans.[158] Charlie was eager to make the trip home, saying that he wanted to fight with the ballot as well as the sword against the "Copperheads & enemies in the rear whose camp fires are burning upon the soil of free Connecticut."[159] Knowing that Republican Governor Buckingham's efforts would be crucial in filling up the newly-authorized regiment, either by recruiting or conscription, Charlie undoubtedly voted for him. Buckingham probably needed the military votes, as he barely won re-election with only 51 percent of the ballots cast.[160]

Charlie was not so focused on garrison duty, social life, and family as to be unaware of the war raging beyond Baltimore. While his brother Fred was fussing about his party finery, the North was suffering yet another catastrophe, this time at Chancellorsville, Virginia, when General Stonewall Jackson outflanked General Hooker's Army of the Potomac in late April and inflicted seventeen thousand casualties. Charlie thought Hooker had been done in by the bad luck of a rainstorm that slowed his troops, rather than by his own poor leadership. Charlie still believed it all came down to the president:

> I think the immediate fear of a revolution is past. Still a dictator would be supported by the army, and by all loyal people, if he prosecuted the war. The only trouble with A.L. is he has no firmness. If he will stand by his order in relation to deserters [i.e., hang them], he will receive the thanks of all good men in the army, but I fear it is all splurge.[161]

> [I]f Abe Lincoln will stand up to the rack [i.e., enforce military discipline] and hold men and officers to their duty, we will come out all right.[162]

Through May and June, Charlie worried about the threat of a massive Confederate attack on his camp, which initially had been set up simply to keep control of disloyal civilians—not to defend against an onslaught. In a foul mood from the uncertainty, Charlie launched his most vitriolic criticism yet of Union leadership: Lincoln was too tolerant, too irresolute, too weak. Every able-bodied man should be drafted and war should be waged relentlessly on the South until its armies were annihilated. Disloyalty should be harshly punished, Charlie thought.

> Why are not deserters shot, spies hung, and paper and copperhead meetings put down? I tell you we are not awake yet, and I fear will not be under the present man.[163]

Yet even as he railed against the president for not taking firmer military action, Charlie sank into a cushy life at Camp Chesebrough. In June, his cabin got carpet and window curtains, thanks to his mother.[164] His bed was draped by day with a white counterpane, which Denny dutifully removed at nightfall. These seductions of comfort made Charlie think that he would be happy to stay in camp for the rest of the war. Still, he wanted the new regiment filled out with three more companies, and hoped that a pending review and inspection by General Schenck and his staff of forty (which included their ladies) would be impressive enough to order it done. At the post-review reception, while Charlie and his staff lobbied their guests for more troops, waiters served cake with ice cream and strawberries, along with pickled oysters, washed down with lemonade and wine. Charlie recognized, on the other hand, that the easy garrison life could end at any moment. "[T]here is some talk of our again taking ground rent-free in Old Virginia, and a blanket instead of a mattress," he wrote his mother.[165]

## Baltimore Threatened

In mid-June 1863 came warnings of impending Confederate attacks on Baltimore. Charlie sent cavalry patrols out twenty miles in all directions and set up outposts to detect any enemy approach. He rode two hundred miles in a week, checking on the deployment of his men. As a further precaution, he closed the camp streets, and put freedmen to work building fortifications. Probably over-working himself, he fell ill, but recovered within a week. To probe far beyond Baltimore, he sent a squad to scout seventy miles northwest toward Hagerstown. There, the patrol ran into a large Confederate force and three men were captured.[166] Without knowing it, they had encountered the screening cavalry of General Lee's Army of Northern Virginia, which was marching north toward the cataclysmic battle at Gettysburg. It would not be long before Charlie himself would run into a similar Confederate force.

Concerned that the Confederates might be aiming not at Gettysburg, but instead at Baltimore, Charlie deployed his troops along the city's perimeter, reinforcing them with five thousand armed civilians. Barricades were erected under the command of engineer Lieutenant John R. Meigs, son of the Union's quartermaster general and a man Charlie would soon meet under even more dire circumstances. Many residents fled the city.[167] But no attack came, although two companies of loyal Delaware Union cavalry were driven back through Charlie's lines by rebel forces. When the fear of imminent attack subsided a day or so later, the barricades were abandoned and the cavalry troops came back into camp. Charlie had spent four nights riding the perimeter of Baltimore's defenses, and was exhausted.[168]

A week later Charlie turned cynical and suggested that a successful Confederate invasion into the north, even as far as New York or Ohio, might teach a useful lesson to the White House. Lincoln would then get tough or would be removed for a dictator. Traitors like former Ohio congressman Clement L. Vallandigham should be hanged, Charlie thought. In May, Vallandigham had been sentenced to prison by a military commission for "implied treason," namely, giving speeches designed to discourage Union army enlistments. When Lincoln stated that his earlier suspension of the writ of habeas corpus could be applied to such cases, and that no civilian conviction was required, Democratic politicians were outraged. Lincoln backed down, slightly, commuted Vallandigham's sentence from imprisonment to banishment, and sent him into Tennessee.[169] Mistakenly believing that Vallandigham had been initially sentenced to death, Charlie thought Lincoln had gone soft with the order of banishment:

> [W]e men are hampered by an easy story-telling ruler, and when we convict men of a death crime and have them ordered hanged, get bluff[ed] by executive interference for political motives, we men know what is wanted and what will win.[170]

## To Harpers Ferry: "Lots of Fun Ahead"

As if in answer to his call for action, Charlie and three companies composed of 184 cavalrymen were ordered out on July 5 to Harpers Ferry, now part of the newly-created state of West Virginia. The cavalrymen and their horses boarded a Baltimore & Ohio freight train adjacent Camp Chesebrough in the early morning hours of July 6 and arrived at Harpers Ferry, fifty miles away, late that afternoon. Charlie predicted, erroneously, that there would be "lots of fun ahead." He showed no sign of knowing that he was being sent close to the path of General Lee's retreat from the July 1-3 calamitous battle at Gettysburg. Brigadier General Henry M. Naglee, over-all commander at Harpers Ferry, put Charlie in charge of all cavalry there, including elements of General George Custer's Sixth Michigan Cavalry Brigade, the famous "Wolverines."[171]

From their campsite on Maryland Heights, the steep northern embankment of the Potomac River, Charlie and his men scouted for retreating Confederate forces up-country from the river to Crampton Gap and to Sharpsburg/Antietam, going as far north as Williamsport. But they failed to make contact, missing Lee's army crossing at Williamsport by a day.[172] By July 13, while still sending out patrols along the Potomac, Charlie had moved his cavalry from the Heights "to a group of pines near the river." He was comfortably encamped in a Sibley tent, a state-of-the-art mobile structure that had been patented for the army by Henry Hopkins Sibley in 1856. Conical in shape, a Sibley stood about twelve feet high in the center, and accommodated about twelve men. (Sibley was stripped of his right to any patent royalties, however, when he joined the Confederacy in 1861.) Sitting in his tent one night, Charlie badly cut himself while engaged in what he called "acuation," i.e., knife-sharpening.[173] This was just one of several times in his writings that Charlie would display an advanced vocabulary and colorful turn of phrase, which seems surprising for someone who had not gone to college.

Perhaps frustrated by a week of mounted patrols without contacting Southern forces, Charlie considered his assignment "foolish" and thought that the army, in dispatching the cavalrymen to such diverse tasks as scouting, was interfering with his goal of building a unified regiment. Blinded by a dream of European-style saber and musket charges by mounted regiments, Charlie was unable to see the importance of cavalry reconnaissance patrols in gathering intelligence for the infantry and artillery units. If such piecemeal detachments continue, he threatened, probably without legal grounds, "I am coming home soon, for it knocks the regiment all over and I won't stay any longer at this child's play of raising a regiment."[174] Still, Charlie expected real action soon because the engineers were building a pontoon bridge across the Potomac to replace the badly damaged Baltimore & Ohio Railroad span. "Should we cross, there will be work as the other side is full of rebs." Very shortly, General Naglee ordered "Captain" Farnsworth (he viewed himself a Major) to saddle up with fifty men for a day of scouting on the West Virginia side of the Potomac.[175] Charlie was about to get the action he was looking for, but his life would be abruptly altered.

At noon on July 14, Charlie led fifty-three men, including his colleague Captain Blakeslee, across the pontoon bridge to the edge of Harpers Ferry, the spot from which John Brown and his raiders had launched their attack on the town several years earlier. Charlie then guided his patrol along the B & O Railroad tracks adjacent the Shenandoah River for about two miles, to a point just below a ridge known as Bolivar Heights. Several versions have emerged of what happened next, but the undisputed upshot was that Charlie's forces did not fare well. According to Charlie, Blakeslee spotted and charged upon some

Confederate pickets, or scouts, capturing all but one of them. When a much larger force then counter-attacked Blakeslee, Charlie and thirty men charged to protect Blakeslee, who escaped with the rebel prisoners. Overwhelmed, Charlie and twenty-four of his men were captured.[176]

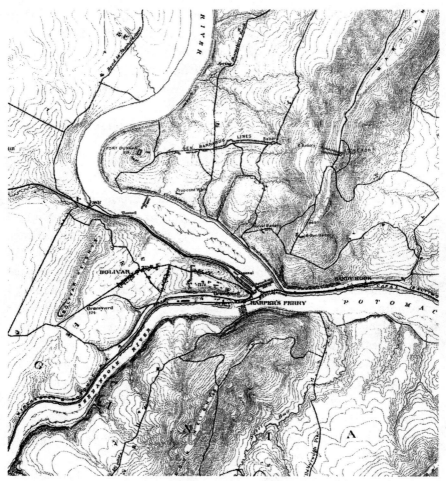

Map of Harpers Ferry, at the confluence of the Potomac and Shenandoah Rivers, showing the pontoon bridge Charlie crossed, and Bolivar Heights, where he was captured, July 14, 1863 (courtesy, George B. Davis, et al. *The Official Military Maps of the Civil War*, republished by Fairfax Press, New York, 1978).

Captain Blakeslee's version differed somewhat and was more dramatic. Instead of initially capturing the pickets, he "drove them in confusion back upon their reserve," and Charlie then joined in a charge upon what proved to be a surprisingly large force of about two hundred cavalrymen. "It became a fierce hand to hand fight," Blakeslee reported. Charlie's horse was shot from under him, but "he fought most gallantly on foot with his sabre until he was overpowered and taken prisoner." The Confederates "repulsed" the Yankees and then captured twenty-six plus Charlie (whom Blakeslee referred to as "Major"). Blakeslee said that he then took four prisoners and got away. A wounded Confederate colonel escaped the melee but was captured later.[177]

A third, more politically-charged, account was later related by Quartermaster Sergeant Weston Ferris, who had been at Charlie's side. According to Ferris, upon spotting the Confederate pickets, Charlie divided the patrol into three squads, one under his command, another under Blakeslee, and a reserve squad under an unnamed lieutenant from General Naglee's staff, "he having accompanied us for the purpose of seeing cavalry reconnaissance." Charlie's and Blakeslee's squads then charged the pickets, leaving the green lieutenant's squad to reinforce them, if necessary. The lieutenant, however, spying another rebel force approaching along the Charlestown Pike, ordered his squad to attack them, while he stayed behind. The reserve squad gave chase, but after about a mile ran smack into "three companies of the 13th Virginia Cavalry," who captured them. They were headed back toward Charlestown when Charlie and his squad made a valiant but futile rescue effort, and were also captured.[178]

If Sergeant Ferris's version was accurate, the whole patrol's failure could be blamed on the young staff lieutenant who disobeyed orders and recklessly committed the reserve squad, instead of holding it in support of Charlie and Blakeslee. General Naglee might then have come in for criticism for sending out such a callow staff officer, who was probably Lieutenant John R. Meigs, an engineer and the son of Lincoln's trusted and indispensable quartermaster general of the Union army, Montgomery Meigs.[179] Perhaps Charlie and Blakeslee thought it good politics to protect General Naglee by not putting the blame for the debacle on the well-connected young Meigs. Even Ferris showed political discretion by not identifying the young staff officer by name in his report.

A fourth version, overly simplified from contemporary letters and reports, simply concluded that Charlie and his whole patrol had spotted and charged upon a six-man Confederate picket of Lee's forces at Halltown, west of Harpers Ferry, capturing four. The two rebels who escaped soon returned with a two hundred-man "screaming countercharge" that split the Union patrol and captured Charlie and twenty-three others.[180]

It is odd that only Blakeslee mentioned that Charlie fought dismounted with his sword after his horse was shot. Had Charlie actually tried to do so, the Confederates would likely have shot him as he tried to whack away at them or their horses. Blakeslee later seemed contrite about his role in precipitating the debacle, so perhaps he was inflating Charlie's heroics to curry favor. Whatever the details, it seems certain that Charlie's fifty-three-man patrol had been over-matched and out-maneuvered by a cavalry battalion of three hundred or so that was screening for the estimated eighty thousand retreating soldiers of General Lee's Army of Northern Virginia. The Confederates had suffered twenty-eight thousand killed, wounded, or captured at Gettysburg and were now desperate to escape to the safe haven of central Virginia. In this sense, Charlie never knew what hit him. But he was about to learn a lot about being a Confederate prisoner of war.

# Chapter III

## A Prisoner of the Confederacy

After a night under guard at a Confederate encampment in Charlestown, West Virginia, Charlie and the other twenty-four prisoners were marched on foot eighteen miles to Winchester, Virginia, where they were held in a second floor room of the Frederick County Courthouse. In the following days, the prisoners were allowed outside under guard, and Charlie was permitted to visit some wounded soldiers of the Eighteenth Connecticut Regiment—many of whom came from Norwich—who had been captured at the disastrous June 15 Battle of Winchester. He himself was visited by two cousins, both probably on his mother's side. Cousin Eunice brought him hot meals, and Jennie, walking about on the arm of a Confederate officer, inquired about Charlie's health when they met at the town water pump.[181] Apparently concerned about retaliation against them in Winchester, Charlie later referred to the two female cousins simply as "true friends." He and Jennie would correspond during his captivity. Charlie's personal servant Denny, who was considered part of the family by this point, was sent back to Norwich after Charlie's capture. "I don't want to lose him," Charlie wrote his mother.[182]

In the coming days, more Union prisoners were brought into the courthouse lock-up. Charlie complained that officers were being confined in the same crowded room as the enlisted soldiers, constituting a breach of military rules and custom. A senior Union prisoner submitted a letter of complaint to the Confederate provost marshal, who predictably passed it up the line to General Lee. The response from Lee is not known, but a week later the provost marshal moved the Union officers to a separate room next to one holding recidivistic Confederate deserters. The officers took Sergeant Ferris with them.[183]

The officers' new quarters lasted only a day, however. On July 18, Charlie and more than three hundred other Union prisoners began the long trip to Richmond, guarded by the famous "Stonewall Battalion." Before leaving the courthouse, Charlie inscribed his name (as "Major") in pencil on the plaster wall of an upstairs room. Others did the same, and their names are still there, maintained as an exhibit by the Winchester Courthouse Museum. One of the prisoners (the handwriting is not Charlie's) also added an original protest poem, "The Curse of Jeff Davis":

> May he be set afloat
> Boat without compass or rudder
> Then that any contents be swallowed by a shark.
> The shark by a whale.
> Whale in the Devil's belly and the Devil in hell.
> The gates locked.
> The key lost.
> And further, may he be put in the northwest corner
> With a southwest wind blowing ashes
> In his eyes for all eternity.

An exhausting first day's march on foot took the Union prisoners eighteen miles to Middleton, Virginia, where Charlie was confined in a house he recognized from his 1862 reconnoitering.[184] Obviously, it was not one of the many he had burned. For the next three days the prisoners were marched south through Front Royal, Sperryville, and Woodville, averaging the customary eighteen miles a day. At one point, they were shelled by Union artillery that was presumably aimed at Lee's forces. None of the prisoners was hit. Reaching the railhead of Culpepper during a rainstorm in the early evening of July 25, they were put aboard boxcars, the train reaching Richmond about 20 hours later. Charlie and the other officers were immediately taken to Libby Prison, where they were greeted by yet more of the Eighteenth Connecticut Infantry officers who had been captured at Winchester. Charlie ate breakfast the next morning with Lieutenant Colonel (later General) William Ely, a family friend, former classmate, and commanding officer of the Eighteenth. Ely showed Charlie around the Libby rooms, which Charlie initially thought were "airy and commodious."[185] He would not always think so.

## Confinement in a Warehouse

Libby Prison stood on the north bank of the James River in Richmond. Built as three separate but connected structures in the mid-1840s, it had served as a tobacco warehouse until the mid-1850s, when Maine businessman Luther Libby rented the buildings and re-opened them as "L. Libby & Son, Ship Chandlers." After the first battle of Bull Run/ Manassas in July 1861, when the Confederacy suddenly needed a place to confine captured Union officers, Mr. Libby was given forty-eight hours to vacate the premises. By agreeing to comply, he was allowed to continue a portion of his business in a small corner of one building.[186]

The Confederacy converted the upper two floors of the four-floor buildings into prison quarters, creating a total of six separate rooms, each of which measured about 44 by 110 feet. During Charlie's confinement, the number of prisoners ranged from 594 to nearly 1,000.[187] Meals were cooked on stoves in each room, twelve officers to a "mess." The prisoners acknowledged traditional military organizational discipline, and the senior officer present, Colonel A. D. Streight, routinely appointed an officer of the day, as well as an officer responsible for each mess.[188] There were no beds and few benches. Each room had about fifteen windows, which were small but, at the beginning, entirely open. To prevent escapes, outside guards were instructed to shoot any prisoner coming near a window. Eventually, the windows were grated with wooden bars.[189]

The first floor of one building was used as a hospital for the sick and injured of both Libby and of Belle Isle, a prison camp for enlisted soldiers, located nearby in the middle of the James River. The number of hospital patients swelled to nearly 900 in early 1864, Charlie estimated. Since the room measured about 4,700 square feet, this would have allowed only a five-by-nine-foot space per patient, a ghastly condition. Dangerous inmates, recaptured escapees, and runaway slaves were confined in Libby's cellar.[190]

Because the provost marshal of Richmond, General John H. Winder, had overall responsibility for Libby, the prison was known as "Castle Winder." Charlie wrote that Winder "runs this place with meanness, harshness, cruelty, etc."[191] Winder once ordered a civilian to be beaten and locked in the cellar for three days for speaking to a prisoner. Another time, three New England captains and a major were chosen at random and sent to a state prison in retaliation for the North having confined four Confederate officers at a state prison in Allan, Illinois. (Whether

Libby Prison, Richmond, 1865
(photograph by Alexander Gardner, courtesy National Archives).

Sectional view of two rooms at Libby Prison (drawing by Captain Harry
E. Wrigley, Topographical Engineers, War Department, c. 1865).

the North had good reasons for such criminal confinements apparently was irrelevant to Winder.) Charlie luckily avoided being selected.[192] And Winder ordered any prisoner caught looking out an unbarred window to be shot. Charlie was thrilled when he heard that Winder's son had been captured by the North because now "we rather doubted them to commence their hangings," an extreme measure that the prisoners had feared.[193] Winder later became military commander of the infamous Andersonville prison camp in Georgia. He had authority over the commandant, Henry Wirz, who was later convicted of war crimes, and hanged. Winder might have been similarly treated, but he died in February 1865, before the war ended and the North imposed its retribution.

Day-to-day authority over Libby Prison lay with two unrelated men named Turner: the military commandant, Major Thomas P. Turner, and the civilian manager, Richard R. "Dick" Turner. The prisoners often mocked Dick by calling him "major," resulting in some historical confusion as to which Turner did what.[194] The Turners punished attempted escapes harshly by clapping the captured prisoners in irons and locking them in small cells for days or weeks. To hamper escape planning, the Turners first ordered censoring of out-going letters, and later, line limitations. But the authorities could act fairly, on occasion. When some prisoners began hogging blankets, the blankets were seized and then re-issued, two to an inmate. And a prisoner's rank was sometimes given surprising respect. When a guard accused Lieutenant Colonel Cesnola (whom Charlie had served under near Fredericksburg) of being a liar, Cesnola grabbed him by the throat, and other officers threatened to throw the offending guard from a prison window. A complaint was taken to General Winder who, instead of punishing the rebellious prisoners, ordered the guard removed.[195]

## Harsh Conditions and Help from Home

In the beginning, Libby Prison provided minimal rations of hash for breakfast, soup for lunch, and rice for supper. With the U.S. currency that they were able to carry into prison, the officer prisoners supplemented this meager diet with outside purchases until their money ran out. While it lasted, each officer contributed a dollar a day toward a cooperative purchase of sugar, butter, bread, crackers, watermelons, tomatoes, beans, potatoes, apples, rice, and coffee, among other foods. In a sign of a weakening Southern economy and a growing black market for a stronger currency, the prisoners maximized their purchases by paying greenbacks directly to the civilian grocers, rather than first exchanging for Confederate dollars at the prison. But the privilege of outside purchasing was problematic and Charlie worried that it might be cancelled any day. It had already been denied to the captured troops of General Robert H. Milroy, presumably because the Confederates despised his ruthless anti-bushwhacker campaign in the Shenandoah Valley—which in itself was responding to ambushes like the ones on Charlie in April and June 1862.[196]

Charlie resented that the South was treating him and his fellow prisoners far worse than the Union was treating equivalent Confederate prisoners. He had heard that Confederate soldiers in Northern prisons were fed better, lived in regular barracks with beds, and enjoyed daily outdoor exercise. They also got three dollars a day to buy additional food, he had heard, while the Confederacy provided the equivalent of three dollars *a month* to the Libby inmates. Charlie thought that if only Lincoln would make the conditions for rebel prisoners at Johnson Island on Lake Erie (considered to be quite bearable apart from its cold weather) as miserable as those at Libby and Belle Isle "then we would not complain."[197]

> We (at Libby) are now full of officers, over 800, and at least 10,000 men are here [at Belle Isle] confined. Their lot is awful—deaths at the rate of 8 & 12 a day has come to our notice. And no relief for them. All the poor fellows get is 1/2 quart of poor soup (made of rotten bacon) and 1/2 a loaf of bread a day. Not a blanket given them, and whilst on the island they laid on the ground through all rain and storms...Even the officers are not furnished blankets sufficient. And the last lot of them (i.e., officers), over 200 men, are now sleeping on floor and no covering. A few poor blankets are distributed, but they are not near so good as a cotton handkerchief. I tell you our condition is awful here, and our government should either attend to it or treat the confederate officer to the same.[198]

Charlie's parents probably passed along these descriptions of the deplorable conditions at Libby and Belle Isle to Governor Buckingham because in late November the governor asked Lincoln to intervene on behalf of the prisoners.[199] Lincoln's response is not known, but the request alone suggests the strength of the Farnsworth family connections.

As conditions in the South worsened generally, so did those at Libby. In November 1863, Charlie reported that no beef had been issued for four days running, although salted pork from the North was available. It got worse in January 1864, Charlie noting that no meat had been issued for eight days and that the senior Union officer, General Neal S. Dow, "was not much pleased."[200]

By agreement between the warring sides, so-called "truce boats" were allowed to bring in foodstuffs from the North, as well as mail, books, newspapers, clothing, and amusements such as playing cards and chess. Letters arrived within a week or two of being sent, bearing six cents postage, although sometimes they were delivered even without a stamp. Boxes of goods took longer, often three weeks. Charlie was desperate for his first box of food, which arrived from his cousin Harry Meredith of Baltimore three months after his capture. From his parents, from cousin Harry, from Governor Buckingham's wife, and from his mother's aunt, Mrs. General William Williams, Charlie got eleven more boxes of provisions in the ensuing months of his imprisonment. This exceeded what he needed, so he shared his bounty with fellow officers and with his men confined on Belle Isle.

To get to Libby, boxes from the North were first routed to Fortress Monroe, near Hampton Roads, Virginia, on a spit of land which remained in Union hands throughout the war. From there, Confederate boats under a flag of truce picked up the goods and carried them up the James River to Richmond. Alternatively, families could send money to General Benjamin F. Butler, commander of the fortress, who would then apply the funds against the government's supplies and ship them to the prison. Libby later barred this monetary form of assistance, and admitted only boxes of provisions sent directly by family and friends.

Charlie's first request to his family was actually not for food, but for comfort items. He wanted a sponge, soap, paper, pencils, pens, clothes, books, newspapers, and his chess pieces.[201] But as prison rations and the prisoners' money dwindled, in October Charlie asked for a box with "10 lbs. sugar, 2 lbs. coffee, 10 lbs. butter, 2 quarts syrup (churned pine apple), a few canned meats," which soon arrived. He received another box in early November with coffee, sugar, grapes, molasses, butter, and some books. Unsurprisingly, the grapes arrived spoiled. He even got a box sent personally by Governor Buckingham's wife, so close were the families. By late November, Charlie reported that he and others were well-supplied with victuals; what they wanted now was news from home. Prison authorities were seizing or censoring communications from the outside, so Charlie instructed his family how to send newspapers and letters in a hollowed-out cake. As the number of captive officers grew, so did the truce boat shipments; one boat brought two hundred boxes for the prisoners. Several others brought the total stock to twenty-five tons! Perhaps because the boxes were keeping Charlie and his friends well-fed, in December he wrote "If I never suffer any more than <u>now</u>, I will not complain."[202]

Sample of Charlie's hand-written letters, this one dated November 20, 1863, to his mother.

Because some officers were getting a lot of boxes and others none, the Libby authorities stopped delivering to the addressees and instead periodically turned over shipments to the highest-ranking prisoner, to be equitably distributed. Reported to Washington by military doctors, the practice was criticized in the North as amounting to a seizure of goods. Charlie, however, defended the prison measure:

> Our commissioned officers superintended it, and the confederate authorities acted in the best possible manner. It was a foul lie about the rations being piled up in sight of prison and not issued. Only such a cracked lot of fellows as our late medical fellow prisoners could spread such a yarn. Give the devil his due. The authorities issued the commissary goods, and made them by their care last 12 days, issuing all that men wanted. There was not that number of days' rations sent. But by the judicious act of them, they lasted longer than at home. This [letter] is a little longer than allowed, but I desired to vindicate persons wrongly accused. [203]

A truce boat with four hundred boxes arrived in mid-January 1864, but Libby authorities asserted a different reason to seize the cargo: a Union army was advancing up the James River toward Richmond under the command of the detested General Butler. The South regarded Butler as a war criminal because in New Orleans he had ordered a flag-burner hanged and also had declared that any southern woman who protested the Northern occupation could be regarded as a prostitute. When Butler's drive up the James slowed, the Libby authorities relented and permitted distribution of the four hundred boxes, although a senior Union officer, as a protest, ordered that they not be opened. Another truce boat, loaded with more boxes, arrived shortly thereafter, and despite some confusion, all the boxes were then distributed.[204]

When southern citizens criticized their government for allowing Libby prisoners, with their gift boxes, to eat better than their own army, Commissioner for Exchange Robert Auld announced that henceforth the prisoners would get the same rations as troops in the field. Libby authorities then seized nearly all existing food boxes, and also barred the prisoners from making outside purchases with the gold coins that kept mysteriously appearing.[205]

Charlie and his prison-mates devised ingenious ways to evade Libby's rules on correspondence. Initially, outgoing mail from Libby was censored, or even destroyed, if the prison censors felt overworked. After several attempts by prisoners to escape, Libby limited letters to a page or less, fearing that they might contain plans for conspirators. But Charlie learned how to slip long letters past the censors, writing them in "invisible" ink (lemon or onion juice that became legible when the paper was warmed), and his family smuggled letters, newspapers, and gold coins into prison by inserting them into canned foods. In late September, Charlie asked his friend Major Fish to have his family send another food box, to include condensed milk, with "a $20 gold piece in one of the cans of milk." Some of the coins got through, but at least one five-dollar gold piece was seized by the guards. By January 1864, prisoners' families were regularly smuggling papers and coins into Libby, concealing them in cans of meat, as well as in hollowed-out cakes.[206]

By late winter, the officers were starved more for news than for food. Referring to interesting news stories sent stuffed into a can of sausage, Charlie wrote, "We opened yesterday the box can of sausage meat, found it very nice indeed. Send one can of same kind in next box. It is better flavored than any we have." He usually had enough provisions, but constantly longed for more "sausage meat in a can," his code for newspapers. When some officers tried to send the newspapers over to the enlisted men at Belle Isle with a re-canning operation in their own kitchen, the Libby guards shut it down.[207]

Mail and box restrictions were tightened even further in March 1864. In addition to limiting prisoners to one out-going letter per week, with a maximum of six lines, and permitting incoming boxes only from individuals (but not from the army or the government), now *all* cans and packages would be opened and searched. The "sausage meat" ploy to smuggle newspapers would no longer work. Moreover, the "invisible letter" technique had been discovered, so letters coming and going were being heated and examined by the guards. To evade detection, Charlie countered by advising his family to hide invisible letters within a whole packet of blank paper, or to write the "invisible" letter on the inside of the envelope, as he would do.[208]

Charlie also used a chance encounter with a pre-war acquaintance to evade the prison censors. Lieutenant Colonel F. T. Cavada of the 114th Pennsylvania Infantry was a Cuban volunteer in the Union army whom

Charlie had met two years earlier at a Norwich party. The two became such close friends at Libby that Cavada, upon being released in early March 1864, carried an "invisible letter" to Charlie's father, written on the back of a concocted note allegedly from *his* father to Cavada regarding "a small package for my son on Belle Isle." The convoluted fake note was wrapped among a stack of letters that Cavada had received during his months at Libby and was allowed to take out. The ruse worked neatly, and Cavada forwarded the "invisible letter" to Norwich when his truce boat docked at Annapolis.[209]

Charlie corresponded regularly from Libby not only with his parents and brothers, but also with his fiancée Georgia Parker. He characterized neither the emotional tone nor the content of the letters to and from Georgia, however, and since none have been found, it is hard to know the nature of their commitment. In a diary entry on December 18, Charlie simply noted "Wrote Georgia 'Merry Christmas.'"[210] He occasionally enclosed a letter to Georgia within a letter to his parents, asking that it be forwarded "should she be absent," which would indicate that Georgia spent at least some of the war years in Norwich.

As he had done from the field, Charlie sometimes wrote from Libby with advice and criticism concerning his brothers and others. When his younger brother Fred turned twenty-one on December 5, 1863, Charlie wrote: "So Fred is a voter, since time flies. It reminds me, I am aged. He will soon meet the world's waves of fortune. May he take the flood tide."[211] Charlie was twenty-eight at the time. As at Camp Chesebrough, his younger brother's attitude often irritated him: "Fred gave me a lecture on not writing oftener, as though we were not restricted as to letters."[212] Charlie felt that his older brother Billings had let him down, complaining that a letter from him was the first he had received "since my migration south." Perhaps the criticism stung; Billings began lobbying in early 1864 for his brother's release. Charlie was critical of a cousin, Walter Loring Farnsworth, age twenty-one, and the comparatively soft life he was living, caustically noting that he "has again gone abroad."[213]

## Belle Isle: Far Worse than Libby

Looking beyond his own welfare at Libby, Charlie worried about his men starving on Belle Isle, and sent much of his own provisions to them. When a box from Governor Buckingham's wife, intended for all Connecticut prisoners, arrived in early December, Charlie made sure that it was shared with those on the island. He took particular care to see that his Company B quartermaster, Weston Ferris, got his share. Charlie felt a special obligation toward some of his fellow Norwich townsmen, especially Private Thomas Carver whose brother Michael had been killed on a patrol that Charlie had ordered earlier that year, and Private George Ward, a schoolmate who had fallen very ill, making sure that provisions reached those two.[214] When it was reported that three Belle Isle prisoners had frozen to death in January 1864, Charlie mistakenly told his parents that Thomas Carver was one of the three, adding a suggestion that Carver's mother not be told how he had died.[215]

There was no housing for the Belle Isle prisoners, numbering between six and ten thousand, and only enough tents for half of them. The others tried to survive in the open, many even without blankets. Provisions were so minimal that the prisoners fought among themselves for scraps. After being allowed to visit his troops there, Charlie smuggled out a letter describing how the prisoners were trying to subsist on one-half quart of soup with bacon flavoring and one-half loaf of bread a day, and that they were dying at the rate of twenty a day from disease and starvation. In addition, three prisoners had frozen to death, and three others were shot, in two days, Charlie reported.[216] A Union surgeon in Baltimore later remarked, upon examining some of the exchanged prisoners from Belle Isle, "Many of them had partially lost their reason...They were filthy in the extreme, covered in vermin...nearly all were extremely emaciated; so much so that they had to be cared for even like infants."[217]

Made aware of the dreadful conditions at Confederate prison camps, the U.S. Congress took action, creating the United States Sanitary Commission in 1861. The ccommission coordinated the earlier volunteer efforts of Northern women in shipping blankets, clothing, and other provisions to Belle Isle and elsewhere. Richmond authorities assigned Lieutenant Colonel James M. Sanderson, a captured Union commissary officer, the task of distributing the commission's shipments to the Belle Isle prisoners. After Sanderson encountered great difficulties in performing the job, he resigned in October 1863. In January 1864, Sanderson's fellow officers at Libby accused him before their self-styled "Indignation Commission of Being Insulted" of "arrogance and mistreatment of our men on the island." Although the accusations were voted down, Charlie noted "Sanderson is very unpopular indeed." When Sanderson went north in a March 1864 prisoner exchange, he was arrested and charged with "cruelty to Federal prisoners," among other offenses. He was found guilty by a military tribunal and dismissed from the army, but was not imprisoned. He later wrote a lengthy defense of his actions.[218]

After Sanderson resigned, distribution of the Sanitary Commission's next shipment to Belle Isle was supervised by one of Libby's highest-ranking officers, Brigadier General Neal S. Dow. Dow had known suffering of his own. Wounded and captured in New Orleans, he had been transported all the way back to Richmond to be imprisoned. After making the distribution at Belle Isle, he told Charlie he had seen men that were "naked, half-starved, lousy. The sick laying upon the ground, a log for a pillow and dying at the rate of 10 a day. Fed upon 2 oz. meat soup and bread. Awfully abused by the guards, knocked down with clubs..." Dow sought to make a second inspection of Belle Isle to see if the men were faring any better, but civilian commandant Turner rejected the request.[219]

In late January 1864, Charlie was allowed to visit Belle Isle to inspect the condition of the First Connecticut Cavalry prisoners. To his joyful surprise, he found that Private Thomas Carver, who had been reported frozen to death earlier that month, was actually alive and reasonably well. (Carver eventually survived the war.) Charlie saw fourteen of his twenty-four men, including right-hand man Quartermaster Sergeant Weston Ferris, Sergeant Franklin H. Monroe, Corporal Amos C. Bradley (who would later die at Belle Isle), Private Peter Miller, and Private Patrick E. Clary, who was hospitalized at the time and was later sent to Andersonville, near Americus, Georgia, where he died. Charlie proudly reported that all of his men "stood up for the Govt. and do not want any backing down."[220]

Charlie was outraged by the Libby guards' treatment of one Belle Isle prisoner, Private George Ward, his Norwich school-mate. Emaciated from illness, Ward was being marched under guard from the Libby hospital room back to Belle Isle when Charlie and another Norwich friend, Colonel William Ely, tossed him a ham they had just received from home. As Ward weakly stooped to pick it up, the guards threatened him with their bayoneted rifles and seized the ham. Ward nonetheless saluted his officer friends at the prison window: "[With] a look of pain, raising his head, hand to cap, he said 'Colonel, the will for the deed.'" Charlie repeated this incident later in testimony before a government commission.[221] Years later, Charlie was lauded in Norwich for his determined efforts to keep the First Connecticut prisoners on Belle Isle alive:

Farnsworth...did what he could to see that those of his own command, captured with him, as well as others whom he knew, shared in the good things sent to him from his own home. His thoughtfulness and zeal in this particular was remembered with devout gratitude by some who returned to speak of it, and who felt that their own preservation from death by starvation was due to him.[222]

Charlie may have received this commendation because his actions were unusual. When a truce boat brought food boxes for two other officers in October 1863, Charlie noted "How much better to have given them to our men. But as usual, officers take it all. Cans of milk, syrup, hams are distributed amongst private messes."[223]

Worried about a Union raid to liberate Belle Isle, the Confederacy in early 1864 began to transfer enlisted prisoners to its newly built Andersonville stockade in Georgia. Thomas Carver, Weston Ferris, and other First Connecticut cavalrymen, along with many Eighteenth Connecticut infantrymen, were sent further south in the first train-load. No one then realized that conditions at Andersonville would prove far worse than those at Belle Isle, and that more than 13,000 Union soldiers would die there from starvation and disease. By the end of February, all of the First and Eighteenth regiments' enlisted prisoners had been sent to Andersonville, Charlie thought, and he asked that families and friends in Norwich be so informed.[224]

## Maintaining Morale

After the Confederacy lost a crucial battle at Lookout Mountain near Chattanooga in late November, 1863, Libby's military guards were sent off as infantry reinforcements and were replaced by the ill-trained Home Guard. Prison rules, and their enforcement, would become less predictable. When Charlie and others shouted to celebrate the news of a Union victory, the quasi-civilian rookie guards rushed in to quash the commotion, and threatened to make the prisoners stand outside all night as punishment for their cheering. Northern papers were now thoroughly censored, or barred completely, just to suppress prison morale. Nevertheless, Richmond papers were readily available, but Charlie read them with a jaundiced eye. He enjoyed a candid report on the fierce debates between the Confederate Congress and President Davis after the South's debacle at Lookout

Mountain, particularly admiring Davis's "long and thorough, well-written, labored article, seeking comfort for large losses with small gains on their side." He thought less of Tennessee Senator Henry S. Foote's vitriolic response that put the blame on Davis personally because he was playing favorites with the generals and demoralizing the troops with his visits to the front.[225]

As time went by, Charlie felt that however harsh Libby's prison conditions and minimal rations were, it was the loss of liberty that hurt the most. Referring to a winter spent three years earlier in a Rocky Mountain blizzard, he reminisced, "Those sufferings sink into insignificance when you add [liberty] to it. Go where you please—that is what makes a prisoner's life so hard." Hardened to the elements, Charlie even thought that the winter weather at Libby "has not been very severe for us up-country fellows." What he yearned for were his carefree days as a horseman: "Lights burn to midnight—having sweet dreams of freedom and old friends. A nice mare assists my pillow as in days of yore. Ah, those happy days and nights will never return—then was my Gala Days." Despite the hardships, Charlie carefully guarded his health at Libby, keeping warm and eating well enough; he boasted that he had never missed a roll-call.[226]

Charlie was willing to suffer confinement for the greater Union cause, asking his family just before Thanksgiving to honor him and other prisoners with the Masons' traditional "vacant chair" observance:

> One week from today as you are drawing chairs around
> the table spread as bountifully, I trust this will reach you.
> Remember the prisoners here confined and look not with
> sorrow upon the vacant chairs, but with joy that they are
> vacant in such a cause.[227]

Six weeks later, he reiterated his acceptance of imprisonment for the Union cause:

> There is little interesting matter for contemplation in our
> present position. We read, and study all it is possible, but
> it is a difficult matter to apply your mind. We now number
> a thousand, and should much prefer serving our govt. at
> some other station. Still, like good soldiers we shall await
> "marching orders."[228]

Charlie observed that events were not going well for the Confederacy. Draft resisters, deserters, and citizens suspected of disloyalty were being hauled into Libby. New conscripts, mostly boys and old men at this point, were brought in in chains for processing into the Confederate army. At least one riot among these new recruits had broken out in an adjacent building.[229] From all this, and from his meager outside news sources, Charlie made a fairly accurate assessment of the looming Confederate defeat:

> The south is evidently growing weak. They are short of men…They seize conscripts to put everyone in the army, do everything in a desperate manner. Their railroads are worn out. Their cavalry is worn down, their supplies gone. Each day loses as we advance upon them from all points. They will make one desperate fight in Virginia and if whipped will move south, concentrate all their armies in one desperate struggle. The end comes within 18 months and not much shorter.[230]
>
> The leads of the papers are blue. They see but little hope for the future, still they fight on. "Glorious victories," but "loss of territories." "Brave troops," still "lose ground." Everything looks blue for them.[231]

Charlie's confident prediction of Northern victory was off by only two months. Nevertheless, he worried about defensive weaknesses in the North, especially in the one city he knew something about, writing to a cousin that "the army must not leave Baltimore."[232]

## Ambition and Resentment

From the day he went to war, Charlie had unabashedly sought to advance in rank and command. One obstacle had been that the First Connecticut Cavalry Regiment had enough men for only one battalion, and the full enrollment of a second battalion—which Charlie might have commanded—had been problematic. But good news arrived in January 1864; a second unit was filling up.[233] Governor Buckingham promoted Charlie to lieutenant colonel in late January, but because of his confinement Charlie was unable to take immediate command of the new battalion, as his new rank would have warranted. The governor was well-aware of the problem and promised to hold the position open, writing that he was looking forward to the day when Charlie would be released "from rebel imprisonment and barbarity, and his entrance upon the more active duty of repressing the rebellion to which he has been so loyally & faithfully devoted."[234]

In Charlie's absence, Major Blakeslee was given temporary command of the new battalion. Regimental Commander Fish reassured Charlie that his "interest is well-guarded" and that his date of muster as lieutenant colonel would date back to December 18.[235] This assurance would have preserved Charlie's right to command the new battalion upon his release, but it proved to be more than Fish was authorized to promise. Charlie's dreams of high command ultimately would be dashed by his imprisonment, personal intrigue, and the realities of the war.

Charlie worried about the battalion commander billet being even *temporarily* filled by Blakeslee, whom he did not trust. "That is one reason why I desire to get out early," he wrote.[236] Charlie now blamed Blakeslee for his capture, and resented that Blakeslee might now gain by it. Writing to his mother Charlie sneered, "I hear of a famous letter from Blakeslee, and wish to hear what credit his failing to sustain gave him."[237] This was a new charge; none of the earlier versions of the Harpers Ferry debacle had blamed Blakeslee for any "failing." Nor did anything come out later to implicate him. In fact, Blakeslee rose to the rank of brigadier general and later wrote the regiment's official history, effusively praising Charlie throughout, all the while undoubtedly ignorant of Charlie's allegations. The two corresponded while Charlie was at Libby, apparently without acrimony.[238] But Charlie had considered Blakeslee a weak leader since at least February 1863 when he wrote to his mother from Camp Chesebrough, "But I can hardly leave camp for an hour, as there is no one but Blakeslee to fall back upon, and as Pope said of Seigle, he is unreliable."[239]

With Blakeslee's supposedly temporary appointment as commander of the Second Battalion, Captain Leonard P. Goodwin took command of Charlie's Company B. Believing that he would soon become the permanent Second Battalion commander, Charlie was not at all unhappy about being replaced by Goodwin. In fact, he was pleased to hear that "all my boys had reenlisted" under their new captain.[240]

Charlie thought he would be confined well into 1864. From the front lines of the First Connecticut Cavalry, Lieutenant Howell Atwater had written to ask Charlie to "stand up" for him at a wedding scheduled for

May 1864 in New London. Charlie doubted that he would be out of Libby by then. "[A] pleasure I looked forward to will be denied me. Such is the fate of soldiers. We are never our own masters after enlisted."[241]

## Gambling and Other Amusements

To pass the long days at Libby, Charlie and three Norwich friends, Quartermaster Lieutenant Dwight W. ("Marlie") Hakes, Lieutenant Colonel Ely, and Lieutenant John T. Maginnis—officers of the Eighteenth Connecticut Infantry, which was composed mainly of Norwich men— came up with a variety of amusements. One was gambling on almost anything. Charlie was particularly successful in taking pessimistic positions in betting on when they would be part of a prisoner exchange, winning a sabre sheath, shoulder straps, one hundred cigars, a pair of size twelve boots, expenses for a "day on the town," and several other wagers of more than twenty dollars. The friends even laid bets on the exact time that would elapse between dinner and breakfast.[242]

A larger circle of the officers amused themselves with politics, publishing, theater, and language studies. The so-called Indignation Commission met frequently to review charges of breaches of loyalty or discipline. One claim alleged that an infantry officer had curried favor with a Confederate guard to get a blanket by proclaiming "under other circumstances, I am a friend of the south." Other officers published the occasional *Libby Chronicle,* a newsletter of humor and commentary. Still others organized the "Libby Troupe," putting on at least one "Negro performance," probably a black-face minstrel show. Ely and others, but apparently not Charlie, studied French, writing out long responses to pedagogic questions.

Sundays were always observed reverently. Amusements were put aside, and the officers read and wrote, "passing the day quietly." In November 1863, the Confederacy had begun to send its own church ministers into Libby to preach to the prisoners, many of whom no doubt thought that God was not being well-represented. But to alleviate their boredom, Charlie's section accepted one of the chaplains, Rev. H. Clay Membull of Columbia, South Carolina, on at least two occasions. After preaching, the reverend actually sat down for dinner with the prisoners. When opposition arose against a return engagement, senior officers took a vote at "a very exciting meeting." Surprisingly, Membull was welcomed back by a four-to-one majority.[243]

A great feast was celebrated at Christmas, the officers dining on a menu of impressive scope in any setting, but especially in a Confederate prison. Drawing from a recent shipment as well as from their substantial stores, Charlie's room of more than 150 officers celebrated, he wrote, with "oyster soup, roast chicken, boiled mutton, vegetables, cold boiled ham with cranberry sauce, pickled peaches, pickled onions, apple sauce, and gerkins." All this topped off with dessert of "apple pie, walnuts, oranges, and raisins."[244] Perhaps the menu and banquet were illusory and the prisoners actually suffered their usual fare, but it was not Charlie's habit to write facetiously.

## Escaping Libby Prison

Many Libby prisoners tried to escape; most failed. Those recaptured were usually punished by close confinement, sometimes in chains, for days or weeks in small, dank, rat-infested cells in the prison basement. In December 1863, Colonel A. D. Streight of Indiana and another officer bribed a guard with a hundred dollars and fled. But, double-crossed by the guard, they were quickly apprehended, "ironed," and thrown into the basement cells. When Streight was still being kept in solitary a month later, his fellow prisoners cut a hole through to his room, enabling secretive communication, at least at night.[245]

During a regular exchange of Union and Confederate surgeons, one infantry major posed as a doctor and walked out. Libby Commandant Turner, in response, threatened to stop all boxes and withhold all rations unless those who helped with the escape were identified. "We would rather starve," Charlie declared.[246] A day later, the masquerading major was exposed and apprehended at City Point, Virginia, about twenty-five miles down the James River. He was returned to Libby and locked in a cell for two days. After two New York infantry officers walked out of the prison hospital and escaped in late October, Major Turner moved the hospital to a more secure location in the basement, and put all prisoners on bread and water for the day. Two months later, several officers bribed a guard with $40 and escaped from the hospital's new location, only to be quickly apprehended. Charlie thought that the corrupted guard would be shot. Clamping down on what he perceived as a misuse of the medical facility, Provost Marshal Winder ordered that "all capable of escape in hospital be returned to quarters."[247]

A plan for an escape from Belle Isle by twenty soldiers in January

1864 "fizzled," according to Charlie, who provided no further details. But nine officers successfully slipped out of Libby later that month. Prison authorities responded by requiring roll-calls every two hours, providing the prisoners with "lots of fun" in creating over- and under-counts for the guards. Two of the nine escaped officers were quickly re-captured and locked in cells; the other seven apparently got away. Charlie never took part in any of these small-scale escape attempts, but he almost fled during the biggest Libby jailbreak of all.[248]

On February 9, 1864, after a herculean tunneling project, 109 officers escaped in what became known as the "Grand Exit" or the "Grand Delivery." Working for seventeen nights, the prisoners dug a fifty-three-foot-long tunnel under the warehouse prison walls, using only a pocket knife, some chisels, rope, cloth, and a wooden spittoon. A chimney extending down to the basement connected with the tunnel, which passed under a road and came up in a nearby carriage shed. Squeezing three floors down the chimney and then crawling through the narrow passage-way in pitch darkness required a lot of courage, strength, and stealth. Colonel Ely, Charlie's close friend from Norwich, was among those who got out. Of the 109 who fled, 59 made it to Union lines, 48 (including Ely) were recaptured, and 2 drowned. The Libby commandant, Major Turner, later suspected that the prison's civilian manager, Dick Turner, and some guards had been bribed to overlook the many nights of tunneling. [249]

Although he never wrote about his role in the break-out, Charlie must have helped in some manner because he had planned to go out with the others, backing out only at the last minute. It was one of the few decisions in his lifetime that he made on the side of caution, and one that he was later unhappy about. An unusual strike-through in a letter a month later revealed a lingering ambivalence about not going: "I started to leave on the night of the escape, but an alarm of the guard deterred me. I am ~~not~~ sorry now, though I at the time acted as I thought prudently."[250]

Libby commanders took various steps after the "Grand Exit" to prevent any future breakouts. One measure was the ultimate weapon: a bomb. Concerned with Union general Judson Kilpatrick's approach to Richmond in early March 1864, Major Turner ordered the basement filled with enough gunpowder to blow up the entire building and its inmates if liberation seemed likely. Turner later admitted, "I would have blown you all to Hades before I would have suffered you to be released."[251]

## The Soldier-Slave Dilemma

In the weeks following his July 1863 incarceration at Libby, Charlie expected that a prisoner exchange would soon have him returning north. The Union and Confederacy had agreed in July 1862 to exchange prisoners on a rank-weighted basis—a sergeant for a sergeant, a major for a major, and so forth. Each side had appointed a commissioner to carry out the agreement. But the system broke down in May 1863 when the South refused to include captured black soldiers in the exchanges, threatening instead to re-enslave or execute them. Still, Charlie thought that his confinement would last only "until after the next battle," apparently believing that thousands of new prisoners of war would force both sides to send some of them home.[252]

Charlie was bitter about the preferential treatment received by some officers, especially Brigadier General Charles K. Graham, who got a quick exchange through his political connections with Massachusetts senator Charles Sumner. But Charlie may not have known of a separate reason for the unusual exchange: Graham was severely disabled by wounds suffered at Gettysburg. In any case, the exchange mattered little because brigadier generals, in Charlie's view, were "useless." Seemingly arbitrary and bizarre decisions by the exchange commissioners increased the frustration of the prisoners. When a captured Confederate major was sent south in a proposed exchange for a Pennsylvania infantry major, Confederate commissioner Judge Robert Auld rejected the deal, probably to punish the Northern major, who had tried earlier to escape. In response, a Southern major was shipped back north.[253]

About a hundred officers and men from Libby and Belle Isle were sent north during a limited exchange in late September 1863, but Charlie was not among them. By October, Charlie had figured out why the exchange system wasn't fully functioning: "I suppose we suffer for the black soldier. Comment is unnecessary." He was becoming resigned to a long imprisonment: "As there is little chance of getting away from here for a long time, a box or so [of foodstuffs] a month will add greatly to our comfort." A rumor spread that Lincoln would accept a Southern compromise to limit the exchanges to captured *freedmen*, but not slave-soldiers; the rumor proved false. In a December 1863 letter to all troops, the Union's commissioner for exchange, General E. A. Hitchcock, stated emphatically that no exchanges would occur until *all* Negro soldiers and their commanders were included. Charlie understood the position clearly, accepting it in the language of the time, while also asserting his toughness and doubting that the impasse would last long:

> Letter of [Exchange Commissioner] Hitchcock distinctly says the negro is the stumbling block in exchange, and until the South delivers our negro soldiers & officers in command of same there can be "no exchange."[254]

> Letter of Hitchcock of 29th [November] shows the real cause of non-exchange to be the Nigger. We feel now as if we understand our ground and could bear it. The chances do not look very bright, it is true, but still there is some hope. The C. S. Congress being in session may remedy this matter.[255]

> Today a letter from Commissioner Hitchcock showed the 'wooly head' in the question of exchange. I thought it would come to it, and them [illegible]. All summer it has been side-dishes served up, but for Thanksgiving we got the big full-grown negro. How it will come out I know not, but trust that that race won't keep 50,000 soldiers in durance rice [i.e., prison rations.] [256]

Despite the impasse on general exchanges, occasional *special* exchanges did occur, primarily for the few captured medical officers at Libby, and for the injured and sick at Belle Isle.[257] Growing more pessimistic, Charlie reacted with one word to a rumor in late December that a major prisoner exchange would soon take place: "Bah." [258]

Represented by Colonel Streight, Charlie and others tried to negotiate with Confederate commissioner Auld for a general exchange of prisoners, perhaps one prison or unit for another. Rebuffed, they were told that only man-for-man special exchanges (excluding Negro soldiers) would be permitted. Auld added that the South was willing, however, to parole more than eighteen thousand prisoners. (Under an agreement between the warring parties, a prisoner sent home on *parole* could not return to action until a prisoner of equal rank from the other side was sent back; a *special exchange* involved swapping a handful of named prisoners; a *general exchange* was an agreement of the two sides to empty whole prisons, or sections of them.) Charlie imagined, somewhat unrealistically, that some agreement for release could be reached "if the Commissioners [of Exchange] would take beard [i.e., experience similar] lodgings in the prisons of each Government. I think they would soon come to their milk [i.e., show some compassion]."[259]

Charlie also became skeptical of the political principles behind the Union's stand that *all* black prisoners must be included in any general exchange. He began to wonder whether there might be some *military* considerations as well. In the most extensive diary entry of his thinking, he wrote:

> The year draws to a close and still we are held within prison walls. Our hopes are daily raised by rumors of being exchanged, only to be depressed by information that an obstacle is in the way. Weekly a special [exchange] goes away, showing there is but little principle in the matter, for if that principle can be ignored for <u>one</u> it can for a thousand. We doubt the existence of any true principle. Yet we suffer for what: Exchange and What. Six months of suffering and no prospect of release. We see the rebel daily giving down, and our Govt. daily raising new issues. Actions to make 46,000 in their hands work wonders.[260]

After a few days, however, he had recovered his spirit of sacrifice:

> The first day of a new year in prison and no prospect of an exchange. We suffer for our country, and I trust everyone here confined are willing to suffer to the last in support of our common country.[261]

And he reiterated his commitment a short time later:

> The feeling here is very strong towards the policy of the govt. Many a hard word comes. This is all wrong. We should suffer as long as our rulers think it necessary, and it is for the good of our government.[262]

One might wonder whether these pronouncements were sincere or if they were propaganda intended for Confederate eyes. Because they were written in tiny script in a private pocket diary, it seems doubtful that Charlie intended for the guards or censors to read these pledges of faith. More likely, he was just trying to keep his spirits up. Charlie understood that the war was not just about maintaining the Union, but about abolishing slavery as well, although he doubted that slaves would do very well after they were freed. "The status of the negro will be settled by the war. I don't think they will stand any higher north after than they did before the war."[263]

In late January, Charlie lost patience and lashed out at the Negro-prisoner principle he had reluctantly accepted a month earlier:

> You see how we hurt. We are in a sorry plight now, since exchange is stopped. I tell you our chances are slim for getting out for the war. We must endure for the sake of these confounded rebs. I wish all the niggers were out of the country. Then this would not happen. But we will brave it.[264]

Trying to lift his mother's spirits, he wrote, in what must have been painful for her to read:

> You must keep up a good heart. We suffer for our country, and are willing to. Even to laying down of life if retaliatory measures come to the [illegible]. Remember we do for the country as much here as in the field, though a bullet is better than a rope for a soldier. Still we will try and stand firm.[265]

In an odd cross-current of the war, the local Richmond citizenry publically demanded that more prisoners be sent north in order to free up more food for themselves. Slaves carrying bread to the hospital were attacked by hungry Richmond citizens. Charlie thought "[We are] eating them out." Partly to reduce the pressure on Richmond food supplies, nearly a thousand Belle Isle prisoners were transferred in November to Danville, North Carolina. Conditions at Danville, a former tobacco warehouse, were extremely crowded, but at least the prisoners now had a roof over their heads.[266]

## Friends in High Places

Charlie decided in November 1863 that he had to push harder to be included in one of the episodic and unpredictable special exchanges. He asked his family to pull strings with influential family friends Governor Buckingham and U.S. senator Lafayette S. Foster. Charlie's father went to work on his son's behalf. (Ironically, Charlie's chances for a special exchange would have worsened in late January 1864 after he was promoted in absentia to lieutenant colonel, because there were few Confederate prisoners of that rank to exchange for.[267] But the South probably was unaware of his promotion.) Charlie also proposed a measure somewhere between a general and a special exchange: an exchange of all prisoners captured before a certain date, namely September 1, a deadline from which he not coincidentally would benefit.[268]

While Charlie hoped that his family's lobbying for a special exchange would succeed, he still thought that a general exchange would be "for the benefit of those confined on both sides."[269] Although the War Department probably agreed that the prisoners certainly thought that they would benefit from broad exchanges, it had come to believe that such agreements were counterproductive in a larger sense. General of the Army Ulysses S. Grant thought that by returning soldiers to the battlefield, general exchanges prolonged the war and resulted in more killing, maiming, and suffering. Grant was especially concerned with the specter of an increased rate of Northern casualties; Confederate captives, owing to the better conditions of Northern prisons, went back to their units in much better shape to fight than did their Union counterparts. The South predictably took the opposite view on general exchanges: it favored them (so long as contraband soldiers were excluded) because it would be getting a rebel soldier in decent combat condition for every emaciated Unionist it sent north.[270]

Charlie realized that he could also call upon another good political contact, his former commanding general, Robert C. Schenck, to push for his release. Unable to recover sufficiently from wounds suffered at Second Manassas to return to combat, Schenck had resigned from the army. A four-term congressman before the war, Schenck went home to Ohio and ran again, this time against the infamous copperhead Democrat Clement Vallandigham, whom he easily defeated. Schenck was promptly made chairman of the House of Representatives' Committee on Military Affairs.[271] Charlie knew that he had made a good impression as commander of the guard when Schenck, trying to recover from his wounds, had served as provost of Baltimore in early 1863. Wasting no time in taking advantage of this new political connection, Charlie asked Chairman Schenck in late January 1864 to push for a special exchange or parole. "I would request of you if not incompatible with your duty that you write Maj. Gen. Butler and request him to parole a Major and allow him to proceed to Richmond and procure the parole or exchange (the latter preferred as I can then be with my regiment) of myself."[272] In late January, Schenck and his wife traveled all the way to Norwich to reassure Charlie's parents that every effort would be made to secure their son's release. Now Charlie had two major Washington politicians lobbying for him: Senator Foster and Congressman Schenck. Governor Buckingham and others would soon join the effort.

Senator Foster felt a special affinity with Charlie, remembering him as a child who often played with the senator's daughter Joanna. While promising to work for a special exchange, Foster reassured Charlie's mother that a recent Libby parolee had reported Charlie to be "in good health and in good spirits." Foster lobbied for Charlie's release with Commissioner of Exchange Hitchcock, with Secretary of War Stanton, and even with the president himself. They all told him to take his plea to General Butler at Fortress Monroe, where many Confederate officers were being held prisoner. Foster then urged Butler to release three equivalent Confederates for Connecticut officers Ely, Nichols, and Farnsworth.[273] No exchange occurred.

Charlie urged his parents to lobby for his release on the specific grounds that "Late developments in the 1st [Connecticut Cavalry] require the presence of Capt. of Co. B. [i.e., himself]."[274] By "late developments," Charlie was probably referring to the pending court-martial of regimental commander Fish for alleged financial malfeasance in Baltimore. Charlie knew that a conviction would lead to Fish's dismissal, opening a command position as lieutenant commander for himself, *if* he were out of prison. Blakeslee would be appointed regimental commander by default, Charlie worried, if he were not soon exchanged or paroled.

What measures Governor Buckingham took on Charlie's behalf are unknown, but the governor did ask the War Department in December to arrange a special exchange for Colonel Ely and a doctor, both held at Libby. He did not include Charlie in his plea. The doctor was released.[275] In early March Charlie's older brother Billings, who had shown little interest in writing to Charlie at Libby, also joined the lobbying effort. He met with Captain W. H. Swift, an aide to General George G. Meade, the former commander of Union forces at Gettysburg, and talked directly with an aide to General Butler, the commander of Fortress Monroe.[276]

None of Charlie's surrogates—not Foster, Schenck, Buckingham, his brother Billings, nor Captain Swift—was successful in arranging for a special exchange. Nonetheless, Charlie's spirits lifted in late February when he read in a smuggled newspaper that 394 Confederate officers from the Union's Ship Island Prison near New Orleans had been transported to Fortress Monroe for an imminent general exchange. Two weeks later, 800 Confederate prisoners, 60 of them officers, arrived at Richmond. The next day, 800 Union prisoners, including 47 officers, were sent north. Charlie was not among them, but he felt part of the "excitement at Libby" because large-scale transfers were being made.[277]

Although no special or general exchange ever came through for Charlie, he was finally paroled and sent north on March 14, 1864. The release came several days after Charlie's brother Billings had spoken to an aide to General Butler, but no one took credit for getting Charlie out.[278] Curiously, Charlie made no diary entry and wrote no letters home to celebrate his regained freedom. Perhaps he was too busy getting onto the truce boat that took him and others to Fortress Monroe, from where he sailed on a Union ship to Annapolis. He was probably also preoccupied by concern that his status as a *paroled* prisoner would indefinitely block the assignment he so dearly coveted—to be the commanding officer of the First Connecticut Cavalry Regiment. Before he could be considered for that appointment, however, a Confederate lieutenant colonel from a Union prison would have to be paroled. Because there were probably few such prisoners held by the North, the high rank to which Charlie had been promoted was now working against his career interests.

# Chapter IV

## Freedom and the Urge to Command

Granted twenty days leave from Camp Parole, Charlie headed home to Norwich, stopping along the way to "make a report" to Congressman Schenck in Washington. He no doubt told of the wretched conditions at Libby, but he probably also wanted to see if Schenck could hasten the end of his parole so that he could take command of the regiment before Blakeslee or some other officer got the permanent assignment. Leaving Washington, Charlie dropped in on his cousin Mary Meredith in Baltimore, and shopped for new civilian clothes and shoes in New York. In Baltimore, he must have momentarily dropped the ingrained vigilance of a cavalry officer, getting "robbed of all my private papers."[279] From New York, he took a coastal steamer to Norwich, arriving on March 22, four days after leaving Annapolis.

Charlie's family and friends undoubtedly turned out to welcome him home. The local newspaper had gleefully reported his parole: "The numerous friends of Lieut. Col. Chas. Farnsworth, of this city, will be gratified to learn that he is at length clear from the abominations of Libby Prison, having reached Annapolis yesterday." Now a local celebrity, Charlie was featured a few days later at a Republican campaign rally, where he was made an honorary vice-president of the meeting and gave a speech about his treatment at Libby.[280]

Charlie recorded nothing in his diary about his homecoming or about seeing his fiancée Georgia. Surprisingly, his next diary entry was made in a code he invented, and it described a rekindling of his love for another woman, Harriet Peck Lester, a young Norwich lady whom he apparently had been close to before the war.[281] The unique code was comprised of a combination of numbers and symbols, along with several uncoded letters.

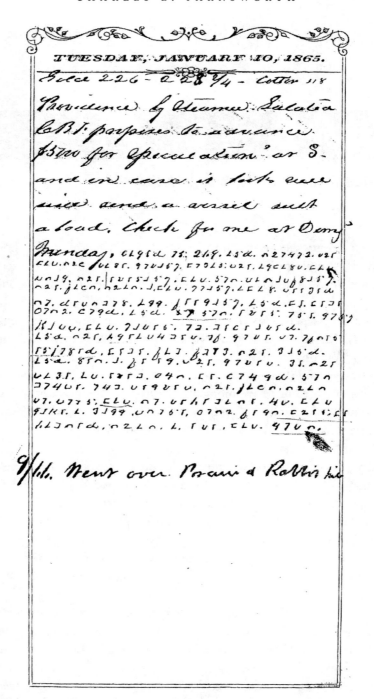

Sample of Charlie's diary entries, with portion encoded, dated January 10, 1865.

| L | ⌐ | ⌐ | ⌐ | 4 | 8 |
|---|---|---|---|---|---|
| A | E | I | O | U | Y |

| ⁹ | 3 | 5 | 7 | 2 | |
|---|---|---|---|---|---|
| L | M | N | G | H | |

| o | 6 | ⊐ | u | ∩ | ⊏ |
|---|---|---|---|---|---|
| B | P | R | S | T | W |

**No code:** J, C, D, F, K, Q, V, X, Z

Charlie's unique diary code.

Presumably to conceal his actions and emotions from prying eyes, Charlie encrypted almost all diary entries concerning his romance with Harriet. The encoded entries are shown here in *italics*. Charlie frequently quoted Harriet verbatim within an encrypted entry:

> *Met HPL and went up with her. The same dear one to me. Where is the woman that has ever entirely forgotten and banished from the heart the memory of a true love? A first true affection. She received me with open arms, a warm kiss. "Ever am I the same to you, Charlie."* [282]

Charlie spent much of the following two weeks courting Harriet, but he also made time to see the parents of his friend George Ward, still confined at Belle Isle. Charlie socialized with other friends, including Colonel Ely, who had been released from Libby with him, but was about to return to his infantry regiment. (Ely would survive the war and achieve success later in Norwich business, rising to treasurer of the Falls & Shetucket Cotton Mills.)[283] Then Charlie headed back to Camp Parole at Annapolis, and waited through April for a full-fledged exchange and orders to return to his regiment, which he expected to command. Trying to fill idle time, he attended a ball in Washington at which Lincoln may have made an appearance, and kept his word to Captain Atwater, by "standing up" for him at his wedding in Philadelphia.[284]

Time was working against Charlie, however. Major Blakeslee had taken temporary charge of the regiment in January after Major Fish was removed. Charlie, who had been promoted to lieutenant colonel in the same month, outranked Blakeslee, but his imprisonment had precluded him from taking command. In early March, about the same time as Charlie was paroled, Blakeslee had been ordered to take the regiment from Baltimore into Virginia, going into action as a unit of General Philip H. Sheridan's cavalry corps. Learning of the regiment's spring successes and Blakeslee's impending promotion to lieutenant colonel (it came through on May 31st), by early May Charlie probably realized that his dream of regimental command had been shattered. The best he could expect now would be as battalion commander *under* Blakeslee, a prospect he could not abide because of what Charlie viewed as Blakeslee's "failure to sustain" at the Harpers Ferry debacle and his general "unreliability."[285]

Frustrated by two months in military limbo, and realizing that he would probably never get the regimental command he had envisioned, Charlie lost patience with the War Department. He decided to seek a disability discharge based on his April 1862 chest wounds and to offer his resignation as a lieutenant colonel. An examining surgeon provided a certificate that gave Charlie's petition only limited support: "[T]his condition of his chest *may* prevent him from discharging active duty in the field for *several months*" (italics added).[286] As chance would have it, however, an order lifting his parole came through while the discharge request was pending, and Charlie was ordered to his regiment. He immediately replied to the War Department, reminding them that he was disabled and had requested a medical discharge. Again, he tendered his resignation.[287]

Although the War Department could have rejected Charlie's application on the ground that he was perhaps only temporarily disabled, it instead decided to grant his request, but with a punitive twist. After a review of Charlie's promotional history, the department discharged him not as a lieutenant colonel nor even as a major, but as a mere captain.[288] Charlie was apparently so eager to avoid the alternative—serving under Blakeslee—that he agreed to leave the army without questioning the two-level demotion. His relentless drive for command had been on display since mid-1862, and he had often threatened to "come home" unless he got what he wanted.[289] Now he was quietly leaving. In the future, however, the War Department's action would gnaw at his sense of entitlement and he would fight back. His forebodings of Blakeslee's rise to power were accurate; within two weeks, Blakeslee had not only been promoted to Charlie's rank of lieutenant colonel, but to full colonel as well—the appropriate rank for a regimental commander. Charlie would have served, at best, as a battalion commander with the rank of lieutenant colonel under Blakeslee, a humiliation apparently too great to be endured.[290]

His military obligations and opportunities behind him, Charlie headed home, stopping in Baltimore again to see friends and to pose for a photograph as a lieutenant colonel, and in New York to socialize. Along the way, he must have felt a jumbled emotional undertow of grief, guilt, and relief, when he learned that his close Norwich friend, infantry lieutenant Alfred M. Goddard, had been killed in combat near the James River.[291]

Charlie as a Lieutenant Colonel, 1863 (photograph by Bendann, Baltimore).

Charlie's arrival in Norwich as a civilian was briefly noted in the local newspaper:

> **Personal**. Col. Chas. Farnsworth, First Connecticut Cavalry, arrived here on Friday, having been honorably discharged the service of the United States, for physical disability brought on from wounds received in the service, aggravated by long confinement in the prisons of Richmond. Col. Farnsworth came from Richmond in March last, and was upon parole at the time of his discharge.[292]

Charlie's first project in Norwich was to shower his attentions upon Harriet. He took her out (or "up," in the vernacular of the time) to hear lectures and music at the newly-opened Breed Hall, the only meeting place in town besides the churches and the town hall.

Breed Hall, Norwich, a popular entertainment and lecture center in the 1860s. Destroyed by fire 1960 (courtesy, Matt Isenburg).

Again and again, he took tea and dined at the Williams home where Harriet was lodging. One evening, on a walk through the grounds of the

Norwich Free Academy, Charlie pressed his ardor upon Harriet, who resisted with a tantalizing demurrer:

> *"The time will come; you shall have all sometime.*
> *When I marry, come and see me."* [293]

Meanwhile, Charlie probably had sealed his engagement with Georgia by giving her a ring purchased in Baltimore from his cousin Harry Meredith.[294] Charlie clearly was torn between honoring his promise to Georgia and his passion for Harriet. It would take a year for the psychic stand-off to be resolved.

## Testimony for the Government

Although discharged, Charlie had one final military obligation, which he no doubt relished. In June, the Sanitary Commission, an arm of the federal government since 1861, asked Charlie to testify about conditions at Libby Prison. Charlie obliged, and submitted two affidavits running over three thousand words that provided details on all aspects of Libby and nearby Belle Isle.[295] He confirmed that the prison room he shared with two hundred officers measured one hundred by forty feet, yielding each officer about seventy square feet, an area seven by ten feet. The prisoners had to make do with the clothing and blankets they possessed when captured; Libby issued them neither. Until the North successfully interceded, there were no benches or stools to sit on, and the prisoners were forbidden to sit on their blankets. In an allusion of the time, Charlie complained that the prisoners had to sit on the bare floor "like so many slaves upon the middle passage." Nor were the prisoners allowed to go near the windows; guards shot at anyone caught peering out. Prison rations were so meager that without the boxes of food coming in from the North, the health of the prisoners would have been dangerously compromised, Charlie testified.

Charlie reserved his most searing criticism for Belle Isle, where more than ten thousand enlisted prisoners were held. Nearly half had no shelter whatsoever, and many slept on the ground without blankets. Hundreds froze to death in the winter. In all seasons, hundreds more died of pneumonia or of chronic diarrhea. Rations were worse than at Libby, and the enlisted received far fewer boxes from family and friends. When the sick from Belle Isle died at the Libby hospital, Charlie could see that they were often not buried but were left on the streets outside the building, where they were eaten by wild dogs, hogs, and rats.

His full outrage was on display when Charlie testified that Richard Turner, Libby's civilian manager, admitted that he had planted mines under the prison walls and was prepared to blow up the building and all of the officers with it if an attack by the North appeared imminent.

As the South had warned many times, it treated captured black soldiers as slaves. Charlie testified that they were flogged regularly, for any small matter. He said that he'd heard from others that some Richmond Negro women were once stripped and flogged for trying to hand loaves of bread to the prisoners.[296]

## Questions of What Might Have Been

While trying to plan a future for himself in mid-1864, Charlie's thoughts no doubt kept turning to the past and he probably wondered if he had done the right thing in leaving his regiment. Since March, the First Connecticut had been conducting a scorched- earth campaign with General Philip H. Sheridan up the Shenandoah Valley and beyond. At times Charlie probably yearned to be there, even as an officer subordinate to the disliked Blakeslee, especially when he heard that the regiment had chased the famous general Jubal Early and two hundred Confederates to the outskirts of Richmond.[297] In June came the sad news of the death during the Shenandoah campaign of another Norwich friend (and prison-mate), Lieutenant John Maginnis. Just a month earlier, Charlie had dined in Baltimore with Maginnis and William Ely, the three celebrating their release from Libby.[298] Charlie probably felt not only relief that he had avoided an order to return to duty like the one Maginnis had received, but also, once again, grief and guilt that another friend may have died in his place.

Restless and searching, Charlie roamed about, visiting Boston, Groton, New Haven, New York, Philadelphia, and Washington. In July he was shocked by news that Annie E. Mallory, clearly an intimate friend, was dead at age 29 in Stonington. The daughter of a family well-established in Connecticut's shipping and shipbuilding industries, Annie had married Jacob Smull, and had died from complications of giving birth to their first child, who also died.[299] Charlie attended Annie's funeral, and afterwards noted in code his abiding affection for her: *"I loved her once so much. I love her today the same. My first, my dearest love. Sleep dear friend. May we meet where partings are no more."*[300] Charlie had never before mentioned Annie in his diary or letters, but she had clearly touched his heart early and deeply. For the moment, memories of Annie overwhelmed his romantic entanglement with Georgia and Harriet. After the funeral in Stonington, Charlie took the opportunity to socialize with friends in the neighboring towns of Watch Hill and Westerly before heading back to Norwich for more evenings with Harriet. He would see a lot of Harriet and little of Georgia in the next six months. He would not mention Annie again.

## Harriet Peck Lester and Her Family

Harriet Peck Lester was born in Norwich in 1837, making her a year younger than Charlie. Her father, Walter Lester, was a Norwich ship captain who descended from a famous sea-faring family. An ancestor, Captain Jonathan Lester, had built a sixty-foot warship, the *Shark*, in Norwich for the revolutionary army in 1776. Years later, after the War of 1812 ended and the British blockade was lifted, Walter's ship the *Dove* was the first merchant vessel to sail out of Norwich, taking horses and cattle to the Caribbean Island of St. Vincent, returning with an enormous, but unspecified, cargo that paid duties of over $9,000.[301] In 1809, Walter married Mary Ann Carpenter of Norwich. After she died in 1829, he married her cousin, Mary Elizabeth Carpenter, in 1833. Harriet was born four years later. After retiring from the sea, Walter turned to farming near Norwich, dying in 1851, at age sixty-nine.[302]

Harriet's mother Mary Elizabeth was apparently unable to care for fourteen-year-old Harriet after Walter died; a guardian was appointed until 1853, when Mary Elizabeth resumed responsibility. Mother and daughter reunited in Norwich at the family home, 236 Washington Street, built in 1790 by Joseph Carpenter, the father of Walter's first wife, Mary Ann. By 1860, the home was headed by Joseph H. Holm, a wealthy thirty-nine-year old Dane and sea captain who was married to the eldest Lester daughter, Louisa. Although sharing a roof with Harriet's half-sisters, she and her mother were not living in poverty; her mother listed $4,000 in personal property in the 1860 Norwich census. (Many years later, as the sole beneficiary of the estate of her half-sister Elizabeth, Harriet inherited the 236 Washington home, its furnishings, and a $1,200 bank account.)[303]

In about 1861, Harriet's mother Mary Elizabeth Lester moved from Norwich to Albany, New York, probably to live with other relatives. Harriet, now in her early twenties, stayed in Norwich, moving from the Holm household to board in the home of Major General and Mrs.

William Williams.[304] (As it happened, General Williams was the uncle of Charlie's mother, Eunice.) Mrs. Williams was the former Harriet Peck, the daughter of Captain Bela Peck, an artillery gunner in the local militia and a Norwich deputy sheriff who lived to age ninety-two.[305] The young Harriet Peck Lester had been given her name as a gesture of friendship for Mrs. William [née Harriet Peck] Williams, so the Williams home was obviously welcoming. But the Williamses had a history of caring for others, so bringing Harriet into his home was not unusual. In 1831, they had taken on the guardianship of the three sons of Rev. Alfred Mitchell, the late pastor of Norwich's prominent Second Congregational Church. Now, having assumed guardian-like duties for Harriet, the general and his wife did their best to restrict to some reasonable number Charlie's ardent visits to Harriet during the summer of 1864.

Harriet was not boarding with just any Norwich family. The William Williams name was famous in southern Connecticut. One William Williams had fought in the French and Indian Wars in 1755 and was one of the four Connecticut representatives who had signed the Declaration of Independence in 1776. Another William Williams built a shipping business and became a general. The William Williams with whom Harriet was now boarding had been appointed a brigadier general in the militia by the Connecticut Assembly at the young age of twenty-eight, the appointment undoubtedly influenced by his social standing rather than by military experience.[306] As a young man, this General Williams had rejected college in favor of apprenticing as a supercargo (i.e., the officer aboard a merchant ship in charge of commercial matters) in his father's maritime business. He and his father later built flour and cotton mills in Norwich, utilizing the hydraulic power of the Yantic River. Although the mills failed, General Williams went on to prosper as a partner in a New London whaling firm and as a bank president. In 1865, he was listed on Norwich's income tax rolls among the town's 50 wealthiest men, out of a population of about fifteen thousand.[307] (By contrast, Charlie's father, Dr. Ralph Farnsworth, was *not* listed among the top fifty.)

Retiring from business, General Williams became a professor of religion and also supervised the Congregational church Sunday school at a nearby Mohegan Indian village. When he died at age eighty-two, his obituary concluded that, "possessed of an ample fortune, he had therefore the power, and more than this the inclination to exercise a wide benevolence..."[308] Williams's benevolence, and that of his wife, were bestowed through their wills upon Harriet, as well as upon Charlie and his brothers, who were grand-nephews of the couple.[309]

Charlie had been close to Harriet before the war. From the frontlines, Captain E. K. Abbott had mentioned their mutual friend Harriet in a letter to Charlie. According to Lieutenant Henry P. Goddard, another friend, Harriet was one of Norwich's most desirable maidens. And Mrs. Williams, related to Charlie's mother by marriage, had taken a special interest in Charlie's confinement at Libby Prison, sending him at least one box of food and sundries. [310] Charlie's family was probably thrilled with his possible marriage to Harriet—someone well-known to them, yet unrelated by blood.

## Romance and Plotting a Future

As summer turned to fall and fall into winter, Harriet was clearly swept away by Charlie's attentions, although she was keenly aware that he was still engaged to Georgia.. Again and again, in coded diary entries, Charlie recorded her words of love to him:

> *Again permitted to revel in charms long sought.*
> *"I cannot deny you what must by law be another's."*[311]

> *"It never can be again but it was. Oh, how*
> *I love. I cannot refuse you though I know I should." *[312]

> *"I cannot say you must not again, for I would not have it so.*
> *You and me will ever always be one."*[313]

> *"I can talk of marrying, but can I never after yours receive*
> *another's embrace except with loathing."*[314]

> *"It is harder to resist each time." *[315]

> *"I cannot refuse you. You first taught me passion. I would give*
> *all that I have or ever shall have for one year with you." *[316]

After a winter sleigh ride three miles north to the town of Baltic, Charlie chivalrously asked if Harriet wanted to slow the pace of their torrid romance. Harriet responded:

*"No, no I do not think it wrong with you. There shall come a time when our blood shall mingle."* [317]

Occasionally, the Williams family would step in to protect Harriet from Charlie's relentless advances. One evening, Mrs. Williams futilely tried to turn him away, settling by limiting the couple to a mere hour together. Harriet felt frustrated, as Charlie noted:

*"I am not cold but you know oh, how I wanted you this evening. I almost despise control. Now how I long for all."* [318]

A poem that Charlie kept with his military papers may have best described this fresh romance with Harriet:

You kissed me! My head had dropped low on your breast,
With a feeling of shelter and infinite rest;
While the holy emotion my tongue dared not speak,
Flushed up, like a flame, from my heart to my cheek.
Your arms held me fast—ho! Your arms were so bold,
Heart beat against heart in their passionate hold.
Your glances seemed drawing my soul through my eyes
As the sun draws the mist from the sea to the skies,
And your lips clung to mine till I prayed in my bliss,
They might never unclasp from that rapturous kiss. [319]

After months of courting Harriet, Charlie took time out to call on his fiancée Georgia in Meriden, spending several days there in mid-December. [320] Their engagement remained intact but problematic, and Georgia may not have known what was going on in Norwich.

Several months later, Georgia wrote to Charlie, seeking an explanation for some "Chicago affair" that William Fish, Charlie's former commanding officer, had written at least twice to her about. The subject of Fish's letters remains a mystery, although it probably had to do with Charlie's business dealings in Chicago, 1857-60. Charlie noted, in code: *"Georgia sent me letters written to her by Fish in regard to the Chicago affair, of which I took copies."*[321] A day later, Charlie added: *"Recd. letter from Georgia in regard to letters of Fish."* [322]

Major Fish's motive for butting into Charlie's love-life probably arose out of his burning resentment with how the War Department had treated him. In April, Fish had been convicted by court-martial of taking bribes in 1863 while serving as Baltimore's provost marshal, in return for releasing citizens from the various trumped-up charges that they had been arrested for.[323] Fish was dismissed from the army, but was not sentenced to prison. Although President Lincoln later rescinded the dismissal, Fish remained deeply embittered. He may have felt that Charlie, having served under him in Baltimore, should have come to his defense at the court-martial, and was now striking back by disclosing a confidence that Charlie had related during their many months together. Such an act of revenge or betrayal by Fish would not have surprised Charlie. Despite Fish's proven qualities as a cavalry leader, Charlie had mistrusted his scruples for a long time, writing in mid-1862 that "[Fish] would sell his best friend for position."[324]

After months of romance with Harriet and a life of ease in Norwich, Charlie made a decision for his future. He had been studying the burgeoning oil, iron, and coal industries of Pennsylvania, and may have considered going into business there.[325] True to his adventurous nature, however, he was drawn toward the more dangerous but enticing challenges of commerce in the war-torn South. Perhaps he felt that he was owed something by someone, after being shot and imprisoned by the South, and unfairly demoted in rank by his own government. Because the war was still raging, getting into Confederate territory would not be easy, but Charlie felt entitled to call on his family's connections for the purpose. He got a letter of reference as a lieutenant colonel from Governor Buckingham, and for good measure, got a similar letter from the governor of Rhode Island. Charlie took the letters to Washington in early January and asked Connecticut Senator Foster to carry them to the White House on his behalf. Charlie's influence with the President could not have been much greater: Buckingham was one of Lincoln's earliest and hardiest supporters and Foster was the Senate Republican majority leader.

Charlie spent January 5 in the Senate chamber listening to Massachusetts Senator Charles Sumner painfully describe the distressing conditions of the families of black soldiers, and what should be done for them. Meanwhile, Senator Foster had met with Lincoln and had gotten the president's authorization for Charlie to go south, specifically to recently-liberated Savannah.[326] The size of a business card, the permit read, in Lincoln's handwriting,

*Will the Commander at Savannah please see the bearer Col*
*Farnsworth, & oblige him so far as consistent with the service?*
*Jan. 5, 1865 A.Lincoln*

Authorization written by President Lincoln for Charlie to travel
through military lines to Savannah, Georgia, January 1865.

Such a presidential pass must have been unusual. Thousands of
northerners went south immediately *after* the war, during the 1865-66 era
of presidential reconstruction, but Charlie was going months earlier, while
General Sherman's troops were still encamped at Savannah and preparing
to put South Carolina to the torch.[327] Charlie seemed nonchalant about
the privilege the president had just extended, however, dryly noting that
he "got card from Abraham Lincoln and a pass from the War Office."[328]
Catching a train to Baltimore, Charlie again socialized, but also laid plans
with his brother Billings for the southern business venture. Billings agreed
to advance $5,000 for a general merchandise brokerage in Savannah, with
a further commitment to ship goods south if the project looked promising.
The brothers' idea was to buy cotton, rice, and other commodities at bargain
prices in devastated Georgia, sell them profitably in the north, and then
ship manufactured goods to sell in Savannah.[329] Although Charlie would
be competing with many well-established merchants along "Factor's Row"
on the Savannah waterfront, he would have the tremendous advantage of
being able to get shipping permits from the Union military commander,
while the locals were still barred by the naval blockade.

With his business plan in place, Charlie returned by coastal steamer to Norwich for one last fling with Harriet, and, it seemed, to say good-bye to her. He was, after all, still engaged to Georgia, and was headed south. Harriet's love for him was as deep as ever, but now was tempered by his imminent departure:

> *Called on HPL and though she was the same loving woman she always was, still the evening was not satisfying. The fact that I was going away seemed to destroy all feeling and we were both cold. Not even one long kiss was given or received and pleasure of love so often enjoyed was far from the mind. And yet I feel she loves me the same as ever. But we could not rouse ourselves. The fact that so soon were we to separate was like a millstone. Both of us felt when we parted that an evening was lost.* [330]

For several nights the young lovers felt consumed by existential anguish over their parting, Charlie describing Harriet's words and his thoughts:

> *"We will go out in a blaze of glory, won't we?" What a real pleasant time we had. We danced, talked, and ignored everyone. And then the walk home and those moments ere we parted forever. What was life or anything? What raptures forever and ever each others.' 'All was mine, dearest, my darling; I die with rapture."* [331]

Charlie somehow pulled himself from Harriet's arms and began his long journey to the Deep South, stopping off to see Georgia one more time on his way. In the library the Parkers's Meriden home, Charlie tried hard to convince Georgia that he was unworthy, and that she should "marry for a better position." But Georgia wouldn't listen to his argument, insisting "I love you and will marry you."[332] She probably still didn't know of Charlie's affair with Harriet, and was simply trying to keep their engagement intact while Charlie was away on business. She certainly didn't contemplate joining him in Savannah. For his part, Charlie couldn't muster the courage to make the necessary clean break with her. He would try, and fail, again in six months. The engagement would remain in limbo.

# Chapter V

## Savannah and the Lures of Reconstruction

On January 17, 1865 Charlie cast off into the unknown world of the war-torn South. During a four-day voyage from New York by coastal steamer, the extroverted Charlie made a point of getting to know his fellow passengers, who included a Massachusetts general, a Florida judge, a doctor, their wives, and the head of the Savannah gas works.[333] Upon arrival in Savannah, Charlie sensed the city's deep economic depression, even though it had been spared the ravages of battle. (In late December 1864, a Confederate army had retreated from Savannah into South Carolina, allowing General Sherman to occupy the city without firing a shot— a "Christmas gift," he called it, for the war-weary president.) Nevertheless, the Savannah harbor lay idle and decaying from the Union's long blockade. It would, however, spring back to life within two years, more than doubling its pre-war shipping activity.[334]

At the time, many Savannahians would not have viewed Charlie's project as the carpetbagging they came to despise. Quite to the contrary, early investment money was essential to reconstruction, and was welcomed. His fellow-passenger the president of the Savannah gas works had told him that the city was barren of goods and had little money to buy anything, implying that Charlie and his funds would be quite welcome.[335] Charlie was not the only Norwich or First Connecticut Cavalry war veteran to seek his fortune in Savannah in early Reconstruction. In February, fellow cavalryman Major George O. Marcy arrived, and in October came artillery General Henry W. Birge.[336]

Charlie managed to find "good accommodations" at the well-known Pulaski House on one of the town's leafy squares, but promptly complained about the hotel's "miserable" food. Losing no time in getting down to business, on the afternoon of his arrival Charlie called on the Union's military commander in Savannah, Major General J. W. Geary, and got a permit to operate as a "general commission merchant." Charlie then rented a store on Factors' Row above the harbor for eight hundred dollars per year, and a storage cellar for five dollars a week.[337]

Coastal steamer *City of Norwich*, c. 1860. Charlie sailed between New York and Savannah several times on similar vessels (reprinted from *The 9-Mile Square*, by Bill Stanley. Courtesy, Norwich Historical Society).

Over four years, war and the blockade had disrupted the cotton industry, and during his march across Georgia Sherman had destroyed vast acres of the current crop. Production had fallen from seven hundred thousand bales in 1860 to forty thousand bales in 1865. Yet thousands of bales—one estimate was fifty thousand—were stored in warehouses at Augusta, one hundred miles up the Savannah River, bottled up by the blockade.[338] Charlie notified his brother Billings that he would be shipping bales of "rags," the type of cotton used for paper stock. His first shipment of "167 bales, 22 crates" generated an enormous profit. Meanwhile, Charlie got a permit from General Geary to ship animal hides as well—up to five thousand of them.[339] To supplement his income as a merchandise broker, Charlie acted as banker for the nearby occupying forces of the Thirteenth Connecticut Infantry, paying cash for the troops' one hundred dollar reenlistment checks, which could not be negotiated for full value until the end of each enlistment. He charged a fee of eight dollars for the service. These "bounties" usually amounted to a little less than one year's pay for enlisted men.[340]

Senator Foster, who had helped Charlie get his southern pass, visited Savannah in March. Foster would become acting vice-president (as president pro tempore of the Senate) less than a month later, after Lincoln was assassinated and Vice President Andrew Johnson was sworn in as president. As acting vice-president, Foster made another visit to Georgia in May, probably to learn more about the ravages of war and the needs of reconstruction, Charlie serving as his Savannah guide for a day.[341]

Savannah riverfront, 1865 (photograph courtesy National Archives).

As Charlie tried to cope at a distance with his romantic entanglements, it became clear which way his heart was pulling him. On an important anniversary, he rather coldly noted "Three years ago tonight I became engaged to Georgia. Tonight I wrote her a letter." Then he wrote to Harriet, undoubtedly with more passion, sending the letter to Fred for local delivery in Norwich. He probably worried that Harriet's protectors, General and Mrs. Williams, might read the letters, or at least lecture Harriet about the propriety of corresponding with a betrothed man, if the letters were delivered directly to the home. Harriet's letter in reply was "full of love." (Charlie never bothered to characterize Georgia's letters.) Another letter to Harriet he labeled "a long and truthful one." Her reply, he thought, was her "last one to me." A few days later, however, he got another letter from Harriet, which he again called her "last" one. Harriet undoubtedly wanted a resolution of Charlie's engagement to Georgia. Despite (or perhaps because of) his complications with the two women in Connecticut, Charlie began to pay attention to the Savannah women around him, taking up with someone named Pery (or Perry) for most of the month of May and then with "C from Florida" for more than a year. He never revealed anything more than that he had spent nights with them.[342]

In April, Charlie sailed by steamer to Charleston to visit Fort Sumter, where the war had begun four years earlier. When news arrived that Lee had surrendered to Grant on April 9, Charlie helped celebrate the victory with a flag-raising at the symbolic fort. Lincoln died of an assassin's bullet a few days later, but Charlie made no note of the tragedy until April 30: "Prayers for the President of U. S. read for 1st time in Christ Church [Savannah]."[343]

After five months as a Savannah commodities broker, in mid-June Charlie returned north to take care of his romantic complications. His frequent letters to and from Georgia and Harriet had resolved nothing. Arriving in Norwich, he promptly called on Harriet. Their love for each other hadn't changed, and Charlie knew he had to face the awkward matter of his engagement to Georgia. He wrote her on a Thursday that he would take the train to Meriden to see her on Sunday—undoubtedly to deliver the bad news. Then he lost his nerve, and instead simply wrote Georgia that "the engagement had better be given up." And thus their long betrothal came to a quiet, sad end. Georgia had waited more than three years for him, lending comfort from afar during the hard fighting of the war and through his long months of imprisonment, and even enduring his wanderings after his release. But it all came to nothing for her. Charlie quickly left for Washington and Baltimore. Georgia answered his engagement-breaking letter, and Charlie responded. What they said to each other is unknown. When Charlie returned to Norwich on July 3, he and Harriet threw themselves into a round of parties, Harriet herself hosting one of them. The pair now obviously felt free to be seen together in polite society.[344]

Georgia was undoubtedly emotionally stricken by Charlie's rejection, and eight years would pass before she married, in 1873. The groom was Augustus P. Day, a former lieutenant of the First Connecticut Infantry Volunteers who, coincidentally, had also spent a few months as a prisoner of war in Libby, just shortly after Charlie was released. After their wedding in Meriden, Georgia followed Augustus to Brooklyn, New York where he was in the coal business. They had children, and lived into the 1920s.[345]

## Rice Farming in Ogeechee Country

After a month away, Charlie returned to Savannah in late July 1865. Tired or bored of being just a commodities broker, he had decided to try his hand at farming along the Ogeechee River about twenty miles south of Savannah, and had formed a partnership with a man named Samuel Edgar Wildman. Known variously as "Edgar" or "Edward," he was the eldest son of a civic-minded and prosperous Danbury, Connecticut farming family. Only twenty-six, Wildman probably came south with personal assets of over three thousand dollars. There is no record of him serving with Connecticut forces in the Civil War.[346] Although a shared military sacrifice might have automatically solidified their friendship in a hostile South, the combination of Wildman's agricultural experience and ready cash probably made him an acceptable business partner for Charlie.

Charlie and Wildman made plans to grow rice in the Ogeechee tidelands, one of the three major rice-growing regions in Georgia. In January 1866, Charlie signed a three-year lease for two hundred acres of a rice farm known as the Prarie Plantation, at the rate of $4,089 per year, half of which was to be paid in gold. The land was probably part of a fifteen-hundred-acre tract owned by the old-line Cheves family who, like other planters, were finding it hard to re-start farm operations.[347] Their fields lay in ruins from inattention, their slave labor force had been liberated, and their Confederate savings were nearly worthless.[348] Renting the farm was an attractive option.

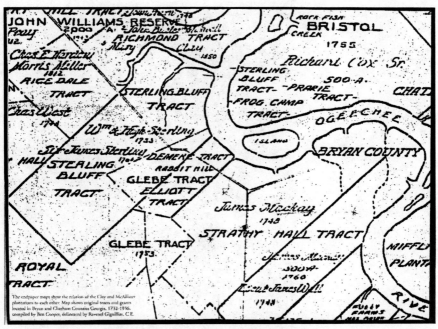

Map c. 1850, showing location of Strathy Hall and Prarie plantation across Ogeechee River (courtesy Carolyn Clay Swiggart, *Shades of Gray*, Two Bytes Publishing Co., 1999).

95

Modern map of Ogeechee River, showing location of Strathy Hall, right-center
(Map image copyright 2014, Craig Williams Creative, Inc. Used with permission).

At two hundred acres, the Prarie farm was far smaller than the seven largest in Bryan County, but it would nonetheless pose a formidable challenge for the two green Yankees. Farming rice was a far cry from Charlie's more genteel commodities brokerage business. Wildman's agricultural background was helpful, but rice-farming differed vastly from any crop in Connecticut that Wildman might have known. Rice had been grown along the lower ten miles of the Ogeechee River since 1745, when slaves were brought down from South Carolina to clear the land of trees and brush and to build five-foot-high levees with flood gates to control irrigation of the fields. Ogeechee tidewater rice plantations came to be known as "marvels of engineering, huge hydraulic machines carved out of the virgin tidal swamps." But much of this infrastructure had been ruined through neglect during the war, as planters fled. Levees had fallen apart, and weeds had taken over the fields.[349] Even after the levees were repaired, they frequently burst under the pressure of heavy rains and high tides, requiring prompt repairs to save the rice seedlings. During a three-week period in mid-1866, Charlie made nine diary entries about the exasperating problem of stabilizing the Prarie dikes.

Rice cultivation required adherence to a strict schedule. Seeds were planted in late April. Freshwater from the Ogeechee River was then drawn on the high tides through horizontal-pivoting levee gates onto rice squares measuring ten to twenty acres. This first flooding was called the "sprout flow." A week later the water was drained on an ebb tide. Two more floodings (the "point" and "long" flows) and drainings followed during the summer; weeds were hoed as the fields dried. A mistake at high tide during any of the floodings could swamp the field with salt water and kill the seedlings. After a fourth flooding (the "lay-by flow"), the rice was harvested in early September: stalks of rice were cut, left to dry, and then bundled and floated on rafts along narrow canals between the rice squares to a barn or mill, to be threshed and husked.[350]

Because rice farming involved working knee-deep in "oozy, putrid, stagnant water," it was considered the most unhealthful kind of manual labor. But skilled workers such as carpenters, floodgate tenders, and rice mill operators were also needed. All in all, Charlie was embarking on a demanding, technical, complex, unhealthful, and risky business. He conceded to his brother Fred that he might fail at it unless he could reap thirty to sixty bushels per acre. Because the average pre-war harvest along the Ogeechee was only forty to fifty bushels per acre, Charlie was taking a big gamble. But the expected profit for rice was greater than for cotton, the other main crop in the region: an estimated 13 percent return on investment versus 6 percent.[351]

Severe labor problems arose with Prarie's freedmen workers even before Charlie signed the long-term lease. "Went to place. Seven people left without permission yesterday—ordered them discharged," he wrote. These freedmen may have simply been following the traditional rice farm "task" system, under which a slave could stop working for the day after he had completed the area of his assignment, usually a quarter-acre. Or they may have been rebelling against the loss of land that they thought General Sherman had given them under Special Field Order No. 15 in January.[352]

*Figure 5.* A Rice Plantation in Operation on the Ogeechee River near Savannah, Georgia. (From *Harper's Weekly,* January 5, 1867.)

Rice plantation operations along Ogeechee River, c. 1867 (reprinted from *Slavery and Rice Culture in Low Country Georgia 1750-1860*, by Julia Floyd Smith, courtesy University of Tennessee Press).

Issued in Savannah on January 16, 1865 partly to keep freed slaves from following the Union army on its march into South Carolina, Sherman's order had effectively confiscated all Georgia, Florida, and South Carolina farms within thirty miles of the coast, redistributing the land in general to the freedmen. But this rendered ownership rights unclear from the beginning because no specific deeds were issued. Opportunity for the freedmen to own the land they tilled was further imperiled four months later by President Andrew Johnson's Amnesty Act, which restored property to former owners who swore an oath of allegiance to the Union. Then the freedmen's hopes were completely dashed by the president's veto of a congressional bill that would have given freedmen possessory titles to lands that had been expropriated from recalcitrant planters.[353]

The Federal Bureau of Refugees, Freedmen, and Abandoned Lands (known as the Freedmen's Bureau) tried to retard this restoration of lands, but it met with only temporary success. By late 1865, most planters in the Georgia tidelands had taken the required oath and had recovered "informal possession" of their land, giving them the right to farm it. But freedmen working the lands between the Ogeechee and Little Ogeechee Rivers in Chatham County (where Prarie Plantation was located) continued to insist that Sherman's order had granted them "40 acres and a mule." Whites were not welcome in large parts of this "Ogeechee District," where they were outnumbered by freedmen, many of whom continued to grow rice on expropriated plantations.[354] Charlie's Prarie plantation was adjacent to some of these freedmen's tracts, and he was probably considered unwelcome, even as a Yankee tenant of a restored plantation owner. To shore up some political support among traditional planters for his vulnerable situation, Charlie got himself elected as an officer of the Savannah Agricultural Society.[355]

Charlie tried to improve worker reliability by following the pre-war rice farm practice of retaining a doctor to treat the freedmen and their families. He paid $600 for a year of a doctor's services, although the promised treatment may have been limited to emergencies. But Charlie's labor troubles continued. Workers left work early or wouldn't show up at all. Responding to what he perceived as their low motivation and high expectations, Charlie decided to sub-rent part of his tract to the freedmen, effectively making them independent tenant farmers. But neither tenant farming nor the wage-labor system proved very effective; freedmen often stopped working when they felt that they had produced just enough to live on, a hangover from the slavery system.[356]

In addition to his labor troubles, Charlie had to keep a wary eye out for potential retribution from die-hard Confederates, who were threatening violence to take back their lost lands. He closely followed the "Heasley" case, in which three Confederate army veterans were tried before a Union military commission on charges of murdering a Freedmen's Bureau agent's assistant, Captain Alex Heasley, by shooting and stabbing him outside his Augusta home in August 1865. Ultimately, only one of the defendants was convicted. He was sentenced to be hanged but the execution was never carried out.[357]

In Washington, alarmed by the resurgence of these Confederate "redeemers" under the relatively mild strictures of President Johnson's reconstruction measures, the Republican Congress enacted the Radical Reconstruction Laws of 1866 and sent additional troops to enforce the freedmen's rights. Georgia became part of a military district commanded by Civil War General John Pope. Congress' tougher measures reaffirmed the rights of freedmen to vote, barred certain Confederates from voting, and mandated loyalty oaths. Georgia redeemers continued to resist enforcement, and the state was not readmitted to the Union until 1870.[358]

## Marriage and Bringing Harriet South

Charlie probably proposed marriage to Harriet during his July 1865 visit to Norwich, after he had finally found the nerve to break his engagement with Georgia. He returned alone to the Ogeechee for several months, and then sailed back north in late October for the wedding. Curiously, he made no diary entry concerning the wedding itself, which took place at Norwich's Second Congregational Church on November 1. The bride registered as twenty-four years old but was actually twenty-eight; the bridegroom was twenty-nine.[359] Officiating at the marriage was the Reverend Malcolm McGregor Dana. Eight years later Dana would write *The Norwich Memorial,* the most authoritative account of Norwich soldiers in the Civil War, lavishly praising Charlie's military service. The newlyweds stayed on in Norwich for several weeks, enjoying themselves and receiving gifts from family and friends. Someone gave them a sterling silver flatware place-setting for twelve in the then-popular medallion style. The handles of the forks and spoons were stamped with the image of Mars, the Roman god of war, an apt symbol for the groom.

Within a month of their wedding, the couple traveled by coastal steamer to Savannah, where Harriet, whom Charlie now called "Hattie," settled easily into that gracious city of lovely, unpretentious homes and small parks, driving herself around town in a horse and buggy, and making new friends. She probably met General Ulysses Grant on his visit the city. Charlie turned back to business, maintaining his brokerage, while traveling a couple of times a week by train and horse to his Prarie plantation, about twenty miles away.[360]

Finally tiring of his long trip to the plantation, Charlie found an abandoned planter's home known as Strathy Hall, on the west bank of the Ogeechee River across from Prarie, and he and Hattie moved in. The house (which is now part of the town of Richmond Hill and listed on the National Register of Historic Places) had been built in the late 1700s by Captain James MacKay, who named it after his ancestral home of Strathnaver, Scotland. Hundreds of the slaves who once had toiled on the plantation are buried in a nearby cemetery. Since the early 1800s, the house and plantation had been owned by the McAllister family, who also owned a large property six miles to the south. In June 1861, when General Lee decided that the Confederacy needed to protect the mouth of the Ogeechee River, the primary southwestern approach to Savannah, the McAllister family donated the southern property. A fort was built there with local slave labor and named for the family.[361]

Joseph L. McAllister, his two sisters, and their widowed mother were living at Strathy Hall when the war broke out. A year later, Joseph accepted appointment as a lieutenant colonel in the Confederate army, raised a cavalry regiment from the local populace, and for two years fought in skirmishes nearby. In the spring of 1864 he was sent off to fight in Virginia, where he was killed at Trevillian's Station, fifty miles south of Richmond, in a tumultuous clash of eighteen thousand horsemen—the largest cavalry battle of the Civil War. The McAllister family was left without a male heir. As General Sherman's army marched toward Savannah from Atlanta in the fall of 1864, Joseph's mother and his two sisters abandoned Strathy Hall and fled to the relative safety of northern Georgia.[362]

Two months later, Brigadier General Judson Kilpatrick, leading a Union cavalry force south along the west bank of the Ogeechee to attack Fort McAllister, set up temporary headquarters at Strathy Hall. In the ensuing two months, his staff ransacked the home, but left the structure intact. Infantry troops destroyed nearly every other home in the area. Some have said that Strathy was spared because Union officers heard that its owners had connections to the north. There was some truth to the rumor: Joseph had attended Amherst College in Massachusetts, and the whole family had often gone north to Connecticut during the hot, oppressive Ogeechee summers. After Fort McAllister fell to Sherman's troops in late 1864, the general walked about a mile north and slept briefly in the overseer's house at Strathy Hall, but he did not stay in the plantation home itself.[363]

After Kilpatrick's group left Strathy Hall in February 1865 to march with Sherman into South Carolina, the house probably lay vacant for nearly a year. Charlie and Harriet moved into Strathy in early 1866 and later brought furnishings from Norwich to make the home more comfortable.

Living at Strathy certainly shortened Charlie's travel to the Prarie rice farm; he could now ride by horse up to a bridge and down the other side to his fields, or simply row a boat directly across the Ogeechee. No more 20-mile trips from Savannah. By spring 1866, the couple seemed quite settled, and they invited Charlie's brother Fred to come down for a visit. "You could have lots of fun outdoors, shooting, fishing, and the like," Charlie wrote him. Fred came in May, but whether he had the fun that was promised is not known. Charlie himself, on the other hand, was enjoying the recreations of rural life, sometimes fishing all day or boating on the river with Hattie.[364]

Strathy Hall main house, pen and ink drawing by Edward W. Wells, 1838 (courtesy, Carolyn Clay Swiggart, *Shades of Gray*, Two Bytes Publishing Co., 1999).

When Fred boarded a steamer in early June for the return voyage to Norwich, he took Hattie along with him. The relentless isolation, hard work, dangers, and unhealthy hot, swampy climate of Ogeechee were taking a toll on her. In early May Harriet had fallen "suddenly ill and quite seriously" after crossing the Ogeechee to tour Prarie. Three days passed before Charlie could get Dr. Phineas M. Kollock, MD, a highly-respected professor at Savannah Medical College, out to treat her. Reassured by the doctor, Charlie noted "Everything straight and safe."[365]

Strathy Hall in modern times. Listed on National Register
of Historic Places (photograph by author, 2009).

To Harriet, Strathy must have seemed even more remote than the
mere twenty miles it was from Savannah. The 1860 census listed only
1,636 whites in all of Bryan County, where Strathy was located; adjacent
Chatham Country, with Savannah, had nearly 16,000. How lonely this
genteel lady must have felt, so accustomed to the comforts and society, if
not the riches, of town life in Norwich. While Charlie thought that Hattie
was "well pleased to live out here," he conceded that "we see no one from
one week to the other."[366] After five months at Strathy, following a month
in Savannah, and with the oppressive summer heat upon her, Hattie was
ready to see Norwich again.

Charlie would spend the summer in Ogeechee struggling to get rice
to grow and battling his recurring "bilious attacks" which were probably
intestinal infections. He was not following the more healthful practice
of most pre-war tideland planters who usually retired to Savannah for
the summer. Other northerners suffered as Charlie did. An agent of the
Freedmen's Bureau had recently resigned and left the Ogeechee area,
calling it "this region of miasma, disease, and death." And there were other

dangers, although Charlie seemed more excited than terrified to come upon (and kill) a rattlesnake he said was "12 feet long, 12 inches around body, 19 rattles." [367]

In mid-1866, Charlie and Wildman expanded their farming enterprise by acquiring a plantation known as Republican Hall, near the Belfast River, about five miles southwest of Strathy. This was a salt-water area, not subject to freshwater flows, with far fewer mosquitoes and less malaria. Because the fields could not be flooded, rice could not be grown, but provision crops like vegetables and corn flourished. Charlie spent the summer tending the two farms, while Hattie first rested in Norwich, and then traveled to Albany in the company of Governor Buckingham's family, perhaps to visit her mother. Charlie took breaks to socialize at the Savage House in Savannah, where he had lodged a year earlier. The venerable Savage family, related to the McAllisters, owned the Tivoli cotton plantation near Republican Hall. Given the cordial relations, it appears that the Savages did not object to Charlie and Harriet living in their kinfolks' house without paying rent to anyone.[368] When Charlie got lonely or restless in late July, he called several times on "C from Florida," whom he had visited a year earlier.[369]

In early August 1866, Charlie decided that he, too, needed a break; he caught a steamer north to New York and another on to Norwich. Curiously, Hattie, accompanied by her Aunt Harriet, left Norwich for Savannah just two days after Charlie arrived in Norwich. Not having a man to accompany them, the two women probably contented themselves with the sights of Savannah without going out to Strathy Hall. They returned to Norwich in early September. These were relaxing months for Charlie up north. He socialized, went bird hunting with friends, attended baseball "matches," discussed finances with his brother Billings, and dined at the home of Governor Buckingham. When Hattie returned in September, the two shopped for household furnishings, which they took south with them in October on a coastal steamer still stubbornly named the *Jeff Davis*.[370] Before departing, Charlie had his picture as a civilian taken by the renowned Norwich photographer W. H. Jennings.

Charlie as civilian, October 1866 (photograph by W. H. Jennings, Norwich)

## A Question of Rank

Charlie had been stewing over the War Department's decision to reverse his promotions to both major and lieutenant colonel. In 1866 he petitioned the department to review its order discharging him as a mere captain, in disregard of the authority it had delegated to Camp Parole for his promotion to lieutenant colonel. The War Department, after making a thorough review of the case, denied Charlie's petition. Acknowledging that such promotional authority *had* been granted, it ruled that the promotion nevertheless was void, the authority "having been given under a misapprehension of the facts of the case." The department implied that it had not known that Charlie, as his doctor stated in a subsequent medical certificate supporting his resignation, was "physically disqualified for field service."[371] But whether or not Charlie could have properly mustered at Camp Parole to confirm his promotion to lieutenant colonel, he *had* mustered as a *major* while in command of his battalion at Camp Chesebrough in the spring of 1863, and the War Department did not convincingly explain why it had revoked that promotion as well.

Despite clearly being discharged in 1864 as a captain, Charlie continued to represent himself to others, including Governor Buckingham, Senator Lafayette, and ultimately President Lincoln, as a lieutenant colonel. His travel permit, in Lincoln's own hand-writing, referred to him as "Col. Farnsworth." Quite possibly, Charlie had kept the truth of his rank at discharge to himself. After all that he had endured in the war, he probably felt that he was entitled to fudge a little on his rank. Many others exaggerated their deeds and their status. Or perhaps Charlie's relentless ambition overwhelmed his dependable integrity.

After the War Department denied the petition regarding his proper rank, Charlie decided that he was at least entitled to an invalid's pension because of his injuries. He obtained a medical certificate in early 1867 stating that his war wounds rendered him "entirely incapacitated for obtaining his subsistence by manual labor." The doctor stated that the musket shot had exited Charlie's torso one and a half inches from his spine; Charlie had nearly been paralyzed by the shot.[372] The report was submitted in support of an invalid's petition to the commissioner of pensions of the Department of Interior. A protracted bureaucratic battle would follow.

## The Storm on the River

To get to the Prarie farm from his Strathy Hall home, Charlie had the choice of two routes: he could ride by horseback four miles north to a bridge, cross over the Ogeechee River, then ride four miles back down the east side to the rice fields; or he could row across the river, which was estimated later by witnesses to be about six hundred feet wide at the nearest crossing, although a modern map shows the width as nearly a thousand feet. Charlie probably opted for the boat most often. In spring, however, the river ran swift with freshets, and winds could make the current dangerously choppy.

On the morning of April 15, 1867, Charlie and Wildman chose the river crossing and set off in a duck boat for their Prarie fields. The freshets were running on the Ogeechee and a stormy wind was building up. The two men probably had some misgivings about making the crossing, particularly in a small craft that rode so low in the water. But Charlie was a skilled boatman, and had boasted of rowing on the river with Harriet. He was also a good swimmer. According to what several freedmen on the Prarie side later said, Charlie and Wildman struggled to row through the waves and wind and nearly reached shore. They may have gotten as close as forty feet. But for some reason, Wildman then appeared to panic and jumped out; he was swept downstream and drowned. Charlie stayed in the boat for a short while but couldn't steer it ashore. When high waves swamped the low-lying boat, Charlie either jumped out or was washed overboard. He, too, was unable to swim the final distance through the swift current and was last seen slipping beneath the water's surface.[373]

Several men on the Strathy Hall side of the river tried to help, but by the time they crossed the river in their flatboat, the bodies had sunk from sight. Coats and hats, which Charlie and Wildman probably shed as they tried to swim, were recovered. Harriet didn't hear of the disaster for nearly three hours because the flatboatmen had to run downstream several miles to get a better boat to cross back to the Strathy side and then run back up to her home. While it may seem curious that the bodies sank from sight just forty feet from shore, modern maps show the river running about fifteen feet deep in that area.[374]

View from Strathy Hall across the Ogeechee River toward Prarie plantation near spot from where Charlie and business partner Edward Wildman attempted to cross, April 15,1867 (photograph by author, April 2009).

As the news of the disaster spread, an up-river rice farm neighbor named Mary Cornelia Talbot hurried to comfort Harriet, taking on the painful duty of notifying Charlie's parents. She wrote,

> Mrs. Farnsworth is very much crushed, it came so suddenly upon her. We trust she will have the strength given her from God to bear up under the dreadful affliction. We hope that she will consent to return home with us. Another would try to be a mother to her, in this sad hour of trial...[375]

Cornelia Talbot was a northerner at heart. At the time, she was visiting her parents, the Richard James Arnolds, at their nearby White Hall/ Cherry Hill plantation. Although Cornelia had been born in Georgia, her parents were northerners who had come south as adults in the 1830s to manage a plantation given to them at their marriage. They eventually became one of the largest Ogeechee rice planters and owned 195 slaves when the war broke out. But true to their northern heritage, the Arnolds fled back to Rhode Island when Georgia seceded from the Union, returning only when the war ended. Cornelia married a northerner during the war. Given their geographical and political affinities, Cornelia and Harriet may have become friends in the small Ogeechee rice farming community. Their two plantations, White Hall and Strathy, had been developed in the late 1700s by the same man, Captain James MacKay. But post-war rice farming was not for Cornelia; she returned to Rhode Island, becoming prominent in patriotic groups, as well as representing her state at two world expositions.[376]

A search party composed of Charlie's and Wildman's friends went out the next day with grappling hooks to troll the rough waters for the sunken bodies.[377] Oddly, no follow-up story appeared in the newspapers about the results of the search-party, but it is likely that both bodies were recovered after a day or two, when the natural process of decomposition would have floated them to the surface. Charlie's father and his brother Fred came down to Savannah to bring Charlie's body home. Harriet undoubtedly accompanied them back to Norwich.[378] From the wording of Cornelia Talbot's April 15 letter, she too may have gone north with them.

Charlie's family buried him in Norwich's Yantic Cemetery a week later, placing a gravestone that aptly captured the essence of the man:

**Charles Farnsworth**
**Born**
**Jan 30th, 1836**
**Drowned**
**Near Savannah, Ga.**
**April 15th, 1867**

**The Lord hath his way**
**In the whirlwind and in the storm.**

Yantic Cemetery, Norwich, with Farnsworth family section
in foreground (photograph by author, 2007).

Gravestone and epitaph for Charlie at Yantic Cemetery (photograph by author, 2010).

Charlie's death was widely noted in Norwich. Local newspapers carried extensive obituaries, calling him "a brave and gallant officer, an earnest patriot, an upright citizen and honest man." Lieutenant Joab B. Rogers, a Norwich friend and one of Charlie's favorite junior officers, wrote a letter on behalf of some of their enlisted men, extolling Charlie as "this esteemed soldier, who served his country in time of need, gaining friends and leaving a glorious record to history…" The regimental chaplain sent a eulogy adopted by a reunion of officers: "We shall ever cherish his memory as a noble & generous friend and a brave and gallant officer." Even the Savannah newspaper reported that "the loss of these estimable gentlemen will be deeply regretted by all who knew them, as they were men of great integrity and honesty. They had been in this country [i.e., the Ogeechee area] but a short time."[379]

Wildman's death was briefly (and somewhat inaccurately) reported in his hometown Danbury newspaper: "A dispatch was received…containing the sad intelligence of the death, in [Savannah], by drowning, of Mr. Edgar Wildman, of this town. The deceased was a proprietor of a rice plantation, and the supposition is that while engaged in its cultivation, requiring, as is well known, the use of dams and reservoirs, he may have been upset in a boat." Wildman also got a brief mention in the New York City press, which may say something of his family's social standing: "Drowned…eldest son of Samuel C. Wildman…in the 27th year of his age."[380]

In her grief, Harriet went to live with Charlie's parents on East Main Street in Norwich, where, less than two months later, on June 11, she gave birth to her only child, naming him Charles after his father. Charlie and Harriet had probably conceived the child in mid-August, 1866, during two days together in Norwich, after being apart for two months, and before Harriet left for a month's visit to Savannah with her aunt. In the end, Harriet had spent a total of thirteen months in Georgia: two in Savannah and eleven at Strathy Hall on the Ogeechee River. Some of the couple's Strathy Hall furnishings were brought back to Norwich.

# Chapter VI

## Reconstruction on the Ogeechee after Charlie's Death

Confederate Major Jacob Motte Middleton, who seems to have been in business with Charlie and Wildman at their nearby Republican Hall plantation, acquired some of the Prarie Plantation acreage after Charlie died. Whether or not Charlie's three-year lease was honored is unknown. Middleton, who had owned 180 slaves and considerable land before the war, was one of the planters who tried to bring economic order to the Ogeechee after the war. At a Freedmen's Bureau conference held at Strathy in late 1867, Middleton spearheaded a labor agreement between a group of local dispossessed freedmen and several "restored" planters. When the settlement broke down a year later, Middleton overreacted by banning the freedmen's union-style meetings. The rice workers, already a more cohesive group than most freedmen because of the inherently shared nature of their work, then organized themselves into the more radical Ogeechee Home Guards and proclaimed that "no white man should live between the two [Ogeechee Rivers]." Outnumbered by freedmen ten to one, many whites now feared to go into certain areas of the Ogeechee tidelands. Major Middleton himself was one of them, and he abandoned the Prarie fields.[381]

In January 1869, a short general strike turned into the infamous "Ogeechee riots," during which two Prarie night watchmen were shot, and stockpiles of rice were looted from Prarie and other plantations. Union military troops under civil war hero General George G. Meade were then called in and nearly a hundred freedmen were arrested. Major Middleton served as a crucial prosecution witness against the defendants in a preliminary hearing, after which twenty-four were charged with the crime of insurrection. After a trial, six were convicted but were promptly pardoned by Republican Governor Rufus Bullock. The episode was a severe setback for the freedmen, but their ultimate defeat came when the plantations they had seized were returned to the former owners.[382]

If Charlie had not died in April 1867, he might have been thrust into Major Middleton's role as a leader of the white planters in the Ogeechee Area. Would he have banned freedmen's meetings, as Middleton did? Or would he, as a former Union officer from an abolitionist family, have taken a more conciliatory approach to their demands? Would he have acted as a pragmatic businessman, seeking to make the best economic deal available? Or would he have reacted brashly, as he sometimes did when challenged? Would he have become discouraged, lost his taste for doing business in the post-war South, taken his losses, and returned north, as others did? (Massachusetts Colonel Henry Lee Higginson—a cousin of Thomas Wentworth Higginson, one of the ardent supporters of John Brown's 1859 raid on Harpers Ferry—gave up and left after two years in Ogeechee, suffering a $65,000 loss.)[383] Charlie's death kept him (and Harriet) from facing these dilemmas. In any case, the McAllister women returned in the mid-1870s to reclaim their house at Strathy Hall, and that would have forced Charlie and Harriet, at a minimum, to find a new home.[384]

# Chapter VII

## Harriet's Long Battle with Washington

The petition for an invalid's pension that Charlie had submitted to the Department of Interior in January 1867 was not promptly acted upon—perhaps because of his death in April of that year. But fifteen years later, in 1882, presumably from Harriet's persistent efforts, the department approved a pension of twenty dollars per month for the three years from Charlie's discharge to his death. While the pension issue was pending, the War Department wrote in 1870 that Charlie was entitled to compensation for any period that he used his own horse while on active duty. The family asked Senator Buckingham for advice, and he pointed out that since Charlie had used his own horse for only one month, a mere fourteen dollars would be due, hardly making it worth the effort to apply.[385]

Many years later, in 1889, Harriet filed for a widow's pension with the Department of Interior, alleging that Charlie had drowned in 1867 because of disabilities caused by his 1862 gunshot wounds. The application and an appeal taken by Harriet were denied, the department ruling that Charlie and Wildman had contributed to their own drowning deaths by negligently setting off across the Ogeechee River during stormy weather, and that Charlie had not died "by reason" of his war wounds because Wildman was not disabled, and he too had drowned.[386] (The ruling was a bit illogical because there was no evidence that Wildman could swim at all. Charlie, on the other hand, knew how to swim, but the gun wounds had weakened his ability to do so.) Harriet did not give up, however, and continued to press the issue with successive interior secretaries. Finally, in October *1908* she prevailed, and her widow's claim was approved at the rate of twelve dollars per month, but only commencing from the prior June. For reasons not stated, she would not receive forty-one years' retroactive benefits.[387] A couple of years after that, the government offered Harriet additional benefits if she could prove that Charlie had employed more than one servant during the war. She declined to apply, knowing that there had only been Denny.[388]

There was other post-war correspondence with the government. Two years after the war ended, and obviously unaware of Charlie's recent death, the Treasury Department wrote twice, demanding that he account for certain weapons, clothing, and equipment issued to his former Company B.[389] Harriet's response is unknown, but it is easy to imagine the scathing tone Charlie would have used, after the shabby way the government had demoted him.

Harriet moved to Colorado Springs in the late 1880s, seeking the salutary mountain air for her son Charles, who had contracted tuberculosis while in law school at Harvard. In the shadow of Pikes Peak, eighty miles from where her husband had once panned for gold, she continued to pound away at what she considered the War Department's wrongful and disparaging reduction of Charlie's rank. In 1886, the department, after a requested reappraisal, reinstated Charlie as a major, effective October 1, 1863, even though had been then imprisoned at Libby and therefore unable to muster with his regiment, a requirement for promotions at the time. Harriet won another victory eight years later when the Department amended the date of reinstatement as major to March 21, 1863, the day he took command of the battalion at Camp Chesebrough. Harriet's ultimate triumph, however, came in 1910—*forty-three years* after her husband's death—when the War Department reinstated Charlie to the rank of lieutenant colonel, retroactive to January 20, 1864, the date Colonel Fish was mustered out because of his court-martial and Charlie became the regiment's highest-ranking officer, although still a prisoner of the Confederacy.[390] Harriet undoubtedly took great pride in winning her long battle for justice and honor for her husband. Although she had always publically referred to Charlie as a lieutenant colonel, she could now do so with official approval. She died in 1916.

Harriet Peck Farnsworth, Charlie's widow age 63 (photograph
by Chas. E. Emery, Colorado Springs, 1900).

# Epilogue

Charlie's short life was filled with adventure and ambition. Whether going into the iron foundry business in Chicago at age twenty, prospecting for gold in the Rockies a couple of years later, commanding a cavalry company in the Civil War, enduring harsh imprisonment at Libby, or rice farming in the Georgia tidal lands, he was willing to take risks and suffer hardships for his goals. He was respected by men for his courage and firmness, and was attractive to women. He knew how to maneuver politically, straining and scheming (unsuccessfully) to become a battalion or regimental commander, and later lobbying (successfully) for a unique presidential permit to set up a business in Savannah.

But Charlie was also prone to rashness and error: both the Chicago foundry and the Colorado gold prospecting ventures failed; his cavalrymen and their horses got hurt during the overzealous early training he conducted; his mounted patrol was ambushed by bushwhackers along a road he erroneously led them on; in defiance of orders against indiscriminate retaliation in the Shenandoah Valley, he burned farm homes for miles around after a second ambush; he led a successful revolt, which could have been deemed a mutiny, against his battalion commander; he led a charge into General Lee's superior forces at Harpers Ferry which ended with his capture; he became impatient with administrative procedures at Camp Parole after his release from Libby Prison, asserted his disability, and resigned just days before he would have achieved his goal of commanding a cavalry battalion; and he undertook the high-risk enterprise of rice-farming along the swampy Ogeechee River amidst the turmoil of early Reconstruction. The only time Charlie clearly showed restraint—choosing not to take part in the "Grand Exit" escape from Libby Prison in February 1864—he later regretted. Ultimately, Charlie's headstrong nature led him to try to cross the fast-flowing Ogeechee River in a small boat on a stormy day.

His unbridled drive and fierce determination were unusual in his Norwich family. Although Charlie's father was a prominent physician and an outspoken abolitionist, Charlie's brothers led quieter lives mostly as businessmen in New England—Fred practicing as a medical doctor for only two years and Billings becoming a doctor only when he was nearly fifty. Although he did not attend college, Charlie's ability to express his thoughts and experiences in long letters home showed how well he was educated in secondary school. He never showed any regrets about not going to college. In his view, real learning came from engaging with the world.

Undoubtedly an abolitionist like his father, Charlie's views on race understandably fluctuated during his eight months in Libby Prison, as his expectations for release oscillated between frustration and hope. He generally supported the government's policy against prisoner exchanges that did not include all Union black soldiers, and was usually stoical about his confinement. But he occasionally expressed resentment over being held hostage to this principle. He doubted that freed slaves would prosper in either north or south after the war. On one occasion, he slipped into utter despair, wishing that all blacks were out of the country. But once out of prison and the army, Charlie showed a northerner's business-like attitude in dealing with free black workers on his Ogeechee plantation during the turbulent early years of Reconstruction.

Charlie's military leadership style reflected his personality. He was decisive, demanded a lot from his men, and could be a harsh disciplinarian, but was greatly admired for his courage and common touch. He sharply criticized colleagues like Blakeslee and Lyon and also some higher-ups, including Lincoln, but he carefully cultivated as patrons those whom he admired, such as Governor Buckingham and General Schenck. A rare change of heart occurred with his former commanding officer, William Fish, for reasons that remain unclear, but probably involved Fish's resentment that Charlie didn't come to his defense at the court-martial .

Only in romance did Charlie show indecision. He allowed a three-year engagement to Georgia Ann Parker during the war to linger another year while he courted Harriet Peck Lester, the woman he ultimately married.

In the occupied south, Charlie sought adventure and financial gain, bringing his brother Billings's investment funds with him to Savannah. He was neither a social reformer nor a political opportunist. As one of the early northern investors who were so essential in restarting the Savannah economy, he was generally welcomed. He paid fair rent for his store, and signed a three-year lease for the Prarie rice plantation. He and Harriet did move into the Strathy Hall home without permission from its owners who had abandoned it over a year earlier, but by occupying it, they probably saved it from further vandalism and neglect. Undoubtedly, southern die-hards or redeemers would have considered Charlie a "carpetbagger," after the term of derision was "pulled out of thin air" by southerners in late 1867.[391] It was convenient to see all northerners in that way. But because the term had not yet been coined when Charlie died, no one would have called him a carpetbagger during his lifetime. In time, some northerners took advantage of southern whites' exclusion from politics to feather their own nests. But Charlie had no interest in that. He simply wanted an exciting way to make money in business, and he invested heavily in the effort. Up north, those who went south to work or invest were viewed simply as American citizens migrating to another state, just as many had gone west earlier, bringing with them "intelligence, civilization, and enterprise." There is no evidence that Charlie ever engaged in what the term carpetbagging generally covered: political corruption, destructive social agitation, or economic exploitation of a conquered people. Charlie was a businessman, and he could deal above-board with both freedmen and former planters. But to the extent that every northerner in the post-war South would come to be considered a carpetbagger by southern redeemers, then Charlie was a carpetbagger. It all depended on timing, definition, and point of view.

Questions remain about the deaths of Charlie and Wildman. A government decision on Harriet's pension appeal years later concluded that the river was only six hundred feet wide and that Charlie had been only forty feet from the far shore when he drowned, but those figures are questionable. A modern map shows the width to be about a thousand feet, and the forty-foot estimate was drawn from an allegation in the appeal, not from eye-witness testimony. The April flow of the Ogeechee is quickened by freshets and drownings there are not unheard of, but Charlie was a skilled boatman and an experienced, if somewhat disabled, swimmer. There was no evidence that Wildman could swim, but the report that he abandoned a wooden boat and jumped overboard makes little sense in any case. Nor does it seem likely that the swamped boat would then capsize and throw Charlie into the water. Perhaps the report was simply based on garbled hearsay. But the possibility remains that some other factor was at work. In the end, Charlie's parents captured the essence of his adventurous short life and early death in the epitaph that they chose from the Old

Testament Book of Nahum for his gravestone at Yantic Cemetery: "The Lord hath his way in the whirlwind and in the storm."

After giving birth to their only child Charles in June 1867, Harriet continued to reside at the Farnsworth home on East Main Street in Norwich. When Charlie's parents Ralph and Eunice died in the 1870s, and Billings took over the house, Harriet moved with young Charles to the home of her mother, Mary Elizabeth Lester, who had returned to Norwich from Albany.[392] Harriet and Charles moved to Providence when he enrolled at Brown University at age eighteen. After graduating from Brown, Charles started law school at Harvard, but dropped out in his first year after contracting tuberculosis. Harriet took him to Switzerland and then to Algeria in search of the clean, dry air that was thought to be curative. Not finding relief, the two headed for California in 1894. En route by train, they stopped off in Colorado Springs and liked it so much that they stayed. Harriet never remarried, nor did she develop an occupation beyond the home.

Within months of arriving in Colorado Springs, Charles had met Edith Winslow, a young lady from a distinguished New England family who had brought her brother west for treatment for his tuberculosis. Charles and Edith were married a year later. He died of the lung disease a decade later in 1906 at age thirty-eight, leaving his widow with four children under the age of ten. One of Harriet's most cherished memories, she once wrote, was of the time she "met Lincoln one quiet morning [in] the second year of the war." That would have been 1862, when she probably had accompanied Governor Buckingham in a trip to Washington.[393] Harriet died in January 1916, at age seventy-eight, at her home at 609 N. Tejon Street in Colorado Springs, the proud widow of a lieutenant colonel who had fought and suffered in the Union cause. She is buried at Evergreen Cemetery in Colorado Springs, next to her son.

Young Charles benefitted greatly over the years from bequests from his relatives, receiving about $30,000 from his grandmother Eunice in 1878 and another $25,000 from Eunice's brother William W. Billings in 1888. Both gifts were held in trust for Charles until he turned twenty-four. Harriet herself inherited $5,000 from an aunt, and a Norwich home from a half-sister. She was also guaranteed $100 a month from the estate of another uncle, Albert M. Billings.[394] These inheritances, worth about twenty-five times as much in today's dollars, allowed Harriet to raise her son without great financial hardship.

Charlie's older brother Billings continued in business for several years after the war. In the 1870 census, when he was forty, his occupation was described as "bookkeeper," and he was living with his parents.[395] Sometime in the early 1870s he began studying medicine in Norwich under his father's tutelage, but he never attended medical school. Two years after Dr. Ralph died in 1875, Billings obtained a medical license of his own and took over his father's practice. A year later, he married Carrie George, a twenty-year-old schoolteacher from Haverhill, Massachusetts, and brought her into the family home on East Main Street. Tragedy struck a year later in 1879 when Carrie died of complications from the still-birth of their only child.

Billings's own life ended shockingly in 1897 when he committed suicide in the barn behind the family home. After lying down on the barn floor, he shot himself in the right temple with a .38-caliber revolver. Reportedly, he had become despondent over financial set-backs, and owned only his home at the time of his death. One newspaper reported that Billings had lost $200,000—many millions in today's currency—while speculating in stocks over the past seventeen years. He was alternately reported as a "shambling...beaten man" or as "happy, prosperous-looking" in the days before his death. Billings was buried near his parents at Yantic cemetery, but as a suicide, his grave was left unmarked—until recently when his descendants had a headstone installed for him and Carrie. An Episcopal minister at the time did conduct a funeral service for Billings at the family home, at which "attendance was very large." The home and its contents, valued at $8,000, were all that Billings owned at this death.[396]

Billings had probably suffered his crushing losses from speculative bets on stock prices at one of Norwich's notorious "bucket shops." In the late nineteenth century, these storefront outfits were not actual stockbrokerages but did have telegraphic connections with the New York Stock Exchange, enabling them to track price movements. Wealthy local men could put down money, often on margin, against stock fluctuations. Oftentimes, however, actual purchases of stock were not made, and customers were betting, in effect, against the house, which was acting like a casino. Worse, the bucket shops often manipulated stock ticker prices by selling their own accounts below market, thereby fraudulently forcing a margin call for the full amount of the bet—a ploy known as a "wash sale."[397] Billings was a sad victim of these frauds over many years. One wonders why he never caught on.

Charlie's younger brother Fred graduated from Yale in 1864, at the height of the Civil War, and then, taking Charlie's advice to stay out of the army, enrolled at Bellevue Medical School in New York, graduating in 1867. After practicing medicine for only two years, he spent eight years in Philadelphia as a businessman, and then retired to New London. He soon inherited substantial wealth from one of his mother's brothers. His wife of ten years, Lydia W. Sanderson, died in 1888, leaving no children. Fred died in 1914 without a will; he owned several New London commercial properties, but was significantly in debt.[398]

A decade after Charlie was buried at Yantic Cemetery, his parents Ralph and Eunice were laid to rest in front of him. Six siblings who had died before age six were transferred from an older cemetery a few years later and reburied under tiny headstones behind Charlie. Charlie's brother Billings and young wife Carrie lie to one side of the plot, under an elegant evergreen tree. Only younger brother Fred is buried elsewhere, in New London.

# Appendix

## The Letters, Diaries, and Documents of Charles Farnsworth*

## Introduction

Over the course of seven years, Charlie wrote his letters and diaries in both pen and pencil—and a few secret ones in lemon or onion juice. Many are now faded or smudged. Although his handwriting is generally legible, occasionally it couldn't be read, and those portions are so indicated with brackets. Charlie expressed himself clearly, although he sometimes fell into archaic words. His spelling tended to be nearly perfect, but his punctuation was his own unique brand, so I have taken the liberty of imposing more uniformity in the use of periods and commas in the transcriptions.

Charlie's diaries posed a curious problem in chronology: he began to make entries in 1863 shortly after his capture at Harpers Ferry, but he used an 1864 edition, adjusting the dates for each entry. In 1865 he used a proper edition but later made entries in it for the previous and following years as well. Many of the diary entries after mid-1864 (mainly to describe his amorous adventures) were written in a code of Charlie's invention, using a combination of symbols, numbers, and switched letters. The code was deciphered by my cousin Frances's husband, Erik Taylor. Most of the encoded entries were about Charlie's romantic life and, in particular, quoted the loving words that his future wife, Harriet, was saying to him.

Apart from two letters in 1860, Charlie's regular correspondence with his family began immediately after he received his commission as a lieutenant in the fall of 1861 and was sent to Meriden, Connecticut for

---

*The collection of Lieutenant Colonel Charles Farnsworth's letters, diaries, and other documents is jointly copyrighted by Frances Hazlehurst Taylor and the author; the commentary is copyrighted by the author.

cavalry training. His mother seems to have saved nearly all of his letters. Charlie regularly destroyed the letters he received from family and friends. Only one of the many letters written to him has been found. To the letters and diaries that follow, I have added occasional explanatory comments.

## 1860

St. Joe
Feb. 28th 1860

Dear Fred,

You must excuse my not writing but I have been very busy indeed. I have bought me a mule here, and I tell you he is a real cunning fellow, a little small chunk of a institution. I am a-going to ride him across from here to Denver City, some 700 miles. The party I am with have a wagon and we have got a stove & fire and shall camp out. We take provisions with us to feed our mules. I will take about 8 qts. of corn a day for a mule, and then eat what dead grass there is to be found on the plains. It is queer what little will keep a mule. A horse would die on the way, while a mule will keep fat upon the amt. I named. We get hay at several places on the way and we can then let them fill up and take enough to last them a day or so. It will take about 30 days to go across. You can put your letter in with Mother's, as the expense is 2 cents a letter from Kearny. Put enough to take it to the end of the mail route, which will be the same as if sent to Chicago.

I know but little of Aiken, but understand he is a clever fellow. I would not say anything about my being any where except Chicago, and if asked say I am travelling, selling goods, and that I am not in Chicago much.

I trust we shall meet soon, but it will not be till I have a little more of the successful than at present.

I have written Mother my P.O. directions.

Much love from
Charles

Denver City
April 1, 1860

My Dear Mother,

I received yesterday your letters of March 2d & 5th forwarded to me from Kearney. The letters sent to Leavenworth have not been sent to me yet. I have sent for them and shall expect them soon. I wrote you last Sunday. On Monday, I started for <u>Mountain City</u>, forty miles in the mountains. Three of us started together on foot. We left in the morning at 9, made Golden City, 15 miles, for dinner and then pushed out. We each carried our blankets and 10 lbs. provisions and a skillet to cook with, making about 25 lbs. of baggage. Monday night we made camp in the mountains some 10 miles, cut down a quantity of brush and small trees and making a shelter, built fire, cooked our supper and putting a large quantity of wood upon the fire, turned in and slept well. The next noon we made Mountain City.

We traveled each day over the mountains where they are working in quartz claims, and through the gulch diggings, some nights getting home to our cabin, and some nights not. One afternoon when about 15 miles from home, a snow storm came up and soon we lost our way and could not see a thing, and we made up our minds to stop for the night. We had no blankets, only an overcoat and our cooking utensil and an axe. We cut down trees, built a huge fire, and then built our shelter. It snowed all night and we had rather a tough time of it. In the morning there were over 4 feet of snow, but we got out safely and reached home by noon.

We staid in the mountains prospecting til Friday morn when we started for Denver and reached there the same night—good walking, I tell you. Saturday I got your letters (they came Wednesday) and today I shall answer them and some from Chicago.

Our trip in the mountains was very pleasant and we think the prospect for getting a little of the sordid metal good, but owing to certain local laws made last fall by miners, little can be accomplished by strangers before June 1st when the laws expire. But owing to circumstances falling in with a member of our order, he showed me around and put me in a way to get information, which I did and got along better than an uninitiated person could.

I do not go much up the quartz claims in this section and think that there are better quick claims west of here. I should start after the next mail comes in Wednesday for Colorado River, some 200 miles west, and may not be in Denver before Fall. Of that as yet I cannot tell. I think that there are better diggings in that direction than here, although I suppose & think a man can even here make from $10 to $100 a day mining the gulches. But I think better diggings lie still further west.

I have left the party I crossed the plains with and am in partnership with one I. S. McHenry from Lane, Illinois. We go to Colorado on foot, packing mules with provisions. We shall cross the Snowy Range. They say the snow is from 10 to 30 feet deep.

We have given up our proposed speculation, at least I have concluded it won't pay at present. I think that business here would pay well and sometimes I think I will stay here and run my chances. I have no doubt but a fortune can be made here in many things. Denver is bound to be the great center of all business from the East and large fortunes will be made speculating in lots & and I think will pay well, although they are held very high even now. Hotels will pay well. I came very near taking one, but my partner thinks it will pay better to go to the Colorado, and so I made up my mind to go. He was in California 6 years and mined most of the time.

If things should not turn out well, I can get back here by June and then the big immigration will be just coming in and there will be lots of chances to buy goods off them at very low figures, as they all will want money upon getting here.

I think that the gift of looking into the future would be a grand idea just now, so as to see what will be advantageous. No doubt next year, if here, I shall pay as I used to in Chicago. Last Spring when I came here that corner lot could have been bought for $500, that block for the same, and now you can't buy it for 10 times that amount. But we cannot see into the future, and must trust to luck. The town is going ahead very fast indeed. There is a great deal of building going on just now and will still continue all summer. Goods now are very high indeed. I believe I gave you a list of prices in my last.

A day or so before I came, there was a duel fought between two men of high standing. One shot the other through the thigh, the ball passed directly through the body. He is still alive. The next day, a man shot another and was hung the next afternoon. Yesterday a rowdy was shot down in the street. He died in twenty minutes. The man that shot him went home. And when the crowd gathered around, he informed them upon his honor that as soon as the excitement was over he would deliver himself up, but if they undertook to arrest him he should defend himself to the last. He soon after left town and this morning he returned, gave himself up and will have a trial sometime today. Public opinion justifies his act and he will be acquitted.

There is no jail here and no courts. The citizens try all cases immediately upon commission and either punish the perpetrator immediately or clear in as short a time. A good deal better law than to let it go through the slow process of law. Stealing is considered here a greater crime than any other and is punished more severely. A man caught stealing is more likely to be hung than one who murders. And you can sleep as easy in a room with twenty hard men characters as at home, for they dare not steal the least thing. Locks are not used at all. A pin in the door is enough, and you can go away and leave your cabin, merely laying a string outside the door and there is no fear of intrusion.

You can call upon Mrs.W. I would say nothing about my short connection with her husband. I hope to be home next fall, if I am successful and have enough to come with.

*I just reached this point when a lady came in and suggested the propriety of my going with her to church and I went to the Episcopal, Mr. Keeler. They meet in a log house and the rector read and preached without his robes. Whether the effect will be the same I cannot tell.*

*Much Love to all. I write thus fine in order to forward it to Chicago.*

*Afft*

*Charles*

---

**Comment:** These two letters, the earliest saved by Charlie's family, describe his adventures during the Pikes Peak gold rush of the late 1850s. Gold in streams in Denver and in the front range of the Rockies west of Denver was discovered in 1857-58, and the rush began in 1859. Actually, the discoveries were made neither at Pikes Peak, nor in Colorado, but rather in what was then Kansas Territory, eighty miles north of the peak. (Colorado's territorial borders were established in 1861.) The miners prospected for gold by panning and sluice-boxing in streams and rivers; it would be thirty years before deep hole drilling would be developed in Colorado. Nonetheless, about $900,000 in gold was taken out in 1859, and about $2 million in 1860. Businessmen from Chicago, where Charlie was selling iron stoves, helped finance some of the early 1859 prospecting, and this may have been where Charlie got the idea to get involved. More than a hundred thousand miners and their families crossed the Great Plains in 1859-60, but only about thirty thousand stayed more than a year.[399]

In the second letter (ninth paragraph), Charlie says that he had come to Denver a year earlier, and notes that real estate prices had risen since then. Yet in the first letter he describes an anticipated thirty-day crossing from St. Joseph, Missouri, as if he were doing it for the first time. One answer to this seeming contradiction: in 1859, he might have been traveling on business by stage coach, a service that had just opened; it was much faster (six days and nights) but allowed almost no room for baggage or equipment. Deciding to leave Chicago to try his hand at gold prospecting in 1860, Charlie needed to carry more gear, so went by mule and wagon train.

The "Aiken" referred to in the first letter is probably William Appleton Aiken, who had recently married Eliza Buckingham, the daughter of Connecticut's governor, a family friend. Aiken would go on to serve as quartermaster general of Connecticut during the war, with responsibilities for outfitting and supplying the many regiments that the state fielded.

---

# 1861

Rocket Mills, Va.
June 6 1861

My Dear friend,

I was greatly pleased to receive a letter from you this morning and have seated myself around the camp fire to answer it immediately. Ever since Tuesday morning it has rained steadily, a regular cold southern storm, which has just cleared off, and we are trying to get dry, for we are completely water-soaked. Our part of the camp is on a side hill, and this morning at about 5 o'clock the rain poured down in perfect rivers, washing through our tents and wetting us through and through. As you say "such is life." But notwithstanding all these little extras camp life is perfectly splendid. I have not seen a sick day yet, and never enjoyed better health in my life. I wish I could just look in on some of the girls in Norwich before I leave this place. We are not a-going to lay here all our three months. I can tell you, we are a-going to fight soon, perhaps before you receive this, our regiment may have seen a battle the result of which will cause more mourning in Connecticut than she has ever yet seen. All the officers in the regiment express their belief that not one-third of us will ever see our homes, a belief which is calculated to excite very many pleasant reminiscences of past life and future expectations. There are at least 15,000 secession troops within fifteen miles of our camp, with Gen. Beauregard at their head, so you see a day's march will bring us right together, the orders for which we have been honestly expecting since we came here. You see, we three month volunteers have got to take all the brunt (you might say) of this war, and then you lazy fellows there at home will come down here and thrash these "secesh," and go home up to your ears in glory, while we lay here a mass of dust, to be the subject of conversation at the fireside of our future children's children. A great consolation to us. I received a letter from Joe Rockwell yesterday dated at La Salle where he is rusticating in great style. Our camp is situated in a patch of woods with a large open field in front for a parade ground. The Harper's Ferry and Alexandria railroad runs right in front of us, and on one side is a river about the size of the Yantic, which is full of fish and is a good place to bathe. There are beautiful boiling springs scattered on all sides of us, so that we are well supplied with fine water, a great luxury in camp life. We send off scouting parties every day of about forty (40) men in hopes of getting some stray seceshinists, but so far in vain. Every night the same number of men go out about two miles from camp on "picket" guard. This guard is the most dangerous position one can be placed in. They are stationed by twos about a quarter of a mile from each other, and have to keep perfectly still all the time in order to detect the approach of an enemy. Every camp has its picket guards, so that they are scattered all over the county and are in communication with each other. For instance, if we wanted to send a dispatch to the War Department in Washington, we could telegraph it in less than half an hour, or if they wished to send a dispatch to us, we could by means of these pickets, carry it to every camp in the same space of time. I did not mean to take so much time to write you, for I was afraid I should not have enough to say. But I will try and scrape up something to fill up part of this sheet. If we are not ordered off within a day or two, two or three of our mess with a corporal are going off in a scouting expedition for two or three days, which no doubt will be a "big thing." How does the Academy get along, do you still flourish there as of old? You must write me all about these things, for anything about old Norwich and the girls there is always welcome. I cannot always write you, but you must not think I forget you, for I never do. But we shall have hard work and little leisure after this work. I shall expect letters from you often, and will answer them when I can. Has Goddard forgotten his old friend, or are his editorial duties so heavy that he cannot send me one little letter? Please read this letter to him, and to all my old friends, or rather I should say male friends, as it was not prepared for the perusal of fair friends. Remember me kindly to Hattie and Mary Williams and all the girls whom I left behind. Don't think me foolish or conceited if I ask you to save this letter till I come home, for it will be necessary for me to refer to it some time or other, as I cannot keep my diary or journal out here. What does Noyes Mines do now since Bob has gone? Please remember me to him. I must ask particularly about Nellie Slater and Helen Reynolds. I am sorry to hear about Jesse, and am afraid he will be worse than before. I do not think there are fifty men in the whole regiment who will enlist for three years, for we have not been fed decently since we left home, but in my opinion had we been treated as much like soldiers as we have like dogs. I have a plan now, which if carried out, I shall enlist for three years but if not successful I shall be home in July if nothing happens. When you write next you can find out of father where to direct your letter; if I am here you can direct as before, but as I am pretty sure not to be you can ask him. I am glad to hear that you are having a new boat built and hope you will use it to advantage, and only wish I was there to row with you. You forget when you speak of having Watch Hill all to yourself this summer. Remember that if I am alive I shall turn up in July and therefore get ahead of you. Would it not be funny if I should be there at the examination at the close of the term. You say you saw that Bob had been appointed paymaster; that is a great mistake.

*He has a 2ⁿᵈ Lieutenant commission in the marine corps, a fine position. He left us yesterday. Talk to Rib like a father about not writing me. I have not heard a word from him since I left. I must now close as I have got to write to father and mother.*

*Yours truly,*

*EKA*

---

**Comment:** "E.K.A." was probably E. K. Abbott, a friend from Norwich, who was then a captain in the Twelfth Connecticut Infantry Volunteers. He survived the war. Charlie would later marry the woman "Hattie" to whom he sends his regards. The reference to "Goddard" could be to either Henry or Alfred Goddard, both Norwich friends of Charlie. This is the only personal letter written *to* Charlie that has been preserved. The inquiry about the "Academy" is odd, because Charlie is twenty-five years old at this point and would not have attended the famous Norwich Free Academy, which opened in 1855, when he was nineteen. The comments about the new boat and Watch Hill are illuminating. Watch Hill is located in the mouth of the Pawcatuck River on the border of Rhode Island and Connecticut. EKA's friendly challenge to Charlie about rowing clearly shows that they were both familiar with boating. This would prove to be important evidence pertaining to later events.

---

*State of Connecticut*
*Executive Department:*
*Hartford, Sept 4, 1861*

*His Excellency*
*William Sprague*
*Rhode Island*

*Sir*

*This will introduce Mr. Charles Farnsworth of Norwich, who calls with reference to business connected with the Quarter Masters Department.*

*He is a young gentleman of integrity and worthy of all confidence.*

*Yours with high regards*

*Wm. A. Buckingham*

---

**Comment:** Before enlisting in October, Charlie briefly pursued a war-time business opportunity, disclosed in the following letter to be the marketing of army field tents. He intended to approach the governors of Rhode Island and Massachusetts, who were responsible for raising and equipping armies for the Union, carrying an introduction from Governor Buckingham of Connecticut, a family friend.

---

State of Connecticut
Executive Department:
Hartford Sept 4 1861

His Excellency
Gov John N. Andrew
Massachusetts

Sir

I am well acquainted with the bearer Mr. Charles Farnsworth who visits Massachusetts for the purpose of exhibiting a new tent for the use of the troops. He is a gentleman of integrity and worthy of all confidence.

I am yours with high regard,
Wm. A. Buckingham

State of Connecticut
Office of the Commander-in-Chief
Norwich, Oct 19th 1861

Charles Farnsworth Esq.

Sir

You are appointed adjutant of the 1st Battalion of Cavalry, Conn Volunteers and will call on Adjutant General J. D. Williams at Hartford on Tuesday for your commission & orders.

Yours Respectfully
Wm. A. Buckingham

---

**Comment:** The lure of adventure and patriotic duty overcame any attraction to wartime business; Charlie enlisted and received a commission in the newly-formed First Connecticut Cavalry, initially in a staff position.

---

General Head-Quarters State of Connecticut
Adjutant General's Office
Hartford, October 21*st* 1861

Special Order )
No. 243 )

Lieut Charles Farnsworth, Adjutant, 1*st* Battalion Cavalry, Conn. Volunteers is directed to report forthwith for duty to Captain Henry Boardman at Camp Tyler, Meriden.

By order of the Commander-in-Chief
J. D. Williams
Adjutant General

Camp Tyler, W. Meriden, Conn
Oct 27*th* 1861

My dear Uncle,

Your letter in regard to the horse was received the day I left, Monday last. And I have not found time to go and see it. But am perfectly willing to trust to you in the matter. Our camp is two miles from West Meriden, which should the owner wish to see me he could bring the horse up there. But if you think it is a good horse you can purchase it, and I will send the amount to you. We have been very much employed since I came here or should have written you before. My love to Auntie.

Afft Nephew
Charlie

---

**Comment:** The envelope was addressed to E. W. Farnsworth. Walter was his father's youngest brother, a businessman in Boston. Many cavalry officers brought their own horses into military service at the beginning of the war.

---

Camp Tyler West Meriden
Oct 31*st* 1861

Dear Uncle,

Your letter of 28*th* came to hand today. In regard to the Middletown horse I would say that from what you said in regard to it, I thought it would be a fine chance to purchase a good horse cheap. I am unable to go to see the horse at present, but will write in regard to his bringing the horse here. According to regulations officers can have their pick from the herd which will be brought here. Should I not be suited in this horse of Allsop's, I can then take my pick from the lot, some three hundred *in number. I think I can get a fine horse in that way. I am very well pleased with my new position, and when I get all my outfit together I shall feel more contented. Much love to Aunt Louisa and Aunt Lydia.*

*Affectionate Nephew*
*Charles*

---

**Comment:** The "uncle" is the same Walter Farnsworth.

---

*General Head-Quarters State of Connecticut*
*Adjutant-General's Office*
*Hartford, November 26th 1861*

*Capt. Charles Farnsworth*
*Co. B. 1st Battalion Conn. Cavalry*
*West Meriden, Conn.*

*Sir,*

*Inclosed I hand you a commission as Captain Company B 1st Battalion Conn Cavalry. You are ordered to report to Acting Major Henry Boardman for duty.*

*J. D.Williams*
*Adjutant General*

---

**Comment:** Within a month of reporting for active duty, Charlie was promoted from lieutenant to captain.

---

*General Head-Quarters State of Connecticut*
*Adjutant-General's Office*
*Hartford, December 4ᵗʰ 1861*

Captain Charles Farnsworth
Co. B, 1ˢᵗ Battalion Conn Cavalry
West Meriden, Conn.

Captain,

Sent the Pistols to you by express. They cost $20 each. The balance amt. is $1.95, as you will notice by the bill inclosed. Will you collect the balance due from Lieut Colburn and remit with yours.

Yours Respectfully
J. D. Williams
Adjutant General

| | |
|---|---|
| Capt. Farnsworth | $1.95 |
| Lieut Colburn | 1.98 |
| | $3.93 |

*Hartford Dec 4ᵗʰ 1861*

Captain Charles Farnsworth:
To J. D. Williams, Lt.:

| 2 | A. M. Navy [illegible] pistols | @ $20 | $40.00 |
|---|---|---|---|
| 96 | " " cartridges | @ 2 ¼ ea | 2.20 |
| 500 | " " caps | @ 1.50 /tb | .75 |
| | Total | | $42.95 |
| | By cash | | 41.00 |
| | Balance due | | $ 1.95 |

Received Payment
J.D.Williams

---

**Comment:** Not only did Charlie bring his own horse, but, like most Union officers, he was expected to pay the cost of his sidearm and ammunition.

---

# 1862

Hd Qtrs Dept of New England
Boston, February 12th 1862

Special Order )
No. 14 )

In accordance with instructions from the Head Quarters of the Army, Major J. M. Lyon, Conn Volunteer Cavalry, you will proceed, without delay, with the four companies of Cavalry now encamped at West Meriden, Conn, to <u>Wheeling Virginia</u> and report to Brig. General Rosecranz.

Major Lyon will apply to Co. D. D. Tompkins, Assistant Qtr Master General at New York for transportation.

By command of Major Gen. Butler
Geo. C. Strong
Asst. Adjutant General

---

**Comment:** This is the order that sent Charlie to the front lines of the war.

---

**TO THE** *Most Ancient and Honorable Fraternity of Free & accepted Masons* around the **GLOBE, GREETING.**

We, Officers, presiding over Meridian **LODGE**, No. 77, in the town of Meriden and State of Connecticut do certify and make known that our WORTHY BROTHER Charles Farnsworth has been legally Initiated, Passed, and Raised to the Sublime Degree of Master Mason in regular constituted Lodge. Therefore, We recommend him to the favour, friendship and good will of all our Worthy Brethren around the Globe.

In testimony whereof, We having first caused our worthy Brother to sign his name in the margin have caused the seal of our Lodge to be Affixed to this Diploma. Given under our hand & seal of this Lodge this 17th day of February A.D. 1862.

Rodney L. Smith, Secretary M. C. Augur W. Master
Leon E. Cox S. Warden
David L. Lyons F. Warden

**Comment:** Before departing with his cavalry unit, Charlie found time to be initiated master mason in the local Masonic Lodge. A seal was affixed, and the signature Chas. Farnsworth appears in the margin.

*Wheeling, Va.*
*1 ½ AM Mar 27 / 62*

*Dear Mother*

*We received orders last evening to report to Gen. Schenck at Moorefield, Hardee County, Va., and leave tomorrow. We have been very busy all night and expect to leave early. From all I learn we are to have active service.*

*Your letter of 22ⁿᵈ received. In regard to letter to F & B do as you think best. Much love from*

*AfftSon*
*Charlie*

*I enclose draft for $20.00 pay for glass.*

*"From Charles at Wheeling, Va. March 27ᵗʰ '62, night before he left for Moorefield, Va. April 3d following, Charles was wounded."* (Note by his mother on the reverse side.)

*Camp Durfee*
*Near Moorefield Va.*

*Dear Mother*

*Here safe and sound and have been out two days scouting. Just arrived tired out. The 82nd Ohio Reg. are here — expect a fight every day. Excuse writing from*
*AfftSon*
*Charlie*

*"From Charles, at Camp Durfee, Moorefield, Va., a few days before he was wounded."* (His mother's note on the reverse side.)

*Head Quarters, Cumberland District*
*Mountain Department*
*Cumberland, April 5, 1862*

*Captain Albert Tracy*
*Asst. Adjutant General*
*Head Quarters, Mountain Department Wheeling*

*Captain:*
*The latest dates I have from Moorfield are to the 3ʳᵈ instant — Thursday. I send copies of two letters from Lt. Col. Durfee of that date, just received. The last written of them gives account of the dangerous, perhaps fatal, wounding of Capt. Farnsworth of the Connecticut Cavalry. I send also a copy of letter of instructions sent today to Lt. Col. Durfee.*

*Very respectfully,*
*Your Obdt. Servt.*
*Robt. C. Schenck*
*Brig. Genl.*
*Camp Durfee Apr 7 1862*
*Moorefield, Va.*

---

**Comment:** On his fourth or fifth day of scouting, Charlie was shot through the left arm and chest when fourteen irregular Confederates, known as "bushwhackers," ambushed his patrol from a hill seven miles along a road through a rocky ravine between Moorefield and Strasburg, Virginia.

---

*Dr. Farnsworth*

*Dear Sir*
*I am happy to inform you that Capt. looked more like himself than he has done any day since the accident. He sat up in an easy chair a short time this a.m. At noon he ate some arrow-root with cream. His nervousness is fast wearing off, if not gone entirely. He is getting used to lying in bed, which is a great point gained. We keep cold water on the wounds all the time. The Dr. Surgeon says the wounds are doing as well as could be expected.*
*We all look forward to his recovery, hoping soon to see him mounted at the head*

*of the Co., as he is the favorite officer of the battalion and loved by his company. Our other wounded man is doing very well.*

> *Your obedient servant*
> *Howell Atwater*
> *1ˢᵗ Lieut. Co. B.*

*1ˢᵗ Cav. Conn./Company Muster Roll*

*Charles Farnsworth, Captain, Co. B, Batt'n 1 Conn. Cavalry, for March & April 1862. Absent. Wounded April 3ʳᵈ /62 by Guerrillas, through left arm & side, 7 miles from Moorefield on Winchester Road. Home on furlough April 17ᵗʰ/62.*

*S. Thompson, Copyist*

> *State of Connecticut*
> *Executive Department*
> *Hartford, April 9ᵗʰ 1862*

*Gen. G. S. Ferry*

*Dear Sir*

*Permit me to introduce the bearer Doct R Farnsworth my family physician who goes to visit his son Capt. Farnsworth of Co B 1ˢᵗ Conn Cavalry who was wounded near Moorefield Virginia a few days since. Doct Farnsworth is a gentleman of high standing and worthy of entire confidence. Any assistance you can render him will not injure the public service and will be highly appreciated.*

> *I am with high regard*
> *your obedient servant*
> *Wm. A. Buckingham*

---

**Comment:** William Buckingham was the Republican governor of Connecticut, a strong supporter of Lincoln, and was responsible for providing troops for the First Connecticut Cavalry Volunteers. Charlie's father, Dr. Ralph Farnsworth, was Buckingham's personal physician, Norwich neighbor, political supporter, and close friend. Charlie was lucky to get such personal medical attention.

---

State of Connecticut
Office of the Commander in Chief
Hartford, April 9th 1862

Gen. N. P. Banks
Virginia

Dear Sir

Permit me to introduce my family physician Doct R Farnsworth, a gentleman eminent in his profession true and devoted to the interests of our country and worthy of entire confidence. He is anxious to see his son, a Capt. in the 1st Battalion Conn Cavalry who was wounded a few days since near Moorefield Virginia.

Any assistance not inconsistent with the public service which you can render in securing the object of Doct Farnsworth will be highly appreciated.

I am Dear General yours
with high regard
Wm. A. Buckingham

State of Connecticut
Office of the Commander in Chief
Hartford, April 9th 1862

Hon. E. M. Stanton
Secretary of War
Washington

Dear Sir:

Permit me to introduce Doct R Farnsworth my family physician, a gentleman of high position in his profession, of great moral worth & a true and loyal citizen.

His son commands a company of cavalry in the 1st Conn Battalion and was wounded at or near Moorefield Virginia a few days since.

If not inconsistent with the public interests and you can give him a pass or in some other way aid him in reaching his son at an early day you will greatly oblige.

your obedient servant

with high regard
Wm. A. Buckingham

*Headquarters Connecticut*
*137 Broadway*
*New York, April 10ᵗʰ 1862*

*Major Genl N. P. Banks*

*Dear Sir*

    *The bearer of this note, Mr. Billings Farnsworth, and his father Dr. Farnsworth, will call upon you to obtain a pass to visit Capt Charles Farnsworth of the 1ˢᵗ Battalion Connecticut Cavalry, who has been recently wounded in an engagement near Moorefield Va. Dr. Farnsworth is the father & Mr. B. Farnsworth the brother of Capt Farnsworth. Any courtesies you may extend to them will be appreciated by Gov. Buckingham whom I represent in this note.*

                    *Respectfully yours*
                    *J. H. Alury*
                    *Asst., Maj. Genl. House*

                  *Head Quarters, Cumberland District*
                    *Mountain Department*
                    *Cumberland, April 12, 1862*

    *Permit Doct Farnsworth & Mr. Farnsworth, loyal citizens of the United States, to pass on the Baltimore & Ohio Railroad, & through the lines of the Army to Moorefield & back.*

                  *Rob. H. Schenck*
                  *Brig Genl*
                  *Comdg*

---

**Comment:** Charlie's father and brother probably traveled by train from Baltimore to Winchester, Virginia, and then by horse to Moorefield.

---

                  *Sunday, April 16, 1862*

*Dear Mother*

    *I am sitting up today and feel quite strong, although my lung troubles me some. I write because I fear no one else will. Father is busy and Billings has gone off on a 60 mile scout. Left last night. Most of the officers and 150 men will be home tomorrow so he cannot write. Father hopes to start for home with me Thursday.*

    *Bear in mind the ball entered the left side, injuring the <u>ribs & lung</u>. When conversing about it the <u>lung</u> is the <u>strong point</u> upon which to make <u>the talk</u>.*

*There is some excitement here today expecting an attack — but still we feel no danger.*

*Much love from*

> *AfftSon*
> *Charlie*

"*From Charles, April 16th 62, at Moorefield, after he was wounded.*" (Note by his mother on the reverse side.)

---

**Comment:** His brother Billings, a civilian, arranged to go scouting with Charlie's Company B while Charlie was recuperating. Note that Charlie felt obliged to justify his inaction to those back home.

---

> *Head Quarters Mountain Department*
> *Wheeling April 19th 1862*

*Special Order )*
*No. 30 )*

> *Leave of Absence for sixty days for the benefit of his health is granted to* <u>*Capt.*</u> <u>*Charles Farnsworth,*</u> *1st Batt. Conn Cavalry*

> *By command of Maj. Genl. Fremont*
> *H. Thrall*
> *Asst. Adjt. General*

*This leave of absence was granted to Capt. Farnsworth to recover from wounds received near Moorefield, Va. He reported for duty the 8th day of June 1862 at Port Republic near Harrisonburgh, Va.* (Unsigned note attached to the order.)

> *1st Cav. Conn./Company Muster Roll*

*Charles Farnsworth, Captain, Co. B, Batt'n 1 Conn. Cavalry, for March & April 1862. Absent. Wounded April 3rd /62 by Guerrillas, through left arm & side, 7 miles from Moorefield on Winchester Road. Home on furlough April 17th/62.*

> *S. Thompson*
> *Copyist*

*May 19ᵗʰ 1862*
*Capt. Thrall*

Sir,

I have the honor to report that upon the 19ᵗʰ of April/62 I received Leave of Absence for sixty days, on account of injuries received near Moorefield, Va. Being sufficiently recovered and very desirous to be with my company in the field, I shall leave here by the 26ᵗʰ instant and therefore am unable to designate my post office for the next thirty days in accordance with paragraph 17b Army Regs.

I am Respt,
Chas. Farnsworth
Capt., Co. B., 1ˢᵗ Batt., Conn. Cav. Vols.

State of Connecticut
Office of the Commander in Chief
New Haven, May 26ᵗʰ 1862

Maj. J. M. Lyon
1ˢᵗ Battalion C. C.

Dear Major

I occasionally hear of the action taken of your Battalion and believe you have had your share of danger & labors for the past few weeks. I am gratified that your command is in a healthy field and that I hear so good an account of the men. Capt. Farnsworth is better and leaves today. I find it a slow operation to get notice from the War Department of resignation. I know that Lieut. Colborn has resigned the duties of Quartermaster. This is a very important position and I trust you will fill it by a properly reliable & competent man. See that he is right for the place in every respect. So with all nominées.

Yours very truly
Wm. A. Buckingham

Baltimore, Saturday May 31, 1862

Dear Mother

I reached this point 5 ½ AM, having enjoyed a fine night's rest. By some mistake in New York baggage was sent on to Washington but is expected here 5 PM. Shall go on to Harpers Ferry tonight. Rumor in town that Jackson has been surrounded & surrendered. A dispatch sent to railroads here for 200 cars to bring prisoners on, 5,000 of them. The city all excitement and threats of killing the whole batch of them when they arrive, freely expressed. Maj Gen Dix can give *no information of Fremont but thinks he is somewhere near Winchester and does not think I shall strike him at New Creek. A regiment of 1800 men raised here in 3 days to avenge the Maryland 1ˢᵗ. I shall therefore go to Harpers Ferry, and then as I hear of my command. Dressed wounds today. They are <u>scabbed</u> over and as dry as bone—feel fine and well.*

*Much Love*
*Charles*

*<u>Lines to Billings</u>: Cannot find Meredith's name in directory and do not know address, so shall not see. Much love to Julia.*

"From Charles at Baltimore on his way to join Fremont and his company, May 31ˢᵗ, 62. Left home Monday May 26ᵗʰ. Letter recd. June 2ⁿᵈ, 62." (Note by his mother on the reverse side.)

*Frederick, Md.*
*Sunday, June 1, 1862*

*Dear Father*

*We arrived at this place last evening amid a very severe rain storm but the day is splendid. Town full of officers and soldiers, some with Banks, others going to join him. He is at Williamsport. General Fremont's advance entered Woodstock a day or so since their getting rear of rebels. I am undecided what to do. May go to Harpers Ferry as there is some fighting every day. Shall at least remain hereabouts until communication is opened with Fremont as it would be useless to try and reach him now. It will be done inside a week. From all accounts the retreat of Banks, though well conducted, was a complete rout, and some of it rivaled Bull Run. There are immense numbers of troops here and near Harpers Ferry and Williamsport, and inside of two weeks we will repossess the ground lost. But that will not save the many killed and the courage given to the rebels from driving us back. The loss of stores etc. was immense.*

*From all I can learn the valley south of Winchester is now in our possession and if Jackson has not got out he is giving up.*

*Much Love to all*
*Charlie*

---

**Comment:** General Nathaniel P. Banks, former Massachusetts congressman and speaker of the House of Representatives, had been appointed commander of the Department of the Shenandoah. Banks's retreat to Winchester was tactically unsuccessful, as the Confederates captured two thousand prisoners, nine thousand rifles, and many wagons of supplies. They then retired with their spoils back up the valley on June 16. [400]

---

Winchester, Va.
June 6, 1862

*Dear Father —*

*I arrived here on the 4th and am detained here, having become separated from Denny and my baggage, although I hear from some contraband that he is in town. But amongst the multitude of 16,000 soldiers I have failed to find him. I left Harpers Ferry in a rain storm and rode to this place and was completely wet through. Slept out first night in a rain storm, but feel well & natural. Cousin Harry M. & Mary & children are here and well. Were here on the retreat and placed under arrest by the Confederates. I had an interview with Banks yesterday and find getting to my command very difficult. Still as soon as I find Denny shall push on on horseback and have him come on after.*

*The story about bad treatment of our wounded here was a lie in toto. I went myself to the hospital and conversed with Dr. Hayes from Maine. He was taken prisoner and paroled. He says he and the wounded could not be treated better than they were. The newspaper correspondents tell more lies than truth. There was but one man butchered, and his throat was cut by a drunken infantry soldier. The CSA army was the hardest looking and according to accounts poor and raw. Mary gives a glorious account.*

> *In Haste*
> *Much Love*
> *Charlie*

*You cannot write me until settled for there are no mails any where here about.*

---

**Comment:** Charlie probably traveled by train from Baltimore to Winchester, and then rode by horseback. The cousins are Mary and Harry Meredith who kept homes in Winchester and Baltimore—southerners who were sympathetic to the North.

*Sunday, June 7, 1862*
*Woodstock, Va.*

*Dear Father*

*Arrived here from Winchester. Fremont is in Harrisonburgh. So through tomorrow PO address is the same as before, Winchester. Mail passed here today from New England, 4 boxes. Much love [to] Julia & Henry.*

*AfftSon*
*Charles*

---

**Comment:** General John C. Fremont had been appointed commander of the newly-formed Department of West Virginia in March. In May, Charlie's Company B was selected to serve as Fremont's body guard. Amos Henry is his first cousin, married to Julia Cushman.[401]

---

*Mount Jackson [Va.]*
*June 10 1862*

*My dear Mother*

*I went from Winchester Sunday and reached Harrisonburg Monday and went to a house for the night. When hearing of a fight at Port Republic and my horse having given out I took it a foot and went over to the place some 12 miles, and saw the result of war in the shape of some 150 of our men dead upon the field and over 500 rebels, and the number of wounded I have no knowledge. I saw one division in our place. The day after the fight Fremont fell back to this place. Everyone is very much dissatisfied with his management. He appears afraid to fight all the time, and such an army you never saw. Nothing but an armed mob, and he pays no attention to them at all. His men are all over the country, straggling everywhere, plundering the people, shooting stock of all kinds for the fun of it, and fighting never. And when you have such an army you will never have anything done. Fremont's march has been the "marching up the hill and down again." He has accomplished nothing at all. Jackson went out of the valley his own way. Fremont lay only one day's march from Strasburg when that day would have cut Jackson off entirely. And he knew it. At Harrisonburgh he lay over a day to give Jackson a chance to get across the river, when advance would have brought on a fight. But it were best as it was, for his mob would have been whipped to death had they had to fight. Jackson could at any time have turned and driven our army out of the valley. But Schenck and Milroy are the*

147

men and have the best troops in the army, not a mere mob. But the balance, oh help us. I tell you Schenck is a tiger in a fight. Write me directly.

Much Love
Charles

Conn Cav Vol
Schenck Brigade
Fremont's Dept.
Winchester

---

**Comment:** Charlie reported back to his unit nearly two weeks before his medical leave expired. Port Republic was as far south and up the Shenandoah Valley as Charlie and his unit advanced. His estimates of the dead at the battle there were accurate. His criticism of Fremont's failure to attack Jackson near the southern end of the Valley was perceptive. Stonewall Jackson's strategy to divert Union forces away from Richmond and then to withdraw safely from the Valley had worked.

General Robert C. Schenck commanded the brigade to which the First Connecticut Cavalry was assigned. General Robert H. Milroy was a counter-guerrilla specialist in General Irvin McDowell's nearby division.[402]

---

Camp near Mount Jackson [Va.]
June 13, 1862

My dear Mother —

We are camped here with great prospects of staying here for a week or more at least and reorganize our army which it very much needs. I am afraid the Gen. has not got the right man in the right place here. But I hope not. He does not seem to have but little military capacity and no order at all. His staff, some twenty or more, are all Dutch, French, and Italian, some of whom cannot speak one word of English — a contemptible lot. All of the officers are very much disheartened at the turn of affairs. Had Schenck had command, Old Stonewall would have suffered severely. As it was he saved us at Port Republic, by going contrary to orders. Otherwise we would have been clean back to Winchester. Schenck is a tip top general. The first trouble with Fremont is want of knowledge of this affair. (He may be brave enough personally perhaps but he was afraid to fight on this advance, that is sure.) Every department is topsy-turvy and no head or tail to it. Our men are all well and have had hard work to do. We are promised a new outfit — horses, arms, etc. — but cannot tell if we will get it, as promises are like water around here.

The battalion are not brigaded as the General says he cannot spare our service; in the fact we are the best he has got. We have a very high standing here, and well *the boys deserve it, save Capt. B who is tied up as a baggage guard to Gen. Schenck, a miserable, lazy life I tell you. I send you my leave of absence, as it may do as a memento in years to come.*

*AfftSon*
*Charlie*

---

**Comment:** In the second sentence Charlie suggested that General Fremont, who was in over-all command of the Shenandoah campaign, had appointed the wrong man, namely General Nathaniel Banks, to lead the fight against General Jackson. Elements of the First Connecticut had been taken from General Schenck and temporarily put under Banks's command, but Charlie's Company B was still Fremont's bodyguard. The Port Republic battle actually occurred at the tiny village of Cross Keys, on June 8. "Capt. B." is Erastus Blakeslee, who later authored an official history of the First Connecticut Cavalry Volunteers.

---

*Camp near Strasburgh*
*June 22<sup>nd</sup> 1862*

*My dear Mother*

    *Up to this time I am in receipt of but one letter from any point, that is a letter from Billings sent to Washington, although mail matter to the 12<sup>th</sup> has been received in camp. Since my last we have fallen back, in plain words retreated to this point and I think will go still nearer the Potomac. There is no fight in our General I am afraid. At any rate, he don't show it. The battle of "Cross Keys" under Schenck would have been a very different story. He is in my opinion as much smarter than our Maj Gen. as can be. What a bully fight we would have had if he had bossed the job. Jackson would not have got away. General Fremont has issued an order to shoot anyone engaged in pillaging or robbery [illegible] and it is understood two have been executed in accordance with it. One thing is certain, the troops are improving very much in manners.*

    *What is the plan of the war I cannot guess. But the end looks very far off to us. How the money goes — here we have Brig Gen and staff for 30,000 and all we can see is 8,000. But the U.S. is rich and politicians must be paid. I tell you corruption is rampant.*

    *I was sent out the other night to arrest a man named Noel. He lived some 10 miles from camp. I had 20 men. As we came upon the bank of a creek near the house, I was challenged by what proved to be rebel pickets. I halted my men, asked who they were, received no answer, asked again and fired upon them. They returned it. Then I ordered my men to charge and we drove them in. Took two horses and rushed for*

149

*the house, surrounded it, and got my man. Gen Schenck & Fremont complimented me very highly for taking my man from inside their lines. I replied, you told me to bring Noel in if at his house, and pickets or no pickets, I must obey orders.*

*The other night he sent me to patrol a road some four or five miles. I went 18 and brought in some valuable information. Says Schenck, "Farnsworth, you're a trump."*

*Much Love from*
*AfftSon*
*Charlie*

---

**Comment:** "Our General" (line 4) probably refers to General Fremont. The battle at Cross Keys is the same as the Port Republic battle that Charlie described in his June 13 letter. Both letters were written after the Confederate forces had escaped south and federal forces had withdrawn north, back down the valley.

Charlie's report of two executions for "pillaging or robbery" might be correct; it is estimated that five hundred executions occurred during the Civil War, the majority probably carried out by the South.[403] However, there are no recorded disciplinary executions by the Union army in the Shenandoah Valley during 1862.

A "trump" is a "dependable and exemplary individual," according to Webster's *Third International Dictionary.*

---

*Mountain Department*
*Head-Quarters, Schenck's Division*
*In camp at Strasburg, Va. June 22ⁿᵈ 1862*

*Special Order No. )*

*Major Lyon, comdg. 1ˢᵗ Batt Conn Cavalry, will detail from his command Capt. Farnsworth of Co. B with twenty five picked men to proceed forthwith to Moorfield, to examine the road between Strasburg and that point, seeing that it is clear of guerilla bands and gathering up any officers or soldiers that may be on that road. Capt. Farnsworth will be accompanied on the expedition by Corporal J. W. Crissey of Co. D, who will return with the party, together with any other members of the Battalion who may be found at Moorfield or on the road.*

*Sergeants J. P. Jones & A. S. Wormley of the 55ᵗʰ Ohio Vol. Infantry will also accompany the party to Moorfield. On arriving at Moorfield, Sergeants Jones & Wormley will be detached to take measures by prepping wagons or otherwise to transfer from Moorfield to New Creek all the Quarter Master's & company stores or other public property that may be at Moorfield, together with all the sick, to be accompanied by such soldiers of the 1ˢᵗ (Schenck) Division as may be at Moorfield.*

*Capt. Farnsworth himself with his command will return to rejoin his Battalion with all reasonable dispatch, by the way of Romney & Winchester or by such other route as he may find most expedient & report to these Head Quarters.*

> *By Command of Brig Genl. Schenck*
> *Comdy. 1ˢᵗ Division*
> *W.W. Este*
> *Lt. & Aide de Camp*

---

**Comment:** Charlie's Company B was no longer serving as General Fremont's bodyguard, it appears. Note that his return route to Strasbourg from Moorefield would have taken him over the spot where he was shot during the April ambush.

---

*Strasburgh June 22 / 62*

*Dear Fred,*

*I am up to date without a line from any one of my correspondents, save one from Billings. What's up? [illegible] avoided me. I begin to fear that there is something wrong.*

*We are doing but little fighting, and lots of retreating, just about now. I tell you there was never a bigger fizzle than John Charles F. He can't fight or won't.*

*Please write me if any thing is wrong and what is the general [illegible] and how the old things work out. Don't run back on me at any time. Post me often. We are moving all the time, and it is hard work to write long letters.*

> *Very Affectionate Brother*
> *Charlie*

---

**Comment:** This apparently was written before Charlie received General Schenck's order to lead another scouting party. "John Charles F." is General Fremont, commanding general of the Department of West Virginia, whom Charlie continues to denigrate.

---

*Camp near Middleton*
*July 1, 1862*

*My dear Father,*

*A week ago last Sunday, the 22ⁿᵈ, I was ordered out as per enclosed. I returned yesterday to camp. During the trip, I was fired upon by and had one horse killed & four wounded. No men hurt. I burned every house within four miles and so reported. At Middleton, saw friend Whiting. I left M[iddleton] Thursday, and Friday a rebel force took possession and took all the force prisoner. On the trip I took one prisoner & a wagon. Viz., seeing a wagon track that turned off the road in a very suspicious place I went into the woods and found the wagon, the horses partly unfastened from the wagon, they having cut and run. I captured the wagon loaded with plunder, three horses, and one man. I delivered this man to the provost marshal at Winchester. I write merely to inform why I have delayed writing.*

*Recd. when I reached camp two letters from you, two from Billings, one Fred, one cousin Julia, & 3 from Georgia and four [illegible] — 13 in all. [Illegible.]*

> *Much Love to All*
> *AfftS*
> *Charlie*

---

**Comment:** By burning houses for four miles around, Charlie may have acted illegally in seeking revenge on the bushwhackers who shot him in the April ambush. General Banks's June 14 order and the general law of war prohibited such indiscriminate attacks. Although Charlie dutifully reported his actions, it does not appear that he was disciplined for his questionable tactics.

"Georgia" Ann Parker was a young lady from Meriden, Connecticut, to whom Charlie became engaged to be married in early 1862. The daughter of a successful silversmith and hardware manufacturer, she was twenty-four at the time.

The "enclosed" was probably the above June 22 order.

---

> *Camp near Middleton*
> *July 2nd 1862*

*My dear Mother*

*I write you a hasty letter to inform you of my whereabouts which have been all around the country. By looking at the map you will see my late trip. Leaving Strasburgh for Moorefield I traveled over the same road upon which I was wounded and passed the very spot. We had a rough trip of it but plenty of excitement. I went over the same road Father came to Moorefield on to Romney and from thence to Winchester, over North river. Denny is all right, as I think you have been written, baggage all safe, except that box of Houghs which I was obliged to abandon.*

*My company, which has been very much scattered, is now nearly all here. But there are some 15 in the hospital. I have lost one a prisoner and one wounded since my return. But as yet not one of the battalion has been killed and only two badly wounded. Voltz is still in the hospital and will never join us, I think, as he is very lame I understand. We are very busy making our musketballs, and Lt. Atwater and myself are at it night and day. Lt. C is no help in that way but he is much improved and is reported as valiant in fight.*

*Suppose that Georgia is with you and trust that a nearer acquaintance will not be unfavorable. I send today letter to her at Norwich.*

*Received a letter from Julia lately. Tell her I will write as soon as I have time. But we expect march orders anytime. General Fremont & <u>eighty-two staff</u>, more than [General] McClellan had in his pannicky day, left here a few days since. Either he is a very unfortunate man or he is ignorant of his business. I hope the former, but the condition of his large army is anything but favorable to his choice in military management. The same farce was tried here that was got up West, to create excitement. But his 82ⁿᵈ staff could not make it go. Everyone felt relieved when they found he was going. And all hoped Schenck would have a Maj Gen command, but Siegel is our boy now.*

*We have rumor of a great battle at Richmond, thousands killed and Gen McClellan amongst them. If so we are gone up sure.*

*Love to all*

*Afft Charlie*

---

**Comment:** Charlie's mention of passing "the spot" on the road between Strasburg and Moorefield where he was shot confirms the April Muster Roll entry describing the location of the ambush.

His note that fifteen soldiers were in the hospital, but only two were there for wounds illustrates the generally accepted view that disease was a bigger threat during the Civil War than battle wounds.

Herman Voltz was the Company B bugler who was wounded with Charlie in the April ambush; shot in the leg, he had not yet improved as much as Charlie had. Voltz eventually did recover, however, and was appointed regimental principal musician, serving until the end of the war.

"Atwater" was Charlie's friend Lt. Howell Atwater of New Haven, Conn. "Siegel" was Major General Franz Sigel, commander of the newly-formed First Army Corps, which included a division of "Dutch" (i.e., German-American) infantrymen. Sigel was born in Germany and had been educated there at a military academy. After emigrating to America, he became a professor at the German-American Institute in St. Louis. Charlie's cavalry battalion now was attached to Sigel's First Corps. Sigel was given this assignment after Fremont refused to serve under the over-all commander of the Army of Virginia, General John Pope.[404]

The rumor of a disastrous battle at Richmond proved false.

It is unknown what "Houghs" refers to.

---

*July 4ᵗʰ 1862*

*Dear Fred*

*Your letter of 29ᵗʰ 1862 was received today. 'Tis true that nearly a month has elapsed since I regained my company, and more than one since I left home, & I too had hardly thought of it. Your remarks in regard to our maternal are full of truth & always known, but still even with the heart swelling with love, there is a something — it is not the want of love. I have received your former letter, and have acknowledged all from home to date, except one from Billings. I generally burn or destroy my letters on receipt and thus forgot. We are all very well indeed and expect to move soon up the valley. I should not be surprised to be in Staunton inside two weeks.*

*March & Strong go home today to recruit for the battalion.*

*Denny is well and how such a report in regard to his running off came out I cannot understand. He is all sound.*

*Herting would not sell my horse for $200. He is a fine animal, though poor in flesh. George Musar of New London was over today from the 3ʳᵈ Conn., an old friend of mine. He is with Gen somebody's brigade.*

*I suppose the Misses are at Norwich at present and I hope will enjoy themselves. Billings is at home and can be if chooses very agreeable to them. And then Julia being there will help some. I wonder how B. Howser will fancy, and what will be the course. I expected she would write me, but has not. I think she is going mad and thus got over it. I wish she had some fine fellow for a husband.*

*Much love*
*Charles*

*Testing letter*

---

**Comment:** Fred is Charlie's younger brother.

Although Charlie had expected to be ordered back up the Shenandoah Valley toward Staunton, he was not.

The comment about a false rumor of Denny "running off" further demonstrates that he was a "contraband," a recently liberated southern slave who had been assigned duties with the Union army, in this case as an officer's servant. Since early in the war, the North had taken the position that if the South considered slaves to be property, then escaping slaves would be retained, just like other seized war matériel.

It is unknown what "testing letter" referred to.

---

*Sperryville, Rappahannock County, Va.*
*Friday July 11th 1862*

*My dear Father,*

*Once more upon the march, our destination, even from day to day unknown. But the map will point out general direction, and I suppose the capitol of the CSA via Gordonsville to be our ultimatum. But to all save our generals it is a mystery and really it is some work to find out under what general we belong. We, the poor Conn cavalry, especially. Since my return we have been under Gens. Schenck, Pratt, McClean, and now we have been divided and two companies are put in a cursed Dutch brigade. And I for one am coming home unless there is a change. The cause is said to exist in a desire to rid us of Lyon and it was supposed that hinting to him of taking away his command that he could resign. But he sticks. Gen Schenck has blowed him up and told him to go home but he won't, he has no pride. A country schoolmaster turned soldier on larger pay than he ever supposed possible for a man to earn is not easily shaken off.*

*But I cannot stand it and I won't. To be put into a pack of thieves a disgrace to our army is more than I'll stand. Before Fremont resigned they had a plan to rid themselves of him, by adding a squadron of cavalry and thus create a Lt Col position which was to go to Fish, thus putting one of his Capts over him a grade, and it was thought he would go home. But that was killed. Now they are on another track. I was told (in fact asked for data) by a person in high position that charges were being preferred against him. A general told me "he must go home—your cavalry is being ruined for want of a decent man at your head," and so it is. He is a decided coward, and no sense. I have written Gov Buckingham for a change of place—that is, to be transferred to one of the new regiments, of course for higher grade, a field officer. And if I cannot get it and no change is made here, I shall be home soon. Though I cannot hardly think of leaving if we are near Richmond and expecting a fight. I would stand anything before I'd resign then, but a change of some kind must take place.*

*But I will give you a memorandum of our march and our present position. Of troops I have no idea, every hill top is covered with camps hereabout, and they say there are three divisions marching this way by three different roads. One by way of Manassas Junction, one here, and up the Shenandoah Valley. It is reported today that Mulligan is here with Western troops, and that a large portion of Gen Rose's Western army is here. We move from here tomorrow for I know not where.*

*The morning of the seventh at 3 a.m. saw our camp deserted and the army en route for Front Royal, the 8th we made Milford, the 9th Luray Court House, the10th we made Sperryville and rested here today, and move again tomorrow.*

*For the life of me I do not know whether we are in Siegel's Corps de Arms or where, and I rather think we won't until we reach our destination. Since I commenced this letter there have [been] over 7,000 men passed by our tent and camped in the field opposite, and they say there are many more upon the road.*

> *AfftSon*
> *Charlie*

*Direct as heretofore*
*Gen Schenck Division*

---

**Comment:** Apparently unknown to Charlie, the Union plan to cross the Chickahominy River and assault Richmond had already foundered in the Seven Days' Battles of late June 1862. Thus, his troops would not be targeting Richmond as their "ultimatum." Instead, they made camp at Sperryville, Virginia until taking part in the Battle of Second Manassas in August. Charlie's complaint that the battalion was being split up and assigned to various commands, thus rendering it less effective in the traditional sense, is shared by some historians.[405]

---

> *Sperryville, Va.*
> *July 14th 1862*

*Dear Father,*

*Yesterday brought letters from Billings of date 2nd & 6th and one from Mother of the 7th and a number of papers from Billings, and some whose address was unknown to me. These are all the letters received as yet. There is a back mail unforwarded. In regard to direction, the papers know long before we do, so continue one address until you see a change announced or directed to make one, but address has been and for all I know is Winchester, Va.*

*Emma Billings has made a very poor choice in young Morgan, but so goes the world.*

*I see today Lilly L. becomes a wife, and I wish her joy and happiness.*

*Denny and baggage were received at Winchester.*

*We expect to move every hour for Richmond I suppose but there is a universal slowness in everything and three days are lost here. It is reported today that a force remain here. If so we may be numbered amongst it.*

*We drew today 10 days' rations and that will take us to Richmond.*

*Nothing new here. I have been out scouting and received a fire from some 15 bushwackers. No one hurt.*

*Maj [Lyon] wanted to take out a battery of artillery to shell them out, but*

*Windham's ideas did not seem feasible. They have disgraced him at headquarters but he hangs on. He is a poor fool.*

> *In Haste*
> *Much Love*
> *Charlie*

---

**Comment:** Major Lyon's idea of firing artillery at scattered bushwhackers was an example of his poor leadership and ignorance about tactics. "Windham" is Lyon, who came from Windham County, Connecticut.

---

*Sperryville Sunday July 20th 1862*

*My dear Father,*

*Since my last letter I have been out on a reconnaissance to Madison, Va. and had a very pleasant trip. Was gone two days but did not find any rebels to have a brush with. Uninterrupted we reached Madison and occupied the town and returned. The usual excitements of a scout were all the incidents although had Maj Lyon done it much would have been said by him in regard to military movements. He is the most forsaken man hereabouts. His command has been taken away from him and he put upon duty of a Sergeant, all to force his resignation. But he won't resign. Gen Schenck is talking of court-martialing him and I think they have a strong case if put through. Neatly speaking, it is about a horse. When in Conn he sold to the Government a horse for $125, since which time he has used the horse himself, commuted its rations in money & the Gov fed the horses. He also drew a saddle for one of the men and has used it himself, never having bought one for himself. He told Gen Schenck that he brought four horses from Conn, when he only brought one, and that one he sent home. He has drawn pay for four horses all the time and 2 servants, and commuted the rations furnished by Government, thus drawing $48.50 per month more than he is entitled to. Of late he has sent his servants home and now he takes care of his own horse, and actually eats with the teamsters. No officer will mess with him for he has never paid a board bill. And when out with men takes one of them to eat at a house with him & asks him to pay as he has no change. He is a disgrace to us all and Gen Schenck has told him so. He is a most consummate coward and some of his operations would disgrace a woman. He was reported at Franklin by a woman for improper actions with slaves, and amalgamation is no new thing to him, if reports from Windham are true. He may be sent home yet.*

*I heard a day since that it was proposed to raise one more Squadron of Cavalry in Conn and then consolidate with ours and make a Lt Col. The Maj said if that*

157

*was so he would be the Col of it. But we can't see it. I wish they would and make me Maj and call me home to tend to the formation of it. That would suit me. But never to be put under Lyon as Lt Col.*

*There are only two Capts who have done anything since we came out, Fish & myself. Middlebrook was never out but once and then failed entirely. And Lyon but once when a fire in the woods so scared him that he rushed to camp and left his advance guard out and reported them cut off. A few hours after, they came in, having gone to the place of destination, taken a prisoner, and awaited in vain for Lyon. Returned.*

*And if any one goes up but Fish or me I shall come home, you bet. I can get the best of recommendations from Seigle or Schenck for my dispatch in my line, and for energy and capability, which Lyon cannot.*

*If there is any such talk please write me. You could speak to Gov. Buckingham and report what I write (easily).*

*We have had no letters since my last to you and they say a week's mail has been captured by rebels.*

> *Afft your son*
> *Charlie*

---

**Comment:** Charlie's scouting patrol to Madison covered forty-four miles, round-trip. Franklin is about thirty-five miles south of Moorefield, the former campsite of the First Connecticut Cavalry. Charlie felt free to express his ambition to be promoted, even going so far as to ask his father, the governor's personal physician, to intercede on his behalf.

The officers had to pay for their "mess," that is, meals, even when they ate at a civilian's house in the occupied parts of Virginia.

---

*Sperryville Va. July 28th 1862*

*My dear Father,*

*Yesterday brought a huge mail and I <u>own</u> the following: Mother's July 19th, Fred's 15th, & Billings 12th, 13th, 15th, & 19th, four from Georgia, and lots of N.Y. papers. Also a letter from Gov. Buckingham in answer to one written to him from Middletown in regard to a position in one of the new regiments. Our major [Lyon] is as usual <u>nihil.</u> I wish you would when conversing with Gov. Buckingham (and you need not be reserve in speaking of Lyon <u>now</u> for his good will is an injury, although he is very friendly to me) say that it is not to better my position that I desire a change. For were I home I should enlist in the ranks as to be removed from an organization that is a stench in the nostrils of our General. He has no idea of the position we* occupy. General Schenck has told Lyon several times he was a nuisance and to go home, and The Battalion would come up. But the fool says he won't. He never had such pay and holds hard. He takes care of his own horse, eats with teamsters, or when he can get in a meal, and draws full pay. He has been complained of for gross conduct with slaves, and has never paid a board bill. He said a month ago that he wanted to go since about the 20th of July, and must. So he was taken sick, and applied for a leave of absence, and as no one would help it along he has been riding around in the sun trying to get it. But as yet no go.

The medical board, from instruction, advise a resignation, saying "one who was as sick as he was and looked so miserable" ought to go home for good. He is as fat as a hog, which in the eating line he is, in reality. He eats 8 qts.of bread & milk one day, besides regular meals. He is a coward of the deepest kind and when riding between two corps some three miles he took two guards and sent one some 30 yds. in advance and one in rear for fear of rebels. But there is no end to his acts, foolish and depraved. He has actually in a round about way kept a nigger wench whilst in camp. This is true, he is a real brute in his passion and yet he could arrest a man for jumping on his horse backwards. Can anyone blame a man who came here (not for pay) desirous of fighting and who has braved the foe wherever found & who has a reputation second to none hereabouts, who is looked upon favorably by his General, for feeling sick of such conduct and such a superior. I want to stay and could not honorably resign now in face of danger even if I would. (In fact, Gen. Siegle has refused to receive it if offered, for I spoke to him about it, as did four others of the Battalion.) And I cannot leave my company without regret, but I think sometimes it is a disgrace to be here. You must excuse the looks of this letter for I cannot write today. Gen. P[ope] has not yet mounted that horse but is expected daily, and I hope we shall soon move forward. There is a great deal in the paper about Gen Hatch's advance to Gordonsville. But I see nothing about a Captain who with a little squad of 50 men went over the same road a day before Gen Hatch got there with his 2,000 men. But the raid on B'dam was a good thing. But the talk about Gordonsville is all bosh. If to any one there is credit, it is to Conn Cavalry.

The Conn Company B passed our camp the other day, and we turned out all the men that were not holding horses for Dutch generals, and exhibited the State flag which brought cheer upon cheer. They said we hear much about you men but everyone says the Maj is a coward and a disgrace to Conn. His fame is wide spread.

Much love from
AfftSon
Charles

159

**Comment:** Charlie counted here four letters from his devoted fiancée Georgia Parker; their engagement would last through three war years.

Charlie's letter to Governor Buckingham, pleading for another battalion and a promotion for himself, shows how well-connected Charlie's family was in Connecticut.

"Gen. Hatch" is Brigadier General John P. Hatch, a division commander under General John Pope.

Charlie's vitriolic attacks on Major Lyon continued, matched now by bragging about his own record of "braving the foe wherever found." The "expected march" by General John Pope toward Richmond did not materialize for Charlie. "B'dam" probably refers to Beaver Dam Station, near Sperryville.

---

*Sperryville, Va. July 29<sup>th</sup> 1862*

*My dear Father*

*Today our camps are deserted, the army save one division having gone out for a field day, some six miles from here. The brigade to which I am attached went out but the Conn. Cav. was left behind. It is composed today of 1 Capt., 2 Lieuts., and 3 men with the Major at their head. The balance are running around as orderlies, dispatch bearers, and such like duty. The Maj had a severe attack last night to favor a leave of absence, but it would not work. Capt. Blakeslee is getting better fast and hopes soon to be out. He looks thin.*

*Yesterday most of the inhabitants hereabouts came in to take the oath or get a pass outside to go south. Whether this will affect anything or not I cannot say as they are generally willing to take the oath rather than move away. Yet if we go out of here and rebels enter the place they are either robbed or taken away unless they swear for the other side. I tell you they are between two fires and are in a measure to be pitied. Starvation will be upon them ere long and they must suffer.*

*Signs of an advance movement began to show themselves but whether from our division or Gen Banks is not apparent. Gordonsville appears to be the end of the present action and possession of that rail road, which could have been easily obtained some two weeks since, but now must be fought for. It is strange that we did not press forward and occupy the place when there were no defence at it, instead of sitting in camp until a force was assembled there.*

*But undoubtedly there was some point to be gained deeper than we little fellows know how to figure, and therefore we cannot judge. But such appears to me to have been the best plan.*

*The talk of Hatch's Cavalry having been to Gordonsville is false for they have not. They went to the rail road, but not to Gordonsville.*

*I suppose next month will see some movements toward Richmond and we will* come towards it from the northwest. But we must have more troops and if our ranks are not filled up immediately a draft should take place. I tell you the rebels have men plenty and everything they want, and the talk of their half fed and clothed army is all bosh. I have never seen a rebel prisoner that was not better clothed than our troops, and their heart is in the work, not for pay but for glory. They are not fighting for money but for glory of the thing. The hundreds of lies in the northern papers of the state of the rebels do more harm than good. The truth is all the towns hereabouts are deserted of the fighting portion — nothing but old men left — and not compelled so much as you think to go. They go willingly. The feeling of '76 is in this section. They are fighting for their independence, they sincerely think, and under the same privation as the old patriots did. Talk as the north will, it is so. But it is all caused by want of knowledge of the real cause. As they become informed upon it, their zeal decreases. But ignorance of the real cause makes better fighters. Here is no freedom of speech and no chance for discussion, and everything is one way.

Much love

AfftSon

Charles

The Major [Lyon] was caught day before yesterday in an attempt to violate the mail. Knowing that Capt. Fish and myself had been in correspondence with Gov. Buckingham, and the mail so long delayed having all come at once, he went to the PO and making some excuse, got inside and sorted out his own letters and tried to appropriate all letters having an Executive Department stamp upon it, but was prohibited.

A short time since, he opened a letter having such a stamp upon it and gave as an excuse that the officer was absent and it might be important, although it was addressed to an officer and on personal business. He is the most unprincipled man I ever saw. He stops at nothing to find out any point. He is jealous of Fish and myself and wanted to know if we got anything from Gov. Buckingham.

---

**Comment:** The "oath" was required by General John Pope; inhabitants who refused to pledge allegiance to the Union were expelled from the occupied territory, to be treated as spies if they returned. This program earned General Pope undying hatred in the South. [406] Charlie's observation that Confederate patriotism reminded him of "the feeling of '76" seems very insightful.

Major Lyon's desperate act of prying into the mail of his junior officers to evaluate his tenuous status seems exceedingly pitiful.

---

Sperryville, Va. Aug 3rd 1862

My dear Mother,

Letters from you of 27th and Billings of 25th at hand, and very acceptable to me. And the news they contained was interesting. The recruiting is carried on in a manner that will do us no good for months. Why not put them into the old regiments and fill them up, and have men fit for service, and under old officers. Now the government has to pay officers for 300 regiments, when the number of men is required in the old regiments, but no, the politicians must have positions, and Government pays the bills. Now mark the future, and see if these men amount to anything for a long time. They have to go through all that we have before they are of much account. But if new officers were to be appointed they should have come from the regiments in the field. But I suppose the State Powers Know best.

There is little new here, the regular routine of camp duty, and short scouts, which keep us moving to but little purpose. But every day hoping for an advance.

Major Lyon is in great tribulation. A letter from the Governor requested him to resign. He went to Gen. Schenck, who told him plainly that it would be for the good of the Battalion, but he won't do it. Charges have been made against him and there is a good chance of his being dismissed in disgrace. The charges are drawn up but he is not under arrest yet. We have some hope of new organization soon.

He seemed "taken aback" on receiving the letter and I do really believe he thought he was a splendid commander. Poor man.

I sent to you today a carbine taken from a _rebel_. It is a US arm, and I send it home for _future use_.

The sword I sent does not appear to have been received.

The day is awful hot and writing is a severe exertion. The sweat runs down a pen.

Much Love,
Charlie


Sperryville, Va.
August 5 1862

Dear Father,

The Major's [Lyon's] days are nearly numbered. Yesterday seventeen charges were preferred against him, for cowardice, fraud, tyrannical and ungentlemanly conduct, and today he verbally tendered his resignation to take effect on the 10th. He was requested to send it in writing, so I suppose he will thus avoid a trial and leave on the ground of sickness. He requested an officer to obtain for him some little testimonial of esteem as a cane or something else, but it does not take well.

He will leave us unnoticed, and uncared, but in Conn. will no doubt talk large of his military career.

His successor will no doubt be Capt. Fish, who is worthy of it, and I judge that it is almost a foregone conclusion at headquarters. It lays between him and [Captain] Middlebrook, and I trust M. will not get it. I think with Fish the Battalion would come up and am sure would be noticed more than heretofore.

There has been lots of fun in connection with the Major leaving. The first thing that seemed to open his eyes was a petition gotten up, requesting to be returned to Conn. and mustered out, pledging themselves to reenlist in the new regiment, but at the same time stating "That if the Battalion could be reorganized under a new commander that they would desire to remain where they were." He got hold of it and his eyes were opened. He called officers one after another to his tent, of whom he asked if they thought his resignation was desired by the majority of the Battalion. Some crawfished, but most answered the question promptly, yes. Upon the heels of which came a letter from Governor Buckingham. At first he was disposed to stand out. But the prospect of arrest brought him to terms.

We are having awfully hot weather but luckily little to do. Marching would be terrible under today's sun. Yesterday we were ordered to march this a.m. but it was countermanded last eve. [Gen.] Pope is some six miles from here and according to reports living in tents, and not on that horse. I hope that there is a little cider at the bottom of his foaming orders, but we don't see it hereabouts. There is not the same strictness in regard to rebel property as before order #5, but still there seem to be loose screws. For the past three days the soldiers have been bringing in negroes by the score who I suppose are to be set to work upon what has heretofore been soldier duty, driving teams and train wagons. This will return to the ranks a large number of soldiers.

As I said before, I hope Fish will get promoted to Major. For myself, I don't want it, at present, and there may be as good a thing ahead. So you will do well to mention my feelings in regard to Fish.

Fred's letter and one from Billings Aug 2, received.

Much Love

Charlie

---

**Comment:** Facing court-martial charges that included cowardice and embezzlement, Major Judson Lyon, commander of the First Connecticut Cavalry, resigned and was dismissed from service, effective August 15, by Special Order #44. Charlie's friend William S. Fish was then promoted to major and given command of the battalion. Major Fish would himself later be court-martialed for fraud and corruption in Baltimore. Convicted, he was dismissed from the army in August 1864, although he was later pardoned and cashiered by President Lincoln. In 1865 his conviction was reversed, and he was restored to rank by President Andrew Johnson.

"Middlebrook" was Lieutenant Louis N. Middlebrook, of Bridgeport.

To "crawfish" meant to back out of a commitment.

Order #5, issued by General Pope, allowed Union troops to seize crops and livestock for subsistence in the Shenandoah Valley. After some soldiers abused the privilege by flagrant pillaging, Pope rescinded the authority with Order #19.

---

*Sperryville, [Va.] Aug 6ᵗʰ 1862*

*My dear Fred,*

*Your letter and paper duly received. I am very glad you are released from study during the hot weather, and hope you will enjoy yourself, and feel refreshed by the recreation of the summer.*

*I am without letters from Georgia since 24ᵗʰ and feel as if it was a long time to be without a word, when mail is all regular. I hardly suppose it would be in the nature of things for a certain person to refer to you of "how beloved." But watch well every action, and see the effect of certain remarks. You have a chance to learn much because you know circumstances. Now see that warm feelings are not always, even when slighted, followed by any deep dejection. I suppose Mrs. Gen & her two young females spend the summer at Saratoga and elsewhere. I should dearly love to be able to follow around. It would be fun to go incognito and from the past. What fun we could get up. I think that I could pass myself off for a middle-aged man. But I am a soldier now.*

*Today there has been a large number of troops pass through this place, and a large train of artillery. I did not learn whether it was Banks' entire Division or not. It went towards Culpepper. I suppose ere long we will skin on a peg or so towards the apex of northern aspiration, Richmond , only to find a deserted pestilential city.*

*We don't know what fight is in our army. With them it means energy, rapid movements, every nerve strained to its utmost; with us a masterly inactivity. I fear Pope has more blow than blows. Today shelter tents have been issued to all of our drivers and the heavy ones taken to Washington. This looks like moving a little.*

*I suppose when we start there will be but little rest for us horsemen.*

*Major Lyon is gone up, and I suppose Capt. Fish will be commissioned Major. At least I hope so, and then we will come together as a Battalion. But the promotion will make me squadron commander. 2ⁿᵈ Squadron. And there is more fun for me in a company than commanding the Battalion, which I think no very envious job. Major Lyon is a crushed man. We tried every way peaceable and he would not let go, so we* *gave him a very severe hint. After the charges were handed in, Gen Schenck sent for him, and said "Major, there is a letter malfeasance for your perusal. I will accept your written resignation any time before sunset." That was to save him arrest & trial which would have ended in his disgrace. As it is, he resigns and is not tried. Before the time was up, Major Lyon had got a surgeon's certificate from Jarvis, who supposed he was helping him out, from the Brigade Surgeon stating that he was unfit for service and resigned on these grounds. But the papers I sent home contain the facts, charges, etc. One coward less in the <u>Grand Army</u>.*

*I am now all right on horses, having captured three. One splendid saddle horse can walk 6 miles, also pace 7, & trot 10 miles per hour. He is splendid & shall send home first chance. He is not handsome, but a splendid saddle horse. Then I have an old fellow made of iron who goes all the time and cares but little. And one for Denny.*

*No pay yet and without spending any thing in the way of horses (considerable) I am entire cat (I save my gold). But still pay day will bring more still.*

> *Much love from*
> *Charlie*

---

**Comment:** Even at this point, Charlie was convinced that he would be part of a great assault upon Richmond. But General Stonewall Jackson's march northwestward along the Rappahannock River, which went undetected by Pope's cavalry, forced the Union forces to turn east to defend Washington.[407]

Charlie felt free to send home a horse captured in battle, just as he had previously sent a captured carbine and sword.

"Mrs. Gen." was most likely the wife of General William Williams of Norwich, Charlie's uncle on his mother's side. The "two young females" probably included Harriet Peck Lester, who was boarding at the Williamses' home, and whom Charlie would eventually marry.

The term "entire cat" probably meant "undiminished." The meaning of "skin a peg" is unknown.

---

> *Head-Quarters First Division Army of Virginia*
> *Sperryville, Va. Aug 8th 1862*

*My dear Father,*

*Today's mail brought letters from Billings and papers from Fred. I saw notice of Brad's death in NY paper. Also saw notice BPL being wounded. Hope nothing serious, and suppose that according to new order of things he will find it hard to get to Norwich, but I trust he will if seriously wounded, for hospitals are miserable places. Gen. Seigle sent for me yesterday and wished to know if I thought another battalion* could be raised in Conn., for he is in for us and wants four more companies. I replied that if Gov. Buckingham was requested to do so I thought it could be done. From what he said I think he or Schenck will write in regard to it. If done, it is proposed to send me home to command which I should hate to do now as we are near a fight. I think we fight within ten days at least. But still if concluded upon, I should go. Seigle of course desires them attached to his corps or he would not mention the raising of it. I trust it will be done. It would make Fish Lt Col and me senior Major. And then our plan is to run in 2 companies more and thus get a <u>Col.</u>

When we move it is through Madison and Gen Schenck told me last night that our wing would do the fighting and, from his manner, it will be big. He is everywhere, up at all hours of the night and riding around the county for 20 miles. I have been outside our lines toward Madison, our outpost, twice on duty and met him at 12 pm going out to look. He is game, and we will make a good fight.

AfftSon

Charles

---

**Comment:** Charlie's plan to raise a second battalion, and thus to secure a promotion for himself, came to naught in 1862. When a second battalion finally was added in 1863, it came too late for Charlie, who was then imprisoned in Richmond.

The planned "move through Madison" toward Richmond would presumably have been along what is now Virginia Highway 231. But the march never occurred.

---

Head-Quarters First Division Army of Virginia

Crooked River Church Aug 14th 1862

Dear Father,

We are encamped here for the night and perhaps two days as we have pitched tents and are living as though no enemy was near. Yesterday they were driven from here and today I guess no one knows their whereabouts unless it is Gordonsville. The late battle was awful. I was on the field on the 12th and know what I say. Pope sent to the NY papers his dispatch, 300 killed and wounded when he knew our loss was nearly 3,000. How about that 10,000 Corinth story, we all say now. The battle was a want of generalship on his part. Banks was all right. Pope sent him forward & did not support him at all. The battle field was an awful sight; their loss was very heavy, perhaps as much as ours, but we cannot tell. I acknowledge the following letters: yours July 25, Aug 3; Billings Aug 2, 5, 9.

Much Love,

Charlie

**Comment:** Crooked River Church is located at the site of the Battle of Cedar Mountain. Charlie was using the church as a temporary encampment. His estimate of losses was fairly accurate: Union dead, wounded, and captured totaled about 2,381; equivalent Confederate losses were about 1,276. General Banks's attack actually achieved a temporary success against Stonewall Jackson's larger force before being repulsed in the Battle of Cedar Mountain. Jackson withdrew to Gordonsville on August 12.[408]

*Head-Quarters of First Division Army of Virginia*
*August 14ᵗʰ 1862*

*I would be very glad if I could give you a detailed report of the march, but I am very tired and will defer until a future time. I have got a splendid horse that I wish you had. I captured it at Madison. It is a fine sorrel, star-faced—a fine pacer and a splendid horse but too high-spirited for war. I will try and get him home if possible. And at any rate will try and keep him carefully, till I get home.*

*I wish Billings would use less paste on papers. Not a paper comes that is not so stuck up that I tear it all to pieces opening it. He seems to think them very [illegible, but perhaps "fragile"] the way he sticks them together.*

*Afft, Charlie*

*Mother's letter of Aug 8 just came in.*

**Comment:** Although lacking an addressee, this letter was apparently written to Charlie's Father. Once again, Charlie felt free to appropriate a captured horse for his family's use.

*Camp Crooked River, Va.*
*Aug 15ᵗʰ 1862*

*My dear Father,*

*Today in conversation with Gen Schenck I mentioned the fact that I thought if to the regiment of infantry & battery for Gen Seigle to be raised in Conn a Battalion of Cavalry was added, Gov Buckingham would be glad to raise it. He said that unless something was done, we, being so small a body, would lose our identity and only the greatest efforts on his part had kept us as much together. He said also he wanted another Battalion added to this, etc.*

*Today Gen Seigle informed Capt. Fish that he would write to Gov Buckingham in relation to it. A crack battalion could be raised this fall in Conn., and for the benefit of this I wish one could be added. We are so small that we are not noticed.*

But eight companies would bring a Lt Col & two Majors which would send us ahead almost as large as a regiment.

> Much Love
> Charles

Should a Captain be taken from this Battalion to command a new one there are many things his experience would suggest and he ought to be on hand to organize it completely.

I think that it would be no more than right to take from each of these four companies an enlisted man or a good Lieut. and make him Captain of a new company, and if possible, one of the Lieuts. also. This would give the Battalion a great start at first and there would be no trouble in filling up companies with only one officer to be elected. Gov Buckingham commands two thirds of this.

The organization of the men should be done by a Capt. from this who should be on the ground from the first. If I could get the appointment I could make a crack Battalion of it, you know, but I would want to suggest some names for officers for this of men I know to be true and of service. No shirks who wear good clothes, but men who fight, and work in camp.

> Charles

---

**Comment:** Charlie continued his plans to enlarge the battalion to a regiment. This appears to be an addendum to the August 15 letter to his father.

---

> Camp near Crooked River
> August 15th 1862

My dear Mother,

Just as I was hurrying off a letter home last evening your letter of August 8th came in. You will see our location on the map left at home. Directly west of Mitchell's Station is Crooked River. Of course it is not laid down right. But we are camped about where the two (oo)s in Crooked are laid down. The river runs more east and west than shown upon the map. Gen Milroy crossed Crooked and Robertson rivers yesterday evening but was ordered back. Gen Siegle is out all the time and in my mind is as much ahead of Pope for commander as Pope is ahead of any of us common fellows. I am afraid he is all gas. He certainly lost us the battle of Slaughter (or Cedar Mount.) which might have resulted in a great victory to us. But still it resulted in showing the rebels that we could fight. It is common report amongst the soldiers that the officers of our regiment Conn. 5th were under liquor.

*How true it is I do not know. At any rate, the 5$^{th}$ was cut up. There was only 450 reported yesterday. They lost the US flag but saved the State flag. Major Lyon is still here, a mere hanger-on and a nuisance. If he had a particle of brains he would remain behind and not try officering.*

*To keep him from the Battalion Gen Schenck has given him 4 men and calls him Provost Marshall of Irwin. He sleeps all day and eats every thing within reach. The amount of business he does amounts to nothing. But still Gen Schenck says he is a Conn Major and therefore he can not kick him out and takes this method of disposing of him. As soon as his resignation is received, which may be two weeks — amongst the press of business at headquarters owing to the present state of affairs it is delayed — he will no doubt take leave of his command, which will be not very affecting. He asked the officers to procure a testimonial of esteem to present him with — any small article, but we could not see it. It was suggested that a copy of the charges preferred be sent to him bound in calf.*

*We expect to move tomorrow. Scouts report the rebels strongly situated across the Rapidan, and if so a river fight is in store for us. But I think that we can do it up for them brown. But what a loss of men is in the future.*

> *Afft Son*
> *Charles*

---

**Comment:** To "brown" meant to shoot indiscriminately.

Modern historians corroborate Charlie's view that General Pope was to blame for the loss at Cedar Mountain by failing to reinforce General Banks's attack. [409]

---

*Head-Quarters First Division Army of Virginia*
*Saturday Aug 16$^{th}$ 1862*

*My dear Father,*

*Gen Siegle as I wrote yesterday said he should write Gov Buckingham in relation to raising another Battalion to add to the one already in the field. Now one reason it should be done is the fact that we are cut up very much because our organization is so small that we have lost our organization completely. A great deal of it is no doubt owing to Maj Lyon being so unpopular and inefficient, but still we are but little better than a large company under a captain. Now, could we add another Battalion to it and thereby gain a Lt Col command, two majors, the eight companies being then full would approximate towards a regiment and therefor a full organization would be maintained. Now we are always attached to some other cavalry, and thus lose our identity.*

*For the officer in charge always makes mention of the acts accomplished as being of the cavalry under his command and that ignores any attached commands. I hope the attempt will succeed and we shall yet have a cavalry formation worthy of a state with 18 regiments of infantry in the field and six in the state subject to call. If Gov Buckingham desires to add to us and thus render our organization larger and more efficient he can do it. For if Siegle writes him as I think he will and he applies to the War Department, it would be granted. I hope that if it is done & I get a promotion that I shall be home to organize it. The idea of taking two of the three company officers from this Battalion will I think strike Gov Buckingham favorably. It would help the formation amazingly. I think the men could be raised as soon as the horses could be procured, for after Sept. there will be a great number of farmer boys to enlist unless the six regiments and large bounties drain the state for the present. Still, picked men are what we want, and if I was in it would surely have. Good country boys, young and healthy, and by the time we were ready for the field we would be well posted, for I think the experience of the field has taught me a great deal. But it is perhaps foolish to anticipate anything. Still, if Fish, as he ought to, is made Major now, there is no one to beat me for the next show.*

*Gen Schenck and Gen Siegle both would recommend me for the position and then a Lt Col would go to Fish, senior Major to me, and in case of our being able to get our two companies out of the NY Cavalry and added to the 2ⁿᵈ Battalion, which is in the plan if we succeed in the first, but is now <u>sub rosa</u>. It would give us a Col's commission when everything would be all right. If our first plan works, then the last can be done by the Gen in the field.*

> *Much love to all,*
> *AfftSon,*
> *Charlie*

*The major's [Lyon's] resignation was today returned accepted, much against his ideas, for he has laid the flattering hope to his heart that it would be rejected and then he would give us fits. He has threatened us, if ever he had command. Poor man, he is miserable.*

> *Camp near Washington*
> *Sept 3ʳᵈ 1862*

*My dear Father,*

*Since my last letter to you, the date of which has escaped me, I have been extremely occupied day and night, and last Friday and Saturday capped the climax. I can hardly relate to you the different expeditions in which we have been engaged, from the time we left Crooked river until we fought at Bull Run. But we have worked all the time, guarding trains, scouting, and fighting. We have one less to report during the past two weeks. The fights of Friday and Saturday were terrible, and as reported to the papers entirely wrong. Friday's fight was fought by Seigel against odds, and was very severe. (I was in it.) But the man was equal for the plan and whipped them and drove them back. The battle of Saturday was fought by Pope although McDowell is supposed to have planned it. And papers to the contrary, we were gloriously whipped. Yes, badly whipped and every thing up to the veteran troops of McClellan and Burnside who held the stress. Bull Run was enacted a second time. The stampede was a sight which pages could not tell. But I know what I write, as I was on the left when this fight commenced and left with Gen Schenck when he was wounded and we supposed the day lost entirely.*

*The fighting, instead of being all day, lasted about one hour, and during that time 75,000 of our men broke ranks and ran like cowards, which they were. It was now that the discipline of McClellan's and Burnside's troops told, and they held the enemy back, and saved the capitol. For our men to the [illegible] did not stop running until the Potomac was reached.*

*Whether there was a traitor in command or not I know not. But I do know the only capable man (in my opinion) that I have seen yet is the Dutchman. The fighting of Friday was more severe than Saturday, but it had a General at the helm that of Saturday.*

*I escaped unhurt, but a fragment of shell struck my curb bit and carved away the lower part of it, and wounded my horse badly in the mouth. But he is not injured. I never thought much of shells until then. Now I have a strong aversion to them.*

*I saw Learned at the fort yesterday, and Zingly. Also lots from the 15th & 16th [Connecticut Infantry] Regiments.*

*I understand that Fish does not join the Battalion but is detached upon staff, and that then there will be no improvement. I have not seen him, but understand that he has staff straps on and that he said he did not care for the Battalion, as he was on the staff. I shall see him soon and learn all about it. If that be so, I am through [with] the military life, for I am completely tired out with work and disheartened by the position and condition of our Battalion. W. B. Sourk I suppose was upon the staff of the late Gen Stevens. They passed me one day upon the Rappahannock but I did not recognize him. Have seen Peale often and passed the time of day, but never long enough to have a confab.*

*I am at present laying by. Not feeling very well and am with the troops from near Washington, with my company.*

*Denny is quite sick with typhoid fever and owing to the exposure of the [illegible], arrived in a wagon, etc., I fear is past hope. But I am attending to him now, having camped and got a tent up. But it is only a chance if he lives. Dr. Barnes is sick and we are without medicines. The latest news from the front. We hold our own.*

*Much love,*
*Charles*

---

**Comment:** This was Charlie's firsthand report on the Second Battle of Manassas/Bull Run, August 29–September 2, 1862. As Confederate forces drove northward, Pope moved his troops, including Charlie's unit, parallel to them. But certain Union cavalry scouts (not Charlie's unit) failed until too late to detect the Confederates' eastward turn toward Washington, and Pope's army was surprised and driven to the edge of the capital in one of the Union's darkest hours.

General Robert C. Schenck, Charlie's commanding officer, was shot in his right arm during the battle. In his convalescence he was assigned to defensive duties in Baltimore. Charlie and his immediate commander, Major Fish, lobbied successfully in January 1863 to have the First Connecticut Cavalry transferred to provost marshal duties in Baltimore under Schenck.

The "Dutchman" whom Charlie saluted was Major General Franz Sigel. (Charlie spelled it Siegel or Siegle.)

Charlie's personal servant Denny did, in fact, survive the typhoid fever he had contracted.

---

*Camp near Georgetown*
*Sept 4ᵗʰ 1862*

*My dear Brother,*

*Yours of 21ˢᵗ received also Mother's of 20ᵗʰ. All nothing from the front since the fight in which Ness & Keany were killed. Seash passed me twice one day and I did not recognize him or he me. I say [illegible] and staff went by, and as I recalled after the [illegible] was on I remember a face that must have been his. No letters of batt[alion] and we are not allowed to send any from the army, but I get my letters through by staff to Washington and then they go all right. [Four lines illegible.] Letter from Cecilia received.*

*I think from present appearance that cavalry is fast going out of service and Conn. will not get in with a Battalion No.2. If not, I shall be in Conn. by winter. I cannot stand my present position. I think that I might have got a position in Infantry before green men, for I understand the drill perfectly, but it is past, and I was not counted in. Still if we do get another Batt[alion], I will go up to a position I shall like.*

*Our army is in awful condition, and Pope is played out. Mc[Clellan] has command and now we will see something. He is the only man the rebels fear. Some difference between 7 days' fight and Pope's 2 hours —2 hours' fight, army in full retreat for a new "line of action", a "new base." I was heartily sick. [Ilegible.] But [illegible] Mc[Clellan] [will] save us. But for him, our capitol would have given up..*

> *In haste (not much account),*
> *Much love,*
> *Charlie*

---

**Comment:** Charlie's company had retreated with Pope's forces to the edge of Washington after the Union's defeat at Second Manassas/Bull Run.

Charlie's admiration for General George B. McClellan's defensive efforts in the Seven Days' War south of Richmond in late June 1862 is not shared by some historians, who think McClelland should have taken the offensive against Lee.[410]

---

> *Camp near Georgetown*
> *Sept 7th 1862*

*My dear Father,*

*I have today to "own" the receipt of letters from Billings Aug 23 & 20, 28th Sept 3rd, Mother Aug 26th Fred Aug 28th. Letter of importance from the army. We are encamped near the city, and will no doubt reorganize before we move. There are all sorts of rumors about us, that we are to stay in Washington, this Fall go to Fort Monroe under Schenck as Military Gov of Eastern Virginia, take the field, etc., and between the whole we are recruiting what good horses we have. If we succeed in getting the Battalion under Fish, and should [we] be sent to Monroe, it would be very pleasant for the winter. I was in hopes the State would start the 2nd Battalion before long and that Gov Buckingham would promote me, but I suppose it is all up and nothing will be done. If we go into service in the field this winter, I shall resign and come home unless another Battalion is raised and given to me. The order from the War Department forbidding officers leaving to take new commands would not affect me, as this would be promot[ion] to the 2nd Battalion of Conn Cavalry which is under one organization, with a Lt Col commanding.*

*Capt. Fish's appointment is in the prospect but he has no communication as yet and your humble servant is in command of the Battalion. Could we have a month's rest to get new horses, clothes, etc., we would be able to take the field to some purpose. The appointment of new officers in their new regiment was a mean thing and all government will suffer for it. The head serves not, for the Government that refused drilled men promotion which would have rendered the troops ready for service in two months where now it will take six. Treason is at the table of our President's advisors. There is no reason why the rebellion cannot be crushed in six months, but for treason in Washington. With Banks for Sec of War, McClelland in command of the army, one half the Brig Gens sent home, Seigle given a big command, etc. Forces concentrated and more fighting, less aspiring for the Presidential chair. And six months ordered [to] close it up. No, our Gov is ruled by politicians and our war is carried on by them. The soldiers of the army begin to cry against the treason in high places.*

*I sent to Billings to come to Washington for that horse, and I think he will please you very much for a saddle horse. He looks hard from the work of the last five or six weeks but will come up. I do not know how good a carriage horse he may be, but suppose he will make a good one. If he does not suit, you can sell him. If we remain here long I shall see Billings. The 8th Conn. is in Washington. I saw Harland, Goss, Edden, Parker, and all the Norwich boys. I hope to see all the 18 before I am ordered off. They say Tyler is the reason for Ely's promotion. Whatever he says must be done in that time is done. His word is law. .*

*In haste, Much Love,*
*Charles*

---

**Comment:** In Charlie's most outspoken criticism yet of the war effort, he alleged treason by unnamed government officials. Oddly, Charlie wanted General Banks to take full charge as secretary of war, despite Banks's failures against Jackson in the recent Shenandoah campaign. Even more surprising, Charlie exempted McClellan (who would run for president against Lincoln in two years) from being overly political.

Charlie seemed proud of Norwich's contribution to the war; he even knew the number of "Norwich boys" in the Eighth Connecticut Infantry Regiment, commanded by his boyhood friend William Ely.

---

*Camp near Georgetown*
*Sept 9th 1862*

*My dear Mother,*

*Little of importance transpired hereabouts, and all we know of war is what we see by the papers. After the exciting scenes of the past two months, a few days of rest is very agreeable. We are promised a month to recruit, obtain horses, and once more put ourselves in condition to take the field, and I suppose we will go back over the ground traveled last summer and spring unless the rebels change the program* from fighting on their soil to living the next winter upon the North. But I hardly think they will stay long North of the Potomac. But this is sure — they have the smartest Generals and the best fighting men, for they fight for their independence and endure everything, whilst our men grumble if they lose a ration once a month.

Sometimes I tremble as I think that the battle is not always to the strong, for energy and skill on their part have turned our hordes to naught. They whipped us Saturday with 60,000 to our 150,000 and some estimate our troops at as much as 200,000 men.

Billings is here and appears to enjoy himself, but he will never learn to take as good as he sends. I hardly know as he will take the horse home. It does not suit him in the least, and would never suit Father; that point was decided before he was on his back two minutes. So that after having had his superior judgment in regard to the animal, I fear to send it home.

Still, if it comes and does not suit, all you must do is sell it. I should kill it here in two months more of hard work. And should it not prove as fitted for you as proper, it can easily be sold, although Billings thinks the expenses of getting it on would hardly pay.

> *Much Love from*
> *Charlie*

---

**Comment:** The Confederate forces were at this moment moving northward across the Potomac toward the Battle of Antietam Creek/Sharpsburg.

Charlie overestimated the size of the armies at the recent, i.e., "Saturday," Second Battle of Manassas. Modern estimates are sixty-five thousand Union and fifty-five thousand Confederate troops. [411]

Charlie's observation that a "fight for independence" will make a soldier endure more hardship was perceptive.

---

> *Camp Buckingham*
> *Sept 13th 1862*

My dear Mother,

Billings has kept you supplied with letters no doubt, as the desk has been entirely at his disposal. My time is nearly all taken up, although duty is not very arduous.

Mrs. Parker and Nellie are here at the Washington base, taking care of Eddie who is sick with fever, but doing well. His fever is of a camp character, very slow going down, and a little more so after he reaches the turning point. I have been in *evenings and shall spend tomorrow PM with him. He is making an effort for a leave home and will obtain it, I think.*

*Billings will leave here today. The horses go next week. The rail road cannot take them now. A letter from Fred of last Sunday received is the last date from him.*

*Much Love*

*Afft,*

*Charles*

**LIST OF QUARTERMASTER'S STORES, &c., No. 27**, *Issued by Lieut. E. Colburn, Acting Quartermaster, 1ˢᵗ Batt. Conn. Cav., to Chas. Farnsworth, Capt., Comdg. Co. B, 1ˢᵗ Ct. Cavalry, at Washington D. C., on the 16ᵗʰ day on November, 1862.*

| Number or Quantity | Articles | Condition When Delivered |
| --- | --- | --- |
| (26) Twenty six | Shirts | New |
| (12) Twelve prs. | Socks | do |
| (10) Ten | Blankets | do |
| (2) Two | Jackets | do |
| (3) Three prs. | Pants | do |
| (7) Seven | Overcoats | do |

*I CERTIFY that I have this day issued to Chas. Farnsworth, Capt. Co. B, 1ˢᵗ Ct. Cav., at Washington D.C., the articles specified in the foregoing list.*

*E. Colburn, Lieut.*

*Acting Quartermaster, 1ˢᵗ Conn. Cavalry*

---

**Comment:** This was the report of the issuance of winter and replacement clothing, to be distributed to Charlie's Company B troops.

---

*Camp Buckingham*

*Sept 18 1862*

*My dear Father,*

*Today Mother's letter of 10ᵗʰ instant was received, having paid a visit to the Conn Artillery Reg. by mistake. Denny is doing fair, and will come out all right I think. I am very glad Mother went to see Georgia, who speaks of her kindness to come "so far" to see her, in a letter to me, the first letter I have received since her illness. Mrs. Parker, Nellie, and Eddie left yesterday PM for home, Eddie having*

176

*procured a furlough through the exertions of Fish and myself. It is for 20 days, and he will be well long before that, I think.*

*Today we, Major Fish and myself, have had an interview with Schenck, Seigel, & Stanton, and shall forward to Gov Buckingham a request approved by them all to increase our battalion to a full regiment, which I trust will meet his approval and will be entered upon. There may be some doubt in the Governor's mind whether he can commission us — Fish (Col), myself (Lt Col) — and get us home to organize it. (As it now stands, I would not serve for less than the 2nd command.) Stanton would not allow us to go home to organize it. But this is the way it can be done. Gov Buckingham issues his call for Cavalry to fill the Battalion to a Regiment, then promotes Fish as the Col., myself as Lt. Col., commissions a Major for our Battalion, and a Capt. for my company. Then we, being useless appendages to this Battalion, would be ordered to our regiment, which would be in Conn. Having issued those commissions, thus filling our present places, we would be at liberty to come home and organize our two Battalions. Now of course if a regiment is raised, Fish would be Col. and there is no Capt. that shall supplant me as Lt.Col., and no citizen in Conn shall. So I talk just as if I was to be Lt.Col., and if passed by shall of course come home.*

*Gen Schenck has today been commissioned a full Maj.Gen. and will be appointed Military Gov of Maryland or Eastern Virginia. He says he shall request of the Sect. of War that we be given to him, so there is little prospect of our being soon in active service in the field.*

*There is little news here, though the heads of Depts. were in session today. But Cabinet day [illegible] for McClellan. Said to be a very hard fight on hand, and reserves called in. If so if successful, they are gone under for the fall. How I hope it may be so. Mother inquires for the Dyes. They are all well. I do not know the Carver mentioned.*

*Much Love*
*Charlie*

*Camp Buckingham near Georgetown*
*Monday Sept 22nd 1862*

*Head Quarters 1st Battalion*
*Conn. Cavalry*

*Dear Mother,*

*We are having an easy time compared with those who compose the advance, who are now each day under the fire of rebel batteries, and meet the foe in the deadly bayonet charges. A bayonet charge is the grandest fighting that troops are called* upon to perform. In it they are said to lose all sense of time or sense, and few can even tell what happens. The news though not as good as we could wish, shows that a master hand moves the sinew of the nation, and a head equaled to the task conceives the great plans. I think the nation must confess that McClellan has done the best of all, and well deserves the praise. To stay a successful army in full pursuit of a demoralized army, a whipped and cowed mob, with that same mob has been no easy task, and none but one whom the army trusted could have done it.

McClellan's name was to every soldier a feeling of security, and they rallied and returned to their duty, and well have they performed their duty. The new regiments have fought well, and I trust will be put into it until they have earned their entire bounty. Some of the 20<sup>th</sup> said to the old troops that they came out from a sense of duty & patriotism whilst we were forced to come for the wages, and therefore they were the best fighting stock. I hope they will have a chance to go through the ordeal the glorious 3<sup>rd</sup> passed through; it would do one good to look at them show their sense of duty.

We have been receiving new clothes to day and our men show up well. Nearly all are fitted out from top to toe complete. There is no chance for homes for at least six weeks, and by that time the fall fighting will be over. Should Maj Gen Schenck accept the Military Governorship of Maryland, and have us with him, an easy winter is before us, and I trust it will be so. He is much better and will be out in a month and that will suit our movements exactly.

Much lover to all,

AfftSon

Charlie

---

**Comment:** Charlie's adulation of a "master hand," which seems to refer to General McClellan's limited success at Antietam on September 17-18, was a bit overwrought, mainly because General Lee's Confederate forces escaped intact. It is generally accepted, however, that "Little Mac" was much loved by his troops, perhaps because of his tactical caution.[412] As for the euphoric effect of hand-to-hand combat that Charlie rhapsodizes about, nearly all of the twenty-three thousand casualties at Antietam came from withering rifle and artillery fire, not bayonet charges.

---

September 22, 1862

Dear Father,

I hardly know what to think of the chances of filling our Battalion to a regiment. My opinion is it will not be done. Still there is one chance to push it through. But now the State has filled her quota and partly by drafting . I fear it cannot be done unless the extra inducements of a cavalry man's life should bring them out.

*We have not heard from the Governor upon the subject and until then every thing is uncertain. But I am all right with Fish and if there is a Lt Col from the Battalion, it's mine. If not, as I said, I'm off. I have been examined and find a discharge is easy enough for me to get from my wounds, and of course should avail myself of it in case of what I should consider miscarriage. You will of course hear the Governor's mind upon the chances of adding to us, and if favorable he will no doubt drop a word indicative of the future. Denny is improving. A letter from Fred says the history of the sword is still unknown. I have written it; the letter must be lost. Will give it again.*

*AfftSon,*
*Chas*

---

**Comment:** Putting pressure on the governor to recruit more mounted troops, Charlie asked his father to tell Buckingham that he would come home with a medical discharge based on his chest and left arm wounds unless another cavalry battalion was raised and he was given a promotion.

---

*Head Quarters Conn Cav*
*Camp Buckingham*
*Near Georgetown*
*Sept 28 1862*

*My dear Mother,*

*Letters from you and Father came to day. I am very sorry that you are to lose the service of the girls that have so long been attached to the household, and fear that a long time will elapse ere you fill their places. I suppose you enjoyed the visit of Mrs. Day. She is always good company.*

*Fred wrote nothing in regard to Miss Bonds wedding.*

*I think Eddie's illness was well-timed, as in his current condition he could not have endured the fatigue of the battles, to say nothing of danger. I see "C.F." suffered some. The death of Marvin Wait was sad, and his poor mother must be in a very deplorable condition, judging from her acts when he left. There is hardly a family that will not mourn some one ere the war ends. The end, I fear, is far off, and thousands are yet to fall, but in a good cause. I suppose ere long we shall again be on the move, as horses are ordered for us and will soon be on hand. Then again for the enjoyments of the field, and service, with its rations of Hard bread and Coffee.*

*The sword I sent home and of which I wrote whilst at Fort Jackson, Va. was taken from a Lt Col of the Georgia Tigers, whilst in the Shenandoah Valley. I* also took his horse, but it subsequently gave out and was abandoned. It is an old fashioned dress sword, and is more particularly a Surgeons' sword. There is but little of interest in their relics now, they are so common, but that was early sent home, so I sent it. The Carbine was taken from a Guerrilla in the last trip to Moorefield.

I shall send home my best and bit by express. The back may be a relic worth keeping. The bit was broken at Bull Run by a fragment of shell. A second would have brought it in range of the body, but I luckily escaped. How often will fortune favor me? At Bull Run whilst lying on the ground shooting at rebel skirmishers, a bullet passed over me just grazing the heel of the boot. I was flat upon the body, and it just passed by my head. I paid no attention to it at the time, but one of the men noticed it and upon examination found it so. The bullets flew around very loose on that day, and the whistle was anything but agreeable.

Much Love
Charlie

---

**Comment:** President Lincoln issued his preliminary Emancipation Proclamation on September 22. Was this the "good cause" that Charlie thought it was worth dying for? Or was it the preservation of the Union? In either case, Charlie almost made the ultimate sacrifice while dismounted at Second Bull Run/Manassas.

Camp Buckingham, described as "near Georgetown," was located in the area of Washington known as Tenallytown. Charlie continued to send war booty home, adding a sword, rifle, and bridle bit to the horses and weapons previously sent.

---

Sept 28 1862

Dear Father,

I wrote you some time since that the application for a regiment had been forwarded signed by Seigle, Schenck, & Stanton, and if so disposed the Governor can easily start the thing. You seem to have this letter when you wrote, though it was written before letter to Child. Though I have written two to him upon different subjects, I am in hopes that it will get through before we are ordered from here, and that Fish & myself can get away. I do not suppose the former sought to build upon me, for there was no need, and he is very well disposed towards me, though he would sell his best friend for position. Still, from motives of interest he will stand by me. At any rate, that is my opinion. All that I hear of his words in quarters are favorable. And as I should not come in contact for the same position, I see no reasons why we should clash.

I expect to hear from the application in many days.

AfftSon
Charlie

*Child could keep you posted confidentially. We have only lost by death (sickness) four. None in battle, but have had some 20 taken prisoners. No Norwich boys hurt.*

---

**Comment:** Secretary of War Edwin Stanton now supported the call for Connecticut to provide another cavalry battalion.

"He would sell his best friend for position" were Charlie's first harsh words about Major Fish, whom he had otherwise admired from the outset.

---

*Head-Quarters First Division Army of Virginia*
*Camp Buckingham Sept 30 1862*

*My dear Billings,*

*I want you to buy me a Sole Leather Valise, Canvass Covered. I should like to have it bound with Iron rod, say 1/8 or 1/4 inch. This will make a valise cost near $20. But it will be the cheapest in the end. My valise cost me $9, and was worn out in six months, and one of the kind I speak of would be good now. In having it ironed, have it strongly done. I will of course say nothing about when it comes by express, being full of eatables etc., say some of those mince and pumpkin pies etc. that they make at Norwich (illegible).*

*Much Love*
*Charlie*

*Have it marked Chas. Farnsworth, 1ˢᵗ Conn Cavalry (one end), and Co. B (other end). There is no great hurry, say two weeks. If not practicable to get what I desire, send what best pleases you, and it will be all right. I only give my idea of something strong. Price $21.*

---

**Comment:** Charlie included with this letter the dimensions of his current valise and drawings for the new one, illustrating front, side, and top views.

---

*Camp Buckingham*
*Oct 2ⁿᵈ 1862*

*My dear Billings,*

*There is but little news in this part of the army vineyard. We are without a horse and the recruits have not yet come. Government is receiving horses very rapidly indeed, and a few days will see us mounted, I fear, for I was in hopes that Schenck would get about before we were ready and take us to himself. If we move to* the front, good-bye for pleasure till next year. But then the excitement of field life will fill up the spaces.

Siegle is I fear to be ignored, and will resign. Why? Because he can fight, will fight, and has fought well. And better than any regular officer we have got. Now that there is a man who will do something, hurt somebody, he is to be crushed by such stand-stills as <u>Halleck</u>.

I hope the regiment will go through and that will show the feelings of a certain man.

Four of my company were Exchanged at Annapolis and have joined the company. They look hale & hearty and though they tell of hard times they do not look any worse than we did when we first came here. We have all got nice clothes and look fine. Then new horses and away for another year of it.

Should you be unable to fix upon a valise as I wrote about, just get as good a one as you can, whatever you think will work, send along. It will satisfy me.

Much Love

Charlie

---

**Comment:** Lincoln appointed Henry Halleck to be general-in-chief in mid-1862. As Charlie predicted, Halleck "crushed" General Siegle's career—but not until two years later and then for retreating, not attacking, in the second Shenandoah campaign of May 1864.[413]

Among those of Company B who were "exchanged" for Confederate prisoners was Pvt. Patrick E. Clary of Hartford. Charlie reported that the four soldiers looked "hale and hearty." Others died later while imprisoned.[414]

---

Camp Buckingham

Oct 4th 1862

My dear Brother,

Your letter of 2nd came yesterday. It was the first intimation of the package, as the letter you refer to had not been received. I have sent today for the package.

The box from Norwich has not been heard from either by letter or express. Our new recruits to the number of 75 arrived last eve and I am very busy organizing them and shall only write to advise you of yours of the 2nd.

The prospect of the regiment looks bad, but from our recruits' appearance, which is far better average than the old Battalion, I think we could raise the men. I hope something will be done.

Much Love

Charlie

*Hi — The package was brought up here today. Many thanks — watch splendid.
Letters of 30ᵗʰ and 3ʳᵈ also received today.*

Oct 15ᵗʰ 1862

*Dear Billings,*

*We are ordered to Fairfax immediately. Send my valise as soon as possible.
Don't wait for anything to be put into it. Send it along. Our order is to report there
immediately, still we have no horses. We may remain here a week and we may move
tomorrow. So send and be sure.*

*Afft, Charlie*

*Camp Buckingham Oct 17ᵗʰ 1862*

*My dear Mother,*

*Although feeling rather weary, having watched last night with Gen Schenck,
I take pen to inform you of our proposed future. We expect soon to be at Fairfax,
having been ordered there, but can get no horses. Today McClellan's order came for
thousands and he is supplied <u>first</u>, gallant men like Seigle <u>last</u>. We may remain here
now for a fortnight longer. Soon it will be winter quarters and a large army raised
late have done nothing. That is the way things go. Oh, I wish some one would take
the thing into his own hand. The army would put him in the <u>White House</u> and hold
him there. I trust we shall have a revolution at the North before spring. I send you
the gallant Kearny & Hooker.*

*Much love,*
*Charles*

---

**Comment:** Charlie recklessly dared to express his desire for a military coup by more
aggressive commanders such as General Philip Kearny, who had opposed McClellan's
order to withdraw during the Seven Days' battle in July 1862, and General Joseph
Hooker, who had led the Union's attack at Antietam in September.[415]

Many of the First Connecticut Cavalry's horses had been killed or crippled
at Second Manassas. Those that survived had been turned over to Captain Niles'
Company C, which was assigned provost guard duty for the Headquarters of General
Sigel at Fairfax Courthouse, Virginia.[416]

---

*Camp Buckingham*
*Oct 20ᵗʰ 1862*

*My dear Father,*

Gen Fremont assigned to Texas, and a letter to Major requesting us to go with him. After much discussion upon the chances of taking him, or Gen Schenck (who takes command soon at Baltimore, and has relied upon our going with him) as our leader, Major said "well, Captain, decide." This morning I gave my word for Texas and have written Fremont to request of the War Dept. to assign us to him. It was hard to decide. Comfort and inactivity, no danger at Baltimore. Work a new field, and to my eye a chance for preferment with Fremont. And if we can be assigned to him without causing Schenck any feeling, I shall prefer it. Fremont will be here soon, when our future will be decided for certain. I wonder if Gov Buckingham would raise three companies (a battalion) of artillery for him if requested.

*Afft. Charlie*

---

**Comment:** "Major" was the just-promoted William Fish.

Given a choice between a horseman's war in Texas or guard duty in Baltimore, Charlie preferred to go west, and showed considerable presumption in writing directly to General Fremont. But Fremont, who had resigned in June after refusing to serve under Pope, never got the assignment in Texas.

---

*Camp Schenck Oct 24 1862*
*Washington D.C.*

*My dear Mother,*

Your letter found us in our new Camp in Washington, having moved from Camp Buckingham yesterday. We are now within the limits of Washington. Our camp is situated upon the branch of the Potomac that runs between Washington & Georgetown on a bluff, and is completely surrounded by heavy timber, in fact is shut in from sight. We have a much pleasanter camp than before, nearer Washington. More beautiful grounds, and only one unpleasant thing—a small pox hospital is located about 1/8 of a mile from us. But I do not think there is any danger from it. I had quite a sick turn for a couple of days, an intermittent fever, but am well now. Our new M.D. has not arrived, but from Jarvis can tell he is a poor stick. Jarvis has gone to the 7ᵗʰ Regiment, south. The 17ᵗʰ is camped near Georgetown, and are engaged building a fort. Washington is well defended.

In relation to the Box, I don't want any clothes at present, save a few cotton socks. Of eatables, send what you think best; anything will be acceptable. The books *or papers will be read by the men and gladly received. Jack in the box. Send it by express to me, Washington D.C., and it will come all right.*

*Valise from Billings arrived all right and is a fine thing, and suits me well.*

*You may send me my dark overcoat, it will come handy whilst we stay here, and when we move I have several articles to send home & can send it with them.*

*Gen Schenck has not been off his back since he was wounded, until last Friday. He was shot through the wrist, completely shattering his arm and all the small bones. And his nerves were so shattered that he has been completely prostrated. Although to anyone but himself it is evident he could have left in four weeks, but he thought not, and he is a perfect Farnsworth when he thinks so & so.*

*AfftSon*

*Charlie*

---

**Comment:** The new camp probably was located along Rock Creek near Kalorama Circle, just off modern Massachusetts Avenue.

---

*Camp Schenck Washington*

*Oct 31ˢᵗ 1862*

*My dear Mother,*

*Your letter of the 21ˢᵗ came duly. I wrote when I sent directions for the box, that my dark overcoat would be very well here, and to send it. Therefore I did not answer your letter upon receipt.*

*There have been no new developments in regard to the Battalion. If we only had horses we would be out where the Confeds were, doing something. Here I wish we were supplied and at work. I knew the brothers well. We first met at Wheeling and have been together much since. Real fine fellows, and whilst they are fighting we lay here idle together with over 100,000 troops within four miles of Washington, doing nothing because we have not got a Westpointer with brains enough to handle so many men, or else it is treason. And to my mind, treason lurks from the White House through all departments. Oh, for a leader even if he wears a crown, and so say thousands. And should such a man spring up, the army will sustain him and place him in a large White building on Pennsylvania Avenue, Washington, D.C. It is so, however strange it may seem. And if it will bring the war to a close and vindicate the North, why I say let it come.*

*I see Gen Banks is to be south. I would very much like to go with him, as he is a General who, but for West Pointers, would have done more and earned a greater name than any of them. And with the soldiers he has the highest place. Should we* be numbered with the Texan expedition I should be satisfied, for the prospects of a lively campaign would be very good, and I think my chances for a better position would be greater under Fremont than elsewhere.

I should not be surprised if there was in prospect a large Southern campaign, for the winter. But it won't work under our present heads of Army & departments.

Much Love,
Charles

---

**Comment:** Charlie obviously disagreed with Lincoln's determination to heavily fortify Washington after the debacle at Second Manassas.

Charlie's disdain for West Point graduates (he was probably referring to Halleck) is clear. But he seems to have gone dangerously too far in charging Lincoln with treason, and arguing for a monarch to "vindicate the North."

General Banks was put in charge of Union-occupied New Orleans in December 1862. Charlie believed, erroneously, that the assignment was part of a larger campaign into Texas.

---

Camp Schenck Nov 3rd 1862

My dear Mother,

Your letter of 30th came Saturday but box did not arrive in time to be brought out Saturday, but will be out this P.M. I doubt not that everything will be good and give great pleasure. My mouth is made up for thanksgiving pies, and shall expect a few about that time. Our going to Texas is all up. Banks and not Fremont has been assigned to that Department. Now we are in for Baltimore and Schenck with strong chances of being there in two weeks. The General's friends mean to get him there, so he can be nominally in command if he is on his back. He is slowly getting command of his nervous system which is nearly as bad as Henry's. He cannot stand pain. [Portion of letter missing.]

I certainly wrote you about seeing the Stones and H.R. Norten at Willards.

Much Love,
Charles

---

**Comment:** Instead of going off on a wild-west campaign, Charlie's Company B got guard duty for General Schenck, the new military provost of Baltimore.

Charlie was socializing at Washington's Willard Hotel, popular then as now for hobnobbing.

---

Camp Schenck Nov 10 1862

My dear Mother,

The box arrived on Thursday just a little behind time but everything was in good order, grapes and all. Mrs. Gov. Buckingham's bundle I sent to Gen Schenck. Much obliged to her for the kindness. I enjoyed everything; gave out the books & papers and men were most pleased with them. We are not going to Texas, but everything looks as though we would move to Baltimore next week. The past week has been very cold in camp and no stove makes writing in one's tent very uncomfortable, and not wishing to buy a stove if we go to Baltimore, have suffered from the inconvenience of want of fire.

Eddie Packer is here, unable to join his regiment. Good that McClellan is removed. Fred has $23 to pay to Father for me in about a month.

AfftSon Much Love
Charlie


If we go to Baltimore, I shall want my white silk and if Fred comes, bring my black pants there also.

---

**Comment:** Lincoln removed McClellan from command of the Army of the Potomac on November 7 primarily because of his failure to crush Lee's forces at Antietam, replacing him with General Ambrose Burnside.

Charlie got boxes and "bundles" of food from family and friends throughout his active duty. This "bundle," coming from the governor's wife, shows the families' close relationship. In asking for his "white silk," Charlie was clearly expecting soft duty in Baltimore.

---

Camp Schenck Nov 14th 1862

My dear Fred

Your last came duly to hand, and I was of course glad to hear from you. I would advise you to take good care of your body and mind, and make the most of your present advantages, for my dear boy the time is coming when it will count. I would advise you to cut off smoking and beer, and thus keep the mind clear. I tell you for your [illegible] sake, take care of every moment, for the battle will be brains against the many, and such condition sometimes works well. So watch every moment & take a deep interest, for I tell you the future is full for strong minds & thinkers. This war and its after-claps will carry down all half-made men.

Nothing new here.

Charles

187

**Comment:** Charlie, age twenty-six, was now giving worldly advice to his younger brother Fred, age twenty.

*Camp Hall Farm, Va.*
*Nov 18<sup>th</sup> 1862*

*My dear Mother,*

*We received orders last night 10 P.M. to move across the Potomac and join the cavalry brigade and receive our horses. And at noon today we pitched our tents once more upon "sacred ground." Horses are expected soon, and we may enjoy a trip south and some fun before we go into winter quarters at Baltimore. For Schenck says he shall have us any way, and that as soon as he assumes command we will be ordered to him. I hope so at least.*

*For we are brigaded under Beardsley, a West Pointer, and I had enough of him last summer. He is a fool, and miserable officer.*

*Letters come as before, Conn Cav., Wash. D.C.*

*Afft in haste*
*Charles*

**Comment:** Most of the battalion, under Major Fish, was already in Baltimore protecting General Schenck's headquarters. The remainder, under Charlie's command, was ordered into Virginia to scout for Confederate forces that might threaten Washington. "Camp Hall" was probably in the Arlington area.

*Camp "Hall Farm"*
*Nov 20<sup>th</sup> 1862*

*My dear Mother,*

*Yours of 6<sup>th</sup> with enclosed came today having been upon a trip to some other section. Every thing in box was very fine and suited me well, the ginger bread especially. I intended sending your tins back, but in our last move was obliged to abandon. My mouth is up for pies about the 27<sup>th</sup> but fear to say send lest we are off. But nothing ventured, nothing gained. If we are anywhere near here, we can get it (and I don't expect to leave here for a long time), and of course if ordered too far off can have it taken out by a friend who will appreciate. So you may send it.*

*Much Love from*

*AfftSon*
*Charlie*

Camp Hall Farm, Va.
Nov 20th 1862

My dear Fred,

I have just sealed my sixth long letter, and take pen that you may know we are again on war ground, and hope soon to be up a war footing and off. We have a rough camp now, all stumps and brush but we are going to clean it up if we don't stay a week. It will look like a farm when we leave. Blasted out 10 high stumps from my street today and have 50 more before my tents are pitched in line. But I do it.

Much Love Charlie

Address as before.

---

**Comment:** Charlie was a stickler for discipline even in field camps, ordering his men to clear tree stumps so that their tents could be "pitched in line."

---

Camp Hall Farm, Va.
Nov. 21 1862
Near Washington

My dear Mother,

Yours of the 13th came a moment since and as but a little more can be said in relation to the box than I wrote in my last. You cannot calculate on a box coming in less than one week. I think we shall be here some time. And as I said in my last, send it. I had not heard of Eddy's being Adjutant and he had not last evening when I saw him. He is a Lieut of "Col. J."

I am sorry to hear of Mrs. Gov. Buckingham's failing health. Hope she will come out of it all right.

[Portion of letter missing.]
[Unsigned.]

Camp Hall Farm
Dec 1st 1862

My dear Mother

The box arrived safely and its contents are all inspected and pass muster. My yes, those pumpkin pies were good, and came just as perfect as could be. How near it brought me to you all when I partook of them.

We are quietly camped here. Was in Washington & passed the evening with the Taylors, a splendid time as usual. Gen Schenck was in the parlor. He is doing excellently, and will leave soon for Baltimore. The approach of Congress has debased

189

*an interview with Stanton, who was not up on report. But now they will soon arrange. How I wish if we are going that we could start.*

*Your letter of 27ᵗʰ came duly.*

[Unsigned.]

*Camp Hall Farm, Va.*
*Dec 12 1862*

*Dear Father,*

*Orders came tonight to move tomorrow, and I am all ready, save rolling up a tent. I expect we go towards the damned city. Seigle is marching towards Aquia-Creek, was last at Dumphries (refer to map).*

*I am glad we are going to take part in the winter campaign. But I think yet that January will find us in Baltimore.*

*All has been excitement getting ready, but the men like it.*

*In Haste,*
*Much Love,*
*Charles*

*Camp Near Falmouth Dec 18ᵗʰ 1862*

*My dear Mother,*

*We have been on the march these 5 days, and have been near to the recent battle field, but not participate in it. We are now awaiting developments. Report says Burnside has crossed again; his last attempt was only a feeler. I rejoice that we have a man that is not afraid to sacrifice life to gain his point. We are too much given to trying to save life. Soldiers are enlisted to be killed, if necessary, and war cannot be reaped unless we are men. I think this month will see the greatest loss of life, and the near settlement of the matter. I am well and contented, but we still feel sure of Battalion. I have a letter from Gov Buckingham, and it will not be a strange thing if I come home for a Battalion ere long.*

*Much Love*

*Charlie*

*Direct Seigle* [illegible]

---

**Comment:** Falmouth lies a few miles north of Fredericksburg, Virginia, site of the bloody December 11-15 battle that cost the North nearly thirteen thousand casualties and the South about five thousand before General Burnside's Union forces retreated back north across the Rappahannock River.[417] Charlie and his unit seem to have arrived too late to participate in this Union disaster. His forecast that the Union is "near settlement of the matter" was more than two years too optimistic.

---

*Camp 3d Brigade Cavalry*
*Headquarters Conn Cavalry Volunteers*
*Christmas 1862*

*My dear Father,*

*There has but little occurred in military circles since my last of note. Our brigade has been on a scout to Culpepper under Col Cesnola.. We found no rebels this side of the river, but a force on the other side. We lost four horses killed in a skirmish, driving their pickets across, but no men injured. I hardly think it means a change of base from Fredericksburgh to Warrenton, though I fear the present base won't win, and when our bad rains come in, there won't be any moving. I fear the rail road from Aquia Creek will not be sufficient to supply forage and (illegible) should the river close up. For myself I think our army is "in status quo" for the next four months, and if we do nothing this winter I fear our cause is gone up.*

*My own idea is that ere six months pass, there will be a clamor for peace from the* <u>*North*</u> *and unless the present administration is overthrown and we have a military power, the Peace party will effect a settlement and all our treasure will be spent in vain. The South will dictate the terms & we will accede to it. Mark me, unless there is a great change, we will be humbled, and all that will do is want of decision on the part of the President. Had we ruled as Jeff has, we should long since have restored the Union & the Government. But no, we have dealt with every thing and every body with gloves and the result is an actual loss to us. If there is any attempt to overthrow the present Administration, McClellan will be the chosen man as a Dictator, and the soldiers will sustain him. To us in the field, and amongst the scenes of the army, we look upon these things as you at home cannot, or dare not. The army is and has been ripe for months for a Military power.*

*Major Fish left here for Baltimore some days since and leaves me in command of the Battalion. I expect we will be ordered there soon., but not for a week at least. There is some hope of increasing our battalion to a regiment or at least one more battalion, and if we go to Baltimore for the present it can easily be done.*

*Much Love to all,*
*No mail here since we left Washington,*
*Afft*
*Charlie*

*What chances are there of the Gov. being elected next spring?*

**Comment:** In the most forceful manner yet, Charlie expressed his frustration with what he perceived as Lincoln's hesitation and softness. He yearned for a dictatorship by General McClellan, who would presumably rule as decisively as "Jeff," i.e., Jefferson Davis. Charlie's estimate that a large "peace" movement would arise by mid-1863 was a year premature.

Attached to his letter is a memo by his mother, undated, but probably written in late 1862: *The sword Chas sent home was taken from a Lieut. Col. of the "Louisiana Tigers" in the Shenandoah Valley by Capt. C. F., who also took his horse, which subsequently gave out, and was abandoned. The carbine was taken from a guerrilla in Charles' second trip to Moorefield after he had been wounded there.*

# 1863

My dear Billings,

Your letter of 28th now at hand, the only letter from home and no more new mail has yet come through. We must have a large one somewhere.

If we go to Baltimore, I shall come home to recruit for a Regiment. If not, there is no aim in trying it. But we shall go, for Fish is hard at work and he hardly ever quits in any thing, queer fellow, but he is always sure, and has got every thing so far he has ever undertaken. He is real busy there but it is the only way. Those kind of men always go up. A letter from him says he is sure of it, and I am just as confident of it as if there. But it will be a couple of weeks any way.

Stationed in Baltimore, it won't be hard to get a Battalion more. That makes me a Major, and if by thy faith a Lt Col. If Fish could get on the staff independent of the Battalion, I should command it and would not want it increased. It will be hard work to raise the men, I fear, yet I think it can be done.

I am glad the Lady Julia pleases, and hope to be home this winter when she is married. I hardly think of the Julia is so uncertain. I hope the Battalion law will go through this session and I get clear of old scenes.

The true conduct of the war now is Burnside to move to Alexandria and Somerville, supported by Seigle & others at [illegible] and along the rail road —5 large expeditions sent south —Charleston, Mobil, New Orleans, North Carolina, & then into Georgia —push into the cotton states, set the niggers free, arm them, and make them fight, thus keep our numbers on the increase and not recruit at home. Consolidate all factions of regiment with the men. Officers put in command of nigger regiments. Those that don't want to, send home. Push through the cotton states, getting away the producing power (of) _slaves_ and destroy the producing country. Burnside, Sheridan, Richmond & the northern line crowd the Western Gen along, and open the Mississippi River. This would bring the rebs into a small compass. We have the men and by the aid of nigger regiments we could have a full million men in the field. The present mode won't work, and the other will crush the rebellion in six months. I am sorry Butler is senior, unless they send him to South Carolina. I trust they will. But what would suit me better would be a new Cabinet, Banks via Halleck; Seward [illegible] Butler —Stanton.

*Our present government won't ever bring things out right. We had a man today killed on picket — Carver of Co. A. Nothing new; rumour says we are falling back to Fairfax or Alexandria next week..*

*I suppose Burnside falls back or moves toward Staunton.*

*Much Love*

*Charles*

*Camp Conn Cavalry*

*Headquarters 3<sup>rd</sup> Brigade*

*Stafford Courthouse*

*January 3 1863*

*My dear Mother,*

*I have been so engaged since we came here, that to tell the truth I have little idea when I wrote last, and now, though a day after the first, "A Happy New Year" to you all. We are doing all kinds of duties, some fun and some danger. Today one of "my" men was shot on picket by the rebels. The first death by the enemy's hands. That has been our lot since we came into service. My men brought in some prisoners from a scout yesterday, and 25 of them are on the rear of the late rebel raid cavalry. We are building huts and barns and there is a strong look of winter quarters, but I think we move ere long — backwards.*

*No advance for us this winter. Held away I am. Oh, that we could go ahead to Richmond. I fear we are losing ground each day. The proper way is to place a strong line of troops hereabout, then send five large expeditions — New Orleans, Charleston, Mobil, North Carolina, and one to Georgia — and then work in and liberate the slaves. Let Richmond go for the present. Let the Western Army, which has Generals that mean something work away and by Spring we could so weaken them that we could move from here with ease and security. But I fear for the result as we are now doing. I wish the Cabinet had been remodeled — Seward & Stanton, not Halleck, removed — Butler & Banks put in, and a reign of Military power for the next year, and all would be well. The main thing now is to get into the Cotton states, free the slaves, and ruin the producing power. But still they are in (illegible) south, united & powerful, and will whip us in the end unless there is a change. Major Fish is at Baltimore, and we are daily expecting to move there. A letter from him today says it is certain, and before the 15<sup>th</sup> I expect to move the Battalion there. As soon as it is done, I am going to Conn to raise the Regiment if it can be done, and I think there is little doubt of the thing being accomplished. If so, of course I go up. I am very (illegible) or before there is a change in the state, for Buckingham won't be elected again even if he seems, which is not likely, not that I fear for myself in case of another governor,* for my position is such that I must get the promotion and my influence is as strong as can be. But under Governor Buckingham I should receive more assistance perhaps, for I fear the next governor will not be very energetic in raising troops.

I should be so glad to get to be Lt Col before he retires.

No mail got, consequently no letters from any one. One letter comes from Billings of 26ᵗʰ; nothing else. We have a (illegible) but where —.

I don't like Butler being removed. He is a better man for Maj. Gen. than Banks. Ain't he bully, so sure and certain when he makes a decision, legal and combative, no backing down. I wish he was in Abraham Lincoln's place. He would soon show Jeff Davis what he meant. He would not <u>retract</u>.

Afft

Charles

John Peak is here as legal staff.

---

**Comment:** Despite Charlie's eagerness to attack southward, there would be no such operation in the winter of 1862-63. To get things done, he now favored a "military government," with generals Banks and Butler replacing civilians Seward and Stanton. These were dubious choices, however; Butler had just been removed from his New Orleans command (to Charlie's dismay) because of allegations of financial impropriety, and Banks had lost battles to Stonewall Jackson in the Shenandoah Valley the previous summer.[418] It is unclear why Charlie thought that these two generals could wage a successful war against the Confederacy.

Charlie's ambition for promotion and command was unrelenting; as a captain, he aspired to jump over the rank of major, and to be appointed lieutenant colonel by Governor Buckingham.

---

Headquarters 3ʳᵈ Cav Brigade

Camp Conn Cav Battalion

Stafford Court House

Jan 6 1863

My dear Fred,

Your letter of 2ⁿᵈ received and much obliged for news. I like to hear from you often. We are having gay times here scouting, have had several severe skirmishes with the rebs since we left Hall Farm. One of our boys was killed a few days since & his body was sent to Norwich.

I trust that I will be placed in a position to come home ere long for a short time . Though I am in no way home-sick here, and am sure I will not be when in Baltimore. There are some gay people there that I knew in Chicago and there will *be fun raised. They are very like the cottage and surely there will be some fun. The two ladies referred to are both in the marrying line. The latter I trust will ere meet one who will save the day. Every thing is lovely in Norwich and progressing finely. I should not wonder if it was a game but it is the queerest one I was ever engaged in. Still after the easy ones of the past, it is refreshing to find a strong and real woman, not carried away by any thing. It is the real wife one wants, not the sentimental school girl. I trust it will be in my power to come home for a few days this winter and if we go to Baltimore you may be sure of seeing me. I see the Norwich boys are going up in the army. It is well, for after the next election I fear they won't have the same influence in their favor. I had heard nothing about the Hakes and see nothing in papers, but if sent home for drunkenness it is all right & ought to be done. There are thousands more who should be served the same way. I always thought Douglas a honest man but the 2nd Department is a very temporary one and may fade.*

*I see by the papers that Rogers is promoted to my company. His commission has not yet come. He is a good soldier and I think will make a good Lieut. He has been a very deserving soldier and ought to have been promoted long since. I do so hope that we get another Battalion raised, that there will be more promotions hereabouts. There is a rumor that Fremont is in Halleck's place. If so, we shall lose Fish 'cause for being a great friend of his, he will get him a good position, I am sure. Not anything short of a Col will suit him and if this change is made, he is sure of it. He is smart and would fill any place he gets well. There is a great deal of Brass in him, sure, but mind, Brass, and selfishness is said to get along. Your open hearted free handed man never gets along. You must cultivate a little of both. I don't mean for you to be a low gravelly man, but close mouth and look out for #1.*

*Charlie*

---

**Comment:** Charlie (age twenty-seven) once again provided brotherly advice to Fred (twenty), this time on choosing a wife and on developing an effective attitude toward the world. Charlie implied that Fred was not yet tough enough, and needed to act more brazenly selfish. It could be inferred that this was how Charlie saw himself.

Charlie's reference to some "gay people" he had known in Chicago suggests the social high-life he led there after leaving Norwich, probably about 1856, and before going to the Rocky Mountains to prospect for gold in 1859-60.

By "[E]very thing lovely in Norwich..," Charlie was referring to his engagement to Georgia.

"Rogers" is Joab Rogers, from Norwich, who was promoted from first sergeant to lieutenant, and eventually to captain, in Company A. Hakes, also from Norwich, was an officer in the Eighteenth Connecticut Infantry. Major Fish did not go onto General Fremont's staff but remained commanding officer of the First Connecticut Cavalry.

---

*Camp Conn Cav*
*Stafford Court House*
*Jan 6 1863*

My dear Father,

Your letter of 31ˢᵗ was received, which was the first since we left Hall Farm. Today one from Georgia & Fred quite warmed me up. Fish is at Baltimore. He is not upon the staff yet, and is there trying to get us transferred, and to get for himself the Provost Marshal Generalship of the Department. He is really a great manager, indefatigable in pushing any thing through he attempts. He is very Brassy and it counts always. Again he is very smart, and long headed. The service allows of a man being taken from his command for staff officers, and that throws the command upon next in rank, though it does not help him any. Harland has been Brig Gen ever since he left Annapolis, and the 8ᵗʰ has been commanded by the Lt. Col. So it will be here: Fish gets Provost Marshal Gen., I command but get no increase of rank. If he can get a commission from the President as a staff officer and resigns here, it will help me. If another Battalion is raised, it will not release me from his command, for the two Battalions would then entitle him to a Lt Col commission. I hardly expect it will be possible to raise more than one Battalion. Still my relations with him are very pleasant, and he knows I understand him, and so we go on well together, and in fact he knows I am the only one on whom he can depend. I trust we can get the other Battalion. He is anxious that I should stand next to him as I am to go up, because our relations are cordial. And I don't think he will throw me off for any one else; I know he won't for any one here. Blakeslee is very underhanded and sly, and has tried several times to euchre him. And Niles he does not like. Marcy he is well disposed to but being the junior Capt he has but little chance of a Majority unless we get a Regiment. We have news that the law allowing us to vote has been annulled and was thrown out. I don't think Blakeslee will run again unless we vote. If he does, I think he will be defeated, though should there be a very strong effort made in the state he might be carried through. Still, my own impression is that he won't run.

As far as I am concerned, any Governor would be obliged to give me my promotion first as justice, being the ranking Capt., next influence, and then say nothing of the justice of the thing, though that won't count much.

I have no idea who will be the "peace man." Perhaps Symian will try again, and New York will <u>Wood</u> up the country for him. You may make up your mind there will be a change unless we vote and that is settled now.

There is little new in relation to Baltimore. Col Robinson 8ᵗʰ Ohio told me he saw Schenck & Fish in Washington on Friday and they told him the order was signed by Stanton for our transfer, and I am daily expecting to receive it, but up to *this hour it is not at hand. If it does arrive and we go there, I shall be home the last of the month. Of course I cannot leave until every thing is arranged in Baltimore & settled down to our regular work. There is a rumour that this corps (Seigle's) moves to Alexandria in four days. I have prospects of an offer being made to get us a Provost Guard for the Corps. But if we go to Baltimore, it will be of no use. It is very unpleasant being in this Corps; it is all Dutch and no one but them stand any chance. It is a real shame that a passive should have so much to say. Seigle is a good man and unbiased but then it is natural that the dutch should put forward in the regiments their own men. They are a very poor set, no understanding of our ways or customs, and then they put on airs because of their rank. We are always fighting. An American does any thing and they ignore it. A Dutch man moves and he is a big man. But they cannot hurt us much at headquarters for we are too well known. But it is not pleasant. Piatt John says there is a continued strife and bickering amongst the American & Dutch on the staff, and that it is a very unpleasant place indeed. They ought to put all the Dutch here and then at the front. The world won't miss one of them if killed, but they manage always to keep out of it some way. Seigle would make them fight if he was in a position.*

*Much Love, Georgia reports Eddy is at home in citizen clothes, inferences resignation,*

*Afft,*
*Charlie*

*I have been writing ever since day light on my many relatives & am very tired. Perhaps you cannot make all out. I have not a stamp and there is not one in the Battalion. I have sent to Washington for some. Excuse my franking this, but I can do no other way, unless a wait for stamps which will be here in three days.*

---

**Comment:** President Lincoln had put the Emancipation Proclamation into effect a week earlier, but Charlie made no comment about it. "Symian" was a derisive contemporary term for Abraham Lincoln's appearance.

"Wood" probably refers to Illinois Governor John Wood, a dependable Lincoln supporter. Charlie was already forecasting the 1864 presidential election, predicting that any "peace" candidate would defeat Lincoln unless soldiers voted.

His low opinion of Gen. Siegle's German-American (i. e., "Dutch") troops has some support among modern historians.[419]

---

Headquarters 1*ˢᵗ Battalion Conn Cavalry
Stafford Court House
Jan 9 1863

The Board of Survey consisting of Capt. Erastus Blakeslee Co. A, 1*ˢᵗ Batt. Conn Cavalry Volunteers, Lieut Wm. E. Morris, Co. D, 1*ˢᵗ Batt. C.C.V., and Lieut. Marcus Sterling, Co. D, 1*ˢᵗ Batt. C.C.V.,

Call by Special Order No. 19 from Headquarters Conn. Cav. Batt. to report upon the loss of three horses Co. B worn out upon the march from Hall Farm to Falmouth and upon scouting parties near there, and when one horse that died in camp.

Have in accordance with said order met and find that upon the 18th of Dec. 1862, the horse of Corporal Grannis gave out upon the road, in the march, and he was ordered to abandon it by his commanding officer.

Also that the horse of private Kemple of said Co. gave out and was abandoned per the order of his commander.

That upon the 22ⁿᵈ of Dec. the horse of private Marggroff gave out upon a scout and was abandoned.

That upon the 9th day of January the horse of Bugler Voltz died in camp of disease,

And that no blame is attached to the commanding officer of said Co.

E. Blakeslee Capt. Co A Conn Cav
William E. Morris Lieut Co. D Conn Cav
Marcus Sterling Lieut Co D Conn Cav

---

**Comment:** This report of damaged or destroyed horses was directed to Charlie, as the acting battalion commanding officer.

---

Head Quarters 1*ˢᵗ Regt. Conn. Cavalry
Dumphries, Va. January 13th, 1863

General Order
No. 1

I.   On and after date the rules of this Camp will be as follows:

| | |
|---|---|
| Reveille | 7 o'clock A.M. |
| Roll Call, feed grain | 7 ¾ A.M. |
| Feed Hay | 8 A.M. |
| Watering Call | 8 ¾ A.M. |

|            |           |
|------------|-----------|
| " "        | 4 P.M.    |
| Feed Grain | 4 ½ P.M.  |
| " Hay      | 5 ¼ P.M.  |
| Roll Call  | 6 P.M.    |

II. Absence from roll call will be reported by the orderly in writing to these Head Quarters.

III. Watering must be done at the call, and by the whole company under charge of the orderly Sergt., who will see that each horse is ridden by its owner or led by some member of the company. At watering call all the horses must be taken to water and no excuses will be accepted, if one is found in the street after the orderly shall have ordered the company to march. No horse except the orderlies' will be <u>saddled</u>. Any violation will be reported to Headquarters by the orderly.

IV. No soldier will be allowed to visit the town unless by permission of his company officer.

V. A morning report will be handed in at these Headquarters every morning. This, under the heading of <u>for Duty</u>, will contain all men who were in camp the night before, and who consequently will be subject for detail that day. Orderly, Quarter Master Sergeant, Commissary Sergt., saddler, wagoner, and artificer shall be reported on daily duty. All men on duty outside camp shall be reported "absent detached." All the horses will be reported present. On ration day the orderly will hand in to these Headquarters the number of in Camp and on duty, who shall draw rations here.

By order Chas. Farnsworth, Capt.
Comdg., 1st Regiment Conn. Cavalry
H. J. O. Walker, Lt. Adjt.


Head Quarters 1st Conn. Cavalry
Camp Chesebrough
Baltimore, Md. January 25th 1863

General Order
No. 2

1st. The name of this Camp will be Camp Chesebrough.

2nd. No enlisted man will be allowed outside of the Camp except by permission of their company commander, approved by the commander of the Camp.

3rd. From and after date the passes of this command will be issued as follows:

Orderly Sergeants of Companies, Q. M., and Commissary Sergeants will receive passes from their Co. Commander each 10 days, good for the next 10 days, *but will not be allowed to visit the City except by the Knowledge of their commander. One Non-Commissioned officer and (4) four men will be allowed passes from Camp from Guard Mounting in the morning until the time for Dress Parade, and one Non-Commissioned officer and three men will be allowed passes from 6 P.M. until 10 P.M.*

*Passes will be written in ink giving names and rank of man and time of ending, signed by Commander of Company and sent by orderly to Headquarters to be approved before 8 A.M. and 5 P.M. No other passes will be granted except as named above.*

*4$^{tb}$. The strictest military discipline will be enforced by the Commander of this Camp and be enforced upon all to do their duty and thereby render his and their position pleasant and easy.*

> *By order*
> *Chas. Farnsworth, Capt.*
> *Comdg. 1$^{st}$ Regiment Conn. Cavalry*

---

**Comment:** Neither the January 13 nor this order was in Charlie's handwriting.

---

*Baltimore, Md. Jan 26 1863*

*My dear Mother,*

*We are here at last, and awful busy. Every moment of my time is taken up. I went to the General once by his order. Except that, I have not left camp, & no prospect of it for a week.*

*Please send by express my white shirts, some 20 handkerchiefs, and my jewelry. Fred either has it or knows where it is. Lend me also 4 towels, 2 or 3 linen napkins, and my cheap silver ring. We have a prescribed table and live in style soon.*

*You may send me any clothing you think will work in.*

> *More when not busy,*
> *Afft,*
> *Charles*

---

**Comment:** The First Connecticut Cavalry, through the lobbying efforts of its commanding officer, Major Fish, had been reassigned to defensive and police duties in Baltimore, under the command of Provost General Schenck. Major Fish was appointed provost marshal, i.e., the chief military law enforcer, and Charlie was given command of the provost guard. Baltimore continued to be troubled by "secession elements."[20]

Charlie's arrival from Stafford on the 26th suggests that he and his troops had been scouting for General Burnside's infamous "Mud March," a failed attempt in late January to cross the Rappahannock River and outflank Lee's forces at Fredericksburg, Virginia. The tactic was called off on account of heavy rains on January 22. [421] Charlie was now clearly looking forward to a period of comfortable garrison life.

---

*Baltimore, Md. Jan 29 1863*

*My dear Mother,*

*I wrote you a line a few days since stating our arrival etc. I will acknowledge yours of 11th instant which was the first letter for a very long time, and nothing since. I do not speak because I feel neglected, for I know a Mother's life and your many duties. So though your letters come less frequent I shall not complain. We are pleasantly encamped but when I get my plans carried out I shall have a camp not equaled any where. I hope to commence tomorrow building barns and officers' quarters. But now we are in the midst of a most terrible storm of snow and rain, and it may hang on for several days. I saw cousin Harry yesterday in the street for a few moments, and shall call around soon. But I am very busy indeed. Men to fit out, camp to arrange, and discipline to enforce. For the men are very wild, just in from the field etc., and require watching.*

*Major Fish is the most indefatigable worker I ever saw. No other man in the army could have got us taken from the front and sent here. It is astonishing what he can do when he sets about it. He never fails. We are wholly indebted to him for our good place now, and I think we shall remain here for the war. The General is in excellent health and giving the very best satisfaction to the Union cause here. Fish makes a splendid Provost, and I am running the Provost Guard & Battalion. I sent three days since a request for office to be commissioner to Co. E, one of the new companies of our proposed regiment. I am anxious to hear from the Governor upon the matter, for if we once start it & this is the starting of it, we shall soon have enough recruits to give me a commission as Major. I don't see how he can delay commissioning a company long. Gen Schenck approved my request and forwarded it. I named Lt. Atwater as Captain.*

*You may dispose of the coat as you think best. It is too bad that I got no more wear out of it, but all the better for the man that gets it. I saw Perkins last summer at Middletown. He was in the regular army; met him again at battle of Cedar Mountain.*

*I wrote you for my shirts. I hardly know what clothes I have at home nowadays. But no doubt some that I could use. If not too much trouble, please let me know. I want white handkerchiefs very much; am entirely out. After we get settled down I* hope you will come on and see the Merediths, when we get our camp all arranged, which will take a month or so. But sometime next spring by May or April come on if possible. I am all alone now. The adjutant of Maj Fish has gone into his office down town so I have a little more work. But if they don't move us from here, I shall be able to make the thing work. I am very anxious to hear from my Co E. If the Governor refuses the commission until a full Company is raised it will be very long before we can get started as it is. I have organized it from what surplus recruits there are here, 25, and want the commission so as to make the start and show that we mean to have a regiment. I think he will do it. Atwater's father is from New Haven and a senator and from political reasons he may think it best to promote.

I do so hope he will be elected next spring for I am very sure of my highest aim under him. I see no reason why next Sept should not see me a <u>Lt Col</u>, and if not too much deceived, it will.

I saw "Falmuth Pawtucket" in the books at the hotel today. Suppose it is Clausen. I left my card for him and if it was him may hear from it. I never saw him as I remember. Oh how the wind howls and the hail strikes the glass to my quarters. A terrible sight! But we have seen the same many times on the front, and now we are very very comfortable.

I have not been out any but there are Union lectures here weekly and I shall make my debut next week.

Much Love

Afft

Charlie

---

**Comment:** The First Connecticut Cavalry was now performing military police duties in Baltimore, with Charlie in charge of the camp and guard, serving under the Baltimore provost marshal, Major Fish. The battalion had become independent, no longer performing scouting duties for various infantry units, and apparently stood a better chance of filling out to the regiment that had been authorized. Charlie noted that fellow officer Howell Atwater's father was a Connecticut state senator, who "for political reasons" might want to help double the size of the battalion. For the moment, Charlie seems to have had enough of the battlefront, and was happy to be patrolling in Baltimore.

"Cousin Harry" was probably Joseph H. Meredith, married to Charlie's cousin Mary Elizabeth Farnsworth, age thiry-six. Harry was from Winchester, Va., but was residing in Baltimore.[422]

---

Headquarters Conn Cav Feb 1 1863

My dear Mother,

Your letter of 27th instant was received yesterday and I will reply to it in detail.

The 3 handkerchiefs will be sufficient. You may send my night shirts, e.g., 3. Of under clothes I prefer [illegible]. The 3 you speak of buying are just what I want and will be enough with the worn ones I have. My life here is just as it would be at home. I am now gentleman soldier. I have or shall have (the building is building) 3 rooms and a kitchen, one bedroom, one parlor, or sitting room, & office. Bedstead, carpet, and every thing same as at home. Sheets, pillow cases and carpet I will send for when I get bed and room completed and up, as I know not the width needed. The dark coat, give away. I am having new clothes made here. I find visiting is be the order of the day. Very fashionable city & staff officers made much of. <u>So, Provost Marshal Staff, General's body guard etc.</u>

Union assemblies every week. Tickets for season $25—very select. Complimentary tickets issued to General & staff. <u>I am in on it.</u> I made my debut this PM at Mrs. Mason's, a very fashionable lady, rich etc., has a marriageable daughter. Next Friday is the Assembly when I shall see all there is. Intended calling at Mary's but it commenced raining and skipped it. Shall go down again for a day. Have just sent 1 Capt & 2 Lieut & 40 men by steamer down the Bay after some rebs that burned a sloop. It is intended as a surprise. So you see the men are not out of service even here. We must have a regiment. The General is high in our praise here. The fact of our coming from the front rather created a reputation of something grand. But a dirtier, poor, ravenous set never tread the city than we were when we came in. It took people down. Right away, coming out, with new clothes and look fine. Our horses are improving very rapidly indeed, and people speak very well of us. My power over men in keeping them in camp and having no guard is the surprise of all. How do you do it says one Col? What a wonder we never had a regiment here before without a guard around camp, says a citizen. How is it done? By discipline; say you will punish if they do wrong and then give the fits if you catch them. I sent one man to work on stone work for the government with ball & chain for a week, for disobeying an order.

Most officers are afraid of their men, fear they must be popular, so are mild. Hence, results like the 26th in Norwich. I bet today I am better loved than that Col. Well. The General told somebody who asked about us, "Those Conn. boys are the smartest in the service. They have saved me more than once. My own life once, and I can depend upon them."

When the rebs made their last raid, he was in Philadelphia. Report came to him that they had entered Maryland. Fish was here alone. The telegraph operator at Phil. could not send cypher and Fish dared not telegraph in full. What to do was the question, and with his usual go-ahead, he assumed Schenck's place and ran the machine, ordered regiment & Battery forward. And when Schenck returned, was very highly complimented by him. He had in fact saved Schenck, for if any thing had gone wrong he would have lost much, in the eyes of all. Of course, that did not lessen the celeb in the eyes of the <u>Hero</u>.

I am getting to write awfully, and must stop this lawyer style or I shall be fit for nothing.

Much Love,<br>Charles

---

**Comment:** Only a week into garrison duty, Charlie had ordered the battalion to rebuild a camp previously occupied by others. According to Erastus Blakeslee's *Official History*, "Captain Farnsworth had charge of the camp. Under his energetic lead the men rebuilt the barracks and erected officers' quarters, paved the company streets with brick, and graded and turfed the ground between. Barns were also built and a hospital and chapel."

The "General" was probably Schenck. As evidenced by mention of the recent Confederate raid and the burning of a sloop in the Chesapeake Bay, the federal government felt vulnerable in Baltimore.

Charlie shows his strict command style here by putting a disobedient soldier in ball and chain for a week. In a slight contradiction, he criticized other officers for wanting to be popular with their men, while bragging that he was well-loved.

The "Union assemblies" were social events intended to lift morale and to raise funds for the war effort from the well-to-do. Charlie seemed pleased to get a ticket to attend.

A note after the second paragraph reads "mother's underscoring," but seems to be in Charlie's handwriting.

---

Baltimore Feb 3<sup>rd</sup> 1863

My dear Mother,

Letter of the 1<sup>st</sup> came today and as it is for immediate answer will clear up the questions tonight. Of outside shirts I am well supplied, and shall only wear occasionally new togs. I intend to call at Mary's tomorrow if possible, but I can hardly leave camp for an hour, as there is no one but Blakeslee to fall back upon and as Pope said of Seigle, he is unreliable. Today I received Mary H. card of address. Will call of course. I am having clothes made here, and my outfit will cost me full $100. Two suits of new, except uniform coat, and boots, etc. My old ones were hardly fit for this post. And every one is coming out new and clean. Quite a pretty trade *for one tailor. 15 officers each full suits. I think I received 6 [illegible] but am not sure as they are distributed.*

*Much Love*
*Charlie*

---

**Comment:** Charlie was devoting a lot of time and attention to getting properly outfitted for his garrison duty, which was a far cry from life in the field.

The criticism of Captain Erastus Blakeslee as "unreliable" is interesting. Blakeslee was later promoted to bevet brigadier general, became an ordained minister after the war, and wrote the First Connecticut Cavalry's official history, extolling Charlie for his leadership in Baltimore. Blakeslee might not have been so complimentary if he had known what Charlie had written about him.

---

*Baltimore Feb 3rd 1863*

*My dear Fred,*

*Your letter of 31st ultimate came duly to this place. I think the letter of 10th ultimate came and was unanswered. As I never keep letters in the field I cannot now tell. We are pleasantly located, and when our barracks are finished there won't be any thing equal to it. I have planned them myself and think they will fill the bill, and make very pleasant abodes for the summer. Our quarters are splendid, compared with tented fields. I hardly know whether I shall come home this winter or not, but think perhaps it best be deferred until May or June. I am so busy and every thing comes on me, and I must be here until my camp is arranged, which will take two months, and then if possible shall come.*

*Capt. Middlebrook has not been here and there is little matter whether he comes or not. You néed not send the ring. What I want is studs & buttons. But send the letters sure.*

*There is little doubt about the kind wishes of Blakeslee, and no one pictures him as I can. My letters are not severe and he cannot complain of one. We are having fair times here, expensive as my bill for clothes. Boots & horse trimmings reaches $150, but it was a complete outfit new. Parties are the order of the day. Union people make much of soldiers and give parties in opposition to secesh. They have balls and parties where the ladies wear secesh flags on their bosoms. Union people are of course excluded. Oh! there is lots of fun here. I have made several calls since my arrival and have the prospect of much amusement for the spring, though we came late as Lent approaches.*

*I am much in the hope the increase of our Battalion will go through. I have nominated Lieut Atwater for Capt. Co. E to the Governor. But the commission does not come. I fear he is not friendly to the move. Still I hope for the best. If I can get it once started I can send it through, somehow.*

*Now once for all stop talking about the army. Don't even think of it. You are ten times better off out of it, and once in it, there is no let up. If the family cannot afford the expense, why, quit, but don't try the army.*

*Paymaster expected here tomorrow and then for 5 months' pay.*

*Denny came back on the 1ˢᵗ and I am once more at home. I have two horses to sell and shall buy a buggy for my other, which is a fine pony, and then with a saddle here I am outfitted for Baltimore.*

> *Much Love to all from*
> *Charlie*

---

**Comment:** His family appears to have chided him for criticizing Blakeslee, but Charlie wouldn't yield.

Charlie was enjoying the political tumult between the Union and "secesh" factions in Baltimore as he watched it played out in genteel society. His enthusiasm for military life was ebbing, however, and he cautioned younger brother, Fred, a twenty-year-old student at Yale, not to enlist, even if financial constraints forced him to drop out of college.

Charlie again expressed his disdain for Captain Middlebrook, who had resigned after Charlie successfully challenged his right as senior captain to assume command of the battalion when Major Lyon was forced out.[423]

---

> *Baltimore Feb 11 1863*

*My dear Mother,*

*Amidst the many every-hour duties of camp, days slip by and we neglect our own desires and wishes. I do not think I have written since the assembly. I went to it and had a real nice time. Cousins Harry & Mary were there; it was the first meeting. I called Sunday and had a pleasant time. They go to Boston this week. I met Miss Hall, whose father knows you all. He left Norwich some years since. A pleasant sweet girl, and they say he is very rich. He is a government contractor. I called at Mrs. Wilson's, a very pleasant, dashing lady whose husband lives in New York, and she here, only this year married. One of those marriages of convenience. She is rich in her own name, and lives splendidly, and keeps open house to Union folks. A sweet woman, but I suppose though married, not <u>mated</u>. She lives with her parents, or they with her. Also, a sister, a Mrs. Thomas, just married.*

*Governor Buckingham came into camp last evening very unexpectedly enroute to Washington. He only stayed a very few moments. I went to town with him. I do* hope he will be elected again. I wish you would send me Bulletins. Say every two days send two half sheets, one paper it would make. I like to keep posted on the "Military Item." If we don't see them every day, we lose our record.

I want to see all mention of the Cavalry. I sent an item a few days since & Bromley said he would stir up a little for us. Letters of 3rd & 2nd received. Bundle came safe. What does the letter on left of Mrs. D's invitation mean? Mr. Carver is well. I see him every day. A real fine fellow; one who always does his duty and will stand well. Mike was a splendid fellow, and a great Corpl. I receive regular letters from Meriden, and if it lays with me alone there will never be any break. Still I sometimes think I hardly deserve so fine a wife.

Denny came back the 1st. He said I saved his life last summer and I was the only man he would have come back to. He is a fine fellow & think dearest of us all. Old Mana & Missus & gray Mane Fred.

> Much Love,
> Charles

---

**Comment:** The Union assemblies were obviously very pleasant social events.

The "cousins" were probably Mary Elizabeth Farnsworth, age thirty-six, and Amos Henry Farnsworth, age thirty-seven.

"Carver" was Private Thomas Carver of Norwich, whose older brother Corporal Michael Carver had been ambushed and killed in January. Charlie probably wanted this compliment about Thomas to be passed along to comfort the grieving Carver family in Norwich.

Governor Buckingham was re-elected and served as governor of Connecticut until 1866. Three years later, he was elected to the U. S. Senate.

"Denny" was the "contraband" working as Charlie's occasional personal servant; he contracted typhoid fever, recovered with Charlie's care for him, and then left his service and went to Wheeling, Virginia, for four months. His devotion to Charlie apparently brought him back.

---

> Camp Conn Cav
> Baltimore March 2 1863

My dear Mother,

Your letter of 17th 1863 is before me. It cannot be that I have not written you since that date. If so, shame on me. Well, for the past two weeks I have been busy as usual. Between calls and camp duty, my time has been well employed.

I was present and saw Commander Wadhaer blown up. It was awful to relate. I called upon Miss Hempstead and had a very nice call. Attended a party at

*Mrs. Sherman's, at which by her invitation I accompanied Miss Higg in her own carriage. Called on Cousin Mary. Attended two Sociables and had glorious times. Made a dozen calls, and three to make. Met Wm. Cencern [spelling uncertain] at the hotel. Saw Morgan, Smith, Ely & Balou at the Easter House. Dined at Mrs. Wilson's and with Col. Fish, and other things in proportion. You can judge whether a soldier with all other duties is not prepared to accomplish all this. When you send bundles by Express after directing to me, enclose in wrapper and direct it to Lt Col W.S. Fish, Provost Marshall, Baltimore, Md., and it will not cost any thing as his bundles come free. Please send me a pair of slippers.*

*Denny left me in Oct and went to Wheeling. Returned Feb 1 1863. He is doing well, and says he is very contented with me.*

*Much Love,*

*Affectionate son, Charles*

*I send two "Cense" for Album.*

---

**Comment:** Charlie maintained a busy social calendar, doubtless as part of his provost duties to boost Union morale and to check on dissidents.

An archaic meaning of "cense" is "rank, rating," i.e., insignia.

---

*Head Quarters 1ˢᵗ Conn. Cavalry*

*Camp Chesebrough*

*Baltimore, Md. March 9ᵗʰ 1863*

*General Order*

*No. 6*

*The following rules and regulations will govern and be enforced in the companies comprising the 1ˢᵗ Regiment Conn. Cavalry:*

*1ˢᵗ. The Orderly, Commissary, Quarter-Master, and ranking Sergts. will occupy the 1ˢᵗ quarters on the right of their company streets. The 4 other Sergts., the opposite ones. Each Corpl. will have apportioned to him a room which will be occupied by his squad. The last room on the line of quarters upon the left will be occupied as the cook house, the opposite ones as a company wash room.*

*2ⁿᵈ. The bunks will be numbered in regular order through the barracks, commencing on the right and each man will be given a number, which number will include his bunk, arms, [illegible], rack, bit pin, bridle pin, shelf, stall for horse and any article of Company property he may receive. This number will in no case be changed, and moving from one mess to another is forbidden.*

*3ʳᵈ. The name and number of each member of each squad will be displayed upon the outside of the building.*

*4ᵗʰ. Any alterations of, or in, the barracks is forbidden, unless first sanctioned by the Comdg. Officer.*

*5ᵗʰ. The utmost regularity will be observed in executing all orders issued from the Headquarters, and all orders issued must be enforced by Company officers, and all delinquents reported to the Commanding Officer, who pledges himself to see enforced all rules made. Non-Commissioned officers must perform their regular duties in accordance with orders issued to them, and they are expected to be well posted up on their duties as laid down in Army Regulations, copies of which will be distributed in each Company.*

*6ᵗʰ. From and after date this Camp will be called Camp Chesebrough.*

*By Order*
*Charles Farnsworth, Major*
*Comdg. 1ˢᵗ Conn. Cavalry*

---

**Comment:** This is a good example of Charlie's insistence on strict attention to military order in the camp, which was named for Lieutenant Colonel William G. Chesebrough, assistant adjutant of the Eleventh Maryland Infantry Regiment. Why he got the honor is unknown.

---

*Inspection Report of Horses, 1ˢᵗ Conn Cavalry*
*Pursuant to Special Order No. 56*
*Middle Department, 8ᵗʰ Army Corps*
*Maj.Genl. R. C. Schenck, Commanding*
*Baltimore, Md. March 9ᵗʰ 1863*

*Inventory and Inspection Report of Horses in the hands of Capt. Chas. Farnsworth, comdg. 1ˢᵗ Batt. Conn. Cavalry at Camp Carrol Baltimore, Md., inspected by Maj. A. B. Smith, 150ᵗʰ Regt. New York Volunteers, 9ᵗʰ day of March 1863, pursuant to Special Order No. 56, Middle Department 8ᵗʰ Army Corps. Dated Baltimore, Md., February 27ᵗʰ 1863.*

| INVENTORY | | | INSPECTOR'S REPORT | |
|---|---|---|---|---|
| NO. ARTICLES DISPOSITION | HOW LONG IN POSSESSION | IN USE | CONDITION | |
| 1. Iron Grey Horse | 3 4/5 mos. | 2 ½ mos. | Too young, stumbles, weak back, unfit for cav. service | Recd turnover to Q.M. for Recuperation |
| 2. Bay Horse | 3 4/5 mos | 2 ½ mos. | Broken down, unfit | " |
| 3. Chestnut Horse | 3 4/5 mos | 2 ½ mos. | Same | " |
| 4. Brown Horse ........... | 3 4/5 mos | 2 ½ mos. | Old, lame, worthless | Recd. to be Sold at public auction |
| 25. Bay Mare Horse ........... | " | " | Foundered | Recd. use as a team horse |
| 42. Black Horse ........... | " | " | Broken down, kidney disease | Recd. sold at public auction |
| 88. Black Horse | " | " | Broken down, may recruit | Recd. turn to Q.M. to recuperate |

| | |
|---|---|
| I certify that the inventory is correct. /s/ Chas. Farnsworth Capt. Comdg. 1ˢᵗ Reg. Conn. Cav. | I certify that I have examined each article in the above inventory, and that its condition is as above stated. /s/ A. B. Smith Maj. 150ᵗᵇ Regt., N.Y.I.V. |

**Comment:** This is a portion of the inspection report. The complete document listed a total of eighty-eight horses that were unfit for further cavalry service.

*Baltimore Md. March 10 1863*

My dear Father,

 Last evening I spent with a party of ladies & gents at Cousin Harry's. We had a pleasant time and a good supper. Mary as usual lively. She is as popular as can be with every one that I have met who number her as a friend.

 Next Friday is the last of our sociables. They have been real splendid. I was at the Masons Sunday and enjoyed myself as usual. If I was a single man, there is no telling what would happen amongst these Baltimore people. The girls are splendid, and as for the papas, they are very indulgent indeed.

 Cousin Walter is expected here soon. We are during along slow with our barracks. Rainy weather and other drawbacks come in and keep us back.

 I saw Dr, Wilson's son in the street today. He said he was going home soon and offered to take any parcels. But not having any thing to send I could not accommodate.

 Gen Schenck is a trump & you can reckon the Uncommissioned people here back him up strong. Oh, that Benny F. and Rob. C. was inplaced. Abraham Lincoln would not as soon show the rebs where we stand. But no, we are, I fear, numbered.

 We had lots of fun here on the holding of the Medical College and Conn. Sabres show the secesh what they meant.

 I am not feeling well to day owing to late hours and supper last night.

    *Much Love*
    *Charles*

---

**Comment:** "During" is an obsolete form of "enduring." A "trump" is a "dependable and exemplary individual." "Secesh" is slang for "secessionists."

 Engaged to be married, Charlie no longer considered himself a "single man" for purposes of the Baltimore social whirl.

 "Cousin Walter" was Walter Loring Farnsworth, age eighteen, who would die in 1866 of what was called "brain fever."

 "Benny F. and Rob. C." refer to Generals Benjamin F. Banks and Robert C. Schenck, Charlie's favorite commanders, whom he thinks should be running the army. Once again, Charlie expressed his impatience with Lincoln's conduct of the war.

---

*Head Quarters 1ˢᵗ Conn. Cavalry*
*Camp Chesebrough, Baltimore, Md., March 10ᵗʰ, 1863*

General Order No. 7

 1ˢᵗ. It shall be the duty of the orderly Sergeant to attend and call all roll calls, assemble the Co. for drill and duty, accompany it to water and exercise a general superintendence over the cleanliness of the street, quarters, and stables. In his absence this duty shall fall upon the ranking Sergt. The ranking Sergeant will attend the Hospital call.

2nd. Each Corporal shall be held responsible for the conduct and character of his squad. He will see that all rules and regulations issued in General Orders are carried out, and any want of attention on his part will be considered sufficient to deprive him of rank.

3rd. Every Soldier is expected to willingly and cheerfully perform all duty, and will be held accountable for any neglect of same. Upon the first sound of the Bugle all men will turn out and commanders of squads will see to it that all their squad mess get up. Upon the sound for roll call the men will assemble in their streets quietly. The men will form in two ranks, Corporals upon the right and left, Sergts. two paces in rear of right. Farriers, saddler, and Bugler two paces in the rear of the left. Officers in front and facing the Co. The Orderly will dress the ranks, command parade rest and call the roll. No noise or talking must be allowed and any disturbance promptly reported. Upon all stable calls the Companies will fall in, in their streets and be marched to the stables. Each Corporal will be held responsible for the appearance of the horse and stalls of his squad. He will see that the horses are cleaned and the stables kept in good order. Each Corporal will see that his quarters are in good order before 9 A.M. each day. Beds made, quarters swept, and street cleaned. He will report any who are [on] other duty in person or in barracks.

In going to and from water the orderly sergeant will see that the men conduct themselves orderly and no running of horses is allowed. Every man will ride his own horse and only those will be fed whose owner is upon duty or sick and excused by the Surgeon which renders it impossible for him to go. Upon the return from water the stables will be chained and locked and no one will be allowed to enter them except by written permission from the Commanders. The saddle of each enlisted man will be kept in the stable, a pin being placed there for that purpose. The bridle will be kept in quarters, and care will be taken that the Bitts and buckles are kept polished.

Saddles must be kept clean, and when ever used in muddy weather will be washed and brushed, the straps always rolled up and fastened.

> By Order
> Charles Farnsworth, Major
> Comdg. 1st Conn. Cavalry

---

**Comment:** Another example of Charlie's rigid rules in camp, this one mainly concerned with the care and feeding of the horses.

---

*Headquarters 1ˢᵗ Regt. Conn. Cavalry*
*Camp Chesebrough*
*Baltimore, Md. March 15ᵗʰ 1863*

*General Order No. 8*

*It having pleased God to remove from our midst Capt. A. H. Niles, we bow in reverence before him, feeling that our Brother in arms who during the past year has been actually engaged in the putting down of the rebellion, and though he has passed unharmed through many a conflict, in yielding to the last Conquerer, has enlisted in the army of the great Captain of our salvation and entered upon quarters not made by hands, eternal in the heavens. In testimony of our respect for the deceased, the colors of this encampment will fly at ½ mast during the day, and the Regiment will attend the funeral this afternoon at 6 P.M. The usual badge of mourning will be worn by the officers of the Regiment for the period of 30 days.*

*By Command of*
*-signed-    Charles Farnsworth, Major*
*Comdg. 1ˢᵗ Regt. Conn. Cavalry*

---

**Comment:** Captain Albert H. Niles, of Hartford, died of typhoid fever on March 15. He was Charlie's good friend and cabin-mate.

---

*Baltimore Md. Mar 16 1863*

*My dear Father,*

*I have not received anything from home for sometime but suppose you are all very busy and do not write. I have been down with a bilious attack and have not got over it yet. I don't feel first rate any way but hope to come out all right.*

*The sudden death of Capt. Niles has made me feel unusual bad. He was one of our (Atwater & self) mess, we three having been together for some time. He was a very gentlemanly and friendly officer. His seat is now vacant, but I feel that he has entered upon better quarters in the mansions above. He died very suddenly indeed. He was buried with Military honors yesterday. I walked through the snow over five miles, and taken all the circumstances in consideration am not so well for it. The shock of his death was very great for Saturday he was pronounced better. Sunday 8 a.m. he was dead. He was first taken with a stoppage, but came out of it. Still he did not recover, and was miserable for a long time, then pronounced on the gain. And six hours after, he was told he could not live 12 hours.*

*His father and two sisters, their husbands and an out-brother were here. He was abroad & acquainted with Walter in Paris.*

*I was invited to dine at Mary's yesterday, but failed to attend.*

*There is a gradually tightening up of the bolts of the machine nowadays, and I think the immediate fear of a revolution is past. Still a dictator would be supported by the army, and by all loyal people, if he prosecuted the war. The only trouble with A.L. is he has no firmness. If he will stand by his order in relation to deserters, he will receive the thanks of all good men in the army, but I fear it is all splurge.*

*Nothing new here.*

> *Please send Bulletins.*
> *Afft Charlie*

---

**Comment:** Although clearly shaken by the unexpected death of his friend Captain Niles, and not feeling well himself, Charlie still found the energy to argue for a dictator to prosecute the war. He was convinced (correctly, as it turned out) that Lincoln ("A.L.") would not enforce his edict that deserters would be hanged.

---

> *Headquarters 1ˢᵗ Reg. Conn. Cavalry*
> *Camp Chesebrough*
> *Baltimore Mar 27/63*

*Colonel:*

*I have the honor to apply for a leave of absence for ten days from March 30ᵗʰ 1863 for the following reasons.*

*A large number of furloughs will be granted to my command during the time asked for, which will render the care of my Regiment less arduous, and it can be easily performed by the efficient officers left in command.*

*And believing that, though we soldiers have drawn the sword for the defence of our Constitution & our national honor, still we may fight a great battle and achieve a great moral victory by the harmless but all powerful ballot. I desire to deposit one, upon the 1ˢᵗ Monday in April in opposition to the "Copperheads" & enemies in the rear whose camp fires are burning upon the soil of free Connecticut.*

> *I am very Respt your Ob Servant*
> *Chas. Farnsworth*
> *Maj. Com. 1ˢᵗ Reg. C.C.V.*
> *Lt. Col. W. H. Chesebrough*

---

**Comment:** Charlie's request for leave was granted, according to a note in his military records. He returned to Norwich, where he undoubtedly voted for Governor Buckingham, a Lincoln Republican, who won re-election.

---

Baltimore April 16 1863

My dear Mother,

I have failed to write you since my return but why I cannot say, though of a truth, I have been very busy indeed, and today have felt far from well. My time has been much taken up. One day I dined at Harry's and it took all day. They are all well and Mary says "I do hope your Mother will come on with Fred; we shall be so glad to see her." They are very pleasant indeed and it were impossible for one to show more attention than they to me. We have had some trouble in regard to organizing the regiment, and whether the section in the Conscription Act which makes all cavalry of less than one half a regiment consolidated will affect us remains to be seen. Some claim one way, some another. I wish Wilson was here; he could tell.

The day of my return Mary gave a large and grand party to the Gen and staff. Invitation was left for me, but owing to circumstances I did not go. They all speak of it as splendid.

Should Fred leave after this is received, send my _spats_ which is all I left this time. If not, send by Express.

Much Love from
Charlie

---

**Comment:** Charlie worried that if the battalion did not quickly fill out to its authorized regimental size it might be consolidated with another battalion, and thereby lose its cherished identity.

Baltimore now seemed so secure that his cousin Mary was urging a visit by Charlie's mother, Eunice, and younger brother Fred, age twenty, a student at Yale.

---

### List of Quarter Master's Property received

**by** LT. COLONEL J. L. DONALDSON, quarter master U. S. Army, from Major Chas. Farnsworth, Comdg. 1st Reg. Conn. Cavalry at Baltimore, Md. on the 27th day of April 1863:

| Number or Quantity | Articles | Condition/Remarks |
| --- | --- | --- |
| 55 Fifty five | Horses | Condemned, turned over to recover |
| 43 Forty three | Halters | Good, been used. |

**I Certify** that I have this day received from Major Charles Farnsworth, Comdg. 1st Reg. Conn. Cavry., the articles specified in the foregoing list.

J. L. Donaldson
Lt. Col. & Q. M.

**Comment:** This document, from Charlie's official military file, shows how frequently his battalion used up its horses.

> *Headquarters, 1ˢᵗ Reg. Conn. Cavalry*
> *Camp Chesebrough*
> *April 30ᵗʰ, 1863*

General Order
No. 9

*From this date untill further orders 1 Non-Com Officer and 3 men from each company will be granted passes from 8 A.M. until 4 A.M., and 1 Non com and 2 men from 6 P.M. untill midnight, or in certain cases untill morning roll call. Under no case will more passes be granted. All passes granted will be returned to the Orderly who will hand them in to these headquarters each morning, and any man failing to return his pass will meet punishment.*

*The Corporal or private in charge of each squad will report each morning any member of his squad not in quarters at and after 8 A.M. to the Orderly Sergt., who unless passes have been granted to them, will report the same to the commanding officer of the regiment. A commander of a squad failing to so report will upon being found out, if a Non Com Officer be reduced, if a private confined and punished.*

*The limits of this camp will comprise the grounds bounded by the railroads upon the north and west, and a line drawn from the crossing below the Q. M. Dept. south to include the Tavern and west in rear of the barns to the railroad. And in future during the day or night any enlisted man found outside the limits of this camp, as so described without a pass will be severely punished.*

*These rules being fairly laid down will be strictly enforced.*

> *By Command of*

C.S.K. [a clerk-Ed.]      -signed-     *Charles Farnsworth, Major*

E.B. [Erastus Blakeslee, Capt.-Ed.]     *Comdg. 1ˢᵗ Regt. Conn. Cavalry*

**Comment:** Yet another example of Charlie's precise orders to maintain strict order in camp. The disciplined troops built or improved the camp's facilities, including a chapel, new barracks with kitchens, streets paved with bricks, horse barns, and landscaping.[424]

## List of Quarter Master's Property received

**by** LT. COL. J. L. DONALDSON, *quarter master U. S. Army,
from Major Charles Farnsworth, Comdg. 1ˢᵗ Conn. Cav'y., at
Baltimore, Md., on the 1ˢᵗ day of May 1863:*

| Number of Quantity | Articles | Cost When New | Condition/Remarks |
|---|---|---|---|
| 24-Twenty four | Horses | Unknown | Condemned |
| 5-Five | Halters | Unknown | Worn |

**I Certify** *that I have this day received from Major Charles Farnsworth, Comdg.
1ˢᵗ Conn. Cavy., the articles specified in the foregoing list.*

J. L. Donaldson

Lt. Col. & Q. M.

Camp Chesebrough

Baltimore, Md. May 4 1863

Dear Mother,

Your letter of 2ⁿᵈ with enclosures came duly. I did not intend to have the amount returned, and am sorry you sent it. I am very glad he had so fine a time whilst in Philadelphia and wish I could feel he enjoyed himself whilst here. But he has got one great thing to learn, and will only learn it by bitter experience. That is not to be so over-expectant, and to be contented with life as it comes. I have learned by some very bitter pills, but I took them, and at the present time there is not a person who takes things as they come more than I do. Fred will have many a rough corner rounded before he does.

I am very glad you are going to Meriden for a visit. You will find them real pleasant people, and will have a good time. I owe Miss P a letter, as I promised her that in the future I would write her at least once a month. Georgia is a very pleasant letter writer and I do my best and some young ladies used to say that I could get up a heavy love letter, but those days are past. I have given up the sentiments of two souls with but a single thought and the terrible romance of the thing, and after all think that the single, free, and easy life of a Bachelor of 28 about the best of it.

Fred said Uncle M was not as well as usual. Is it so? And is he going down gradually?

Tell Fred that relying upon his judgment in the horse matter, I shall not send the "cow" home. It is lucky for my reputation that the horseman of the family happened around just as I had selected a piece of stock, and condemned it for family

218

use. But I find that the "cow" will bring a good deal of money, but would never "do for Father to drive." As he has such splendid stock on hand, my horse would shame the family. Some funny fellows!

I have been to the Opera for the past three evenings. Splendid house. One night with Mrs. Wilson, one with Miss Mason. Fred knew them. Took tea at Mary's Sunday, who seems very much disappointed that you have not come on. I said you would no doubt prefer fall or winter to go south.

Much Love
from your son
Charles

---

**Comment:** At Charlie's invitation, younger brother Fred, age twenty, had come to Camp Chesebrough for a visit, but he was not the model guest, perhaps expecting too much "action" in garrison life. Charlie seems to have cooled on his plans to marry Georgia, and was paying ever greater attention to the Baltimore ladies. His social life in Baltimore had now expanded to include regular attendance at the opera.

Once again, Charlie had planned to send home a horse and then sarcastically deferred to his younger brother's judgment of the horse's poor quality.

---

Baltimore May 8th 1863

My dear Mother,

Your letter of the 5th came today and as it is raining splendidly I will endeavor to answer it immediately. It has rained here nearly all the time for four days. I have not been off camp since Saturday when I went down to the Opera, and from appearances, shall not for two days to come. This storm which is always on hand when our army moves has ruined Hooker's plans, but there is not one half the cry over his 10,000 killed that there was over Burnsides, and yet he failed. Whereas Burnsides would not, if such men as H. Frank and hundreds of Brig Gens had done their duty. Conn has suffered again in the 17th & 20th which is all there is there at present.

I answered your letter enclosing money immediately. As to the ticket, please do not send any money, for it did not cost me that, though it was the price of the tickets, and they were scarce at that. So don't send any thing. And even if it had, I like to spend for Fred, and better there than for some foolishness or other. I can stand all he cost me

I am sorry that Fred was so tired out with his journey, but perhaps it showed a good time. I supposed from what he said that he was against taking a trunk, therefore was short of clothes. But after he has traveled as long as I have (if he learns by experience like the present) he will take a trunk, for they cost no more

219

& are much less trouble than a half team, a valise. Live & learn. I think his stay would have been longer and he would have felt better had he been able to appear in full dress at the ball. But sensitive as he is to such things, it wore upon him. I was very sorry but did the best I knew how towards rigging him out.

A letter from Georgia saying you are expected 3ʳᵈ week in June. I trust your teeth will not interfere with your enjoyment this summer.

My gloves are certainly missing and I don't find any left in their place. I rather suspected him, after giving Denny a blessing for his carelessness in the matter. He can keep them if they fit. I have only used them a few times.

Little news of importance here save the exciting "war news."

We hope for the best, but it looks dark at times. Though I believe Hooker is a good general and has a fine army, if Abe Lincoln will stand up to the rack and hold men and officers to their duty, we will come out all right.

There is no city news of interest.

Harry & Mary are well. I took tea there Sunday last.

AfftSon

Charles

---

**Comment:** The Union had suffered a disastrous loss at Chancellorsville, Virginia a few days earlier when Stonewall Jackson's Confederate army outflanked General Joseph Hooker's troops, driving them back and inflicting seventeen thousand casualties.[425] Charlie thought that Hooker's mistakes were worse than General Burnside's at Fredericksburg, but that Hooker was getting off with less criticism. Nevertheless, Charlie retained his confidence in Hooker. Charlie was optimistic, even in those "dark times," but thought that Lincoln needed to "stand up to the rack," i.e., endure the mental stress of command, and to enforce military discipline.

Charlie tellingly devoted substantial space to explaining that if Fred had brought a proper wardrobe he would have enjoyed Baltimore society life more. Fred inadvertently took home a pair of Charlie's new dress gloves, the absence of which was initially blamed on the personal servant Denny, who was given an undeserved "blessing," i.e., scolding.

---

May 26 1863

Dear Mother,

Bundle came last evening. Carpet suite is down and curtains up.

Well,

Love

Charlie

**Comment:** Carpet and curtains for the officers' quarters! Very swank.

*Headquarters 1ˢᵗ Reg. Conn Cav*
*Camp Chesebrough*
*Baltimore June 10 1863*

*My dear Mother,*

*Your letter came this evening and just as I sit down to answer it, Denny comes in to remove white counterpanes from bed and prepare my resting place for the night. Well, I suppose he wants to go to bed, as has got to go to market tomorrow at 4 a.m. to buy 15 quarts strawberries. Now of course you will wonder what we, Capt. Goodwin & wife, self & Rodger are going to do with that number of strawberries. Well, Gen Schenck and a party of 40 ladies & gents are coming out here tomorrow morn to review and inspect my camp, and we prepare. Ice cream, strawberries, cake, pickled oysters, lemonade, & wine for a refresher. And so off he must go tomorrow early to have them picked over & culled ere* <u>10 a.m.</u>

*We are expecting grand times here tomorrow. Our men look fine, our camp splendid, and we prepare to use the General well and see if we can't get rid of a notion he has that the Government should not support 4 Companies here, when two are enough. Therefore send two away to Winchester. But though there is some talk of our again taking ground rent-free in Old Virginia, and a blanket instead of a mattress, still we hope to be retained here until we are a regiment, or at least until we get six full companies. I will write you at length in relation to tomorrow.*

*The Bulletins come regularly and much obliged. My quarters are fine and I am content to serve the Reg. for life if kept here. But I don't want to go to the front but can't resign now when so summoned and no way if we should go.*

*The photograph is Atwater since his engagement. I don't much wonder you don't know it. He is fine looking.*

*I saw Mr. Gilman's death in the papers. It is sometimes strange how a family will pass away so near to each other. Mr. Gilman was a very fine man indeed. Does he leave much property?*

*I don't like my photograph but have given them all away to persons whom I cared little for. I will have some new ones taken here. No one liked them, and I was lucky to get rid of them. If I get a good one I will send you some.*

*The Merediths go north 1ˢᵗ of July. They are expected here tomorrow. They send love whenever I see them.*

*Gen Tyler & Co. are here. They must enjoy Schenck and staff. They love each other so much.*

*Fish will remain here a Marshall even should we go, which I trust is rumour. I shall be sorry if we do that you did not come down with Fred in the Spring. It is Hot here now, I tell you.*

> *Much Love*
> *Charles*

---

**Comment:** Charlie had grown accustomed to garrison duty and to Baltimore social life. He happily prepared for the "review" of his camp by the provost general and commanding officer of the Middle Military Department, Robert C. Schenck, and he intended to ply the general and guests with sweet desserts in hopes of gaining their support for a full regiment. The General Tyler who was General Schenck's guest was probably Daniel Tyler, former president of the Norwich & Worcester Railroad.

Charlie predicted that one-half of the battalion would be sent back to the front but frankly admitted "I don't want to go." Three weeks later he would be sent, and he went happily.

---

> *Baltimore June 20 1863*

*My dear Mother,*

*Your letter of 19ᵗʰ just received. We are all in a foolish excitement over the approach of a "baggage train," [illegible] the General & staff. There is no danger here for a long time and I doubt if the rebs are thinking of us. Their plan is Washington first, Baltimore if necessary.*

*But we are OK. Conn Cav is on every road for 20 miles out, permanently located in squads on picket. I have ridden over 200 miles this week, and am laying over Sunday.*

*We have streets barricaded and all the blacks <u>under</u> spade.*

*I am so tired I can hardly hold a pen.*

*We have heard nothing of the 18th Conn. Did not know Ely was taken, but supposed they were badly used up.*

*Will write more tomorrow if I have time.*

> *Much Love*
> *Charlie*

---

**Comment:** Confederate forces, under General Lee, were on the move by "baggage train" and otherwise, but toward Pennsylvania, not toward Washington or Baltimore. General Jeb Stuart's cavalry successfully screened Lee's advance from Union cavalry— composed of units other than the First Connecticut Cavalry.[426] Unaware of Lee's intentions, and under pressure from fearful Baltimore citizens, Charlie ordered freedmen to build defensive fortifications.

"Ely" was Colonel William G. Ely of Norwich, a friend of Charlie and commander of the Eighteenth Connecticut Infantry, which was overwhelmed and captured at Winchester, Va., by General Lee's forces in mid-June.

---

*Baltimore June 21 1863*

*My dear Father,*

*Everything is quiet on the line, and for myself I think it one great scare. When will our government settle down to a sense of war and up and at them using, and keep using, men & have them always in hand until the last man is under arms and then we will use the rebs up. Why when old regiments were leaving Hooker by the 3-a-day were not a draft made and a large army made ready and their places supplied? Why are not deserters shot, spies hung, and paper and copperhead meetings put down? I tell you we are not awake yet, and I fear will not be under the present man.*

*The policy (diplomatic) may be OK, but a war policy of a little more stuff would be better. Still our city is full of excitement, building forts, rifle pits, and all sort of defenses. Streets barricaded and every thing in readiness. But still no rebs, and what is more there won't be any this way for a few days, I will bet. I laugh at them for their fears, but it is no use. You would think Lee was already here. Schenck is cool, and has not fully satisfied himself that they are across the river. But the inhabitants want forts and forts they are building.*

*Much Love*

*Charles*

*I am well, though tired.*

---

**Comment:** Charlie believed that the Union should use its superior numbers to overwhelm and wear down the South. But because their terms of enlistment were expiring, 130 regiments raised by the states were due to go home in early 1863, which was what Charlie referred to as "leaving Hooker by the 3-a-day." [427] In response, Congress enacted the first national conscription law in March. Lincoln issued the first draft order in July.

---

*Baltimore June 24, 1863*

*My dear Father,*

*Your letter of 22nd comes duly. I wrote either upon that day or day before. Therefore you will have learned where and how I am.*

*We are still in status quo in regard to the rebels, and all is excitement here* still, but they don't come. Lt Upson and a squad of men were sent up the rail road in cars, then to scout towards Hagerstown, which they did splendidly. They went into Hagerstown whilst it was full of rebels but discovered them and after a few moments both broke and got out.

They scouted all around that county for five days and sent the only reliable news we had here of the movements of the enemy. But they paid for their daring in the loss of three men taken by the enemy. They had a good run for them, some twenty miles, the rebs taking fresh horses on the way at last ran them down. You see, the boys ahead could not get start enough to get a fresh horse. But the rebs would pick one up and then follow them up, thus crowding their horses all the time.

Nothing new here of late. We hear no news of the 18th at all. All I got is from Norwich papers.

Capt Atwater came here with his Company, which has been in Philadelphia for some time, and now we have the whole Company here, and the Regiment all in Baltimore.

We are having plenty of work and lots of riding, and it does not look much like being sent away from here very soon except on scouts, etc. I wish the Governor would give a bounty to men enlisting. We can never fill up until he does. I tell you recruiting is very slow. I never expect this regiment will fill up entire, or, at the rate we have recruited it will take a year.

> Much Love
> Charles

---

**Comment:** At Hagerstown, Lieutenant Manton D. Upson's Company E patrol encountered the screening cavalry forces of Lee's Army of Northern Virginia on its thrust into Pennsylvania. Lee would engage General George G. Meade's Army of the Potomac at the Battle of Gettysburg two weeks later. Despite losing three soldiers in the twenty-mile cavalry chase, Upson's patrol was successful and probably was part of the reason that Meade had better information about enemy positions than Lee did.[428]

While now called a "regiment," the First Connecticut Cavalry was still of battalion size, and Charlie doubted that it could "fill up" at this point in the war unless the state paid bonuses for recruits. Scouting assignments for the battalion continued, as Charlie predicted, and would soon involve Charlie himself.

Although Charlie did not mention it, a news story about this time reported that he was "quite sick."[429]

---

*Baltimore June 28 1863*

*My dear Father,*

We have reached another Sunday and still no rebs, but for all that, we see them in our dreams. We are preparing for their reception, but unless an army of men not there this month follows but men who are soldiers from force of habit come this way there is nothing to prevent Lee riding in any day. We have nothing here but these volunteers sprung upon a night, and one good warm day's fighting and they will melt away. As I look at it, we are going to get a sound thrashing this time, and for my part I'm glad of it. I would not, if I was not in the army, turn my hand to prevent their going to the center of New York, thence around through Ohio, home. And I hope they will do it, and burn every house in the route, and such burn and destroy. And after it is done, perhaps our government will learn this is no child's play, but that war means something and that harsh means must be used. Perhaps it will learn that to protect itself it must hang Wood & Sigman and Vallandigham. Oh! how I do hope they will drive us all across the Susquehanna river and keep us there for a month. Take Washington & the President if it will learn the men high in power anything. Perhaps then the People would take hold & some man would get up & be sustained as a Dictator. Then you would see an earnest prosecution of the war.

I know this is a little strong, but we men that are hampered by an easy story-telling ruler, and when we convict men of a death crime and have them ordered hang(ed), get bluff by executive interference for political motives, we men know what is wanted and what will win.

The Rebels will capture & destroy enough on this raid to have kept a large reserve force of 500,000 men the past year.

I trust it will wake Abe up and he will find a rain storm in earnest.

The other day he said (when he heard some news from Maryland) that he thought like the man who asked Noah to take him in the ark, and Noah refused; he said he could go along with his old <u>ark.</u> "He did not think there would much of a shower." He will find a heavy rain up this way if he comes along.

*Very AfftS*
*Charlie*

---

**Comment:** In his strongest criticism yet of the government's prosecution of the war, Charlie called for a dictator who would hang dissidents, and yearned for a Confederate pillaging of New York and Ohio (and, presumably, Pennsylvania en route) which he thought would stiffen the northern spine. He acted a bit incautiously in putting such thoughts onto paper.

Former Ohio congressman Clement L. Vallandigham had been sentenced to prison in May 1863 by a military commission for "implied treason," i.e., giving speeches that discouraged Union army enlistments. Lincoln's earlier suspension of the writ of habeas corpus was interpreted as applying to the case, and a political uproar over the use of military tribunals followed. Lincoln responded by commuting the sentence from imprisonment to banishment, and sent Vallandigham into Tennessee.[430]

---

*Headquarters 1ˢᵗ Reg. Conn Cav*
*Camp Chesebrough*
*June 30 1863*

*My dear Father,*

*Last night we were all under arms, and lots of excitement. Rebels reported within seven miles, and the city deserted. Well, we all assembled inside the barricades and waited long and anxiously, but no Rebs.*

*Our camp was left and I suppose few expected to see it standing in the morn. My trunk and papers were buried in a hole long-prepared, and the women fled in terror. But this morn we are at our table and no one would suspect that last night was one of alarm.*

*I tell you the citizens turned out good, and 5,000 concerned men were under arms. But as usual only a false alarm. Some Delaware cavalry had a brush and rushed in through my pickets and reported 10,000 rebs coming. But they did not come beyond my pickets 25 miles out, for our boys held them and they left. They had no idea of coming in town but drove the Delawares in, and then left. It was only a little cavalry squad, say of 150 or so.*

*All well and every thing lively.*

*I have just received pieces of Artillery and intend to hold my hill.*

*Much Love,*
*Charles*

*Mary goes North tomorrow; excuse haste. But I was up all night for 4 nights and have ridden over 150 miles in the time. C*

---

**Comment:** The "Delaware cavalry" consisted of two companies of the First Delaware Regiment.

To defend Baltimore from the feared Confederate attack, Charlie's battalion mounted positions behind barricades at the city's edge.

Anticipating an attack, Charlie buried his "papers," presumably including personal correspondence. Later, he would routinely destroy letters written to him, and none from his war years have survived. In typical understatement, he casually noted the strain of his duties—no rest for four nights, and riding nearly forty miles on patrol a day.

---

*1ˢᵗ Cav. Conn. / Company Muster Roll*

*Charles Farnsworth, Captain, Co. B, 1ˢᵗ Reg't., Conn. Cavalry. May and June 1863. Present. Commanding Regiment.*

*O. J. Markle, Copyist*

---

**Comment:** This document from Charlie's official military file shows that he commanded the First Connecticut Cavalry, now formally a regiment, during May and June, 1863, but as a captain, not a major. It is unclear why the re-designation as captain was made.

---

*Baltimore,* [date illegible; probably June 30]

*Dear Fred,*

*Arrived all well and sound. Go to Harper's Ferry tonight.*

*No official here knows Gen Fremont's whereabouts. I guess he is near Winchester or thereabouts.*

*Write Billings often. He said he had done everything for you and you hardly noticed him, but was thick with me. He felt bad and cried very much. He is nearly as badly broken down as Henry. Poor boy, he thinks we are all against him. He is very tender and loves to help us all when able. I am sorry for him. Please write him.*

*Be a good boy and go ahead, and you may have to help us all out yet.*

*Much Love*

*Chuck*

---

**Comment:** Charlie returned to camp after a night behind the barricades in Baltimore and was immediately sent out to scout General Lee's drive into the North.

General Fremont had resigned his commission in July 1862, so it is odd that Charlie is pondering his whereabouts.

As the middle son, Charlie seemed to be mediating (even as he left for the front) between his older brother, Billings, and his younger brother, Fred, over some lack of communication or other misunderstanding. We are given possible insights here of their personalities: Billings felt unappreciated and Fred may have been overindulged.

---

July 1.[Diary] *Left Baltimore with 184 men for Harper's Ferry 6 p.m. Capt. B.A.G., Lt. B.J. Collins, Chaplain & Doctor.*

---

**Comment:** This is the first entry in Charlie's diaries, which he probably began after his capture on July 14, backdating and recording some entries from memory. From contemporary letters that he wrote home, this entry should have been dated July 6.

The cavalrymen and horses probably traveled on the Baltimore & Ohio Railroad, reaching Harpers Ferry, West Virginia, fifty miles away, later that day.

---

*Head Quarters, Middle Department, 8ᵗʰ Army Corps*
*Office Provost Marshal*
*Baltimore, July 5, 1863*
*12 P.M.*

*Dear Father-*

*We are off at 4 a.m. tomorrow for the front. Everything lively and lots of fun ahead.*

*Love to all.*

*Afft*
*Charlie*

---

**Comment:** General Meade's forces had already fought Lee's army in the bloody Battle of Gettysburg, July 1-3, but Charlie seems not to know that. His boast of "lots of fun ahead" proved inaccurate, to say the least.

His mother's note on the envelope of this letter reads: *"Charlie's July 5th just before leaving Baltimore to join Gen. Meade's army."*

---

July 5. *Arrived Harper's Ferry, 6 p.m. Reported to Gen. Briggs.*

---

**Comment:** Brigadier General Henry Shaw Briggs was severely wounded a year earlier at the Battle of Seven Pines and was probably serving here in an administrative role.

---

July 7. *Reported to Gen. Naglee. Assumed command of all the cavalry detachments at the post. 6ᵗʰ Michigan. Capt. Dean*

---

**Comment:** Brigadier General Henry Morris Naglee had been a banker and vintner in the San Francisco region before the war. The Sixth Michigan was a cavalry regiment, part of the famous "Wolverine" brigade, which was commanded by Brigadier General George Armstrong Custer. It would appear that Charlie was put in charge of various cavalry detachments at Naglee's headquarters, including some from the Wolverines.

*July 9. Took 50 men and went to Crampton Gap. Found that 2ⁿᵈ of our Corps were coming through. Met Gen. Slocum. Returned by west road.*

**Comment:** Camped at Maryland Heights, just across the Potomac River from Harpers Ferry, Charlie was patrolling along the eastern shore of the river. Major General Henry Warner Slocum, only thirty-five years old, was second in command under Meade at the Battle of Gettysburg; he was now moving his infantry corps south.

*July 11. Sent scouts towards Sharpsburg, Antietam, and no news of enemy.*

**Comment:** Charlie's scouts found no Confederate forces near Sharpsburg/Antietam because Lee's retreating troops had crossed the Potomac River further north, at Williamsport.

*July 12. Sent scouts up the Potomac towards Williamsport. No news of enemy.*

**Comment:** Charlie's scouts just missed Lee's troops crossing the Potomac at Williamsport. The Confederates then passed to the south toward Falling Waters, where a rear-guard skirmish with Meade's pursuing forces would be fought on July 13-14.

*July 13. Brigaded under Col. Wells, of Mass. Moved camp to a group of pines near the river. Have a good Sibley tent, and all the men have cover. Collins is Brig. 2ⁿᵈ Mass. Hurt myself in tent with acuation. Sent a picket guard up the river.*

**Comment:** Charlie had moved his encampment down Maryland Heights toward the Potomac.

A Sibley tent stood about twelve feet high, was conical in shape, and accommodated about twelve men. It was patented by Henry Hopkins Sibley in 1856 for the U.S. Army. Sibley, however, later joined the Confederacy and lost his patent royalties.

"Acuation" is another term for knife sharpening.

*Maryland Heights*
*July 14th 1863*

*My dear Father,*

*We are at present at this <u>hole</u> expecting to cross into Virginia soon. All news from the army is in a fog. We are having lots of fun, doing little of any account. Our coming out was very foolish, though it fills up a space someone must fill. I was in hopes to join Gen. Pleasanton's cavalry, but we are located here. Should we cross, there will be work as the other side is full of rebs. The Gen proposes to put a pontoon over and we go over first, of course. We want it done well and hearty, though it rains all the time and we brought nothing with us but a rubber and one blanket, expecting to remain only a few days. But it looks as if we were booked for the campaign. If so, I am coming home soon, for it knocks our regiment all <u>over</u> and I won't stay any longer at this child's play of raising a regiment.*

*Much Love to all*
*Charlie*

*You need not write as I am not sure of letters. But if any thing urgent, send to Fish and he will get it to me. C*

---

**Comment:** Harpers Ferry was generally known as "the hole" because of the surrounding steep cliffs. Along with a large swath of western Virginia, it had become part of the new state of West Virginia three weeks earlier, on June 20, 1863. Charlie, however, thought it was still part of Virginia.

A pontoon bridge was necessary because the only other nearby bridge was the Baltimore & Ohio Railroad's. It had been destroyed and replaced nine times during the war and probably was unavailable for Charlie at this time.[431]

Major General Alfred Pleasanton took command of all Union cavalry in June 1863, serving directly under Meade at Gettysburg. Most of Pleasanton's cavalry was now leaving the area, but the First Connecticut Cavalry detail stayed at Harpers Ferry, under General Naglee. It was Naglee who ordered Charlie's detachment to cross the Potomac on July 14 to scout Lee's retreating rebels.

Charlie's overweening goal still was to build a full regiment, even as he was about to engage in combat. He abhorred having the battalion split up and ordered about in small units, however useful that might have been in scouting for the infantry.

---

*Hd Qtrs.Harpers Ferry*
*July 14th 1863*

*Special Orders)*
*No. 10 )*

*Capt. Farnsworth with fifty (50) men will report at the Bridge at Harpers Ferry at 1 P.M. this day with one day's rations.*

*By Order of Brig. Gen. Naglee*
*by W. T. [illegible]*
*Asst. Adj. Gen.*

---

**Comment:** Confederate troops still occupied the town of Harpers Ferry, just across the Potomac from Maryland Heights, but the size of their force apparently was unknown. This one-day reconnaissance was intended to probe, and probably to harass, the Confederates. Charlie's detachment crossed the pontoon bridge under cover of a Union artillery barrage.

---

*July 14. Ordered to cross the river at noon. Capt. Blakeslee and 52-man detail moved down the railroad and came in rear of picket. Capt. B charged it and captured all but one. I saw a force of Rebels come down the road. I saw they would capture us all unless checked, so I charged with 30 men upon the 12th Va. Reg. Cav. Saved Capt. B and his prisoners, but I was taken prisoner with 24 men. In charging, my object was to give B time to get back to the crossroads before the Rebels divided us. It worked well. He escaped with the prisoners, 1 colonel and men. There was the 5th Reg. Cav. at Charlestown under Jones. Was well treated by my captors.*

---

**Comment:** This was the pivotal day in Charlie's military life, even more decisive than the day he was wounded. He would never again command troops in combat. Charlie's version of what happened differed somewhat from later reports by Captain Blakeslee and by Sergeant Ferris, which follow:

---

## Captain Blakeslee's Report on the Skirmish and Capture

*"Major Farnsworth, myself and 50 men crossed the Potomac, by order of General Naglee, to reconnoiter the enemy's position beyond Bolivar Heights and to ascertain their strength. About two miles from Harper's Ferry, the advance guard, 18 men under myself, charged upon the picket of the enemy numbering about 30 and drove them in confusion back upon their reserve. Major Farnsworth coming up*

231

now charged upon the whole reserve of the enemy about 200 strong. The enemy also charged and it became a fierce hand to hand fight, in which, owing to the disparity of our numbers, they repulsed us, rescued several prisoners whom we had previously taken, and, I am sorry to add, captured Major Farnsworth and 26 men. The Major's horse was shot from under him, and he fought most gallantly on foot with his sabre until he was overpowered and taken prisoner.

"I took command of the remainder of our men and fell back, bringing with me one Captain, one Second Lieutenant, and two privates, all of whom were captured by the advance in their first charge upon the picket, in which we also shot several horses, and wounded the Colonel of the 12th Virginia Cavalry so that he was afterwards found and brought in a prisoner.

"Allen F. Phillips, Co. A 1st Sergeant, deserves especial mention for his courage and good conduct in the affair." [452]

## Quartermaster Sergeant Weston Ferris' Report

"July 14th, General Naglee ordered Major Farnsworth and Captain E. Blakeslee, with 40 men, to cross the Potomac and reconnoiter the enemy's position on Bolivar Heights. A pontoon bridge was laid across the river which we crossed a little after noon and followed the Shenandoah R.R. track for some distance, coming upon a steep bank behind some woods about two miles from Harper's Ferry. After the officers had seen the position of the picket posts, the Major divided his men into three squads, one commanded by Captain Blakeslee and one by himself. The reserve was in charge of a lieutenant on General Naglee's staff, he having accompanied us for the purpose of seeing a cavalry reconnaissance. Major Farnsworth and Captain Blakeslee charged into the picket posts. I was left with the reserve.

"Our lieutenant saw some rebs running up the Charlestown Pike so he ordered the reserve to charge up the road and up the road we went. After a ride of about a mile, in a sudden turn of the road, we came upon three companies of the 13th Virginia Cavalry. As we numbered but twenty men and our lieutenant was left behind us, we thought it best to retreat. I found that my horse was giving out for he proved to be wind-broken. In ascending a hill, he came to a sudden stop without orders and I found myself in the hands of the rebels. This was more provoking as behind the hill was a brigade of our troops. We were hurried back to Charlestown. On the way, we met Major Farnsworth and some of his men who had been taking prisoners. He saw us charging up the road and knowing the danger we were in, tried to head us off by crossing the fields but he was too late. So the Major and twenty-four of his men fell into the hands of the rebs. He said that if the lieutenant had been either killed

232

*or taken prisoner, he would have not felt so badly. After we reached Charlestown, we were obliged to turn over our horses. After dark, we were marched to General Jones' headquarters where we spent the night in a soaking rain. The next morning we were taken to Winchester and confined in the old Court House, where prisoners were constantly coming in. We saw a great part of Gen. Lee's army pass."* [433]

July 15. *Reached Winchester. Was confined in Courthouse. Allowed to go around town with guard. Saw Malvern, Bowen, Ripley, [illegible], and others of 18th in hospital. Cousin Eunice came and called, sent me meals each day. Found Lt. Norcross of 2nd Mass. Cav. with 14 men the only prisoners. Was confined in same room with our men.*

---

**Comment:** Nearly the entire Eighteenth Connecticut Volunteer Infantry Regiment had been captured in the disastrous Battle of Winchester, Virginia on June 15, 1863. Many of the prisoners were paroled within two weeks, presumably because the Confederates did not have the facilities to hold them, with the Battle of Gettysburg looming, but the four named by Charlie (from Norwich, as was most of the regiment) were hospitalized and presumably unable to be transferred. Others were sent to Richmond prisons.[434]

Charlie's mother was Eunice Williams Billings, so presumably this cousin Eunice is from his maternal side. She was living in Winchester, about eighteen miles from Harpers Ferry.

The old courthouse in Winchester still bears Charlie's name, as well as those of other Union prisoners, handwritten by pencil on the plaster wall of a second floor room.

Thus far, Charlie seems to have been treated well, his main complaint being that he was confined with his enlisted men in a breach of military custom.

---

July 16. *A member of the 1st New Jersey Cavalry came in, reported that our men captured a Col. and 15 men. That a large force of cavalry crossed at evening and drove the rebels back. Lt. Meigs, who hid himself (one of our party), reached our lines safely. Maj. Pope 8th New York, Lt. Potter & Kellogg 6th Michigan came in.*

---

**Comment:** "Came in" was a euphemism for "captured." The New Jersey cavalryman's report was exaggerated—only the Confederate colonel and four others had been captured in the skirmish that led to Charlie's capture.

---

July 17. *Lt. Hammond Ringold, Baltimore Cavalry, came in today. Also Capt. Scoffield 1ˢᵗ Vermont Cavalry, captured at the charge upon the [illegible], Williamsport.*

*Depot, Prisoners of War*
*Winchester, Va. July 17, 1863*
*Major Bridgeford*
*Provost Marshall*

*Sir*
  *I take the liberty of addressing you on behalf of the Federal officers 5 in number confined here as prisoners of war. We are unable to avail ourselves of the conditions permitted to get a conveyance for transportation to Staunton, and I am desired to request that if it be not contrary to your regulations, we be allowed to proceed at once to Staunton or such other place as we may be destined, there to report in such time as you may specify. Our object is to be able to get conveyance after leaving Winchester for all or part of the route.*
  *We will give parole to keep to the direct public road and any thing you deem proper in regard to communicating etc.*

*I remain sir*
*Very Respectfully your*
*Obd sv,*
*E. H. Pope*
*Major, 8ᵗʰ N.Y.*

*Hd. Qtrs. Winchester, Va.*
*July 17, 1863*

*Gentlemen,*
  *I am directed to say to you that Maj. Bridgeford has written to Gen. Lee with regard to the disposal of Federal officers & men now at this point.*

*Very respectfully,*
*M. S. Stringfellow*
*Adjutant*

---

**Comment:** In this exchange of letters, the senior captured Union officer requested permission for Charlie and the other officers to travel on their honor by "conveyance," so as not to have to walk to their ultimate place of imprisonment; the request was forwarded to General Lee who no doubt denied it.

---

*July 19. Whilst at the pump today Jennie and a Confederate officer passed. She spoke to me and inquired after my health. Miss [blank in original] was with her. Our room is becoming very crowded indeed. We ask for a separate room, but the Provost Marshal will not furnish one.*

---

**Comment:** Jennie was the second cousin—also on his mother's side—to visit Charlie.

Over-crowding in the courthouse room was probably an additional reason why the officers were requesting to be "paroled" to travel on their own to a Confederate prison.

---

*July 20. Lt. Gamble 113ᵗʰ Penn., Lt. Small 1ˢᵗ Maryland came in today. A large number of men have been brought in. We now have about 150 enlisted men.*

*July 21. After repeated requests made to the Provost Marshal to remove officers from the same room with soldiers, he at last gave us the choice of a room leading out of the Confed. States' guard house where their thrice deserters are confined, and we moved in, taking Ferris and Van with us. We are a little more select here.*

---

**Comment:** Under pressure, the Confederate provost marshal complied with the customary rules of war and separated the captured officers from their enlisted men. Charlie and the other officers made an exception for Quartermaster Sergeant Weston Ferris of New Canaan and for Van, apparently also a senior enlisted man.

---

*July 22. Left Winchester for "Libby." Nine officers and over 300 men, under guard of Stonewall Battalion. Marched to the fork of road that runs to Middletown. A large spring house that I remember well when the army moved from there last summer. Very tired indeed. Capt. Henderson was in command of the guard.*

---

**Comment:** "Libby" was a warehouse in Richmond that had been converted recently into a prison.

The Stonewall Battalion (officially, a brigade) was named for General Thomas (Stonewall) Jackson, who was killed earlier in 1863 at the Battle of Chancellorsville, Virginia.

Middletown is about fifteen miles south of Winchester, but it is hard to know where "the fork" was located. Charlie apparently was confined for the night in a house he recognized from reconnoitering in the Shenandoah Valley a year earlier. At this point, he was within about forty miles of the scene of the April 1862 bushwhacker ambush.

---

July 23. *Pushed through Front Royal. Turned to left of Chester Gap. Received cannonading. Our cavalry is reported near. Camped near crossroads. A pontoon is at the crossing of Shenandoah River at the identical spot we crossed last year.*

---

**Comment:** Charlie and the other federal prisoners, numbering about three hundred, were still marching on foot, along with Lee's retreating soldiers. Front Royal is about ten miles southeast of Middletown, at a narrow point of the Shenandoah River where the Confederates had built a pontoon bridge.

As happens in many wars, the prisoners became the unintended victims of friendly fire.

---

July 24. *Passed through Sperryville. No fences appear and the country though green shows the scars of last year's camp. Camped for night near Woodville.*

---

**Comment:** At twenty-five miles, his longest day's march yet.

---

July 25. *Reached Culpepper at evening and stopped near the railroad. Heavy rain. Were here furnished cars and started 9 p.m. for Gordonsville.*

---

**Comment:** After marching seventy miles in four days, Charlie and the other prisoners were put aboard a train at Culpepper, bound for Richmond.

---

July 26. *Left Gordonsville in morning and reached Richmond in evening. Confined in the far-famed "Libby." Found most of the officers of the 18<sup>th</sup> Conn. here. Assigned to Mess #5.*

---

**Comment:** Charlie traveled the final ninety miles by train from Culpepper to Richmond, including a lay-over in Gordonsville, in about twenty hours.

---

July 27. *Took breakfast with Col. Ely and spent most of the day in taking an inside view of our prison and learning the ropes. Weather warm but I do not consider our confinement as bad for the rooms are airy and commodious.*

**Comment:** Constructed about 1850 for use as a tobacco warehouse on the James River, the building was comprised of three connected structures, each four floors high, with each floor measuring about 110 by 44 feet. In 1854 Luther Libby, of Maine, had bought the facility and converted it into a shipping chandlery. In July 1861, the Richmond government gave Libby forty-eight hours to vacate his property so the Confederacy could use it to confine Union officers captured at the First Battle of Bull Run. Libby substantially complied, although he may have been allowed to retain a small space for his business. (Enlisted prisoners were taken to nearby Belle Isle in the middle of the James River, where they were held almost entirely without shelter from the weather.) Libby's upper two floors were converted into prison quarters—a total of six rooms. The officers had no beds and few benches. Windows were left open at first, but were later grated with wooden bars. A hospital room was set up on the first floor of the east building. Captured slaves and dangerous inmates were kept in the cellar.[435]

July 28. *There are two departments, the East Col. Streight and the West Col. Tilden. The west has 12 messes of 25 each, who cook upon 2 stoves. Rations issued are meat, bread, salt, rice or beans, and vinegar. Our meals consist of Breakfast-Hash, Dinner-Soup, Supper-Rice.*

July 29. *We purchase potatoes, apples, rice, coffee, onions by assessing each member of the mess and so keep a decent table. We also send out for articles and the bill amounts to $1,000 per day—Confed. money, 5 for 1.*

July 30. *One man in each mess acts as commissar and the others order through him. One officer is detailed as cook for mess each day.*

**Comment:** Charlie and about three hundred other officers were confined in one of the west rooms. Each mess of twenty-five officers cooked for themselves, on two stoves, spending about $200 per day, or about eighty cents a day per prisoner. Much of the officers' personal money had been taken by guards, but the remaining cash helped supplement the prisoners' diet until that money ran out.[436]

*July 30, 1863*
*Libby Prison, Richmond, Va.*

*Dear Mother-*
*You are of course aware of my capture upon the 14th near Harper's Ferry. I arrived here on the 21st, having marched from Winchester to Culpepper Court House. I find quite a number of friends & old school mates here, and am quite*

contented. Our fare with what we buy is good, and our treatment here is far better than I expected from reports. Contentment is more than half of it. Of course we look for an exchange soon & wish the Governments will soon come to an understanding. 'Tis so foolish to keep such large numbers on both sides idle. There is 500 officers here. Ely is well. Hakes went to Hospital yesterday. The balance are in good health. Friends at W. were very kind indeed, and were true friends. There were 24 men taken with me, but suppose you are aware of it. They are all well. Take care of Denny till I come home. I don't want to lose him.

Much love,

Charlie

Write G. S. common.

---

**Comment:** "Friends at W," was probably code for the Winchester cousins who came to see Charlie while he was detained there at the courthouse.

Colonel William G. Ely and Lieutenant Dwight W. Hakes, officers of the Eighteenth Connecticut Infantry, were from Norwich and probably are the "friends & old school mates" mentioned. Ely attended Monson Academy in Monson, Massachusetts, so Charlie may have been his schoolmate there. This is the only evidence known of Charlie's formal education.

His personal servant Denny was apparently sent to Norwich after Charlie was captured.

---

August 2. *Surgeon Holbrook of the 18th came in with Bowen. Also 10 who were taken at Winchester.*

August 5. *Capt. Bowen, Malvern, and all the surgeons left at Winchester, also sick officers, came in today. Maj. Purcell, 4th N.Y. and several others escaped at Staunton. Purcell and myself went up the Valley together in June '62. Recd. letter from Jennie.*

---

**Comment:** "Up the valley" refers to the Union campaign against Stonewall Jackson's forces in the Shenandoah Valley during the summer of 1862.

Jennie was the cousin who spoke to Charlie by the water pump in Winchester.

---

August 27. *Wrote to cousin Jennie, Georgia, and Mother. Also to Col. Fish.*

August 30. *Wrote Georgia.*

*Sept. 1863*
*Libby Prison*

*My dear Father,*

This letter is intended to run the blockade and I trust will. You can note receipt by saying "letter" without date was received. We are in a hard old place, but managing. We live along, waiting patiently for our governments to exchange us. But few desire any concessions on the part of the government, stand boldly for its rights, and we will suffer. Still we have strong hopes of an arrangement being effected soon. There are 558 officers, 27 surgeons, and 9 chaplains. They have given us 4 oz. of meat, ½ pound of bread per day, salt & vinegar. We also get a pull of rice or beans, poor wormy ones. But for what we buy, about $1,000 per day, we should all be sick. We buy sugar $5 a pint, butter at $10 a quart, paper 25 cents, bread 25 cents per loaf, soda crackers 25 for $1.00, watermelons $4 each, tomatoes 8 for $1.00, beans $2 per quart, etc. Shirts $10, common hickory ones. Shoes $10. We send out and buy as I say $1,000 a day, which keeps us up. We exchange our greenbacks for Confed. at the rate of 6 or 7 per one. But the government is very much down on our trading in their money and try to force us to send our own coin for goods, but we have so far always had what we wanted for their money.

Since we came here we have been allowed to send out for stuff, except Milroy's men; they are not allowed to. They have never kept us very clear on this though; they often say they shall shut down on us as a retaliatory measure against Meyar. Only think: "he" has coffee (good Java), we have to buy old rye and peas at $1.50 per lb. or Java over $6. He has sugar, we buy at $5 a lb. He has all the meat he can eat, we get 4 oz. He a good accommodation, we are housed in a loft. He has the run of a prison yard, we are shot at if we put our arm outside the sill of the window. But we only wish our government to give them the same as us. Contrast Johnston Island with this old tobacco warehouse with its grated windows and close confinement. How willing would we give a month there for a month here, and still they talk of cutting off our only comfort, purchasing outside. But I think our government in the future will feed them as we are fed, and then we would not complain. But even then they would have the advantage of prices on us. Give Confed. Officers ½ lb. bread, 4 oz. meat, and water to drink. All that the C.S.A. furnishes us. We buy all our comforts.

We have the southern paper every day at 25 cents a paper and so poor and full of lies that but for the few lines of some fight where they always whip us and which we can sift out some little advantage for us, we would seen [illegible] of them. Northern papers of less than a month's age we seldom see. Oh, how mean is their spirit, but it makes soldiers of us. We long saw the power of a magnanimous government here; now we see the small mean nicks of a government falling. Oh, could our government only now go out there [illegible], we should soon put out their light. They have only a shell of an army, but they make it all count, moving their troops from one part to another for a few weeks, then back again. They work hard and are always rewarded. An army like Meade's could come here easily if only thought so. We could have taken Richmond easily had they not made mountains of molehills. There was not 5,000 men within 40 miles of here at that time I wish it were possible for our government to use their prisoners as we are used. Butler, Schenck, & all the "Brutes" don't begin with the man who runs this place in meanness, harshness, cruelty, etc. A man hailed to me in the street one day, and the man was put on bread and water to find out who it was. At last a man was hired who would own it. Payed for it, and he was put by Winder in the dungeon for 3 days, and bucked by a guard 2 times. Such is our treatment when it pleases them. Oh, how glad it made us when we learned that his son was held as a hostage and we rather doubted them to commence their hangings. There are men here in Castle Winder who were put there at the beginning of the war and are there still. Citizens are put here and no attention paid to them for months. Capt.Wolfe (of Mystic). He has not heard from home. He is a merchantman Capt. These are handled the same way. There is no use in sending money here. They steal all we had that they got for we are searched clean when we enter and what has been sent by friends has never been sent in — stopped outside for some excuse or other. Boxes of clothing have come in. These are [illegible] watched, but money, that they won't allow. And this too when we couldn't live unless we bought outside. Oh, what a rotten, miserable concern this CSA is and one more so every passing day the whole time and down it falls. I wish the people only could see the inside of it as we do. They would never say one word about desertions and one word of fault with the process for except for peace [unintelligible], and all that holds this nation together is the deception that binds on all and the army to enforce. The country is cleaned up of men and to all the old men who came here now to fill up the army would rampage [illegible]. Boys and old men are brought here every day in chains and put in the army. There is no exemption here. Crowd them in somewhere for one more desperate [illegible]. Oh, I hope now [we] may succeed under Meade and crush their forces.

No news to assess here anyway. And there are an immense number that are here for desertion or resisting the draft. But with a strong pride we care for them. How I wish I was out and in it. Would I not give them a pull. We hardly expect our government will exchange until after the next battle so we shall hardly expect to be out before November. While we hope they will soon do so and that such day to becoming somehow. I don't want anything for a while yet. Will send when it is néeded. We are in for the war.

Ely and all his officers are well and desire very much one more blow at the rebs. Hakes is in Hospital but not very sick. I am in good health.

*Major Thomas who died here had in the office of Gen. Winder taken off his person when he entered $400, and they would not allow it to be used to bury him and we made up the bill, $300. Did Schenck ever excuse this, or old Benjamin F. Butler? Who would not be sick after such treatment?*

*Much love to all,*

*from Charlie*

---

**Comment:** This was Charlie's first letter criticizing prison conditions, and he somehow got it past the censors. He wrote it horizontally and vertically across both sides of two pages—making his script even harder to read—but not using the "invisible ink" that he later employed

The Confederates had imposed especially harsh restrictions upon General Robert H. Milroy's men because Milroy had organized a ruthless Union anti-guerrilla force in the Shenandoah Valley to combat southern bushwhackers such as those who had shot Charlie in April 1862.

The repeated references to "he" obviously meant Confederate prisoners in the North. Charlie was quite right in describing the conditions of federal prisons as being better, even though a slightly higher percentage of prisoners died in Northern (15 percent) than in Southern prisons (12 percent).

General John H. Winder was the provost marshal of Richmond, which had been under martial law since 1862. Commodity prices and exchange rates, as well as the prison, were under his far-reaching jurisdiction. Thus the term "Castle Winder." The commandant of Libby Prison was Major Thomas P. Turner. The manager of daily prison operations was a civilian, Richard R. "Dick" Turner, no relation to the commandant. "Dick" Turner was often disparaged by the prisoners, who mockingly called him "Major," adding to the historical confusion.

The theft of $400 from a Union major was so abhorrent to Charlie that he compared it to Union General Butler's infamous order in occupied New Orleans that women who insulted northern troops were to be regarded as prostitutes. Charlie provided eye-witness testimony of the unpopularity of the draft in Virginia, as elsewhere in the South, when he observed "old men and boys" being brought into Libby in chains for the Confederate army.[437]

---

*September 6, 1863*
*Richmond, Va.*
*Libby Prison*

*My dear Mother,*

*The first Sunday of autumn finds me in as good health as could be expected under the regime of the C. S. Govt. Little did we think in early June or July that our captivity would extend so long. But we are in the hands of our government and*

*await, without even a feeling of complaining their exchange. I wrote Georgia the 27th of August, and receiving one from her, answered it on the 30th August.*

*I hope the next boat will bring letters from you, and extracts from papers. I hear of a famous letter from Blakeslee, and wish to hear what credit his failing to sustain gave him.*

*Truly,*
*Charlie*

---

**Comment:** For the first time, Charlie criticized Captain Blakeslee for a "failing to sustain" in the Harpers Ferry skirmish that led to Charlie's capture, and showed contempt for what he imagined Blakeslee's explanation to be. Three versions of what happened there are set forth verbatim at the July 14 entry above. While Sergeant Ferris' version blamed a green lieutenant for the disaster, both Blakeslee's and Charlie's accounts described Blakeslee as having made a headstrong assault upon a slightly larger force of Lee's cavalry pickets (i.e., scouts or outlying guards) only to encounter a much larger force, from which Charlie then had to extricate Blakeslee. Charlie thus had good reason to be unhappy with Blakeslee's performance, and had cause for deep resentment if, in fact, Blakeslee was going around tooting his own horn.

Based on the practice of prompt prisoner exchanges in 1862, Charlie expected a short confinement. It was his bad luck, however, that the system had broken down in May 1863 over the South's refusal to include captured black soldiers in the exchanges.

*Sept. 6, 1863*
*Richmond, Va.*
*Libby Prison*

*Dear Fred,*

*Perhaps a letter, of the heading that this page bears, will be of interest in years to come, for we sometimes prize such little things. Of news none reaches us of late, no truce boat, no assurance of a "meeting of the commissioners," and at times we feel down, but we suffer for our country and should bear it with patience. But it is true there is not a cloud so dark that has not a silver lining and so we poor prisoners have some cheerful times. But we long for our native hills. They say the darkest hour is just before the day appears. So now we may be on the eve of a reunion with our friends. We hope so. I trust you had a pleasant vacation. Rockwell sends love. Ely and the 18th are in good health. Rumour says the 1st is full and that a lot of new commissioned officers are out. What has it done for us.*

*Truly,*
*Charlie*

**Comment:** Charlie strained to remain stoic in this letter to his younger brother, now almost twenty-one, even sending best wishes for Fred's vacation.

*September 7. Wrote Mother, Fred, & Billings.*

*September 10. Wrote Mother.*

> September 10, 1863
> Richmond, Va.
> Libby Prison

*Dear Mother,*

*My stay seems indefinitely prolonged. Please send the following: 20 lbs. sugar, 5 lbs. coffee B&G, 8 lbs. G tea, etc. Send me sponge, 2 cakes soap, all the papers and books you can put in. Send some paper & envelopes, lead pencil, and pens and holders. I sent for clothes to Billings. I hardly expect we are out for 2 months and if sooner the box will be shipped at Fort Monroe. Send my small chess men — no board — and 2 packs cards. This box should be strong, about the size of a soap box, top screwed on. Direct same as letters.*

> *With much love,*
> *Charlie*

**Comment:** This letter was addressed to Mrs. E. W. Farnsworth, Norwich, Conn., without a stamp, and arrived with six cents due. Charlie had probably run out of cash to buy supplements to the meager prison diet of hash, soup, and rice, and was counting on truce boats to bring family donations. He was also clearly having trouble filling the long, boring hours of confinement in the Libby warehouse.

*September 14. Recd. letter from Fish & one from Mother.*

*September 20. Noisy day. Blankets are taken away and reissued, 2 to each officer, some having 8 and others none. Won a bet today of Lt. Marlie Hakes 18th Conn. (that we would not be released before today) of 1 sabre steel sheath ($20). Won one of Goldsboro, surgeon 5th Maryland, of one pair shoulder straps ($12).*

**Comment:** The Libby authorities enforced an equitable distribution of blankets upon the prisoners, who had been unwilling to do so themselves.

The confined officers tried to pass the time by placing bets on their likely exchange dates, Charlie always seeming to take the most pessimistic position. "Marlie" was Dwight Hakes' nickname.

---

*September 22. Gen. Graham, Capt. Wrigley, & about 100 men, Leach, Childs, went north. Leach took a letter to Fish, Childs to Mother. Sent a letter by Quigley. Letter to Fish was in regard to promotions.*

---

**Comment:** These men "went north" as part of limited special exchanges or in paroles after the prisons swelled with captives from battles at Gettysburg and Vicksburg. But repatriations were stopped again in late 1863 over the Southern refusal to include captured slaves.[438]

---

*Richmond*
*September 23, 1863*

*Dear Mother,*

*Your letter of Sept. 6 came on the 15*[th]*. The reason you did not hear from me was there was no boat. You will with this receive my letter of no date. We have passed through another hopeful time, but the meeting of commissioners brought no relief and now we are booked for another month or more. Well, perhaps a good time will come 'ere long. Why* *we* *are* *held* *and* *Gen. Graham* *exchanged is a question a number of our officers will answer by their resignations. This favorite business has "played out." Many Cols., etc., who have been here from one to three months more than him are left. But Sumner's "pet" gets out. Out with such business. I am well: looking for that box every boat. Ely & Hakes and Norwich boys in good health. Much love,*

*Charlie*

---

**Comment:** Brigadier General Charles K. Graham, commander of a New York infantry brigade, was wounded at Gettysburg, taken prisoner, and confined at Libby. He was exchanged on September 19 for Confederate general James L. Kemper, who also had been wounded at Gettysburg.[439] Charlie was bitter about this exception to the freeze on exchanges, but may not have known that both generals were hospitalized with serious wounds.

Why Charlie believed that Graham was the "pet" of Massachusetts Republican senator Charles Sumner is unknown.

---

Attached to the letter was this note by Charlie's mother:

*From Libby prison*
*Sept. 23ʳᵈ, '63*
*Recd. Oct. 6ᵗʰ*
*Ansd. " " a.m.*

*Did not know what was meant by expecting "that box;" supposed he meant one he had ordered from Baltimore. Left of same day as a letter of earlier date which explained.*

*Richmond, Va.*
*Sep. 1863*

*Dear Mother,*
 *The last truce boat brought nothing from you although I was very anxious to hear. I have written regularly, but letters missing, very often in fact when they have more than they can to examine. They just destroy as fast as handed in so one hardly knows when one gets through. I hope to receive box soon. I wrote you a <u>long</u> letter a few days since — and received your last by the last boat.*
      *Love — Charlie*

---

**Comment:** Censorship by prison officials was erratic, probably due to the volume of letters and the number of soldiers available for guard duty.

---

 *September 23. Wrote Mother and sent a letter by 7ᵗʰ Conn. to Georgia. Also enclosed a few lines leadpencil to Mother. This letter went on 28ᵗʰ.*

*Head Qrtrs. Libby Prison*
*Sept. 25 / 63*

*Special Order No. 25*
 *Major Farnsworth is hereby detailed as Officer of the Day.*
    *By Order of*
    *C. C. Tilden*
    *Col. Comdg.*

*Mess*
*No. 1 Capt. Atwood*
*No. 2 Master Haines*

*No. 3 Capt. Sprague*
*No. 4.Capt. Pollock*
*No. 5 Lieut. Cary*
*No. 6.Lieut.Savingston*

---

**Comment:** The prisoners maintained a daily military routine, appointing an officer of the day, as well as an officer to take charge of meal preparations for each room at Libby.

---

*Sept 25 1863*
*Baltimore, Md.*

*Dr. Farnsworth*
*Norwich, Conn.*

*Dr. Sir*
*I received two letters from the Major your son this morning by "under ground Railroad." He is ever hopeful of exchange & I am in correspondence with the commissioner to hurry the matter up. Says the rations are neither very plentiful or excellent, but he will be permitted to receive a box directed to him. He says send me a pineapple cheese, 2 cans condensed milk, 1 lb. tea (green), 2 lbs. coffee. Also his overcoat and citizen's suit of clothes, a good felt hat no. 7 ¼ , paper, envelopes, pen & ink & pencils. Books & newspapers. Also put a $20 gold piece in one of the cans of condensed milk. You can have the can unsoldered, put in the money & solder up again & put my initials on the top of the can. This is necessary as they would take his money away if they found it. I think also you had better send him a pair of boots & some sugar. You can direct the box to me & send by express. I will forward it by flag of truce.*
*Very respectfully yours*
*Wm. S. Fish*
*Colonel & Provost Marshal [Baltimore]*
*Don't make too large a box.*

---

**Comment:** Charlie's commanding officer urged Dr. and Mrs. Farnsworth to send provisions to Libby, and they responded by shipping a series of boxes.

---

*September 27. Lt. M. Hakes came from Hospital and sleeps with me. Recd. letter from Georgia of date 17th.*

**Comment:** Charlie never expressed in his diary any emotional reaction to the letters from his fiancée Georgia.

---

September 28. *Recd. letter from Fred. Went to hospital today. Sent a letter by 7ᵗʰ Conn. to Georgia, letter dated 23ʳᵈ.*

September 30. *Went to hospital today. Sent a letter.*

---

**Comment:** Charlie's ailment is unknown.

---

October 4. *Answered letter of cousin Jennie. Also wrote Fred.*

> *"Libby Prison"*
> *Richmond, Va.*
> *Oct 4/63*

*My dear Mother,*
> *Your letters of Aug 11 & 8 came duly. The 1ˢᵗ answered since. I wrote you for a box and as yet have not received though. Some Conn. boys who ordered two weeks after have received. Perhaps the letter miscarried. But I should like it if possible soon. There is no prospect of an exchange for us, though a Brig. Gen. can get one. (We call it a compliment, as that rank is easily made, and generally useless.) We stand no chance for months, though if they would send a prisoner from Johnston Island & let him meet one from here, they would not be long apart. But well-fed commissioners on wine dinners can't see it. I tell you red tape is a big institution. I suppose we suffer for the <u>black soldier.</u> Comment is unnecessary.*
> > *Affectionately,*
> > *Charlie*

---

**Comment:** Johnson Island Prison, located on Lake Erie in Ohio, was used mainly for Confederate officers. Except for the cold weather, conditions there were not generally considered harsh.[440] Charlie felt that both he and his imaginary Confederate counterpart were treated with indifference by their governments.

Descending into bitterness, Charlie resented suffering for the "black soldier."

Attached to this letter was a five-cent note issued by the State of Georgia.

An excessive number of Union officers probably were promoted to the rank of brigadier general, but Charlie's comment still seems a bit insubordinate.

---

October 5. *Wrote Mother & Col. Fish and sent by John M. Recd. letters from him of date Sept. 28th. Made an order to Fish for box.*

October 10. *Won of Capt. Lucas 5th N.J. Cav. one day's expenses in Baltimore or Washington after we get out. Time from Dinner until after breakfast next day.*

---

**Comment:** The gambling was now focused on the exact time between meals!

---

October 11-16. (Here Charlie listed the dates and number of letters he had written from Libby Prison through January 1864, and then summarized them.) *To Georgia (24), to Mother (35), to Col. Fish (13), to brother Fred (10), to cousin Jennie (1), to brother Billings (1), to Goodwin (4), to Blakeslee (1), and to cousin Mary (1).*

*Richmond, Va.*
*Oct 16 1863*

*My dear Mother,*

*I again use the U.G. R.R. to communicate with you. I am well and in fair condition, hopeful for the future, though 3 months of prison life is as much as I want in one year. I am in hopes each day will bring my box from home. Then I shall live again. But new beef broth & bread has played out and I long for a box with coffee etc. There is no show for an exchange. If there was, it could have been effected long since. Well, we are content to remain here through the war if any principle was up, but only yesterday two more officers were notified of a "Special Exchange." Oh, how our government is given to favoritism and it may some day get its reward. We are now full of officers, over 800, and at least 10,000 men are here confined. Their lot is awful — deaths at the rate of 8 & 12 a day has come to our notice. And no relief for them. All the poor fellows get is ½ quart of poor soup (made of rotten bacon) and ½ a loaf of bread a day. Not a blanket given them, and whilst on the island they laid on the ground through all rain and storms. Some have buildings, but no covering. Even the officers are not furnished blankets sufficient. And the last lot of them, over 200 men, are now sleeping on floor and no covering. A few poor blankets are distributed, but they are not near so good as a cotton hankerchief. I tell you our condition is awful here, and our government should either attend to it or treat the confederate officer to the same. Now think of it at Johnston Island. I have it from an officer confined there, since exchanged, that the Confeds. have beds. All here sleep on the floor, with one or not any blanket. We have meat, bread & rice furnished by*

C.S. Govt. They get meat, bread, coffee, [illegible], vegetables, etc. Our government allows them $3 greenbacks a day to spend. Here we get $35 Confed.a month, equal to about $3 of our money. Now see what $35 will buy and then see how long it would last: 7 sweet potatoes $200 confed; 12 eggs $250; 2 lbs. sugar $800; 2 lbs. butter $1,000; cup, plate, kit, etc. $1,000. A fine bill of fare for a month. Oh, this damnable government that cannot take care of its prisoners, and ours gives them all of the delicacies etc.

This is what we suffer here. These officers speak of the fine times they have on the island. Now the vermin here is enough to kill a man, and no relief. The destitution here is awful. Prices all above the reach of anyone. They say themselves that they are unable to give us any better fare, that it cannot be had and that they wish our government would take its men away for they cannot feed them. Oh, it is awful to see them as they pass our building for their rations, stagger under a <u>Pail</u> full of soup. Oh, they are all weak, poor, and dying. How long shall these things be? One day they brought 16 men from the island sick and 8 of them died that night. This comes under our notice—since then the hospital has been moved from our building. Three of my men—Leach, Childs & Williams—were there and I saw them often. They are great F. men in the regiment. Should you hear of them sick in [illegible] Norwich [illegible], have Fred go and see & do for them.

The 18th are in good health. Hakes and myself are chums. Ely is in hospital, not sick but for a bed to sleep on. What we call bumming is a favorite practice here, but I prefer the floor and fun of 5 rooms to run in than a bed in one and that amongst the sick. The M.D.s expect soon to go out exchanged. The ministers have gone some time since. There has but little officers died here since I came.

I wish you would send me on receipt of this, if you have not sent already and even if you have, send in a week 10 lbs. sugar, 2 lbs. coffee, 10 lbs. butter, 2 quarts syrup (churned pine apple), a few canned meats, etc. Send to me. Paste upon box "Not to be furnished if exchanged" and it will come or be stopped, and even if lost, why the chance is worth all. We suffer here. Send a few books and plenty of papers. Send my love to Meriden.

Much love,
Charlie

Acknowledge this as "2nd letter without date".
Then I know it got through.

**Comment:** This indictment of Libby and of its hellish annex on Belle Isle was smuggled out with an exchanged prisoner, probably someone Charlie thought would not be searched. The "U.G.R.R." is the Underground Railroad. Once again, he contrasted Libby's conditions with those at the Federal prison on Johnson Island, this time emphasizing the vast differences in nutrition. His anguish was evident over the eight to ten enlisted prisoners dying daily on Belle Isle, but Charlie does not mention whether any of his twenty-four captured cavalrymen were among the deceased.

"Send my love to Meriden" refers his fiancée, Georgia.

*October 17. Asst. Surgeon Worthington 14ᵗʰ Pa. Cav. went north on truce boat today. "Special Exchange." Lt. Col. Erwin 10ᵗʰ New York Cav. also went on this boat. Wrote Fish a letter introducing Worthington.*

*Office Commission for Exchange*
*Fortress Monroe, Va.,*
*October 19th 1863*

*Mrs. Farnsworth*
*Norwich, Conn.*
*Madam,*

*I am in receipt of your letter of 16ᵗʰ instant advising me that you have forwarded a box for your Son, Maj. Chas. Farnsworth, now in Libby Prison.*

*The box shall be duly forwarded to him, on its arrival here.*

*Respectfully,*
*Your ob'd't Serv't*
*S.A. Meredith*
*Brig. Genl. & Comm. for Exchange*

*October 20. Won a bet today of Lt. John Maginnis 18ᵗʰ Conn. that we would not be released before today of money $20.*

**Comment:** Consistently taking the pessimistic position on his bets, Charlie continued his winning streak.

Richmond, Va.
Oct 20/63

My dear Fred,

Everything is as usual here, about nothing new in regard to our being exchanged, and in fact we do not expect it during the war, from the present status of commissioners. Please preserve all newspaper items in regard to the capture of Maj. F and all that relates to the regiment as he deserves to see it. I hear Marcy is about to resign and that Atwater has. Kindly remember me to them. Ask them to write.

Truly,
Charlie

---

**Comment:** Charlie seems to be referring to himself at "Major F." He was slightly misinformed about Marcy and Atwater. Major Marcy was captured on October 17, escaped three days later, and then resigned from the regiment in November. Captain Atwater did not resign until January 14, 1864.[441]

---

October 22. Received box from Baltimore, made up by cousin Harry and Col. Fish. Contained S.T.C., clothes, a new pair of boots, etc. Recd. letter from Mother, Georgia, & Col. Fish. Answered them same day. Also wrote to cousin Harry thanking him for sending box. Sent letter by Dr. G. who goes north on parole on account of sickness in family.

---

**Comment:** "S.T.C." probably stood for "sugar, tea, and coffee." An exception to the freeze on exchanges was occasionally made for humanitarian reasons.

---

Richmond, Va.
Oct 22 1863

Dear Mother,

Your letter of 7th came today. Box from home came same boat as one from Billings. I am well supplied with clothing by Fish from Billings. If you have not sent me a box before this comes, send one with <u>butter</u> 10 lbs., <u>sugar</u> 10 lbs., not crushed but coffee-sugar 2nd quality. <u>Syrup 2 gallons, molasses, condensed milk 5 lb. can</u>. Send to Billings in N.Y. for it. (That gingerbread is splendid, you might send a candle-box size of it <u>entire</u>.) Smoked beef & salmon, 2 lbs. candles. As there *is little chance of getting away from here for a long time, a box or so a month will add greatly to our comfort. The butter you can put in a pail, syrup in a can.*

*Truly,*

*Charlie*

---

**Comment:** His mother noted that this letter left Libby Prison on October 25 and arrived in Norwich on November 8. It was sent free as "soldier's letter" to "Mrs. E. W. Farnsworth, Norwich, Conn." She also noted that her October 16 letter to Charlie had gotten to him within five days.

---

*Richmond, Va.*

*Oct 22 1863*

*Dear Mother,*

*Yours of 7ᵗʰ came today. Box from Meredith came duly. I sent to Fish for clothes and have received them. Am now quite comfortable. All the 18ᵗʰ are well. Hakes received a box today. We are chums. I have one reported as at the office; will receive it tomorrow. Send box with eatables. Clothes do I have enough of.*

*Much love,*

*Charlie*

*October 23. Box from home came and bore testimony of a Mother's love. Box contained sugar, coffee, tea, clothes, books, etc. Letter from Blakeslee.*

*October 24. Am enjoying the pleasure of clean clothes and good things of our boxes. Rumors say we are in for the war, as our Govt. will not exchange. Small gave dinner party — had wine and felt high.*

---

**Comment:** These rumors were well-founded; the prisoner exchange and parole program was frozen for the remainder of 1863 over the South's declaration that it would execute or re-enslave captured black soldiers.[442]

Charlie was now receiving delicacies from home, providing the means for a "dinner party" with wine. Meanwhile, many prisoners on nearby Belle Isle were starving.

---

*October 25. Reported the meeting of the Commission Indignation meeting on Being Insulted: a 11ᵗʰ Michigan Infantryman who in sending for a blanket says "under other circumstances I am a friend of the south" rather than in opposition*

*to it. White in chair. Speeches by Dow, Henry, & White. Major Warren 32ⁿᵈ NY*
*and _____ 4ᵗʰ NY Cavalry escaped from hospital. Kitchen moved and hospital is*
*established in lower room. Wrote Mother, Georgia, and Fish. Warm late in evening.*
*Guard doubled. Sanderson has an officer put in cell.*

**Comment:** The Indignation Commission was an ad hoc group formed to enforce discipline and loyalty among the prisoners. It would later convene to hear charges against Lieutenant Colonel James M. Sanderson, who is mentioned here.

Libby tightened control over its hospital after the escape of Major Warren and another prisoner, whom Charlie did not name. A more spectacular escape would occur in February 1864 when 109 officers tunneled 53 feet under the walls to freedom. Forty-eight were re-captured, two drowned crossing the James River, and fifty-nine safely reached Union lines.[443]

October 26. *Wrote Blakeslee. Lt. Meen 6ᵗʰ Michigan came in. Was taken at Charlestown 9ᵗʰ May. Meen reports that Atwater has resigned. Also that one of my captains was killed at "6."*

**Comment:** Lieutenant Atwater may have submitted his resignation in October, but he did not actually resign until January 1864. It is unknown what "6" referred to.

October 27. *The officers are only allowed bread today because they fed the men who were confined on account of the escape of the 2 from the hospital. Great excitement on the No Exchange policy of Stanton. Recd. letter from Mother of Oct. 16. Wrote Denny. Sanderson resigned. A lot of sick and wounded sent north last night. My letters of 5ᵗʰ went by them.*

**Comment:** Authorities punished all the prisoners because some had shared their food with the two who were caught after trying to escape. Despite the no-exchange policy, the South was unloading sick and wounded prisoners, probably to unburden its hospitals.

Lieutenant Colonel Sanderson resigned his commission, but was still a prisoner. His life would get worse.

October 28. *Guard heavily reinforced. Bread riot last night. As the niggers were taking bread to hospital, the citizens attacked and took it from them. Negro performance of the "Libby Troupe" in the dining room. Dwight quite sick.*

**Comment:** This was not the first of the Richmond bread riots. In April 1863, Confederate President Jefferson Davis himself had to intervene to disperse a crowd of more than a thousand women who broke into stores, stealing clothing, shoes, and jewelry as well as food.[444]

The "Libby Troupe" was an entertainment by and for the prisoners, who also published the occasional "Libby Chronicle," which was "devoted to facts and fun" according to its masthead.

---

*October 29. Morning papers complaining of the action of USA on exchange and complain still more of the expense we are to them. Eating them out. A barge arrived with boxes of clothing for our men.*

---

**Comment:** The Confederate government's dilemma was that it needed to capture a lot of Union soldiers to win on the battlefield, but providing them with even minimal rations deprived southern citizens of adequate food, which in turn caused significant civil unrest.

---

*October 30. Papers talk loud on next exchange. Letter from 22ⁿᵈ. Wrote Mr. P. Wrote two letters for the R.R., Col. Fish and Georgia. Maj. Stowe, 88ᵗʰ Indiana Reg. died last night. Col. Ely up to raise money to pay funeral expenses — $200. Wrote to Capt. Goodwin.*

---

**Comment:** The "R.R" (i.e., underground railroad) was Charlie's term for smuggling letters past the guards by concealing them with the few specially-exchanged or paroled prisoners.

Captain Leonard P. Goodwin was a junior officer in Charlie's Company B.

---

*October 31. Maginnis reports a boat up and that the U.S. Commissioner is aboard and will accept the proposals of the Govt. and an exchange will be effected. Bulk boxes of clothing and stores sent to Lt. Randolph and Gen. Dow were distributed today. How much better to have given them to our men. But as usual, officers take it all. Cans of milk, syrup, hams are distributed amongst private messes. John took a letter (Oct. 20) for Col. Fish.*

---

**Comment:** "The proposals of the Govt." may have been the Confederacy's concession that it would not re-enslave or execute captured black freedmen, but only slaves.

Contrary to the report, the North did not accept this proposal. Thus, the freeze on general exchanges continued.[445] For the first time, Charlie conceded that although the officers had enough food, the enlisted men on Belle Isle were in great need.

---

*November 1. Won box of cigars (100) of Lt. Palmer. Won 1 pair boots size 12 of surgeon Goldsboro. Clothing given out by Gen. Dow. The authorities would not allow it to go to the men. Made a bet with Capt. Warner 18th Conn. that we would be in the Union lines Jan. 1, 1864. $10.00. Bet was cancelled on the 15th of Nov.*

---

**Comment:** For unknown reasons, Libby initially barred the officers from sharing a large shipment of clothing with the enlisted prisoners on Belle Isle. The garments got distributed a few days later.

For the first time on record, Charlie placed an optimistic bet on being exchanged, but then agreed to cancel the bet two weeks later.

---

*November 2. Troops are passing through here today. Supposed to be Lee going West. Boat reported.*

---

**Comment:** Prisoners were prohibited, on pain of being shot at, from looking out of Libby's windows, but Charlie successfully peeked. It was not General Lee, however, who was marching by; he was one hundred miles to the north, facing Union forces across the Rappahannock River. The troops in view may have been reinforcements for General Braxton Bragg at Chattanooga. Bragg had just won a victory there at Chickamauga Creek, but would be driven out of the important railhead of Chattanooga in November.[446]

---

*Richmond, Va.*
*Nov. 2, 1863*

*My dear Father,*

*There is confined within this building Lt. Col. F. T. Cavada, who was in Norwich the spring of Joel White's party. He spent a number of weeks at the house of Dr. Fuller, acquainted with the Ganman (children). From his description I think he was at the Doaners for a few weeks. He is a Cuban gentleman, resides now in Philadelphia. How strange the fortunes of life. We meet at different stages and under far distant skys the same actors, in very different situations. He knew the Kennys. All well.*

*Charlie*

**Comment:** small world, Civil War era.

*November 3. A number of enlisted men went north last night. Letter given to John Maginnis on Saturday. I suppose went in this boat.*

**Comment:** These were probably paroles.

*November 4. Col. Ely returned from hospital. Bishop of Richmond preached.*

**Comment:** Confederate ministers often preached at Libby, and the Union officers came to resent political instruction from the churchmen.

*November 5. Gen. Dow visited Belle Island and distributed clothing sent by the Sanitary Comm. He reports the condition of the men as awful: naked, half-starved, lousy. The sick laying upon the ground, a log for a pillow and dying at the rate of 10 a day. Fed upon 2 oz. meat soup and bread. Awfully abused by the guards, knocked down with clubs and otherwise abused. Mail. Dr. Pierce 5th Md. died.*

**Comment:** General Neal Dow's vivid description of conditions on Belle Isle matched other eyewitness reports. The United States Sanitary Commission, an agency of the government, coordinated the work of civilians (mainly women) who were trying to provide humanitarian aid to the soldiers.

*November 6. Dr. Goldsboro 5th Md. left this morning. He took letters to Fish, Horne, Meriden. He is paroled 40 days. Riot amongst the privates in building opposite. Three surgeons paroled by Lee, and a Lieut. who came inside the Reb line by invitation to exchange papers, and was returned, went north. Recd. letter from cuz Jennie. Letters recd. but none for me.*

**Comment:** Doctors were being specially exchanged, probably to increase the over-all medical care in the North, which would benefit Confederate prisoners as well.

*November 7. Boxes came up. A premeditated escape on Island was betrayed* by one of the men. Gen. Davis yesterday distributed 700 blankets and 500 suits to men on Island. Col. Irwin Asst. Comm. Dwight much better.

November 8. Recd. box from home containing coffee, sugar, grapes, molasses, etc. books, etc. Butter. Dwight received box from home. Made table. Quiet. No service.

---

**Comment:** An impressive box of provisions for their Sunday dinner. "Dwight" was Lieutenant Hakes of Norwich, who had been sick.

---

November 9. Received letters today from Mother Oct. 26 & 27, Fred Oct 28, Fish Oct 28. Chaplain H. Clay Membull came here from Columbia. Chaplained 2 Brigades. Neal Dow refused by Capt. Turner to go to the island. Read a letter written by him and endorsed by Turner. Assigned to Mess #23.

---

**Comment:** A high-ranking Confederate chaplain had come to preach.

It is odd that "Captain" Turner, who was actually the civilian manager at Libby, approved of General Dow's letter, but then prohibited a second visit to Belle Isle.

---

Richmond, Va.
Nov 10 1863

My dear Mother,

Letters of 16, 21, & 27 were received. Box containing butter came 8$^{th}$. No letter in box. Should this arrive before 1$^{st}$ proximate, send a ham in next box, provided you send one before that date. Do not send a box during December. Send no more tea. Grapes spoiled, everything else grand. Hakes' box came same day as mine. H. Clay Membull is eating at same table with me. Send papers entire. Have sent to Billings for blankets. Do not think I meant complaint in regard to boxes. I only wrote so as to notify in case one letter missed. I am well supplied now. No hopes of Exchange.

Much love, Charlie

---

**Comment:** It is not surprising that the grapes spoiled during the week or so aboard a truce boat.

H. Clay Membull was the Confederate chaplain who was visiting Libby. It is hard to tell whether or not Charlie was actually pleased to share a meal with him.

---

November 10. *Wrote Mother, answered 16th, 26th, and 27th letters. Not to send a box during Dec. Wrote Fish, Jennie M. & Chas. Johnson. Sent. H. Clay preached. Men were not furnished any rations today. Clothing issued and guards were instructed to trade it away from them.*

---

**Comment:** Confederate minister H. Clay Membull continued to preach to the Union officers, even as the enlisted prisoners went without food. Does "trade it away from them" mean that the guards seized the clothing from the prisoners? Hard to know.

---

Richmond, Va.
*Nov 16, 1863*

Dear Father,

I have a chance to send "on the sly" though it may not get through for some time. Don't mention letter post-marked "Old Point." They are underground ones and the authorities here seeing it in your letter, knowing it is not the regular mailing place of their letters, come back on me. Dr. H 1862 will write you not to send me any more boxes unless ordered after date. Except send me a small box with a ham (boiled) and a ½ dozen cans to <u>Lewis</u>.C. Meek [illegible]. Bake a cake of some kind. Cut out a portion of it. Write a long letter full of news, just as you think. Send to M, saying we have a chance to send a sealed (no matter how long) letter. Put them and any extracts from papers inside the cake. (Leave it in a pan.) Then put in the portion cut out & <u>frost over.</u> I shall receive it all right.

There are ways of getting through if you only think of it. I have searched every envelope in the pack, emptied out the sugar, coffee, tea, everything, but cannot find anything. You should take some chances. Write as I say. Send me all the news of 1st Conn. Cav. Gov. Buckingham, Senator Foster, and others could, if they set about it, get us out on a "Special."

Bring all the influence possible to bear and [illegible] pull and I guess it will come OK. Remember, don't send me any more large boxes of tea, coffee, sugar, etc.. A small box and a frosting with a cake with letter. Some milk, can fruits would do and put you in communication with me. Take a can of peaches, unsolder it, take out peaches, fill with letters packed in sugar or salt, so as to get [illegible] <u>weight.</u> Put your initial on the paper. I should then know what to open first. There are ways to do it. Only [illegible] be careful not to mention except by hint in any letter coming regularly. Stamp the Enclosed J.B. Cent.

*Much love —*

*I find that with Hakes' boxes and mine we have enough coffee and tea to last us 2 months. That is the reason for countermanding orders. With what we have and only a small box with [illegible] milk & __Cake__ inside awhile I can winter here. Remember me on the 20th.*

---

**Comment:** It seems that Charlie was hungrier for uncensored news than for provisions. Letters from home were not getting through, so he concocted this elaborate scheme to conceal correspondence in a cake. Hakes seems to have become Charlie's closest friend at Libby.

---

November 11. *No issue of beef today. Excuse was "none to be had." All we have is one half loaf corn bread. Membull left today. Letter from Mumford to White says "I hope to see you all en route north." __Bah.__ Preaching by Rev. Mr. Membull said he was very much pleased with Commissioned officers. Gave letter for Georgia to Lt. Col. Nichols.*

---

**Comment:** Although Charlie was skeptical of the official excuse for not issuing beef, food supplies in fact were running low for the civilian population, and food riots had broken out in Richmond. The boxes from home were now a godsend for Charlie.

Confederate minister Membull finally left Libby after four days of preaching.

Lieutenant Colonel Nichols, apparently paroled, agreed to carry out a letter to Charlie's fiancée Georgia.

---

November 12. *Wrote Father, sent by Capt. Warner, Ret. Surgeons reported going on next boat. Wrote Father in regard to Col. Cavada 114th Penn. Wrote Georgia & Fred. No beef yesterday or today. Sweet potatoes as an egaisaterry.*

---

**Comment:** An "egaisaterry" might have been a term for "substitute."

---

November 13. *A large number of privates left this a.m., supposed that they go to Danville. Ration today was corn meal mixed with water, no raising, and 2 small sweet potatoes. Wrote to Father & gave it to Warner for a surgeon to take. This is same letter mentioned yesterday.*

**Comment:** The Confederate prison at Danville, near the North Carolina border about fifty miles south of Richmond, was composed, like Libby, of tobacco warehouses. The former Belle Isle prisoners now at least would have a roof over their heads.

*Richmond, Va. Nov 14ᵗʰ 1863*

*My dear Billings,*

*Time moves on and still we are stationed at Richmond with no prospect of an immediate Campaign. Four months have passed and still we are not exchanged. I think some arrangement would be arrived at if the Commissioners would take beard lodgings in the prisons of each Government. I think they would soon come to their milk At any rate, we should like to <u>bet</u> on it.*

*Truly*
*Chas*

**Comment:** Charlie was suggesting that the Exchange Commissioners should come and experience life as prisoners with similar ("beard") lodging, so that they would learn to show some compassion ("come to their milk") for prison conditions on both sides.

*November 14. 700 more Yanks went to Danville this morning. Boxes being issued. Hakes has one. Meat issued today for first time in four days. Wrote Billings. Recd. letter from Georgia, Nov. 1, 1863.*

**Comment:** The Danville prison soon became so over-crowded that inmates had little room to move around.

*November 15. No Preaching. Sent word by Dr. Millbrook to Father: "Send no boxes, all back order included" unless requested to by a new letter of instruction. Four months ago today reached Winchester. Col. Nichols returned letter given on the 11ᵗʰ.*

**Comment:** It appears that Nichols was not paroled after all, and that Charlie's letter to Georgia did not get out yet.

*November 16. Wrote Father re GAP, Nov. 11, 1863. Enclosed a letter to Georgia, the one given Nichols on the 11ᵗʰ. Wrote not to send boxes but send one with ham and a cake containing letters. Letter went with some 300 sick and wounded. A very exciting meeting in regard to calling rebel ministers to preach. Streight and Henry appeared. Voted that they be invited here by a majority, 4 to 1. My letter given to John, but it did not go until today. Letter mentioned above I gave to Loomis to go by Cutter. Returned on 19ᵗʰ. Sent again by Wheeler.*

Charlie now was having more trouble sending and receiving letters than getting boxes of provisions; prison authorities welcomed the food assistance, but worried that correspondence could generate security problems and bad press.

Colonel A. D. Streight of the Fifty-First Indiana Infantry was one of the senior officers imprisoned at Libby, and often submitted complaints about conditions to Confederate authorities on behalf of his fellow prisoners.

The lop-sided vote in favor of "rebel" ministers may have demonstrated Chaplain Membull's popularity, or perhaps just a high level of prison boredom.

*November 17. Boxes given out. Ely got one. Fire in the room where the boxes were kept burned two of them. Report that Gen. Winder will inspect today. Warner learning chess. Ely received $25 gold.*

*November 18. Preaching by Rev. Membull. He preached a week since. Thompson went past here from hospital. He has had small pox. Wrote Fish not to send box, but cans of milk.*

---

**Comment:** By popular demand, Confederate minister Membull returned to preach.

Charlie urgently wanted gold money, hidden in sealed milk cans, perhaps to bribe guards for an escape. His friend Ely had received twenty-five dollars in gold the day before.

---

*Richmond*
*Nov 19 1863*

*Dear Father,*

*One week from today as you are drawing chairs around the table spread as bountifully, I trust this will reach you. Remember the prisoners here confined and look not with sorrow upon the vacant chairs, but with joy that they are vacant in such a cause.*

*Nothing new. I am well as possible and take real comfort in the articles received from home. We hear nothing new on the great question of exchange. Send no more boxes for the present.*

*Much love,*
*Charlie*

---

**Comment:** Charlie's most eloquent dedication yet to the Union war effort.

---

*Libby Prison*
*Richmond, Va.*
*Nov 19, 1863*

*Dear Father,*

*One week today you will gather together the family. One chair will be vacant. No new thing, to see <u>that vacant chair</u> employ upon the Thanksgiving noon. But it is not because of any indisposition of its occupant to be there, for very unhappy days have I past when you were so seated. I remember one spent in the far West, and many others I recall. <u>Now</u> a prison's walls hold me, and bayonets restrain my actions. Little will it surprise me if a returning anniversary finds me here. I pray not. Think of us all, for we shall think of you. You will recognize the mode of sending this, but as there is some uncertainty against these going out, you may receive at times, a letter of an earlier date, after one of a later. You see by that, we Yanks are up to tricks. You were very cautious in your boxes. You can easily send a letter concealed, for rest assured however secure you conceal it, <u>we</u> can find it. One good way is unsolder a can of peaches and fill it with letters, filling it up with sugar, salt, or something to make weight. It will be found by marking your initials upon the paper (of that can), will show us that <u>it</u> ought to be opened first.*

*Now you might inform Hakes, Ely, Woodward, & Lindsay's folks there to do it, and then send all the cans in one box to me (just a small box) and writing each officer's name on his can, I would distribute it. Long letter etc. will do us more good than anything else. You could keep up this custom weekly and afford us much comfort. Or, say, one send a can, another a cake, a third a loaf of bread, etc., with letter inside. The box being small would go through quick. Strap it well so it would be a hard box to open, for guards all not [illegible], now by one seen.*

*Well, there is nothing new here. The Govt. sent about 5,000 blankets and lots of clothing for the men. It has been delivered to them and affords some satisfaction to them of interest in their welfare by the Government. It is hard for men to suffer what prisoners do here in Richmond. The [illegible] federals were treated and* most insulting of all, the guards having such, few would not believe it possible for men to live upon the rations issued to us. Mine, just laid beside, me consist of two sweet potatoes, honestly not as large as two gingers and no longer. A chunk of meal & water, mixed up. That is regular officers' rations. (Soldiers one-half that.) Honestly, were it not for money spent by us, many would actually have starved. Our soldiers do, at the rate of 20 a day. Will God suffer such a government to live? Napoleon used to say, "Success is on the side of the most men & heaviest artillery." Oh what a recourse will they have against them when the leaders of this rebellion stand before the White House..

Col Ely and myself could be yet out on a Special Exchange. If the Governor, Foster, and Fish, Schenck and others took hold of it, we could easily get out. But I suppose now it would be harder work than it would have been months ago.

Our govt. have sent down rations for these men prisoners here. But the rebs will as a matter of course get more than one half. Steal it! But what the men do get will help them. Yesterday Geo. Ward 18ᵗʰ [illegible] went past our prison from the Hospital, tottering along. I saw him, spoke to him. Col Ely had just recd. a box, it had a large ham in it. He dashed to the window. Threw it out for Ward. But when he stooped to pick it up, a Confed. bayonet prevented him. A look of pain, raising his head, hand to cap, he said, "Col., the will for the deed." Col. afterwards recovered his ham. I have given much of my stuff to our men as they pass the prison, throwing it out of the windows and when large numbers pass; some will get it before the guard can stop them. Nearly all pass our prison when they come in and are distributed according to the various buildings and at guard towers.

This letter is supposed to reach our lines inside a plug of tobacco, there to be mailed to you. Winship, Ward etc. of Norwich 18ᵗʰ Cav. are still here, the only ones of that regiment we know of that have not gone North. Col. Ely & Hakes are well and hearty. Hakes is my bedfellow and chum generally. We get along finely, play chess, read, and walk — the latter quite necessary for health. We number now nearly 1,000 officers confined in six rooms, 100 to 150 for each. Eat, sleep, wash & everything. Fine fellows these rebs.

That was a fine article for Mrs. Higgins to publish about how she got a letter compromising a high line gentleman and one who had given his word. He had no communication. Foolish in Bulletin to publish name and mode. Should it ever reach here, all our letters would be returned. People should be careful how they publish our tricks. It harms us more than they know of. But the world is full of just such fools. After they get out, they think it is smart to expose the tricks of prison life. But there is more than one means of getting around the matter. Since a commission is writing the néed in regard to change of commissioners. Hitchcock being Com.;

*Meredith — a miserable, decrepit, haughty old fagg. Auld says he has hopes from a letter recd from H that an early exchange will be effected. We hope so. The Times is about right — the North cannot become barbarians and treat reb prisoners as ours are treated. And their fellows can do anything they choose. Bless you, they are a hard-hearted set, the whole lot of them.*

*The weather here for the present month has been fine and we have not suffered very much from cold, though there are times when a fire would well please us. But stoves are luxuries that the C.S.A. cannot afford for prisoners, and even if they should put up an old wood stove they won't give us fuel. You would be pleased to see the stove pipe on our cook stove — you can pick up better in any receptacle of rubbish North. [illegible] all [illegible]. I cannot do it justice. Well, they'd rather stay in their power than feel any shame.*

*Nov 22nd Sunday. All quiet along the lines. Learn lot of letters brought nothing new or cheery from friends on the momentous question of Exchange. The surgeons are expected to arrive on the next boat and then ours will go north. We hope everything will be counted on the list. But if not, combatants only get rid of surgeons for a mid- November sort of headline. Then these M.D.s you never saw. Well, they have had a taste of Jeff living and I hope are pleased.*

*Fondly,*

Note by his mother on the envelope, which was addressed to R. Farnsworth M.D., Norwich, Conn. reads: *"Left the prison in a plug of tobacco. Don't know who brought it. Written Nov 19 & 22; Recd 29th/63."*

---

**Comment:** This long letter, written vertically as well as horizontally across the front and back of two sheets of paper, was smuggled out, perhaps under cover of the preceding letter to his father of the same date. The prison may have imposed a one-page limit on out-going letters, short enough for quick censorship.

Charlie was clearly irritated that a former prisoner would publicize how letters were being smuggled out of Libby.

Firsthand documentation here of the Libby prison population: 1,000 officers in six rooms of one of the warehouse buildings. Thus, there were about 170 prisoners per room.

George Ward was a Norwich friend. Charlie would later testify before a government commission regarding the cruelty of this incident involving the ham.

When officers tried to share their boxes, they were sometimes barred by Libby authorities. One wonders why.

"Jeff living," in the last paragraph, referred to war-time conditions in the South under Confederate President Jefferson Davis.

---

*November 19. Letter written and sent on 16ᵗʰ returned, unable to get it through. Made Father a letter for Thanksgiving day. Col. Cesnola is distributing clothing upon the Island. Papers report a large number of Yanks escaped from Danville. Letter referred to above was given Loomis who sent it to hospital for some men to take, but was returned. This letter was afterwards sent by Holbroke Nov. 22ⁿᵈ.*

Richmond, Va.
"Libby Prison"
Nov 20 1863

*My dear Mother,*

*Your letter of 8ᵗʰ came yesterday. All the boxes have come in good time. Hakes had one from Bolt that will last us over a month. We are very comfortable now. At times we look hopefully upon an exchange, but not knowing the points at issue, only judge from newspaper items. At any rate we see no harm in a special exchange of all captured to, say, Sept 1ˢᵗ, thus leaving in the hands of the C.S. over 300, securing good treatment and good faith from the U.S. towards their prisoners. If the C.S. would consent to such an exchange, we from our standpoint see no harm. It would restore a large number of prisoners to their homes, and lessen suffering. It does seem as though some such arrangement could be made, with honor to both sides. All your letters recd. My kindest regards to Gov. Buckingham and Mr. C. Lehman. Oh that it were possible to be with you on the 26ᵗʰ. Have written Billings, but receive no response.*

Much love,
Charlie

---

**Comment:** Engaging in a bit of special pleading, Charlie argued for a "special exchange" of soldiers captured before September 1, which would have included him.

The twenty-sixth was Thanksgiving Day in 1863.

---

*November 20. Geo. Ward 18ᵗʰ C. V. passed here today, returning from Hospital. Col. Ely threw a ham out to him, but the guard charged bayonets on him and refused to allow him to pick it up. He tottered along, very weak indeed.*

*November 21. No meat issued today. Article in Whig in regard to exchange. Col. Cesnola visited the Island again today. Wrote to Winship to inform me if any of 1ˢᵗ Conn were there. Won $25 of Palmer on bet on getting out. (Whist.)*

**Comment:** The *Whig Magazine*, edited by Horace Greeley, continued publication even after the demise of the Whig party in 1860.

November 22. *No preaching. Today cold drizzly rain. Sold gold $2 for one. Made bet with Col. Ely upon the 20th that we would not be exchanged before Jan. 1, 1864. Had a long talk with Scoffield. Norcross but little better. Gave Holbrook a letter for Father. Also one to Uhler for same, containing one for Georgia. Recd. Georgia Nov 26th /63, Father Nov. 11, 1863, Father Nov., enclosed in plug of tobacco.*

**Comment:** Charlie's father got into the spirit of smuggling letters, this one sent in a plug of chewing tobacco.

November 23. *Papers speak of our exchange near at hand. Col. Cesnola choked the guard for calling him a liar. Crowd came to rescue and said they would go throw him out of window. Col.Cesnola complained to Gen.Winder who had the man removed. Two canal boats loaded with boxes arrived, over 200 private boxes.*

**Comment:** Rank had its privileges: an imprisoned colonel assaulted a prison guard, and the guard was disciplined for impertinence. Many families were now sending boxes of provisions.

November 24. *Boat up. Surgeon on boat. Federal surgeon left this a.m. Major White took a surgeon's place and went out. Some one blowed. Turner threatened to put us on "No rations," stop all boxes, unless we told. Starve. Letter of 18th returned.*

**Comment:** The Confederates typically refused to complete an exchange until they had received a prisoner of comparable rank and duty from the North. In this case, the Libby prisoners helped Major White pull a fast one, but someone "blowed" the scheme. "Dick" Turner, the Libby civilian manager, had tried to coerce the officers into revealing the ringleaders, but they refused. Although White got away from Libby, he was re-arrested when the truce boat landed at City Point, Virginia, at the mouth of the Appomattox River, below Petersburg.

*November 25. Major White returned and confined in the cell. Taken when boat reached City Point. He is confined in same cell Col. Purcell was. Salt pork from U.S. Govt. issued to us. We have not had any beef for four days.*

*November 26. Thanksgiving. Major White released. In evening, Libby Minstrels.. Sanderson and Cesnola had a grand dinner. Ham, turkey, chicken, oysters, fruits, peas, wines, etc. Issue of beef today.*

---

**Comment:** Hard to believe the menu, but it does not seem that Charlie was being facetious.

---

*November 27. Boxes. Mail. Recd. letters from Col. Fish 19th, Fred 17th, Mother 9th & 16th, Georgia 12th, Meredith 13th, 22 boxes & barrels from 882nd Co., also a box from Mrs. Gov. Buckingham. Lt. Poland died in hospital.*

---

**Comment:** As evidence of his family's political connections, Charlie received a box of provisions from the governor's wife.

---

*Richmond*
*Nov 28 1863*

*Dear Mother,*
*Your letter of 9 & 10 came yesterday. I am well and in good health. I had lost sight of Bennett. Glad he called. He is a fair sort of a man. Good address & education. Married a Harris. [illegible] New London. Box from Billings had a cheer. We have a great feeling now. Hakes has box from JMB, Ely a box for Hakes, me, & self from Mrs. Gov. Sunday School contributes enroute. We are well supplied. I should like ginger bread, <u>cake,</u> and milk. The latter article we are always short on. Send it when you send. But do not send any more large assorted boxes.*
*Much love,*
*Charlie*

---

**Comment:** Charlie's emphasis on <u>cake</u> and his special plea for more canned milk probably were coded requests for more smuggled letters, newspapers, and gold coins.

---

November 28. *Answered letters of yesterday. Rumor came in this evening of advance of Meade, Grant, and the safety of Burnside. Prisoners captured report the army is at Chancellorsville. Issuing boxes today. Guard relieved to go to Lee. Home Guard now on duty. Reported advance of Butler. About 100 more prisoners came in today. Poor fellows.*

---

**Comment:** Charlie was mistaken: The Union army was not at Chancellorsville but rather was at Chattanooga, where Grant and Sherman were winning a major victory. Charlie's First Connecticut Cavalry was not there, however; since July, it had again been patrolling once again in the Shenandoah Valley.

A loosely organized "home guard" existed in every Confederate state, and was generally given the task of tracking down deserters. Its assignment here to replace the regular military prison guards would have been unusual, and demonstrated the Confederacy's desperate need to send every soldier in uniform to the frontlines.

---

November 29. *Cold rain. Lt. Col. of 15th Mass. Cavalry came in, reported Lee falling back. No regular preaching today, as we are without chaplains. Dinner: pork stew, baked beans, coffee, cake, tomatoes, peaches, etc.*

---

**Comment:** The lieutenant colonel was correct. Lee tried to attack north toward Washington, but was forced to retreat south, across the Rapidan River when Meade assaulted his right flank.[447]

---

*Nov 30 1863*

*Dear Mother,*

*Your box came and was recd. today. Everything was in good order and made us all happy. Little of news here. All well. Do not send any more assorted boxes. I am abundantly supplied.*

*Much love,*
*Charlie*

Note by his mother: "*Charles acknowledges receipt of my box intended for Thanksgiving, sent from here 18th of Nov. It was 12 days in reaching him.*"

November 30. *Box from Mother came. Ginger broken. Cranberry, meats, sugar, books, etc. Wrote acknowledging receipt of it. Good news today.*

December 1. *Dates of letters received: Mother Aug 11, 30, etc., Sept 6, 28; Oct 7, 11, 21, 27, Nov 8, 9, 24, 29, Dec 2,5,5,5 17, 24, 28; Georgia Aug 16, Sept 17, Oct 7, 22, Nov 1, 12, 29, Dec 21, 27; Fish Sept 2, Oct 13, 28, Nov 19, 23, Dec 12; Fred Aug 30, Sep 21, Oct 28, Nov 17, 20, Dec 2, 13, 16; Blakeslee Sept 28; BHM Nov 12, 19; Cousin Bennie Aug 24, Sept 19, Oct 23.*

*Mother Jan 1, 8, 24, 27; Georgia Jan 21, 23; Fred Jan 15, 24, 28.*

---

**Comment:** This was a thorough accounting by Charlie of his correspondence since his capture. The last line of dates was undoubtedly added later.

---

December 2. *Box received from Mrs. Gov. Buckingham addressed to Col. Ely was distributed between Hakes and myself. Wrote Georgia & Mother. News from the armies is good. Malvern, Warner, Rockwell, Cols. Scranton and Woodward all received boxes today. Lent Ferris $5 U.S., have receipt. Made up a box for men on island.*

---

**Comment:** The "good news" was probably smuggled in with the boxes, which were now arriving in large numbers. Charlie again shared his box of provisions with his men on Belle Isle.

---

December 3. *Letter from Nov. 23 and also 20th came. Boxes sent from Mother for me. Also a box from the General for commissioned officers. Invoices received today. Recd. note from Stone. Sent him a box with coffee, sugar, tea, etc. He is confined in building nearly opposite. Geo. Ward of 18th Conn. is in same building. Recd. letter from Secession. Answered it immediately.*

---

**Comment:** "The General" was probably Schenck, Charlie's former commanding officer.

Henry T. Stone, of Putnam, Connecticut was a private in the First Connecticut Cavalry who was captured and then imprisoned at Libby in August. He was later transferred to Andersonville, where he died in March 1864.

It is unknown who "Secession" was.

---

December 4. *Recd. box from Mrs. P. & C.S. Onions, jelly, etc. Wrote acknowledging receipt. Also one to G. Packed box for Ferris. Lt. Col. Chas. Holton 5th Md. died today, making 3 officers from that regiment since Sept. Recd. [illegible] from Mrs. Lee. Box from Mrs. Albert Cates for Dwight, gave everything from her away. Boxes from S.S. received.*

**Comment:** Foodstuffs were now arriving from many sources, most of them unidentifiable. "G," however, was his fiancée Georgia.

Quartermaster Sergeant Weston Ferris had been captured with Charlie at Harpers Ferry and was imprisoned on Belle Isle.

*December 5. Barrel of flour, potatoes from Sunday School and several boxes came. Gave flour to Chickamauga officers who are out of money and have not received boxes. Two boxes for Ferris went to the island today. Col. Cavada goes over with Sanderson. Cold day. Col. Streight had interview with Auld. The same old story. Exchange man for man, parole excepted — counting 18,000 paroles as valid.*

**Comment:** In September, the Confederates had won the battle of Chickamauga Creek, fifty miles south of Chattanooga, and had taken a large number of Union prisoners. Two months later, the Union successfully struck back at Chattanooga itself.[448]

Colonel Streight, the senior imprisoned officer at Libby, was now negotiating for exchanges directly with Judge Auld, the Confederate representative to its commission on exchange.

Lieutenant Colonel Sanderson's earlier attempt to resign went unrecognized, and he was still one of the senior Union officers at Libby.

*December 6. Wrote Capt. Goodwin, [blank in original], Fred, & Georgia in answer to letter Dec.3ʳᵈ. Recd. letter from Ferris on the island thanking me for money and boxes, both of which were received all right. Filed all my letters and made memorandum of all written and received.*

*December 7. Wrote Mrs. Buckingham thanking her for the box of eatables sent us. Letter of Hitchcock distinctly says the negro is the stumbling block in exchange, and that until the South delivers our negro soldiers & officers in command of same there can be "no exchange."*

**Comment:** General E. A. Hitchcock was the Union's commissioner for exchange. The South had offered to return black freedmen soldiers, but not fugitive slave soldiers or their white commanding officers. The North rejected the compromise.

*December 8. Recd. letter from Mother Nov. 24th. Rebel Congress met yesterday. The papers of today do not have the message. Not sent in yet. Rebel guard came into building to quiet noise. Said they would take us out and make us stand under guard out of doors all night.*

---

**Comment:** The prisoners were probably celebrating news of Grant's stunning victory at Missionary Ridge, near Chattanooga, with the Confederates fleeing south in disarray. The Confederate Congress blamed President Davis for the debacle.[449]

---

*Richmond, Va.*
*Libby Prison*
*Dec. 8th/63*

*My dear Mother,*

*Fall has closed and I feel as we used to in Chicago after the close of navigation. Well, if we "close up accounts," "balance book," and come out with a "new card" in the Spring, I'm satisfied. But though business is "suspended" we do not find the range of enjoyment equaled to a residence in the city. I shall I hope see you about May 1864, hardly before. But I pray then. I sent to some of my men on Belle Isle a box of eatables. Sgt. Ferris of New Canaan is there. I sent it to him for distribution. Make mention of it in Bulletin.*

*Truly affectionately*
*Charlie*

---

**Comment:** Before he was twenty years old, Charlie was a partner in a Chicago foundry that made cast-iron stoves. Here he employs metaphors from that time to underscore his current dilemma. His forecast as to when he would be released from prison would prove fairly accurate.

Parents of the First Connecticut Cavalry troopers apparently published a "bulletin" about their sons; Charlie wanted public acknowledgement in it for having shared his provisions with more needy prisoners.

---

*December 9. Wrote Mother in answer to letter Nov 24th. Jeff message in papers. A long and thorough, well-written, labored article, seeking comfort for large losses with small gains on their side. Confederate money the day of the excitement of battle at "Lookout" was down to 21 x 1 greenbacks.*

**Comment:** Confederate President Davis opened the fourth session of the First Confederate Congress on December 7th by calling for increased conscription, higher taxes, and a reduction in the money supply to control inflation. He reassured the assembly that the North's "progress has been checked," despite the loss of Tennessee.[450] After Union General Hooker won the battle of Lookout Mountain as part of the seizure of Chattanooga, Confederate inflation had surged.

*Richmond, Va.*
*Dec 9 1863*

*My dear Mother,*

*Your letter of Nov 24 came today. I wrote that the box came OK. Many thanks to Mrs. Gen. Williams. I look only for a small box, say with a* cake, *or a boiled ham & canned milk, or a few* cans *of* fruits. *Of general articles we are supplied for the present. The boxes of Mrs. Governor Buckingham, the Greenes, & S.S. with what DWH and myself have received are enough for the present, but I should like to taste a "light frosted cake" of your make. All your letters except Aug 30 are received. Too much credit cannot be to given the authorities here, in the attention they show us, and willingness they exhibit in delivering our boxes, forwarding our letters, etc. There are trials & unpleasantalities, but on the whole it is a great deal better than "grumblers" released give credit for. If I never suffer any more than* now, *I will not complain.*

*Affectionately,*
*Ch. Farnsworth*
*Maj / Conn Cav*

**Comment:** General William Williams of Norwich was related to Charlie's mother.

Charlie may have been dissembling here by fulsomely praising the prison authorities for admitting boxes and innocuous letters, while at the same time asking for informative letters, newspapers, and gold to be smuggled in cans of milk and fruit.

"DWH" is Dwight Hakes of Norwich.

*December 10. Today's papers full of congressional proceedings. Foote of Tennessee pitches into the Prez and administration very severely. Reports to them on his visit to the army, on Pemberton & Bragg, on the issue of rations to prisoners. He finds that for 8 days no meat was issued. Potatoes, onions, hams, etc. came today. Cans are all inspected now for liquor. Stacks of cans labeled French peaches are confiscated. Order of Winder issued that in consequence of the U.S. stopping money to their prisoners, there would be no issue to us in the future.*

---

**Comment:** Tennessee Senator Henry S. Foote, a long-time critic of Confederate President Davis, gave a vitriolic speech to the Confederate Congress on December 9, castigating Davis for the loss of Chattanooga and Vicksburg, for retaining favorites among the generals, and for demoralizing troops with his visits to the front.[451] Foote also may have argued that if Union prisoners were denied adequate rations, the North would retaliate in kind, just as General Winder, the provost marshal of Richmond, was doing here with regard to sending money to prisoners. Winder would soon be sent to take charge of Andersonville prison camp in Georgia. Conditions became so bad there that Henry Wirz, its commandant, was later convicted and hanged for war crimes. Winder might have been charged as well, but he died in February 1865.

---

**December 11.** *Letter of Judge Auld to Commissioner [for Exchange] Meredith saying that in the future the C.S.A. will not receive any boxes from the North, but will deliver what is on hand. After that, the prisoners would receive the same rations as their soldiers in the field.*

---

**Comment:** The Confederacy tried to justify this new standard on the grounds that citizens were complaining about prisoners eating better than Confederate soldiers.

---

**December 12.** *Last night Lt. Skelton, shot through the head at [blank in original], with Capt. Anderson, bribed a guard for $40 and escaped from hospital. The guard was arrested and will be tried by court martial. Will in all probability be shot.*

**December 13.** *Quiet. Attempt of several officers to escape from hospital was discovered and a lot of them returned to their quarters. Lt. Col. Nichols returned from hospital.*

**December 14.** *All boxes ordered removed from building. Afterwards, 15 allowed to a room. Great commotion in the Commandant emptying articles and putting away things. Ordered that the purchasing of articles by prisoners be stopped. The last bill sent out was for $20,000.*

**Comment:** Libby commandant Major Turner enforced the new rule on rations, with predictable resistance by the prisoners. At an exchange rate of 20:1, this food bill for the Union officers was about $1,000.

---

*December 15. Letter of Hitchcock of 29*[th] *shows the real cause of non-exchange to be the Nigger. We feel now as if we understand our ground and could bear it. The chances do not look very bright, it is true, but still there is some hope. The C.S. Congress being in session may remedy this matter.*

---

**Comment:** Union Commissioner for Exchange Hitchcock made another announcement of the North's policy. Charlie now willingly accepted the North's principle that *all* prisoners must be treated alike in exchanges.

---

*December 16. Recd. letters from Mother Dec 2*[nd]*, Fred Dec 2*[nd]*, Georgia Nov 29*[th]*. Sent them a receipt. Rumors currently reported that an exchange is about being made.*

---

**Comment:** Just a day earlier, there seemed no possibility for exchange, and then came this hopeful rumor.

*Richmond, Va.*
*"Libby Prison"*
*Dec 16 1863*

*Dear Mother,*

*Your letter of 2*[nd] *came today. I have acknowledged yours of 24*[th] *Nov. You say nothing of letter of date Nov. 16 1864 so suppose you have not received it. Though I should think it is on hand as of the date of your last. Have you letter of mine making mention of "Col. Cavada" as friend of Dr. Fuller's and the Lanmans? He was in Norwich at Joel W. party. The contents of last box were OK, came in good order. Books just what needed. Mrs. P's box was just the neatest thing out, everything so nice, appropriate, and so well packed. It would have done your heart good to see me open it. A campstool duck of a thing; boiled ham, pickles, jelly—everything fine. I wrote a reply. Also wrote Governor Buckingham; you may hear of it. We try to be [illegible] even here. Today a letter from Commissioner Hitchcock showed the "wooly head" in the question of exchange. I thought it would come to it, and them [illegible]. All summer it has been side-dishes served up, but for Thanksgiving we* got the big full-grown negro. How it will come out I know not, but trust that that race won't keep 50,000 soldiers in durance rice. But from the tone of the letters that is the only hitch; get that out of the way and paroles won't keep the Commissioners apart long. We are all well here nowadays. All the clothing & rations sent here by U.S. has been delivered by the Confed. authorities, Surgeons' report to the contrary. Our commissioned officers superintended it, and the confederate authorities acted in the best possible manner. It was a foul lie about the rations being piled up in sight of prison and not issued. Only such a cracked lot of fellows as our late medical fellow prisoners could spread such a yarn. Give the devil his due. The authorities issued the commissary goods, and made them by their care last 12 days, issuing all that men wanted. There was not that number of days' rations sent. But by the judicious act of them, they lasted longer than at home. This is a little longer than allowed, but I desired to vindicate persons wrongly accused.

Much love,
Charlie

---

**Comment:** "Durance rice" meant prison food.

The North now had made it completely clear that no exchanges would be made unless *all* Negro prisoners were included.

Charlie seems to be sincere in his defense of the Libby authorities who had been accused of starving prisoners.

---

Richmond, Va.
Dec 16 1863

My dear Fredrick:

Your letter of 2nd came today. I've desired the name etc. of Alfreds de Satiens. Send all the news you can rake or scrape, we are hungry for news. Glad that you were home 26th ultimate and had so fine a time. Also that "B" is doing well. I suppose that Atwater will get out of service this winter, if he desires to. Oh, how I want to be with the regiment. The late correspondence of commissioners shows the "nigger" in the fence. Well if fate keeps us here allright. I hope that some settlement will be reached. The status of the negro will be settled by the war. I don't think they will stand any higher north after than they did before the war. The reception of boxes from the North is stopped. I hardly think officer boxes are included.

Truly,
C.F.

**Comment:** Another in a long line of line letters in which Charlie accepted the North's uncompromising position that all Negro prisoners must be included in any exchange agreement.

"B" was probably Erastus Blakeslee, whose promotion to major had just been announced. Charlie probably was both envious and resentful.

---

December 17. *General cleaning out of the hospital. Winder's order reads "All capable of escape in hospital be returned to quarters." Maginnis came up, messes with Col. Ely. A rainy day. Article in Enquirer of this morning says to recognize the negro soldiers. Free ones, not slaves. Made a bet of $20 with John Maginnis that we would not be out of here on the 1ˢᵗ of Feb.*

---

**Comment:** Several escapes had been made by prisoners feigning illness so that they would be transferred to the lightly-guarded hospital section at Libby. The *Richmond Enquirer's* editorial position had already been accepted by the Confederate commissioner for exchange, but the two sides would continue to disagree on whether or not "contrabands" who joined the army were free soldiers.[452]

---

December 18. *Wrote Georgia "Merry Christmas," also Col. Fish.*

*Richmond, Va.*
*"Libby Prison"*
*Dec 19ᵗʰ 1863*

Dear Mother,

*Ere this comes to you, bringing news of my good health, familiar voices will shout in your ear "Merry Christmas." Accept one from our "prison house." I find myself as each day comes, thinking of years ago and time points to one in the field, one in Norwich, one in the wilds of the mountains, others in C. Such is life "checkered." Well the past experience has fitted me for such life. Three years ago now, I was truly suffering, a camp fire in the "rocky." Well this is luxury to it. Excepting Liberty. Those sufferings sink into insignificance when you add to it. Go where you please — that is what makes a prisoner's life so hard.*

*I am every day looking for a small box from you, and trust it will come before the 25ᵗʰ. Much love to you all and may we meet ere autumn leaves again cover the ground. But if we do, it will surprise the most of us. Ely, Hakes & all the 18ᵗʰ Cav are in good condition. One of the "Lenny's" of Philadelphia (Trott's friends) is here.*

*He introduced himself to me a few days since. Heard Katie speak of me often. Fine fellow, of 6ᵗʰ Pa. Cav.*

> *Much love,*
> *Charlie*

---

**Comment:** "C" probably referred to Chicago, where Charlie was a partner in the cast-iron stove business for several years before 1860. "The rocky" refers to the Rocky Mountains near Central City, where he was prospecting for gold in the spring of 1860. This was his most poignant testimonial yet to the value of freedom.

---

December 19. *Wrote Mother & Col. Fish. Col. Streight and Capt. Reade made an attempt to escape last night. Gave guard $100 and his watched guard peached, and after they were over in the street, fired in the air, when they found themselves surrounded by a squad of men who were in waiting, under the command of Lt. Furche He was returned to prison, confined in cell and ironed. Judge Auld says officers' boxes can come through.*

---

**Comment:** Colonel Streight, the senior imprisoned officer, was probably the escapee who was put in chains after being recaptured.

---

December 20. *Wrote Misses Graines thanking them for box.*

> *Office Commissioner for Exchange*
> *Fort Monroe, Va.*
> *Dec 21ˢᵗ 1863*

Mrs. Farnsworth
Norwich, Conn.
Madam

*I have the honour to acknowledge the receipt of your letter of Dec. 14ᵗʰ. The Rebels are still receiving packages for our prisoners sent by <u>individuals.</u> I will therefor forward the box alluded to in your letter to Maj. Farnsworth at Richmond.*

> *I am, madam*
> *Very Respectfully*
> *Your obed't servt*
> *S.A. Meredith*
> *Brig. Gen. Comm for Exch.*

**Comment:** Brigadier General Meredith was the North's agent for exchange, serving under General Hitchcock, the commissioner for exchange.

*December 21. Recd. letter from Mother of date Dec 5th. Rumour says a proposition has been made of our side and accepted for an exchange of prisoners. Maj Ferris came in to see Col. Cavada and so informed him. He says we go soon. 25 tons of boxes came up. Made a bet with Warner that we would be out of C.S.A.M.P. before April 17, 1864 of $35.*

**Comment:** A shipment of twenty-five tons of boxes from individuals showed a very high level of citizen support for these prisoners of a Confederate States of American Military Prison (i. e.,"C.S.A.M.P.").

> *Richmond, Va.*
> *"Libby Prison"*
> *Dec 22 1863*

*My dear Mother,*

*Your short letter of Dec 5th came today. I expect the box will be here ere long as we learn Officers' boxes will come through. So don't worry over the matter. I am very much in hopes to receive it ere the 25th so as to remember you all upon that day in a dinner from that box.*

*So Fred is a voter since time flies. It reminds me, I am aged. He will soon meet the world's waves of fortune. May he take the flood tide. We have received boxes from many of our friends and are in good condition since they came.*

*The Gaines' box was splendid, and the S.S. came in good time. But we are glad they sent them, for without it our table would be* scant.

*We wait patiently for our deliverance, and it cannot come too soon. I trust the box contains a few late papers for we get but little news from home.*

> *Much love,*
> *Charlie*

*Ely, Hakes & 18th well.*

**Comment:** Charlie's younger brother Fred turned twenty-one on December 5, becoming eligible to vote. Charlie, the "aged" middle brother, would turn twenty-eight on January 30, 1864.

December 23. *Order from Gen. Winder to select 3 of the most influential "Captains" from New England regiments to be held as hostages for 3 of same rank held by us at Allan, Ill. Capt. Turner selected by lot. It fell on Capt. Litchfield 4ᵗʰ Inf., Capt. Chase R.I. Cav., and Capt. Kendall 7ᵗʰ Ind. They are to be taken to Salisbury, N.C. or some state penitentiary.*

---

**Comment:** In an act of retaliation, Richmond provost marshal Winder sent three New England captains to harsher confinement. Lucky for Charlie that he was registered as a major, not as a captain.

---

December 24. *Recd. box from home of Dec. 5ᵗʰ. Contained $5 gold, which was retained by C.S.A authorities. Grand concert by Minstrels. Christmas. Warner and Ely indecisive as to leave, but gave up the idea. Major White taken as a hostage, sent to Salisbury. Usual officers and 150 men came in tonight.*

---

**Comment:** Not all smuggled gold coins got past the guards.

The "Minstrels" were blackface prisoners, presenting an entertainment for the holiday.

---

December 25. *Gave dinner party for Col. Cavada and Maginnis:*

Soup

Oysters

Roast Chicken                          Boiled Mutten

Vegetables

Potatoes           Onions            Cabbage

Entrees

Cold Boiled    Ham

Cranberry sauce                Pickled peaches

Apple sauce                 Pickled onions

Gerkins      Piccadilly      Chocolates

Chicken pie               Oyster pie

Celery

Pastry

Apple Pie

### Dessert

Walnuts                                          Raisins

Oranges

---

**Comment:** A stunning menu at any table, but especially at Libby Prison! Or was Charlie being facetious?

---

December 26. *Accident on canal—boys drowned. Rumour after rumour comes in today, favorable to exchange. A truce boat up with 500 prisoners, a like number returned. Also Capt. O'Keef, Lt. Cameron, and Lt. [blank in original]. Rumour says the cartel is agreed upon and that we all go north within a month. Bah. Wrote Mother in answer to hers recd. 24*[th] *1863.*

---

**Comment:** Although general exchanges were not yet agreed upon, apparently large numbers of prisoners were being paroled. In theory, they would be eligible to return to action only when the same number and rank of Confederate prisoners were sent south.

---

Richmond, Va.
"Libby Prison"
Dec 26 1863

*My dear Mother,*
*    The box of Dec 5 came on the 24*[th] *and was very opportune for "Christmas." The ham was in centre of table. Col. Cavada dined with us. We had a splendid table from goods sent from home. The remittance sent in box was taken by the authorities. We are not allowed money now, since as reported by our keepers, the U.S. does not allow their prisoners to receive money. As much obliged to you as though I was allowed it. Much love to Aunt H for can of meat. Dwight received every thing in good order. Well, but oh! how anxious to see home and friends. Weather has not been very severe for us up country fellows.*

Much love,
Charlie

*18th all well.*

---

**Comment:** The Eighteenth Connecticut Infantry was composed mainly of Norwich men, among them three friends of Charlie—Colonel William G. Ely, Lieutenant Dwight W. Hakes, and Lieutenant John T. Maginnis. Charlie's family would have been interested in hearing about all three in order to pass news on to their families. All three would be paroled in March 1864. Ely and Hakes survived the war; Maginnis was killed in action at Piedmont, Virginia in June 1864.

---

December 27. *Made a bet with Bowen of $20 that we are not paroled or exchanged by the 1ˢᵗ of Feb 1864. Made a bet with Loomis of $1 — money in hands of Hakes — that we are here Feb. 13, 1864. Made bet with Loomis of $5 gold in hands of Hakes that we are not paroled or exchanged by Feb. 1, 1864. Released Maginnis from $20 bet on Feb. 1, 1864. Made bet with Adams 12ᵗʰ Cav. that we are not exchanged on Feb. 1, 1864. Wrote a letter to Father for U.G. This letter sent by [blank in original].*

---

**Comment:** Betting among the friends had reached casino levels, with Charlie almost always making a pessimistic prediction as to the date they would be released from Libby.

---

December 28. *Recd. letter from Fish 10 Dec. Wrote Fish. Cancelled bets with Loomis, he paying me $1. Wrote a letter under date of 25ᵗʰ to Georgia and sent in one to Father under date of Jan. 1. Sent by Lt. M. Jan 15ᵗʰ.*

December 29. *The year draws to a close and still we are held within prison walls. Our hopes are daily raised by rumors of being exchanged, only to be depressed by information that an obstacle is in the way. Weekly a special goes away, showing that there is but little principle in the matter, for if that principle can be ignored for one it can for a thousand. We doubt the existence of any true principle. Yet we suffer for what: Exchange and What. Six months of suffering and no prospect of release. We see the rebel daily giving down, and our Govt. daily raising new issues. Actions to make 46,000 in their hands work wonders.*

---

**Comment:** Charlie accepted the principle that Negro prisoners must be included in any exchange agreement, but after witnessing a number of "special exchanges," he began thinking that the North benefited inordinately from the general freeze. The South needed its prisoners returned more than the North did because the South lacked the huge pool of manpower that the North enjoyed.

---

December 30. *The south is evidently growing weak. They are short of men [illegible]. Many of their own issue worth 15 for $1 greenback and 20 to 35 for $1* *gold. They seize conscripts to put everyone in the army, do everything in a desperate manner. Their railroads are worn out. Their cavalry is worn down, their supplies gone. Each day loses as we advance upon them from all points. They will make one desperate fight in Virginia and if whipped will move south, concentrate all their armies for one desperate struggle. The end comes within 18 months and not much shorter.*

---

**Comment:** The third sentence seems garbled, but the meaning of the overall entry is clear. Charlie knew the South was losing men and matériel. His forecast of the end coming in about June 1865 was only a couple of months off the mark.

---

December 31. *The last of a year. What a cold rainy day. The leads of the papers are blue. They see but little hope for the future, still they fight on. "Glorious victories," but "loss of territories." "Brave troops," still "lose ground." Everything looks blue for them. Capt. White was put in cell for trying to bribe guard. Two officers go north tomorrow. Lights burn till midnight — having sweet dreams of freedom and old friends. A nice mare assists my pillow as in days of yore. Ah, those happy days and nights will never return — then was my "Gala Days."*

---

**Comment:** In his view, the southern newspapers were emphasizing hope over reality. A true cavalryman, Charlie's thoughts turned to his horse on New Year's Eve.

---

# 1864

*January 1. A clear cold day. Col. Ely had a dinner party. The first day of a new year in prison and no prospect of an exchange. We suffer for our country, and I trust everyone here confined are willing to suffer to the last in support of our common country. Wrote Father, enclosing a letter to Georgia with a post-script of Jan 4. This letter to G was of unopened date Jan 25, recd. Jan 25; left here Jan. 15, recd. Jan 23<sup>rd</sup>.*

---

**Comment:** Charlie started the New Year with this rededication to sacrifice for the Union cause.

It is unclear what the odd reference to Jan. 25 in the letter to Georgia indicates, but apparently the January 4 letter was delivered eight days after it left Libby on the fifteenth.

---

*January 4. Recd. letters: Fred Dec. 11, Mother Dec. 17, Cuz Harry Dec. 19. Answered them this evening. Reports are bad. Warner betting on April 1<sup>st</sup>. Wrote Cuz Harry that army must not leave Baltimore. Wrote home. This letter was received at home on Jan. 27. Georgia speaks of a letter of this date as having been recd. by her upon the 23<sup>rd</sup>.*

---

**Comment:** Charlie's worry about Baltimore's security may have been greater than the Lincoln administration's; Marylanders in general had cooled in their support for the Confederacy since the Battle of Antietam in September 1862. On the other hand, Erastus Blakeslee's report, written after the Civil War, stated "The secession element being strong in Maryland, the business of the [First Connecticut Cavalry at Camp Chesebrough] was large [during January 1863-February 1864]."[53]

---

*Confederate States Military Prison*
*Richmond, Va. Jan 4 / 64*

*My dear Mother,*

*Your letter of 17<sup>th</sup> ultimate came today, glad to hear you have dates to 3<sup>rd</sup> ultimate. Both boxes came duly, of this have advised. Geo. Ward is here, saw him a short time since. We (E, H, and myself) sent him a box of tea, sugar, etc., for which he was very much obliged and expressed himself in a note. Carver is on Belle Isle; well yesterday. I sent them some things not long since. Glad H.M. has seen you.*

*Heard of him in service through letter of his to Col. Ely. See by letter of cousin Harry that Walter has again gone abroad. Conflicting reports in regard to boxes. Some understand officer boxes are allowed to come; others, all boxes stopped. I suppose private boxes will be allowed as our govt. allows permission to receive packages from their friends. Fred gave me a lecture on not writing oftener, as though we were not restricted as to letters. Of course it would not do, to write oftener than once in ten days, as the authorities could not examine them.*

*All well,*
*Charlie*

---

**Comment:** "E and H" were Colonel Ely and Lieutenant Hakes. Private Thomas Carver of Norwich, a member of Blakeslee's Company A, was captured in a skirmish at Waterford, Virginia in August 1863. Thomas's brother, Corporal Michael Carver, had been killed in a First Connecticut Cavalry skirmish at Stafford Courthouse, Virginia in January 1863.

"Walter" was Charlie's cousin Walter Loring Farnsworth, age nineteen, the son of his uncle Walter, a Boston businessman. Charlie is unimpressed that this military-age relative had "gone abroad" for at least a second time. Charlie also seems irked that his twenty-one-year-old brother, Fred, was whining about not getting enough attention from him.

---

*January 6. Wrote father, also sent a letter to N. H., in Washington. Today a complete list of officers was taken to be forwarded to our govt. This does not imply an exchange, or any steps toward one, as they send these lists quarterly. There appears but little show of an exchange, at the present writing. The feeling here is very strong towards the policy of the govt. Many a hard word comes. This is all wrong. We should suffer as long as our rulers think it necessary, and it is for the good of our government.*

*"Libby Prison"*
*Richmond, Va.*
*Jan 6th / 64*

My dear Father,

*Letters received by last mail from home, Fred & cuz Harry. Glad to hear from you all, and as often as you can. Letters, though short, are very earnestly sought, and looked for. My last letters from Fish giving me the list of recent promotions. They are all good ones, and will give the regiment as fine a lot of officers as I know of. I suppose it will be full ere I reach it. And that next spring it will be at the front.*

*How much better will I feel there, than here. There is little interesting matter for contemplation in our present position. We read, and study all it is possible, but it is a difficult matter to apply your mind. We now number a thousand, and should much prefer serving our govt. at some other station. Still, like good soldiers we shall await "marching orders." We are all well. Ward is still here, well when last seen. I think there has not been any boxes received since 11ᵗʰ ultimate. My best regards to all. Last letter from Mother was date Nov. 29, recd. 16ᵗʰ ultimate.*

*Much love,*

*Charlie*

---

**Comment:** Although the First Connecticut Cavalry battalion was officially enlarged to a regiment in December 1862, about five hundred recruits were needed to fill out this second battalion. Charlie seemed resigned to the reality that the positions were filling quickly and that someone else would be appointed commander of the new battalion.

The Libby buildings, which housed about six hundred Union officers when Charlie arrived, now had about a thousand and had become suffocatingly over-crowded. With six rooms of about five thousand square feet apiece, Libby now provided about thirty square feet per prisoner, the equivalent of a 5 x 6-foot space.

---

*January 9. General Morgan, Adj. Hill, Colonel Alston, and others visited prison today. He is a well-built man. Morgan proposes to exchange Streight for Col. Duke. Three men froze to death upon Belle Isle last night. Great indignation meeting on sale of sanitary goods. Heard of death of Thomas Carver—froze to death.*

---

**Comment:** It is unclear which Confederate General Morgan that Charlie is referring to.

Private Thomas Carver in fact was not one of the prisoners who froze that night. He survived the war.

---

*January 12. Great indignation meeting against Lt. Col. Sanderson, owing to specified acts of arrogance and ill treatment of our men on the island. Severe resolutions offered by Capt. McKee, voted down. Sanderson is very unpopular indeed.*

---

**Comment:** The "indignation meetings" were initiated by Libby prisoners in 1863 to raise morale. Here, the officers leveled a very serious charge against a senior officer. Lieutenant Colonel James M. Sanderson, a captured Union commissary officer, had been given the task by Confederate authorities of distributing clothing and other provisions to the thousands of enlisted prisoners on Belle Isle. His fellow officers thought Sanderson had not performed well. Arriving in the North as part of a prisoner exchange in March 1864, Sanderson was arrested and charged with "cruelty to Federal prisoners," among other offenses. After a trial before a military commission, he was found guilty and dismissed from the army.[454]

*"Libby Prison"*
*Richmond, Va.*
*Jan 13th 1864*

*My dear Brother,*

*We are without a truce boat for nearly three weeks, and hardly know when one will come. I write so that you may hear of my continued good health to the date of this. We have been having a cold snap and did not suffer over-much, our clothes and blankets from home being a great acquisition. My last box was Dec 5th and my stock is running down. I am in hopes the next boat will bring those necessaries again. I am anxious to hear from you, but suppose some good is intended by this stoppage of communications. Our prison life was varied by a visit from Gen. B. H. Morgan. We saw the general, he has been receiving the hospitalities of the city, and from paper accounts has had a gay time. He is very fair, well-built, quiet man. My last from you was Dec 16, home 17th. You will report me at Mother's when you are there as well to date. Say I wrote a letter giving our "bill of fare" for Christmas. Please inform me if received. Write all the news you can. Use letter paper instead of note. Regards to Lt. C. and any of the 1st you may meet. Th. Carver of Norwich is dead; Monroe, Ferris & others well.*

*Much love to all from Yours Affectionately,*
*Charlie*

---

**Comment:** Charlie repeated his earlier mistaken report; Private Thomas Carver was not dead, but was still confined at Belle Isle.

Further identity of General Morgan is not known.

---

*January 13. Wrote Georgia and Fred and Mother. Capt. Metcalf, N.Y, is reported going north on parole. L and Geo. go today. A confederate Major was in today. He came here on parole to effect an exchange for Major White of Penn. He says he is going back as Auld will not send White north. This does not look well for exchange.*

January 14. *Six months ago today I was captured. Little thought we that today would see us here. I have been well since, not missed a roll-call since I came here. Of the men taken with me, some still remain in Belle Isle. Several have gone home, owing to exchange of the sick.*

January 15. *Papers report a truce boat and a meeting of the commissioners yesterday. Capt. Gregg L. Metcalf and a Lt. in hospital go north today. Rumors say that exchange is more complex than ever. Grand fizzle of some 20 soldiers' escape.*

January 16. *Boat up with some 400 boxes. A large mail, but no prisoners. U.S. refuses to remove Butler. Confed. States firm. No exchange for a long time expected. Boxes will not be issued owing to reported actions of Butler. Sanitary goods all issued. There has been very poor use made of them. Officers have used them, when the men on the island are suffering.*

---

**Comment:** General Benjamin F. Butler, already infamous in New Orleans as "the beast" for hanging a civilian flag-burner, was preparing to move his Army of the James up river toward Richmond, as one prong of the 1864 Union offensive that would feature Sherman's drive across Georgia, Sheridan's drive up the Shenandoah Valley, and Grant's assault upon Lee's forces. Libby officials retaliated against Butler's action by withholding boxes that had just arrived.

Poor hygiene, as well as lack of nutrition, was prevalent on Belle Isle. By "sanitary goods," Charlie may have simply meant soap.

---

January 17 (Sunday). *No issue of meat today. No service today. Spent in reading. Sunday is even observed in prison; very little card playing on that day. Everyone reads and writes, passing the day quietly.*

January 18. *No meat today. Sanderson rescinded his boxes unopened. No one else can have any.*

---

**Comment:** Sanderson, the Union commissary officer condemned in Charlie's January 12 diary entry, may have been retaliating against his fellow officers for their criticisms.

---

January 19. *Mail recd. Letters from Mother Dec 29th, Georgia Dec. 21st & 27th, Capt. Goodwin Jan. 3rd. Wrote Mother a letter. Also answered Capt. Goodwin. A truce boat reported up. Auld goes down tomorrow to learn if our boxes will be issued if Confed. prisoners can receive them. Ould thinks this is the last boat for a long time, that all negotiations are suspended. If so we are in for it sure...*

---

**Comment:** Colonel Robert Auld (sometimes spelled "Ould" by Charlie) was the Confederate commissioner of exchange. General E. A. Hitchcock was his counterpart in the north. The two sides negotiated for months but failed to reach agreement for a general exchange in 1863 or 1864. They did, however, arrange a number of special exchanges.[455]

---

*"Libby Prison"*
*Richmond, Va.*
*Jan 20th 1864*

*My dear Mother,*

*A boat with mail and boxes came Saturday. Mail came in today. There is some question about the delivery of the boxes, and it may end in none being delivered. The present complicated state of the exchange question makes everything doubtful. You may soon be cut off from writing even. This action of the Govt. may be right. Of course we unlucky prisoners cannot question it. I wrote to Father Jan 1st and addressed a letter to G in his care same time. Both will be received together. Should she be absent, please forward. Answer if you received it, please. Your letter of Dec. 29 came in today; more to come in tomorrow. Glad you received my letter of North as it was important. I wrote you in regard to the same matter about Jan 1st (mentioned above), hope you have it. Sorry to hear of Father's illness. Trust he will be better, and that I shall soon meet him. Lennig is well. I do not remember your writing in regard to him. I have letters from G of Dec 21st & 27th. Also a letter from Capt. Co. B saying all my boys had reenlisted. Glad to hear it.*

*Hakes and E are well.*

*Much love from*
*Charlie*

---

**Comment:** "Capt. Co. B" was probably Captain Leonard P. Goodwin, who took command of Charlie's company in October 1863. "Lennig" is unknown.

Enclosed with this letter was the following one, written in "invisible ink:"

---

*I wrote you to warm my letters, this will explain why.*

*Write in this way on opposite side, writing at the reverse angle so as to correspond with start of the reverse page, which should be written heavy. Also write across the* lines and write lightly; it will pass. Write with lemon or onion juice, [illegible] water. Heating will bring it out. Iron the letter with a hot flat iron. It will then appear OK. Then you can write a long letter giving much private news. I sent you a few days since a long letter enclosing one to Georgia. Did you receive it? I ask the same question on other page. You see how we hurt. We are in a sorry plight now, since exchange is stopped. I tell you our chances are slim for getting out for the war. We must endure for the sake of these confounded rebs. I wish all the niggers were out of the country. Then this would not happen. But we will brave it out. I am well supplied with eatables for the present, nothing elaborate. But when we come down to regular rations, oh we have not [left blank]. We have not had meat for 3 days, only cornbread , just such as Pat mixes for Old Gray every morn, baked. That is all we get from the Govt. How I hope Jeff will some day get the same kind of diet. Please write Georgia to [illegible] my letter after this date. Also impart to her the <u>art</u>. Please inform Mrs. Magginis, Marcia Vale, also Mrs. Hakes, of this as her husband will write in this way. Also how and with what to write. You can by this means. Write me long letters, giving me all the news.

I send this letter as an experiment; if successful, I shall be glad. Please write Georgia in regard to it and who to detect this, and as how to do it, and request her to write to me. Winter is fine, and it will pass

Love, Charlie

Write Col. Fish to iron with a hot flat iron my letter of Jan. 22$^{nd}$.

---

**Comment:** In his first "invisible ink" letter, Charlie wrote with onion or lemon juice, horizontally and vertically across both sides of the letter. His family followed instructions to apply a warm iron to the paper, and the writing became legible.

Charlie, despairing of any general exchange because of the South's punitive policy toward black prisoners, lashed out for the first time at the African-American presence in general.

"Pat, who mixes for Old Gray every morn," was probably a colorful metaphor comparing the prisoners' rations to a horse's. Charlie wished upon Confederate president ("Jeff") Davis a meal of the same cornbread that he was getting.

---

January 20. Recd. letter today: Mother Dec. 28, Jan 1 & 8; Fred Dec. 29$^{th}$; Fish Dec. 27; Goodwin Dec. 22$^{nd}$. All the mail here has been delivered. Another expected in a few days. Letter of Fish says my interest is well-guarded, that Battalion muster is Dec. 18, and that mine will date back to the same as his.

**Comment:** The "interest" that Lieutenant Colonel William S. Fish, commander of the newly enlarged First Connecticut Cavalry *Regiment* (after the creation of a second battalion in December 1863), was referring to was Charlie's promotion to major in March 1863. It appears that Charlie was worried that the promotion would not be recognized if he was not present for duty when the new regiment formally mustered. In fact, the promotion *was* later revoked, and apparently for that reason. Years would pass before the War Department reinstated the promotion.

---

*January 21. Wrote Georgia. [Illegible.] Recd. today Mother's letter of Dec. 5ᵗʰ, also Father's. Wrote Georgia that letter of Dec. 3ʳᵈ just received. Wrote Mother, answering receipt of sausage meat. Also sent reply to [illegible] on the consumption of a heavy amount of apple duck.*

---

**Comment:** "Sausage meat" and "apple duck" were probably code words for Northern newspapers that were smuggled in with the boxes of provisions.

---

*"Libby Prison"*
*Richmond, Va.*
*Jan 22ⁿᵈ / 64*

*Dear Mother,*
  *Your letters of Dec 28ᵗʰ 1863 Jan 1 & 8ᵗʰ 1864 came today. You are I trust in receipt of letters settling the Dec 5 box question; it came for "Christmas." You need not enclose five cents for letters. They do not pass through the mail here. A few stamps, two (2) on a letter might reach me. Please rescind <u>immediate</u> notice of any receipt of box — I am not generally behind in such matters.*

*Much love, affectionately from*
*Charley*

*We opened yesterday the box can of sausage meat, found it very nice indeed. Send one can of same kind in next box. It is better flavored than any we have. Dwight was glad to receive his share of it.*

*C*

The following letter, undated, was enclosed with the January 22 letter to his mother and apparently written with invisible ink:

*I know you wished to write but feared it would make me trouble if found natural. The searching is not severe and if sent as this was will come all right. If you have called my attention to the can by saying you had better open such a thing first, I should have found it before. As it was, we had a can open and did not find it until today. Send more the same way; many should have come same way. As it was, they got it but will return it when we leave, I suppose. But when the letter sent you I suppose H.R. told you the way we wished it. This way is another dodge, and may work well. But when Mrs. Hakes or you send, please enclose in each other's boxes. Then we shall always have news.*

*I did not suppose that you had my letter informing you of this means of communicating as you said nothing in open letters, so not finding any thing in bread, supposed the next box would have the letter requested. I sent you 3 letters with 2 by Hakes and one covering one to [illegible]. Have sent one since on "ocean paper," please so mention in open letter. Thomas Carver was frozen to death, another victim to rebel barbarity in not giving prisoners sufficient covering. You will not so inform his Mother. Poor woman. [Illegible] you in regard to death in war open [illegible]. I did all I could for the men, gave them all the money I had and sent two large boxes to them. Carver was a fine soldier. I pity his mother, poor woman.*

*We do not understand Kempt's marriage; suppose the woman was very poor.*

*Mrs. Schenck is a fine woman and a great friend of mine. She does not hansome much but has a good heart. Miss Taylor is from Washington, a splendid family. I wrote you about them when in Washington. The general was there when sick. I thus became acquainted. I am very glad Father showed the General so much [illegible]. He has been very kind to me and will always help me when in his power. He is a fine man. I hope he will be in the field again and we under him. But I fear he cannot return to Baltimore again. If not, Fish will have to rejoin his regiment for no one else would keep a Colonel in that [illegible] unless personally friendly, and then Schenck would be willing for me to have command of the regiment. Any other General Command dept. would order Fish to it. That is one reason why I desire to get out early.*

*You must keep up a good heart. We suffer for our country, and are willing to. Even to laying down of life if retaliatory measures come to the [illegible]. Remember we do for the country as much here as in the field, though a bullet is better than a rope for a soldier. Still we will try and stand firm.*

*Sad news of Capt. Theo. Glad CPW has child; one also would [illegible] the name would have suited him better.*

*Was W.D. in the army as a private or as an officer? Has he taken the oath or is he a rebel prisoner only?*

*I suppose you and yours have letters to expect from N & WWB; well we must work the harder. But I do not see how they can stand it should they cast us off.*

*Much love,*
*[unsigned]*

---

**Comment:** In this secret letter, Charlie again reminded his mother to send letters hidden in cans of provisions.

"Does not hansome much" probably means "is not easily handled." Nearly two weeks had passed since January 9, when the death of Thomas Carver on Belle Isle was erroneously announced, but Charlie still did not know that he had survived.

Charlie apparently believed that his close relationship with General Schenck and his wife would get him assigned to command the new regiment if Fish were ordered elsewhere.

"A bullet is better than a rope for a soldier" seems a grim thought to write to any mother.

---

*January 22. Answered Fish letter of Dec. 25. Wrote Mother to write Fish. [Illegible.] Wrote Georgia a letter on ocean card. Streight's room was shut off from ours. Doom all chance. But yanks saw-cut a half of up stairs clear, and after night we have full communications. Small taken out by McGill and went around twice, is to be paroled and sent home soon.*

---

**Comment:** Colonel Streight, being punished in solitary confinement for his attempted escape on December 18, was reconnected with his fellow prisoners through their ingenuity and courage.

---

*"Libby Prison"*
*Richmond, Va.*
*Jan 23ʳᵈ 1864*

*My dear Fredrick,*

*Dec 29ᵗʰ your last date. I saw that Marcy was with the regiment. I suppose from recent letters that Colburn meets with more success than Marcy did. I rec'd. names of some new officers from Goodwin. By the way, Co.B have reenlisted, and will all be home on furlough. Remember when you meet them that they were my old company—a good set of fellows remain. A. is to be married in May, wants me to stand up with him. I wish I felt it possible, that our exchange would come before that time. But a pleasure I looked forward to will be denied me. Such is the fate of soldiers. We are never our own masters after enlisted. My kindest regards to him when he returns. I am glad Father is better. I notice that the grim angel is making many a victim in our circle. [Illegible] — Norwich — is that stock at par now. Watch well, years come fast after 21. Much love. G speaks of your visit with pleasure,*

*Charlie*
*Major, 1ˢᵗ Conn.*

---

**Comment:** Major George O. Marcy became one of the First Connecticut Cavalry's top staff officers when it was enlarged to a regiment in December 1863. Charlie thought that Marcy had been a failure as captain of Company D.

Captain Leonard P. Goodwin took command of Charlie's Company B in October 1863.

Charlie was proud that his Company had reenlisted in the newly formed regiment. "A" is Captain Howell Atwater. "G" is Georgia Parker.

---

*January 23. Wrote Fred and Capt. Snider two letters to [illegible] to read together. Guard came in and stopped canning in the kitchen. Kept them under guard for a long time. Congressman here in regard to our rations. Saw Dow, he was not much pleased with our bread. He said we should be exchanged soon. No meat for 8 days. 3 men shot on Belle Isle. Recd. letter from Huntly.*

---

**Comment:** The Libby prisoners had been receiving letters from home in cans of milk. They were now trying to send messages to the Belle Isle prisoners in "excess" canned products, but were caught in the process.

General Neal S. Dow, wounded and captured near New Orleans in July 1863— and transported all the way to Richmond for confinement—probably was now the senior Union officer at Libby.

It is unknown why three Union soldiers were executed on Belle Isle.

---

*"Libby Prison"*
*Richmond, Va.*
*Jan 24ᵗʰ 1864*

Dear Father,

*Your letter came today and gave me great pleasure. For the interest Senator Foster has shown I am very thankful, and feel if efforts were made, the end could be gained. I have hoped a general exchange would be effected for the benefit of those confined on both sides, for there is little fun in being cooped up when the excitement of the field is preferred.*

> *Much love, affectionately,*
> *Charlie*
> *Major, 1ˢᵗ Conn. Cav.*

---

**Comment:** U. S. senator Lafayette S. Foster was a friend of Charlie's family.

Although Charlie naturally believed that a general exchange would be "for the benefit of both sides," General of the Army Ulysses S. Grant was coming to the conclusion that such exchanges were counterproductive because they prolonged the war and increased the bloodshed.[456]

---

January 24. *Gave letter written to Georgia upon ocean paper to Col. P. who will deliver letter of this date.*

---

**Comment:** "Col. P" is Colonel Powell, who went north on parole to try to arrange a special exchange of prisoners.

---

> *Richmond, Va.*
> *Jan 25 1864*

*Hon. R. C. Schenck*
*Washington D.C.*

*Dear General*

Since my confinement here there has been a number of Special Exchanges. The authorities here are willing to return a man of equal rank for one sent here on parole by our Govt. with the understanding that he procure the parole of a specified officer. I would request of you if not incompatible with your duty that you write Maj.Gen. Butler and request him to parole a Major and allow him to proceed to Richmond and procure the parole or exchange (the latter preferred as I can then be with my regiment) of myself. If such an arrangement can be effected and I know it has been done in a [Remainder of letter is missing.]

---

**Comment:** Robert C. Schenck, Charlie's former commanding general, was now an Ohio congressman. Charlie was trying here to cash in on his long and loyal service to a man he greatly admired.

---

State of Connecticut
Executive Department
Norwich, Jan 25th 1864

R. Farnsworth, M.D.
Norwich

Dear Sir

I take pleasure in enclosing for your son Maj. Charles Farnsworth a Commission as Lieut. Colonel of the 1st Regt. Conn. Cavalry and trust the way will soon be open for his release from rebel imprisonment and barbarity, and for his entrance upon the more active duty of repressing the rebellion to which he has been so loyally & faithfully devoted.

I am with high regard
your obt servt
Wm. W. Buckingham
Governor of Connecticut

---

**Comment:** This was the promotion that Charlie was hoping for, one that would have entitled him to take command of a battalion in the new regiment. Unfortunately for Charlie, he was still imprisoned, and this fact would later affect the War Department's view of the governor's promotion.

---

January 25. Recd. letter from Frank [illegible] enclosing $5 for his brother. Exchanged for $75 Confederate, retained by the authorities in hands of Capt. Moffet. Wrote Father, also General, in regard to a special exchange.

---

**Comment:** Charlie is referring here to his letter to Congressman (formerly "General") Schenck.

The Confederacy/Union currency exchange rate now was about 15/1.

---

January 26. Long walk with Capt. Adams downstairs. All of our cavalry scouts talked over. Capt. Carraway of Conn. escaped from [illegible], captured, brought here.

---

**Comment:** "Talked over" probably meant that the troopers were convinced to reenlist.

---

*January 27. Visited Belle Isle with Col. St. Louis. Saw Ferris, Carver, Monroe, Phelps, Bradley, Bishop, Lavof, Rutter, 2 Millers, Clary (in hospital), Wesson, Sutterman, Huntly (in hospital) still here. The camp is in a fine location, but much crowded. All stood up for the Govt. and do not want any backing down.*

---

**Comment:** Private Thomas Carver of Norwich had previously been reported dead on Belle Isle, so Charlie was probably surprised to see him. Quartermaster Sergeant Weston Ferris, Sergeant Franklin H. Monroe, Corporal Amos C. Bradley, Private Peter Miller, and Private Patrick E. Clary had been captured with Charlie at Harpers Ferry. Corporal Samuel G. Phelps and Private Ebenezer Bishop had been captured at Waterford, Virginia in August. Bradley died on Belle Isle. Clary was sent to Andersonville, where he died. The others survived their imprisonment. All were members of the First Connecticut Cavalry. Lavof, Rutter, the other Miller, Sutterman, and Huntly cannot be further identified.[457]

Charlie limited his admiration for Belle Isle to its location, which few would disagree with. But the camp had neither enclosures nor sanitary facilities; prisoners lived and slept in the open, exposed to the elements.

---

*Libby Prison*
*Jan 28 1864*

*Dear Mother*

*Well to date. Carver is not dead as reported. Well, and has not been sick since he came here. Little news to communicate except continued fine health. Remember me to all. Letter from Billings came today. 1ˢᵗ from him since my migration south.*

*Much love,*
*Charlie*

*Boat reported, so I send these few lines.*

---

**Comment:** It seems odd that his thirty-four-year-old brother, Coddington Billings, had not written to Charlie during the first six months of imprisonment, even though Billings had come with their father, Ralph, to attend Charlie after he was wounded in the Shenandoah Valley in April 1862.

---

*January 28. Wrote Col. Fish a letter in regard to exchange. Also Mother in regard to Carver's death. Also to write Gideon Ferris, New Haven. Also a short letter containing names of soldiers on Belle Isle to Bulletin for publishment. All the letters in code. They are putting in window bars in all the windows. Reported — that an equal number of officers to Major command are to be confined in cells.*

**Comment:** Surprisingly, the Libby warehouse lacked bars on its windows until this time. "Letters in code" probably meant that they were written with "invisible ink."

Nothing is known of the rumor about an apparent retaliatory lock-up of junior officers.

---

January 29. *Boat up. Col. Powell, Capt. Hunter, and four others go north today. The news by the morning papers favorable for exchange. Letter written to Georgia on the 24ᵗʰ goes by this boat. Saw Fish's account in morning papers. Nine hundred sick prisoners in hospital. Major Bates and Capt. Porter made their escape.*

---

**Comment:** One Libby warehouse room, measuring about 4,700 square feet, was used as a hospital. With 900 patients, each prisoner would have had about a 5 x 9 foot space for himself. A ghastly sight, if accurate.

---

January 30. *Twenty-eight days ago today I made my first appearance in this world. Lt. King, Capt., & brothers followed Bates' example and left for better quarters. Great excitement in Libby roll calls. Every two hours the Rebs find their count over [at] new 4R and next time fall short as many. Lots of fun. Bates was retaken and put in cell this morning.*

---

**Comment:** It was his birthday, but he misstates his age as twenty-eight *days*.

With escapes becoming more frequent, the prison authorities were now requiring more musters and head-counts. (A major escape by tunneling in February was being planned; Charlie probably knew of it at this point.)

"4R" is probably the warehouse section where he was confined.

---

January 31. *More roll calls today. Total number of missing: nine. Maginnis received his letters.*

February 1. *Lt. King captured and returned to prison. Mail distributed. Recd. letters from, and answered Fred Jan 15ᵗʰ, Goodwin Jan 18ᵗʰ, Mary Jan 20ᵗʰ, and Georgia Jan 23ʳᵈ. Order issued that only one letter a week be allowed each prisoner and that only six lines. Order speaks of the "so-called United States."*

*"Libby Prison"*
*Richmond, Va.*
*Feb 7 / 64*

Dear Father,

Order issued limiting letters to six lines. No letters from Mother by last boat. Through G learn of receipt of letter sent by Mother. Trust you have my last letters. Expect box soon. We are also allowed but one letter a week.

*Much love, Charlie*

---

**Comment:** The Libby authorities had tightened the rules on prisoner correspondence, limiting outgoing letters to six lines and allowing only one incoming letter per week. The limitations may have been punitive or may have been necessitated by the prison's inability to read and censor the large volume of mail to and from a growing prison population.

---

*Senate Chamber*
*Feb. 3 1864*

My dear Mrs. Farnsworth,

I have just made the acquaintance of Col. Powell, who left the Libby Prison on Friday last, where he has been confined as a prisoner since last July. The rebels allowed him to come on his parole for 30 days, to see if he could effect an exchange for the rebel Col. Lee whom we hold prisoner. The exchange will no doubt be effected.

Col. Powell knows your son well, and says he is in good health and in good spirits. I inquired particularly for him, for my memory often recurs to the time when he wore a long-sleeved apron and came often to our house to hold in his lap our little Joanna. Those days are now far in the past. Sad changes have since come over us and over our country. And God reigns over all nations and individuals, and doeth all things as it pleaseth Him. To submit to his will is a duty not attained without painful struggles.

I have frequently been both to the President and the Secy. of War to see if something could not be done to relieve our unfortunate prisoners. Nothing has been accomplished. I now mean to try if something cannot be done by way of special exchange. Col. Powell says that all the supplies now sent by individuals to the officers in prison are delivered. Nothing will be received from the Government nor from societies such as the Sanitary or Christian Commission.

I drop you these line, my dear Mrs. Farnsworth, knowing your solicitude for *your son, and thinking it possible you might not have as late news from him as last Friday.*

> *With kind regards to the Doctor,*
> *I remain very truly your friend*
> *L.F.J.Foster*

---

**Comment:** This personal letter from US senator Foster of Connecticut to Charlie's mother showed clearly how well connected the family was.

---

**February 9.** *Grand exit of 109 commissioned officers, 21 Field officers, discussed at roll call. Col. Ely left, also Gamble, Small, & Good. Lots of fun during the evening getting ready & watching the guards.*

**February 10.** *Roll call in the rain. Two officers recaptured early. One in the navy-yard. The mode of escape unknown till late P.M. Guards placed under arrest — supposed they were bribed. Turner in a [illegible, but perhaps "account."].*

---

**Comment:** Charlie was referring either to Major Thomas P. Turner, the prison's commandant, or to Richard ("Dick") Turner, the civilian manager of the prison. It was probably the latter, who could have been held to "account" for not knowing whether the guards were bribed to overlook the tunneling that went on for seventeen days.

---

**February 13.** *Recd. mail today. Letters from Mother Jan 24ᵗʰ, 27ᵗʰ, Fred Jan 25ᵗʰ, 28th, Mary Jan 27ᵗʰ, Georgia Jan 31ˢᵗ. Col. Ely returned today. The whole number recaptured is 44.*

---

**Comment:** Seeing his friend Colonel Ely recaptured after the mass escape may have reassured Charlie that he hadn't missed out on anything good. The total number recaptured would reach forty-eight.

---

> *"Libby Prison"*
> *Richmond, Va.*
> *Feb 14 1864*

*My dear Mother,*

*Yours of 24 & 27 ultimate came 18ᵗʰ. Glad to hear from you, often as possible. My last was written on 7ᵗʰ. Col. Ely is here, returned yesterday. Please speak to*

*W.A.B. and Senator F in regard to the matter of conversation when he left for Washington. I have written R.G.S. in the matter. Late developments in the 1ˢᵗ require the presence of Capt. of Co. B. Urge the matter.*

*Much love*

*Charlie*

*Maj 1ˢᵗ Conn Cav*

---

**Comment:** Although one line longer (in the original) than the prison limit of six, this letter got through the censors. Charlie conserved space by using initials: "W.A.B." was Connecticut Governor Buckingham; "F" was Connecticut Senator Foster; "R.G.S." was his former commanding general, now Congressman, Robert C. Schenck. "Capt. of Co. B." was Charlie himself, who was trying to pull all the political strings he could.

---

**February 14.** *Wrote Mother, Fred, Georgia, Major Marcy. Made memorial of letters.*

**February 20.** *Truce boat at City Point. Boxes and mail. Col. Loer for whom Col. Pearce was paroled came on this boat. Papers contain accounts of several officers from Schnider Island to Baltimore — 394 of them. Supposed they will be sent here for exchange. We have had a week of extreme cold weather. Capt. Day recaptured & returned to quarters.*

*Libby Prison*

*Richmond, Va.*

*Feb 21 / 64*

*Dear Mother,*

*I wish very much for you to see and obtain all the influence of W.A.B., L.P., & F and others in regard to the matter of our thought. I wrote RGS a second letter. If F was not in trouble he could do a good deal. Still S can effect it & will do his best. Carver and others of 1ˢᵗ and 18ᵗʰ have been removed to Americus, Ga. All well. Boxes are still unsettled.*

*Much love from, affectionately,*

*Chas. Farnsworth*

*Maj 1ˢᵗ Conn Cav*

**Comment:** Although again exceeding the prison's six-line limit in the original (by two lines), this letter passed through the censors. As in his February 14 letter, Charlie economized here on space.

Charlie probably did not realize it at the time, but the transfer of Thomas Carver and others of the First Connecticut Cavalry and the Eighteenth Connecticut Infantry to Americus, Georgia was bad news. They were going to the infamous Andersonville prison, where thirteen thousand of a total of forty-five thousand Union prisoners died. Carver, however, survived.

"L.P." is unknown.

*February 21. Wrote Mother & Georgia. Ferris & them of the regiment were removed today from the island and placed in the Pemberton building. Supposed they go to Americus, Ga..*

**Comment:** Charlie's Quartermaster Sergeant Weston Ferris probably was not sent to Andersonville prison in Americus, Georgia; he was released from Confederate confinement in November 1864.[458]

*Senate Chambers*
*Feb 24 1864*

*My dear Mrs. Farnsworth,*

*Many thanks for your kind letters.*

*From inquiries made, I can inform you that Charles did not escape from the prison at Richmond . He was well, when the others left.*

*The subject of special exchanges has not been overlooked by me. I have conversed with the President, the Secy. of War, and General Hitchcock who has the special charge of the matter. All gave me encouragement. Gen. Hitchcock advised me to write to General Butler at Fortress Monroe, as it would be through him that any thing could be accomplished. It is some time since I did so, and asked him if he would not name a rebel Colonel, a Lieut.Col., and a Major to exchange for Col. Ely, Lieut. Col. Nichols, and Major Farnsworth. I have not yet had an answer to my letter. I shall write again if I do not hear soon. I did not inform you of this before, fearing that nothing would come of it, and I should be raising false hopes.*

*There is nothing more to add at this moment. I write in haste while an exciting debate is going on in the Senate.*

> *With kind regards to the Doctor,*
> *I remain yours very truly*
> *L. F. S. Foster*

---

**Comment:** Senator Foster, at the family's urging, had carried Charlie's case all the way to President Lincoln, who probably sent Foster to the Union's commissioner for exchange, General Hitchcock. Hitchcock then suggested that the senator take up the idea of a three-officer special exchange with Major General Benjamin Butler, commander of the Union's Department of Virginia and North Carolina with headquarters at Fortress Monroe, located at the junction of the James River and the Chesapeake Bay, just north of Norfolk. Despite Senator Foster's intervention, the effort apparently came to naught, as he informed Charlie's mother. (It was Charlie's mother, not his father, who corresponded with the politicians on the matter of their son's imprisonment.)

---

> *Libby Prison*
> *Richmond, Va.*
> *Feb 28th 1864*

*My dear Mother,*

*Your last letter received is 27th ultimate. The last mail recd. on the 25th brought Dwight letters of the 12th, but not one for me. There is a mail here not delivered, which I trust has come. I learn of a box which left 9th (by Dwight's letter), not yet received. I am out of sausage meat, hope it contains a can. We are again in receipt of boxes and are well supplied. Press the exchange with all your power. Cousin Harry has sent me a box. Trust to receive it soon. Also boxes ordered by Ely, M., H., and myself from Baltimore. Write me all news you can. I wrote you that members of 1st & 18th here have gone to Americus, Ga., so inform friends.*

> *Much love,*
> *Affectionately,*
> *Charlie*

---

**Comment:** "Dwight" and "H" refer to Lieutenant Hakes. "M" is Maginnis.

By writing that he was "out of sausage meat" Charlie was signaling that he wanted more *news* smuggled in the cans.

---

February 28. *Wrote Mother & Capt. Marcy. Capt. Postin went north.*

*Annapolis, Md.*
*March 10 1864*
*R. Farnsworth, Esq.*
*Norwich, Conn.*

*Dear Sir:*

*It affords me great pleasure to enclose a letter from Major Farnsworth. It is written in invisible ink & will require the application of heat to render it legible. I was paroled on the visit, at which time Major F. was in good health. Major Norris of the Confederate Exchange Bureau promised me that he would procure his release at an early day. You will oblige me by acknowledging receipt of enclosure, addressing me at "Continental Hotel, Philadelphia."*

*I am, very Respectfully,*
*Your obedient servant,*
*H.F.Cavada*
*Lt. Colonel 114ᵗʰ Pa. Vol.*

*Norwich, Conn*
*Sept 10 1863*
*Col Cavada*
*114ᵗʰ Pa. Vol.*

*Sir:*

*I forwarded to you today a small package for my son on Belle Isle. Will you please confer a favor by seeing it committed to him.*

*With many kind regards,*
*Your sincere friend*
*R. Farnsworth*

---

**Comment:** Charlie wrote to his mother, using invisible ink on this old letter to Colonel Cavada, who was allowed to leave Libby with his personal correspondence. Cavada later added a note before forwarding the "invisible letter" to Charlie's mother: "The above was 'concocted' in order to enable me to pass it out of the prison as an old letter, previously recd. by me. HFC." The smuggled March 6 "invisible ink" letter follows:

---

*Libby Prison*
*Mar 6 1864*

*My dear Mother,*

I again appear to you through the medium of the underground railroad. One word about boxes: a new regime is in force. Our boxes are now more rigidly enforced. Now the boxes are searched before delivered, and out of our sight. Every article is opened and emptied out. Sugar, coffee, can fruits, everything. It is almost impossible to conceal anything. We do not get one half sent us, as they steal it, confiscating whole boxes upon merest pretext. They use us awfully since the "grand delivery," shooting anyone who comes in sight of the window, and using the most contemptible means to annoy us. I started to leave on the night of the escape, but an alarm of the guard deterred me. I am ~~not~~ sorry now, though I at the time acted as I thought prudently. We are now only allowed to write one letter a week, and that only six lines. So you see it is hard work to keep up a correspondence. Writing in this style has been discovered and all our letters are examined. I have not received any from you in this style. This I send by a officer who goes on a truce boat who will forward to you. Perhaps you see the dodge—a letter evidently received from the north, but written here is goes out with his letter, and is mailed at the north. The best way for you to write when you send box is in this style upon a sheet of paper, sending it as part of a quantity of same. Sending it as part of a quantity of paper in box, I can find it and bring it out. In future I will write with this upon the inside of the envelope of a letter and you can do the same. So in future, heat the envelope of my letter. Remember and write on inside of envelope and test all mine of later date than this. I would not advise you to send anything but small boxes with sugar, coffee, ham, &milk, and a few small articles as paper. Envelopes & paper etc.

These will come through without much trouble, and if lost will not involve much expense, and will do as good. But they are sharp now and look into everything, but you can write a letter as I tell you on the inside sheet of a quantity of writing paper and I shall get it without doubt. Remember the envelope way.

---

**Comment:** The letter was left unsigned, in case it was discovered among the papers of Col. Cavada, who carried it out of Libby. The prison authorities had obviously tightened restrictions on correspondence since the February 9 escape, which Charlie called the "grand delivery." For the first time, Charlie revealed that he had been part of the escape plot but had changed his mind when he thought he had been detected. Despite knowing that nearly half of the escapees had been recaptured, Charlie confessed (with a strike-through in the original) that he actually was sorry that he had acted prudently by staying in his room.

His mother noted on the bottom of the letter: "*No. 14. Charles March 6th '64; Recd. March 16th '64.*"

---

*"Libby Prison"*
*Richmond, Va.*
*Sunday March 6 1864*

*My dear Mother,*

*Your letter of Feb 9th came on the 2nd instant. The box has not come to hand. Perhaps it is, but not to send any more boxes. I see Fish is all right again. Fred wrote me on the 18th, little of interest. I trust W.A.B. will succeed [illegible] north. Our kind wishes to him. Regards & thanks to Mrs. S.S.P. for contents of box.*

*Love from*
*Charlie*

---

**Comment:** "W.A.B." is Governor Buckingham, upon whom Charlie had based his hopes for exchange.

His mother noted on the reverse side: "*The last letter Charles wrote from Libby Prison, March 6th, 10 days before he was exchanged. Came after he did.*"

---

*March 6. Wrote Mother two letters, one went north by returning officer. Arrival of paroled rebel prisoners — 800 men, 60 officers. Excitement in Libby.*

*March 7. 47 officers & 800 men went north today. Col. L. F., Lt. Col. Cavada. Sanderson, Archer, & Stratton, Major Nuper, Morton, Kobach, Edmander, & White. And Capt. Hubbell of 17th Conn. Won a bet of $25 with Warren that a commissioned officer would go amongst this 1st group.*

---

**Comment:** Mass paroles were suddenly taking place.

---

*11 West 16th Street*
*New York March 9 1864*

*My dear Mrs. Farnsworth,*

*Billings came yesterday with your letter; you may be certain that I will do all that is my power to cooperate with your other friends in soliciting the aid of influential persons capable of promoting the exchange of your son Charles!*

*I have no acquaintance with any of the "powers" in Washington, great or small, but I know General Meade. He was a member of my old corps, Topographical Engineers, while I was in the army, and it is to him that I will address myself. I do not know that he can exert any special influence in this case. Nonetheless, he is in a high position at this moment, and I feel assured that he will do what he can, and this for various reasons!*

*Billings told me that he had seen Mr. Myers again [illegible] and of General Butler, and that he would interest the general in the case. I think this the most direct & important move that can be made, it being the promise of General Butler, rather than that of any other person, to arrange with the rebel authorities for these exchanges, but, in such cases it is better to use with the affiliations which can be brought into action, if sometimes a very much and quite unexpected and [illegible].*

*I repeat that I will do what I can. I think with you that Charles has been quite long enough in prison to entitle him to consideration. The "powers" must be made to know the grounds upon which his friends work for his early exchange.*

*I do not know what policy the government intends to pursue in this question of exchange of prisoners, upon grand principles, and would suppose that no unnecessary delay should be allowed to take place, but I have been told (by a southern man) that the rebels say every prisoner in our hands is a good fighting man to them, while a large portion of the Union prisoners in their hands are very poor soldiers! Hence, according to their reasoning, our people do not desire an exchange, and to prevent it, that we are continually throwing obstacles in the way of such exchanges! Now this came to me through this union southern man, of the expectation that we hold unexchanged more than 30,000 of their men, against about 16,000 of ours!*

*If this theory be true, it will serve to account for the very slow progress which has been made — this matter of exchange of prisoners.*

*With kindest remembrances to you personally & the doctor from myself & my wife, I am very truly your friend,*

*W.H. Swift, Capt.*

---

**Comment:** Captain Swift, a well-connected family friend, had served under General George G. Meade, who was still one of President Lincoln's top generals. Nonetheless, Captain Swift also advised the family to lobby with General Butler, the commander of the Department of Virginia and North Carolina at Fortress Monroe.

---

## MEMORANDUM FROM PRISONER OF WAR RECORDS
### War Department
### Washington

*Farnsworth, Chas., Major, 1ˢᵗ Conn. Cav. Captured at Halltown, Va., July 14, 1863. Brought from Culpepper July 26-August 5, 1863, and confined at Richmond, Va. Paroled at City Point, Md., March 14, 1864, reported at Camp Parole.*

*Copied by R. B.*

---

**Comment:** Although his mother had noted earlier that Charlie was exchanged on March 16, the official records indicated that he was *paroled* on the 14th. The discrepancy in dates was insignificant, but the manner of release was important. If he had been exchanged, he could have lawfully returned to duty; if paroled, he had to wait until a Confederate of equal rank was sent south. Ordered by the War Department to report to Camp Parole, Maryland, it was clear that Charlie had been paroled, and was thus temporarily ineligible for action.

---

*March 18. Went to Washington and received leave for 20 days, and pay — as Captain to Feb. 29, 1863. Capitol. Gen. Schenck — made report to him. Denny, Farn., Bran, and all the accountables.*

---

**Comment:** Charlie was not paid for his time as a prisoner of the Confederacy—nor even beyond February 1863, for some unknown reason. But at least he was free and able to go on leave for three weeks.

---

*RE: CHARLES FARNSWORTH, Capt., Co. "B", 1ˢᵗ Conn. Cav., Baltimore, Md. March 19, 1864.*

*F. 247 ) Asks that an order may be issued to muster him in as Major, 1ˢᵗ Conn. Cav. to date from Oct. 5/63, and also to be mustered as Lt. Col. to date from January 20/64.*

*Forwarded by Lt. Col. W. H. Cheeseboro.*

*I am cognizant of the facts contained in the within statement. Major W. S. Fish was mustered in a Lt. Col. 1ˢᵗ Conn. Cav. on Oct. 5/63, & Capt. Farnsworth, at that time a prisoner of war at Richmond, Va., held the commission of major & was eligible to be mustered in as such. The organization of the regt. was completed Jan.*

*21 /64 & Lt. Col. Fish was mustered as Col. Major Farnsworth still a prisoner at Richmond as eligible to muster as Lt. Col.*

*Submitted by Honorable R. G. Schenck, Maj. Gen.*

*Upon the return of Capt. Farnsworth to his command, this will be authority for the C of M for his Div. to muster him into service as Major from date of Oct. 5/63 & as Lt. Col. from date January 20/64.*

*RE: CHAS. FARNSWORTH, Lt. Col. 1ˢᵗ Conn. Cav., Annapolis, Md. April 14/ 64.*

*F. 303 ) States that he is a paroled prisoner of war & requests that the order of March 31/64 giving the Commander of his Div. authority to muster him as Major from date of Oct 5/63 & Lt. Col. from date Jan 20/64 be modified so as to enable him to be mustered by Commander of the 8ᵗʰ A. C.*

*Resolved, that this will be authority for the C of M. 8ᵗʰ A. C. to make the muster in accordance with the previous decisions of the officer.*

---

**Comment:** These two hand-written memos were found in Charlie's official military records on file with the National Archives, and reveal varying opinions on what his proper rank should have been.

"C of M" probably meant Commander of Muster. "8th A.C." probably referred to the Eighth Army Corps.

---

March 19. *Baltimore. No [illegible]. Mary's to dinner. Rec. [illegible] and settled affairs with Haley. Rec. from him $200. Ordered [illegible]—robbed of all my private papers. Balt. 8-10.*

---

**Comment:** It was ironic that Charlie was robbed in the town that he formerly policed.

---

March 20. *Baltimore #88. Kibby & 50, self at [illegible]. $7.50 Hotel. Left 6 p.m. —fall.*

March 21. *New York. Hat $5. Clothes. Boots. Home fare 3.00.*

---

**Comment:** Charlie made the social rounds in Baltimore, shopped for civilian clothes in New York, and then went home to Norwich, probably by steamer.

---

*New York*
*March 21, 1864*

*My dear Mrs. Farnsworth,*

*I was truly glad to hear that Charles had escaped from the hands of the Philistines, and hope he may now be with you and the doctor to comfort you after the long period of anxiety which his captivity and suffering in prison must have produced in the minds of both while awaiting the tardy movements of the "exchange."*

*I enclosed my note for General Meade to Captain Bache, one of his aids, a nephew of the general, and a friend of mine, considering it probable that the case would be kept in mind more certainly if entrusted to the case of two, rather than one! I enclose from the note of reply from Captain Bache, which came this morning, that you may see, even in the case of General Meade himself, that his efforts to produce the exchange of this man's nephew came without results!*

*All this serves to add to the gratification you must feel that the thing itself has been successfully accomplished! With best wishes for you all in this happy ending of your pain, I am dear madam,*

*Your faithful servant*
*W. S. Swift, Captain*

---

**Comment:** The referenced note from Captain Bache has not been found, but Swift's letter suggests the family was able to at least plead (however unsuccessfully) with General Meade on Charlie's behalf, even though Meade at this time was under General Grant's command and was pursuing Lee's army in Virginia.[459]

---

March 22. *Arrived home from Richmond. Lecture. Phillips in evening.* Met HPL and went up with her. The same dear one to me. Where is the woman that has ever entirely forgotten and banished from the heart the memory of a true love? A first true affection. She received me with open arms, a warm kiss. "Ever am I the same to you, Charlie."

---

**Comment:** Charlie was finally home in Norwich. Recorded here is the first of many diary entries (mostly concerning his romantic life) made in his own homemade code. The entries have been decoded and set forth here in this separate font. Charlie's code was a unique combination of numbers, symbols, and substitute letters, along with several uncoded letters. Presumably to conceal his actions and emotions from prying eyes, he encrypted diary entries about his romance with "HPL," Harriet Peck Lester, whom he clearly had known before the war and whom he would later marry. (A copy of the deciphered code appears as an illustration.) He particularly enjoyed quoting verbatim

Harriet's professions of love for him. Charlie was still formally engaged to Georgia Parker, but he made no mention of her during this brief visit home. Harriet was born in Norwich in 1837, making her a year younger than Charlie. Her father, Walter Lester, was a famed Norwich ship captain. Walter's father, Captain Jonathon Lester, had built a sixty-foot war ship, the *Shark*, in Norwich for the revolutionary army in 1776.

---

March 23. *Meeting @ Breed Hall. Dined Mrs. & Geo. Ward. HPL at meeting.*

---

**Comment:** The Wards were the parents of Private George Ward, still imprisoned at Belle Isle.

Breed Hall, opened by John Breed in 1860, was a Norwich theater that produced lectures and entertainments.

---

March 25. [Illegible] *Meeting. 20th March. Allen* [illegible] *called. Fare .50, 1.75. Ret. .50, 1.75.*

March 26. *Self to H.* [Illegible.]

---

**Comment:** Charlie called on Harriet.

---

March 27. *At home all day.*

QUARTERMASTER GENERAL'S OFFICE
*Washington City, D. C.,*
*March 29th 1864*

Sir:

*Your Return of Clothing and Camp and Garrison Equipage rendered as commander of 1st Conn. Cavalry Vols. from 2nd April 1863 has been received and examined at this Office, and sent to the Second Auditor of the Treasury for settlement.*

*Remarks: Stoves (other than Sibley) and Regimental books should not be entered on Return of clothing account.*

*Very Respectfully Your Obdt. Servant,*
*By order of the Q. M. General*
*A. N. Robinson*
*Capt. & Asst. Q.M.*

*Capt. Chas. Farnsworth)*
*1ˢᵗ Conn. Cavl. Vols. )*

    *This is the last action of the Q/M Stores made of me, as I was captured soon after and have not drawn any since.*

*Ch. Farnsworth, Lt. Col.*

---

**Comment:** This document (with Charlie's response) was found in Charlie's official military records at the National Archives. It is unclear what the quartermaster thought Charlie had failed to return. Note that the War Department addressed Charlie as a captain, while he responded as a lieutenant colonel. The dispute over his proper rank would continue for years.

---

    March 30. *Meeting* [illegible]. *Nichols, 18 Aland, New London. Fare 1.00*

    March 31. *New London party. Good time. [Illegible]. Ward. Ely. Steadman. Breed Hall. Book & pen $3. Stamps .50.*

---

**Comment:** Colonel Ely was released from Libby with Charlie. "Ward" must refer to George Ward's father; Ward the son was still imprisoned at Belle Isle.

---

    April 2. *Harriet. Gay time. [Illegible.]*

    April 6. *Ball. Mary's dinner.*

---

**Comment:** This was probably his cousin Mary, of Baltimore and Winchester, Virginia. Charlie was en route back to nearby Camp Parole; his twenty-day leave would expire on April 7.

---

    April 10. *Called with F & K on Mason—tea.*

    April 13. *Returned from Annapolis.*

    April 18. *Ball Fair. Lincoln.*

---

**Comment:** Charlie may have attended a formal party in Washington where President Lincoln made an appearance.

---

SPECIAL ORDERS)

No. 160)

WAR DEPARTMENT,
ADJUTANT GENERAL'S OFFICE
*Washington, April 27ᵗʰ, 1864*

\*        \*        \*

45. Leave of absence is hereby granted the following officers:—
Lieutenant Colonel *Charles Farnsworth*, 1ˢᵗ Connecticut Cavalry, a
paroled Prisoner of War, for five days.

By order of the Secretary of War:

W. A. NICHOLS,
*Assistant Adjutant General*

April 27. *Left for Philadelphia. Atwater. Miss Chase. Miss Mitchell.*

April 28. *Atwater married. Stood up with Miss Mitchell 1338 Walnut at
Philadelphia. Miss Chase 1118 Girard at Philadelphia.*

---

**Comment:** Captain Howell Atwater, who resigned in January 1864, had been a junior
officer in Charlie's Company B. When Atwater asked Charlie to "stand up" for him
at his wedding, Charlie was imprisoned at Libby and thought that he would not get
out in time to attend. But he made it.

---

April 29. *Camp Parole.*

*1ˢᵗ Cav. Conn. / Field and Staff Muster Roll*

*Charles Farnsworth, Lt. Col., 1 Reg't Connecticut Cavalry. Jan and Feb. 1864.
Absent. Commissioned Lt. Col. on Jan. 19, 1864, but not mustered. Now a paroled
prisoner.*

*Merrill, Copyist*

---

**Comment:** From Charlie's military records, showing that he was still on parole and
suggesting that he was not entitled to the rank of lieutenant colonel.

---

May 1. *Miss Hibler.*

May 2. *Dined at Harrys.*

---

**Comment:** Harry Meredith was the husband of Charlie's cousin Mary; they kept a home in Baltimore.

---

May 4. *Beacher and Small. Small since killed.*

---

**Comment:** Charlie made this entry, and some others, long after the fact, using a subsequent year's diary for the notation. Here, he recorded in 1865 that he had seen these men in May 1864, but that one of them had since died.

---

*"Camp Parole"*
*Annapolis May 6th 1864*

*Col. A. R. Root*
*Commander, "Camp Parole"*

*Sir:*

*I have the honor to resign my commission as Lt. Colonel, 1st Conn. Cavalry Volunteers, for the following reasons.*

*Upon the 3rd of April 1862 whilst scouting near Morefield, Va., I was severely wounded by a ball passing through my left arm and side. I have suffered considerable pain and inconvenience from it, but have always been on and performed duty, though whenever mounted I suffer from pain in my left side and lung.*

*I was taken prisoner upon the 14th of July 1863, and having suffered from eight months' close confinement in the crowded rooms of "Libby Prison," Richmond, Va., I find my lungs so affected that it is impossible for me to ride without excessive pain in my left side and lung.*

*Believing that my command would be benefited by it, I tender my resignation. Being a paroled prisoner at this time, my command would be the gainer of a field officer, much needed by them.*

*I am very respt*
*Your Ob. Servant*
*Chas. Farnsworth*
*Lt. Col. 1st Conn. Cav.*
*"Paroled Prisoner"*
*Annapolis, Md.*

**Comment:** Perhaps tiring of being a useless parolee for almost two months, undoubtedly in poor health from his wounds and imprisonment, realizing that the regiment would benefit from the promotion of someone else into his position as lieutenant colonel—or perhaps disappointed and resentful that Erastus Blakeslee had been promoted ahead of him—Charlie decided to resign. The report of the medical examiner, which follows, was intended to support the resignation, although it seemed to find Charlie only temporarily disabled (i.e.,"for several months").

*"Hospital Camp Parole"*
*near Annapolis, Md., May 6, 1864*

*Medical Certificate:*

*Lt. Col. C. Farnsworth, 1ˢᵗ Conn. Cavalry (paroled prisoner), having applied for a certificate on which to ground the tender of his resignation, I do hereby certify that I have carefully examined this officer and find that he has two "cicatrices" of the left arm and lower portion of his chest —the result of a perforating gun-shot wound, which he states he received about two years ago; that two months ago slight [illegible]; and that he suffers severe pain when riding on horseback or taking other active exercise.*

*It is, in my opinion, quite probable, although his general health is good, that this condition of his chest may prevent him from discharging active duty in the field for several months. Two scars in his left arm, the result of a flesh wound, are of no consequence.*

*This officer is not physically disqualified for service in the "Veteran Reserve Corps."*

*F. H. Gross*
*Surgeon U. S. Volunteers*
*In charge of Hospital*

**May 12.** *Exchanged. Ordered to regiment.*

*Washington, D. C. May 14, 1864*

*Col. E. D. Townsend*
*Asst. Adj. Genl. U.S.*

*Sir:*

*Having upon the 6ᵗʰ instant tendered the within resignation, upon the enclosed surgeon's certificate to Col. A. R. Root, commanding Camp Parole. Whilst awaiting my certificate from the Ordnance Department, I was declared exchanged, and ordered to my regiment. Being incapacitated, for the reasons set forth in my resignation, from doing duty, I respectfully request the immediate acceptance of my resignation as Lt. Col. 1ˢᵗ Conn. Cav.*

> *I am very Respt*
> *Your Obt. Servt.*
> *Chas. Farnsworth*
> *Lt. Col. 1ˢᵗ Conn. Cav.*

---

**Comment:** A Confederate prisoner of Charlie's rank (whether lieutenant colonel or captain is unknown) apparently had been sent south, allowing Charlie's status to be converted from "paroled" to "exchanged," and thus making him immediately eligible for active duty. But having taken the position just a week earlier that he was physically disqualified from active cavalry duties, Charlie could not now take advantage of his new status, even if he wanted to. (Blakeslee was now in command of the regiment, and Charlie at best would have been a battalion commander taking orders from Blakeslee, a prospect Charlie undoubtedly dreaded.) On the other hand, Charlie's hasty decision to resign had cost him the opportunity to muster with his regiment and thereby confirm his status as a lieutenant colonel, a loss that would haunt him in the future.

---

May 14. *Tendered my resignation.*

May 15. *Lt. Goddard, 8ᵗʰ Conn. Vols., killed south side of James River.*

---

**Comment:** Lieutenant Alfred M. Goddard, an infantry officer from Norwich, was a friend of Charlie, and of Harriet.

---

SPECIAL ORDERS)                     WAR DEPARTMENT
No. 178)                     ADJUTANT GENERAL'S OFFICE
                             *Washington, May 16ᵗʰ, 1864*
                                        (Extract)

\*     \*     \*     \*     \*

7. Major *C. Farnsworth*, 1ˢᵗ Connecticut Cavalry, having tendered his resignation, has authority to await in Baltimore the decision of the War Department thereon.

> By order of the Secretary of War:
> E. D. Townsend
> *Assistant Adjutant General*

SPECIAL ORDERS)                   WAR DEPARTMENT
No. 179)                ADJUTANT GENERAL'S OFFICE

*Washington, May 17*[th]*, 1864*

(Extract)

\*      \*      \*      \*      \*

33. Captain *Charles Farnsworth*, 1st Connecticut Cavalry, having tendered his resignation, is hereby honorably discharged the service of the United States, on account of physical disability, with condition that he shall receive no final payments, until he has satisfied the Pay Department that he is not indebted to the Government.

By order of the Secretary of War:

E. D. Townsend,

*Assistant Adjutant General*

---

**Comment:** Charlie had submitted his resignation as a *lieutenant colonel*. Two days later, the War Department granted him leave as a *major*. The following day, his resignation was accepted, and he was discharged as a *captain*. The War Department gave no explanation at the time for these rapid reductions in rank. Disregarding these official actions, Charlie continued to hold himself out as a lieutenant colonel.

It is not clear how Charlie was supposed to prove that he owed the government nothing, as the War Department was demanding.

---

May 17. *Baltimore.*

May 18. *Ely, Maginnis, Warren in Baltimore.* [Illegible] *for regiment. Ely on to G.G. Bot ring of Meredith.*

---

**Comment:** One day out of the cavalry, Charlie went to see some of his Norwich friends of the Eighteenth Connecticut Infantry Regiment with whom he had been confined at Libby Prison. It was the last time he would see Maginnis.

---

May 22. *Capt. McCall buried. Masonic and military (ceremonies).*

June 10. *At Norwich.*

June 11. *"I was determined to ask you on this drive. Now I am satisfied."*

---

**Comment:** Back in Norwich, Charlie was seeing one of his women. Because this entry was not encoded, Charlie was probably not quoting Harriet. More likely, he was quoting Georgia, to whom he probably gave the engagement ring he had acquired in Baltimore. His heart, however, was clearly being drawn to Harriet.

---

June 14. *New Haven. Atwater's.*

June 15. *New York. Made a loss of $4,672 on stocks.*

---

**Comment:** After his release from the army, Charlie had started to watch commodity prices (oil, gold, steel), but he had never before mentioned the stock market. How he suffered this enormous financial calamity is unknown.

---

June 18. *Heard of Culver and Maginnis' death at Piedmont.*

---

**Comment:** Officers of the Eighteenth Connecticut Infantry, Culver and Maginnis had been imprisoned with Charlie at Libby and probably had been paroled with him. They were killed as infantrymen in General Philip H. Sheridan's victorious drive up the Shenandoah Valley in the summer of 1864. Charlie had seen Maginnis just a month earlier.

---

June 24. *Billings sent for. Fred home.*

June 25. *Mother very low. Billings came. Miss Jane Deaner came.*

---

**Comment:** Charlie and his two brothers were now with their mother, who had fallen ill. Billings was a businessman, although he would become a doctor a decade later. Frederick had just graduated from Yale.

---

Charlie submitted the following affidavits to the Commission of Inquiry by the United States Sanitation Commission, which was investigating treatment of prisoners of war by the Confederacy:

# NARRATIVE OF PRIVATION AND SUFFERINGS OF UNITED STATES OFFICERS AND SOLDIERS WHILE PRISONERS OF WAR IN THE HANDS OF THE REBEL AUTHORITIES

Being the Report of a Commission of Inquiry, Appointed by the United States Sanitary Commission With an Appendix Containing the Testimony And Also Copies of Photographs of Returned Union Soldiers after Their imprisonment at Belle Isle (1864).

Testimony by Letter of Lieutenant-Colonel Farnsworth, 1st Connecticut Cavalry (at p. 155):

Norwich, June 29, 1864

**Gentlemen**: In reply to a letter from one of your Committee, I have the honor to make the following statement of what I saw, heard and felt of the treatment of prisoners of war by the Confederate authorities at Richmond, Virginia:

I entered service October, 1861; was captured on the 14th of July, 1863, in a cavalry skirmish near Halltown, Va.; was conveyed to Richmond, and confined in Libby Prison; was paroled and sent North on the 14th of March, 1864.

My treatment by my immediate captors was gentlemanly in the extreme; even going so far as to assist me in concealing money, so as to prevent the Richmond authorities from robbing me.

Upon reaching the Libby, we were rigidly searched, and all moneys and attractive jack-knives, nice overcoats and meerschaum pipes were kindly appropriated by the prison authorities; rubber blankets, canteens, spurs and haversacks were taken from us. Lieut. Moran, for complaining of this treatment, was knocked down by Richard Turner, inspector of the prison clothing.

There was never an issue of clothing or blankets made by the Confederate authorities during the time I was there confined. We did receive one hundred (100) each of tin plates, cups, knives, forks (mostly damaged by bayonet-thrusts, they having been picked up from battle-fields), for the use of one thousand officers.

ACCOMMODATIONS—In six (6) rooms, one hundred by forty, there were confined as many as twelve hundred (1200) officers of all ranks, from Brigadier-General to Second Lieutenant. This space was all that was allowed us in which to cook, eat, wash, sleep, and exercise. You can see that soldierly muscle must fast deteriorate when confined to twenty (20) superficial feet of plank; we were not allowed benches, chairs or stools, nor even to fold our blankest and sit upon them; but were forced to sit like so many slaves upon the middle passage.

This continued until the appointment of General Butler, Commissioner of Exchange, after which time we were allowed chairs and stools, which we made from the boxes and barrels sent us from the North.

There was plenty of water allowed us, and a tank for bathing in four (4) of the rooms.

There were seventy-six (76) windows in the six (6) rooms, from which in winter there was no protection.

SUBSISTENCE—Our rations consisted of one-quarter (1/4) of a pound of beef, nine (9) ounces of bread of variable quality, generally of wheat flour, though sometimes of wheat flour and corn meal, a gill of rice, and a modicum of salt and vinegar per day. This continued until the 11th of November, which was the first day that meat was not issued, and bread made entirely of corn meal was substituted for wheat bread; this meal was composed of cob and grain ground together, and when mixed with cold water without salt or any raising, made the bread. Meat was next issued on the 14th, and issue suspended on the 21st. On the 26th we received slat pork, sent to the prisoners by the United States Government; from this time out, meat was like angels' visits; sometimes it was issued at intervals of ten days, and sometimes not in thirty (30) days; the longest interval was thirty-four (34) days.

The amount of rations first issued will undoubtedly sustain life; but their long continuance without exercise will produce disease of a scorbutic nature.

The rations issued after the 11th of November will not sustain life, and without the aid sent to us from the North, the mortality would have been great. Nine ounces of such corn bread and cup of water per day, are poorer rations than those issued to the vilest criminal in the meanest States Prison in the Union; yet this was considered fit treatment by the *hospitable* chivalry of the South to be extended to men taken in honorable warfare, any one of them the peer of the arch-traitor, Jeff. Davis.

BOXES—We began to receive boxes in October. These came in good order, were inspected in our presence, and delivered to us entire; they came regularly, and were delivered in good order up to about the 1st of January; after this time boxes were sent regularly from the North, and were received by Col. Ould, Commissioner of Exchange, but they were *not* issued to us; they were stored in the building within sight of the prison, and at the time of my leaving, three thousand (3,000) had been received there and not delivered to us; what was the cause of this non-delivery of boxes we were never informed. They keep up a semblance of delivery, however, by the issue of five (5) or six (6) a week, they receiving from the North about three hundred (300) a week.

The contents of these boxes were, undoubtedly, appropriated to the private use of the officials in and about Richmond. Here is simply one instance: Lieut. Maginnis, of the 18th Reg., Conn., since killed in battle, recognized a suit of citizen's clothes which had been sent to him from the North, on the person of one of the prison officials, and accused him of the theft, and showed his name on the watch-pocket of the pants. Such cases were numerous.

BELLE ISLE. Upon the 26th day of January, 1864, I visited Belle Island, as an assistant in the distribution of anything sent by the Government and by the Sanitary Commission of the North; this was my first time outside of the prison walls in six months. The island is situated just opposite the Tredegar Iron Works, in the James River. The space occupied by prisoners is about six acres, enclosed by an earth-work three (3) feet in height; within this space were confined as many as ten thousand prisoners. The part occupied by the prisoners is a low, sandy, barren waste, exposed in summer to a burning sun, without the shadow of a single tree; and, in winter, to the damp and cold winds up the river, with a few miserable tents, in which perhaps one-half (1/2) the number were protected from the night fogs of a malarious region; the others lay upon the ground in the open air. One of them said to me: "We lay in rows, like hops in winter, and take turns who has the outside of the row."

In the morning, the row of the previous night was plainly marked by the bodies of those who were sleeping on in their last sleep.

Fed upon corn bread and water, scantily clothed, with but few blankets, our patriotic soldiers here suffered the severest misfortunes of this war. Here, by hundreds, they offered up their lives in their country's cause, victims of disease, starvation and exposure—sufferings a thousand times more dreadful than the wounds of the battle-field. As many as fourteen (14) have been known to freeze to death in one night. This I have from men of my own regiment, and it is perfectly reliable.

The hospitals upon the island are Sibley tents, without floors, the ground covered with straw, and logs of wood placed around for pillows, to which, when about to die, the men were carried; and here, with logs for their pillows, the hard, cold ground for their bed, death came to their relief, and the grave closed over the victims of rebel barbarity.

The officer in charge of the island was well spoken of by the men. He deprecated the condition they were in, but said he could do no more, for the authorities gave him no more to do with; and yet it is a fact that the men were stimulated to work at their trades, as blacksmiths, &c, for the benefit of the Confederate Government, by the offer of double the quantity of rations they were then receiving, thus acting out, in their treatment of Northern soldiers, the great principle of Slavery and of the South, that the lives of the poor and helpless are in their eyes of no more value than the amount of interest they will produce on capital.

The facilities for washing were good, a sandy beach all around the island, and the whole number of prisoners could have washed in the course of the day; but, under the management of the authorities, only a limited number (say 75 men per day) were able to wash, being conducted under guard to the water, in squads of five (5) or six (6).

The sickness caused by the above treatment was of the respiratory organs, pneumonia, &c., and chronic diarrhea.

Men were without medical treatment on the island until disease was so far advanced that when taken away in ambulances to the hospital, in squads of twenty (20), one-half (1/2) of them have died within five (5) hours—some of them while their names were being taken at the hospital.

Men were returned from the hospital to the island when so weak that they have been obliged to crawl upon their hands and knées a part of the way.

On the 20th of November, 1863, a squad were passing the prison (Libby) in this condition, going from the hospital to the island; among them was George Ward, a schoolmate of mine and of Col. Ely, of the 18th

321

Conn. Vols. Col. Ely threw a ham to him from the window. As the poor fellow crawled to get it, the rebel guard charged bayonets on him, called him a damned Yankee, and appropriated the ham.

The bodies of the dead were placed in the cellar of the prison, to which there was free access for animals from the street. I have known of bodies being partially devoured by dogs, and hogs, and rats, during the night. Every morning the bodies were placed in rude coffins and taken away for burial. Officers have marked the coffins thus taken away, and have seen them returned twenty (20) times for bodies. You may draw your own inference as to the rites of burial extended to a Yankee prisoner in the Capitol of the Southern Confederacy.

Officers dying, their brother officers procured metallic coffins and a vault, in which they were placed until they could be removed North. An officer, (Major Morris, of the 6$^{th}$ Pennsylvania Cavalry, I think,) who had in the hands of the Confederate authorities several hundred dollars taken from him when he entered the prison, died in the hospital, and the authorities refused to use his money for a decent burial, and we raised it in the prison.

LIBBY MINED—Upon the approach of Kilpatrick on his grand raid on Richmond, about the 1$^{st}$ March, the greatest consternation was produced among the inhabitants. The authorities felt sure of his ability to enter the city and free the prisoners.

We were informed one morning by the negroes who labor around the prison, that during the night they had been engaged in excavating a large hole under the centre of the building, and that a quantity of powder had been placed therein. Upon inquiring of certain of the guards, we found it the general impression among them that the prison was mined.

Richard Turner, inspector of the prison, told officers there confined, that "should Kilpatrick succeed in entering Richmond, it would not help us, as the prison authorities would blow up the prison and all its inmates."

The adjutant of the prison, Lieutenant Latouche, was heard by an officer (Lieutenant Jones, 55$^{th}$ Ohio,) to use the following words to a rebel officer with whom he had entered and examined the cellar where the powder was reported as placed: "There is enough there to send every damned Yankee to hell."

Major Turner said in my presence the day we were paroled, in answer to the question, "Was the prison mined?" "Yes, and I would have blown you all to Hades before I would have suffered you to be rescued."

Bishop Johns said in the prison, when asked if he thought it was Christian mode of warfare to blow up defenceless prisoners: "He supposed the authorities were satisfied on that point, though he did not mean to justify it."

> I am very respectfully,
> Your obedient servant,
> CHAS. FARNSWORTH
> Late Lieutenant-Colonel 1st Connecticut Cavalry

> Norwich, June 30th, 1864
> State of Connecticut, )
> County of New London )

Personally appeared Charles Farnsworth, signer of the foregoing instrument and statement, and made solemn oath that the facts stated therein are true, before me.

> DAVID YOUNG
> Justice of the Peace

## ADDITIONAL TESTIMONY BY LETTER OF LIEUTENANT- COLONEL FARNSWORTH

> NORWICH, CONN., *July* 16th ,1864.

Rev. TREADWELL WALDEN,
Philadelphia:

**Sir**—Your favor of the 14th inst. received. In answer to your request for a written statement of facts, related to you by myself in conversation, in regard to the conduct of the guards at Richmond, Virginia, and the provision made for the sick upon Belle Isle, I submit the following:

In what is known as the "Pemberton buildings," nearly opposite the "Libby," there were confined a large number of enlisted men. Hardly a day went by that the guards did not fire upon the prisoners. I have known as many as fourteen shots to be fired in one day. They were thus subject to death if they merely came near the window to obtain fresh air. It was a very common occurrence to hear the report of a musket and then see the sergeant of the guard bring out a wounded or dead soldier.

The guards would watch for an opportunity to fire upon their prisoners, and, without warning the prisoner to leave vicinity of the window, fire.

Lieutenant Hammond, of the Ringgold cavalry (better known to Libbians as "Old Imboden,") was at the sink, which is constructed upon the outside of the building. From the upper part of the sides, boards are removed for the purpose of light or ventilation. The guard below caught sight of Lieutenant Hammond's hat, through this opening, showing that the guard was intent upon striking his man; but a nail gave the bullet an upward turn and it passed through Hammond's ear and hat-brim. From the position he was in, there is little doubt that but for the ball striking the nail he would have been struck in the breast.

The attention of Major Turner was called to it, but he only laughed and said, "The boys were in want of practice." The guard, when spoke to about it, said, "he had made a bet he would kill a damned Yankee before he came off guard." There was not the least attention paid by the commander of Libby prison to this deliberate attempt at *murder*.

Lieutenant Thos. Huggins, of a New York regiment, was standing at least eight feet from a window on the second floor; the guard could just see the top of his hat. To be sure of his man, the guard left his beat and stepped into the street. Being seen, a warning cry was uttered, and Huggins stooped and the bullet buried itself in the beams above. This was the same guard that fired at Hammond.

Richard, or as usually called, Dick Turner, was the inspector of the prison, and acted under the orders of the commander. There was nothing too mean for him to do. He searched you when you entered, knocked you down when you grumbled, took your blanket from you if found lying upon it after morning roll-call, never spoke of you except as damned Yankees— told you "you were better treated than you deserved."

This "high-toned Southron" was employed as the negro-whipper of the prison.

Colonel Powell, 2d Virginia cavalry (Union), Colonel Streight and Captain Reed, 51$^{st}$ Indiana, and others who had been confined in the cells, used to witness the whippings, (the cells were at one end of the cellar where the whipping-block was,) and they could hear,—even if they shut their eyes to the horrid exhibition.

Colonels Powell and Streight hold me of as many as six negro women

324

having been stripped and whipped, at one time, for having passed bread to our soldiers as they marched through the street.

The flogging of the negroes that worked at the Libby was an every-day occurrence.

These blacks were free negroes from the North, who were employed as servants, but fell into the hands of the enemy. He flogged one of them so severely that he was unable to move for two weeks, and walked lame months after. His offence was resisting a white negro-driver.

The hospital tents on Belle Isle were old Sibleys. These were not temporary hospital, for many died in them each day; but when they could not contain all the sick some sick were removed to Richmond hospitals. These tents were awful places for human beings to be placed in—without floors, a heap of straw for a bed, logs of wood for pillows—men died with less attention than many a man pays to a favorite dog. The hospitals in Richmond were much better, being in buildings, and were furnished with bunks and straw beds,—some of them with sheets. But though treated with kindness, compared with Belle Island, the want of proper medicines was visible, and many died for the want of the most simple remedies.

Upon the 25th October, 1863, two officers, (Major Hewston, 132d New York, and Lieutenant 4th New York Cavalry),escaped from the hospital. Immediately, upon its being known, all the sick who were well enough to sit up or stand, were removed from the room and placed in an empty room under our prison. Here they were kept for twenty-four hours, without food or blankets, as a punishment, it was said, for not reporting the contemplated escape of the officers named. From this treatment, Surgeon Pierce of the 5th Maryland died.

The officers in the room above, removed a portion of the floor and furnished the sick with food and drink, and shared their blankets with them. This coming to the knowledge of Major Turner, we were deprived of rations for one day—October 29th, 1863.

This was not the action of the surgeons of the Libby, for, with one exception, they were kind and attentive, and did all in their power for our comfort, but of the commander of the department, Brigadier-General Winder, and of Major Turner, commander of the prison, who, I am informed, was dismissed from West Point, by orders from the Secretary of War, having been convicted of forgery.

I was informed by men whom I knew—Ward and Winship of the 18th Connecticut, and Ferris and Stone of the 1st Connecticut—that the enclosure in Belle Isle was a mass of filth every morning, from the inability of the men to proceed to the sinks after evening.

Many of the guards would fire upon the prisoners for the least violation of the rules. The men were in a miserable condition and looked sickly, worn out—starvation and exposure was expressed upon their features.

Trusting that the above will assist you in your report,

I am respectfully yours,
CHARLES FARNSWORTH

Sworn to and subscribed before me, this 18th day, of July, A. D.1864,
DAVID YOUNG,
Justice of the Peace.

---

**Comment:** The United States Sanitary Commission was formed in early 1861 by a group of New York women to provide clothing for Union troops. The commission's mission expanded to include disease prevention, and then was made a governmental agency in June 1861. Charlie provided his testimony in mid-1864 to a Commission of Inquiry that was clearly interested in more than prison hygiene. Charlie reported here, for the first time, that captured freedmen were regularly whipped in the Libby cellar.

---

July 4. *Tea at Mrs.Gen. Evening at Martha. Boss & E.P.*

---

**Comment:** "Mrs. Gen." is the wife of General William Williams, the uncle of Charlie's mother, at whose home Harriet was boarding. "Martha" is probably Martha Ripley, a childhood friend of Charlie and Harriet, and who was still unmarried.

---

July 6. *Billings at Abbots with HPL.*

---

**Comment:** "HPL" (or sometimes "H") is Harriet.

Curiously, his brother Billings attended a party with her. Captain Abbott, who wrote to Charlie as "EKA" in June 1861, also had come home from the war.

---

July 16. *Barker came.*

July 17. *Church a.m. H's evening.*

July 19. *Tea. Mrs. General. Called on Mrs. Abbots. Cemetery bank.*

---

**Comment:** Once again, Charlie had tea at Mrs. Williams's home, for the obvious purpose of seeing Harriet.

---

July 20. *AEM sick.*

---

**Comment:** "AEM" was the former Annie E. Mallory, age 29, married now to Jacob Smull of Stonington, Connecticut, on the coast. The Mallory family was well-known in the shipping and shipbuilding industries. Annie was suffering from complications of childbirth.

---

July 21. *Party at W. Williams.* [Illegible.]

---

**Comment:** Another social event at General and Mrs. Williams's home, undoubtedly with Harriet.

---

July 24. *Church a.m. Evening walk, "remember the promise."*

---

**Comment:** Because the entry was not encoded, this was probably Georgia speaking, reminding Charlie of his engagement vow.

---

July 26. *Stonington. AEM buried today. Was at funeral.* ˉI loved her once so much. I love her today the same. My first, my dearest love. Sleep dear friend. May we meet where partings are no more.ˉ

---

**Comment:** Annie Mallory Smull and her baby daughter died of complications three days after childbirth. Charlie concealed his love for Annie from prying eyes by encoding his deepest feelings, shown here in a separate font. Although currently romancing one woman while engaged to another, Charlie seemed still to carry a torch for Annie.

---

July 27. *Watch Hill. Mrs. B. Burr. Lt. Due* [Illegible].

July 28. *Westerly.*

July 28. *Stonington breakwater. Eve--a service. Home.*

August 1. *Ride Fort Hill. Noank. Mystic.*

---

**Comment:** Watch Hill is located on a narrow peninsula in western Rhode Island, just across a small bay from Stonington. Watch Hill and nearby Westerly were famous in the late 1800s for their mansions and social life. Having attended his friend's funeral on Friday, Charlie crossed the bay to Watch Hill/Westerly on Saturday and then returned to Stonington Sunday, where he attended an evening church service. Then he started the eighteen-mile ride home. Three days later, Charlie rode fifteen miles, presumably by horseback, to the coastal towns of Noank and Mystic.

---

August 2. *Head of River—Milltown.*

---

**Comment:** Milltown is the town center of North Stonington, on the Pawtucket River, which drove the town's hydaulically-powered mills.

---

August 4. *Brand and paint.*

August 5. *Home.*

August 7. *Mrs. Chapin. Eve. H.*

August 8. "Sometime." Talked this evening on academy steps. Requested a favor. "The time will come; you shall have all sometime. When I marry, come and see me."

---

**Comment:** In this entry, shown in a separate font, Charlie was clearly quoting Harriet, who promises to be available to him even after she married someone else! The "academy" on whose steps they sat was the Norwich Free Academy, a public high school founded in 1856 with strong support from General Williams, at whose home Harriet was living. The academy remains today the main public high school of Norwich.

---

August 9. *Off for* [illegible]. *"U. Cash."*

August 10. *Tea at Mrs. Ripley. Home with HPL.*

September 2. *In Boston.*

September 6. *Cousin Mary. Athenium.*

---

**Comment:** Charlie was in Boston, at the Anthenaeum, a membership library founded in 1807 that also presented lectures, readings, and other literary events. It is still in operation today.

---

September 7. *In Boston. Grand Organ.*

September 8. *At Parkers in evening. Macumbers, Mrs. & Mr. Meredith.*

September 9. *In Groton to visit Miss Butler.*

---

**Comment:** The reference is to Groton, Connecticut, not the Massachusetts town of the same name where Charlie's father and grandfather were born.

---

September 10. *Norwich in evening.*

September 12. *In New Haven. Frank Ives party in p.m.*

September 15. *Hemlock Grove. Renfries.*

September 18. *Perseverance and compassion in persons of strong natures is like graneri. The passions of the same are wild when aroused* [illegible] *and consume their* [illegible] *when they are divided.*

---

**Comment:** Charlie's attempt at moral philosophy ended in some confusion—partly because it is unknown what "graneri" is or are. But he seems to be telling himself that unless he harnesses and directs his strong drives toward some worthwhile project he will self-destruct.

---

September 21. *Capt. D of* [illegible].

September 22. *Party at Osgoods. Home with H. James Day at house.*

October 3. *Dinner Party at house for The Days.*

October 4. *Called. Kinney. Went up the road with party to America. BFM.*

October 6. *Met CBF in New York.*

---

**Comment:** "CBF" is his older brother, Coddington Billings, a businessman who would later become a doctor. The meeting probably pertained to financial matters because Billings would soon make a loan to Charlie to start a brokerage business in Savannah, Georgia.

---

October 8. *In Philadelphia.*

State of Connecticut
Executive Department
Hartford, Oct 8th 1864

*To the President*
*Washington, D.C.*

*Sir*
*Permit me to commend to your confidence Col. Charles Farnsworth late of the 1st Reg. Conn. Cavalry, a highly loyal & respectable citizen of Conn.*

*I am with high consideration*
*your obt servt*
*Wm. W. Buckingham*
*Governor of Connecticut*

---

**Comment:** This letter of reference from the Governor of Connecticut was the first indication that Charlie was going to seek a favor of the president—as it turned out, a permit to go south while the war still raged.

---

October 10. *At Fort Delaware.*

---

**Comment:** Fort Delaware is on the Delaware River, near the town of Salem, New Jersey.

---

October 10. *Went to Washington to release Geo. B.*

---

**Comment:** It is not known who Geo. B. was, or what Charlie did for him.

---

October 25. *Sick in ears. Deaf as a post.*

November 7. *Returned from New York where I was under the care of Agnew.* Again permitted to revel in charms long sought. "I cannot deny you what must by law be another's."

---

**Comment:** Having recovered from an ear infection, Charlie once again could hear Harriet's loving words, which he encoded, as was his practice.

---

November 20. Rainy evening. Called L. Extract from a letter: "It never can be again but it was. Oh, how I love. I cannot refuse you though I know I should."

---

**Comment:** "L" is undoubtedly Harriet Peck <u>L</u>ester.

---

November 25. Sick. Destroyed letters. *Slight estrangement — <u>Cor.</u>*

---

**Comment:** It is unknown what "Cor" refers to, but this was the first sign that Charlie's plan to go south was creating tension between him and Harriet.

---

November 27. Well, but we were quiet. Fussed over monthly.

November 29. *Lunch at General's.*

December 2. Sat in her lap. "Shall we change seats?" Then came loose the arm chair.

December 5. Lunch at Norton's. "I cannot say you must not again for I would not have it so. You and me must ever always be one."

December 6. Walk up Franklin Street. "I can talk of marrying, but can I ever after yours receive another's embrace except with loathing."

December 7. Dance. Rode down. Tom up with driver. "Not now; when we go back." Broke window of carriage.

December 8. Awful windy. Met HPL at Gen. Went up. "I love you for this act, to go such a night as this..." *Met. Left Gen. At Learned's. Awful windy.*

December 9. Called HPL. "It is harder to resist each time."

---

**Comment:** For an entire week, Charlie recorded nothing in his diary except encoded descriptions of his love affair with Harriet.

---

December 11. *Recd. Martha. Evening with H.*

---

**Comment:** Martha Ripley and Harriet were reputedly two of the most desirable unmarried women in Norwich.

---

December 12. *In Providence.*

December 13. *Evening at Dunnell.*

December 14. Dance hall: "I cannot refuse you. You first taught me passion. I would give all that I have or ever shall have for one year with you."

December [undated, but probably the 15th]. *Sleigh ride in Baltic in the afternoon. If you say never again, it shall be so.* "No, no I do not think it wrong with you. There shall come a time when our blood shall mingle."

---

**Comment:** Charlie continued his practice of encoding Harriet's most intimate words. Baltic is a small town about three miles north of Norwich.

---

December 16. *Went to Meriden.*

**Comment:** Meriden, where his fiancée Georgia Parker lived, is forty-five miles west of Norwich; Charlie had mustered there with the First Connecticut Cavalry in October 1861. He probably made this trip to see Georgia, staying several days. But to keep the visit secret, he made no mention of seeing her, and even encoded his destination.

December 20. Fair. Meriden Hall.

December 21. *No dance. Steng came from New Haven.*

December 22. With Martha in p.m. Mrs. W said not to call. Went up in evening. "One hour." Had a pleasant time. Dull. Sick soon. "I am not cold but you know oh. how I wanted you this evening. I almost despise control. Now how I long for all." *New Haven 141 lbs.*

**Comment:** Back in Norwich, Charlie called on Martha Ripley in the afternoon and later went out with Harriet in the evening, despite Mrs. Williams's attempt to shield her from Charlie's advances.

December 24. Went to Westfield with HPL en route to Albany. Took sleigh ride spring. Returned via Worcester. Recd. a long note three editions. "I will never change towards you. Live and see."

**Comment:** Harriet was going to Albany, New York to spend Christmas with her mother, who had moved there from Norwich several years earlier. Charlie accompanied Harriet part way on the train.

December 25. Should be sick about now. again. for four weeks.

December 26. *Dinner party at Mrs. Aiken's. A real pleasant party. L.L. Festener, Hakes, Stanton, McKibbon there.*

**Comment:** This Stanton was surely not the secretary of war, whom Charlie had met in Baltimore, but probably a brother of J. L. Stanton, an infantry captain from Norwich who had been killed in the war. Mrs. Aiken's husband, William Appleton Aiken, served as the quartermaster-general of Connecticut during the war.

December 27. Georgia sent me letters written to her by Fish in regard to the Chicago affair, of which I took copies.

---

**Comment:** This was Charlie's first diary entry in months that specifically mentioned his fiancée Georgia Parker, and it creates new mysteries. Why had Charlie's former superior officer, Lieutenant Colonel William Fish, been corresponding with Charlie's fiancée? What was the "Chicago affair?" Did it pertain to some business problem during the years before 1860 when Charlie was involved in the cast-iron stove business there? Had Fish divulged something that Charlie had confided to him? Why would he do that? One potential reason: revenge for Charlie's failure to go to Fish's defense when he was charged with extortion in a court-martial.

---

December 28. Mailed a long letter to HPL in Albany. Recd. letter from Georgia in regard to letters of Fish. *Gold 229-227 ¾* .

---

**Comment:** Charlie apparently tried to explain the "Chicago affair" to Georgia, and she had responded, but it does not seem that the air had been cleared.

---

# 1865

January 1. *Mr. Dana preached his first sermon today, to the 2ⁿᵈ Congregational Church. He was installed last Wednesday. He is a young man, talented, apparently a good logician, and a fair orator, evidently earnest in his calling.*

Wrote a letter to HPL at Albany hoping to see her on the 11ᵗʰ at the dance.

*Received letter from Mr. Foster in relation to going to Savannah.*

*Export of oil from Pennsylvania in '62 was 10,182,020 gallons; first 10 months, '63 was 26,070,569 gallons; and in first 11 months '64 was 30,182,020 gallons. Number of barrels found in Pennsylvania in '64: 2,000,000 @ $11 per barrel. The iron found in Pennsylvania and dug in 1864 was 700,000 tons @ $50 average, $37,500,000. Coal 12,000,000 at $6.50 average, $78,000.000. Making the product of Pennsylvania for one year from these articles $130 million.*

It was reported that Joe Starweather was found in Lib. Webb's room at four a.m. She has left town.

---

**Comment:** Malcolm McGregor Dana was the well-known minister of Norwich's Second Congregational Church. He later wrote *The Norwich Memorial* and *Our Brave Boys,* two books that celebrated Norwich's contributions to the Union effort. Charlie and his family were members of the church. In 1845, his mother had donated a silver baptismal chalice to the church, after a devastating fire.

Harriet was still in Albany, with her mother, but Charlie was expecting to see her in ten days.

Nothing more is known about the unfortunate LibWebb. Although Charlie had been watching the booming Pennsylvania economy, he decided to go south to Savannah and was collecting letters of reference. The letter written by Senator Foster has not been found, but presumably it read like the following three from the governors of Connecticut and Rhode Island.

---

**State of Connecticut**
**EXECUTIVE DEPARTMENT**
*Hartford, Jan 2ⁿᵈ 1865*

*Maj. Gen. W. T. Sherman*
*Commanding U. S. Forces, Georgia*

*General,*

*I commend to your confidence the bearer, Lt. Col. Charles Farnsworth, a respectable & loyal citizen of this state.*

*Col. Farnsworth entered the military service of the government in 1861, for his energy and ability was promoted to be a Lieut Col and as such commanded the 1ˢᵗ Regt. Conn. Cavalry. In that position he rendered valuable service until his health became impaired by wounds and severe labor and made it necessary for him to resign, upon which he received an honorable discharge.*

> *I am, General, very respectfully yours,*
> *Wm. A. Buckingham*
> *Gov. of Conn.*

---

**Comment:** There are some curious inaccuracies and omissions here by Governor Buckingham. First, the War Department considered Charlie to be a captain, not a lieutenant colonel. Second, Charlie never actually commanded his regiment; the battalion was enlarged to a regiment while he was imprisoned, and when he was released he was on "parole," barred from taking command. Third, the governor made no mention of Charlie's imprisonment, even after all his efforts to get Charlie released. Would eight months at Libby have "tainted" Charlie in General Sherman's eyes?

---

**State of Rhode Island**
**Executive Department**
Providence, Jan. 4ᵗʰ 1865

*Col. Wm. Ames*
*Commander 3ʳᵈ Rhode Island Infantry*
*Hilton Head, South Carolina*

*Colonel*

*I am instructed to bring to your favorable notice the bearer Col. Charles Farnsworth late of the 1ˢᵗ Conn. Cavalry.*

*He is thinking of establishing himself in business in Savannah, Georgia and any assistance you can render him through your official position will be esteemed a personal favor.*

> *With the compliments of the season,*
> *I am, my dear Col,*
> *Very truly yours,*
> *Charles S. Bailey*
> *Col. & Adj.Gen.*

> State of Rhode Island
> Executive Department
> Providence, Jan. 4th 1865

*Maj. Genl. Geary, U.S. Vols.*
*Military Governor of Savannah, Ga.*

*General,*

    *I have the honor to bring to your favorable attention Mr. Charles Farnsworth, late Lt. Colonel of the 1st Conn. Cavalry, as a gentleman of sterling integrity and unquestioned loyalty.*

    *He desires to engage in business in Savannah or vicinity and any facilities which you can consistently afford him will be appreciated as a personal favor by*

> *Your Very Obedient Servant*
> *James Smith*
> *Governor of Rhode Island*

    January 4. *Called at* [illegible] *and saw Mary. Purchased the articles requested by Mother.* Sixty-five. *Left Norwich for Washington.* [Illegible] *a Libbian* [illegible] me. He escaped. *Saw Mr. Foster in evening. He said he would start my thing immediately. Governor* Hale here. Saw him in Baltimore buying plated ware. *Commissions* must pay well.

---

**Comment:** Charlie's partially legible entry about a "Libbian" probably was a reference to a fellow former prisoner at Libby. It is a mystery why he encoded only portions of the entry.

    Charlie sailed from Norwich to Washington in a day and immediately went to see Senator Foster, apparently about getting a travel permit to the South ("my thing") from President Lincoln.

---

January 5. *Wrote Georgia.* Sent a letter to Harriet Peck Lester. Spent the day at the Capitol. Sumner speaking on freeing the families of black soldiers. No quorum in the house. Saw Schenck. He will do what he can for me to help me south. *Met Mr.*[illegible] *family of Chicago. He said he was in Colorado. Has mail address there; has a store in West Denver and is a member of the legislature.*

---

**Comment:** After writing to both his fiancée and his current lady-friend, Charlie spent the day observing a Senate debate on the breadth of the proposed Thirteenth Amendment, which was intended to abolish slavery throughout the country. Senator Charles Sumner of Massachusetts, who had barely survived a severe physical caning on the senate floor by a South Carolina congressman in 1856, was speaking in strong support of the amendment. Charlie undoubtedly approved.

Charlie also got a commitment from his former commanding general (now an Ohio congressman), Robert C. Schenck, to help him go south.

---

January 6. *Gold at $228 to 233. Obtained letters from Foster, Sherman, and Farnsworth. Got a card from Abraham Lincoln and a pass from the War Office. Went to Alexandria and stayed there with Bob.* Colonel Harde said this is the first pass issued direct to Savannah.

---

**Comment:** The second sentence makes no sense: Charlie didn't get letters *from* Sherman and himself; he got a letter from Senator Foster addressed to General Sherman *about* himself. Perhaps Charlie was flustered from getting one of the first passes to Savannah issued by Lincoln. The permit, in the president's handwriting, read:

---

*Will the Commander at Savannah please see the bearer Col. Farnsworth, & oblige him so far as consistent with the service?*        *Jan. 5, 1865 A. Lincoln*

January 7. *Arrived in Baltimore. Called upon friends in Sharpville. Called at Meredith's store. No train to New York this p.m. Flood at river is the cause.* S___ spent the night with Yallie Hibler and myself until 12 p.m. She accused me of sitting with Lydia Knowles the evening at Hares with my head in her lap. *Remember the conversation I had at the doctors with Hibler.*

**Comment:** His cousin Mary's husband, Harry Meredith, apparently owned a store in Baltimore. Charlie enjoyed an exciting evening in the city where he had encamped with his battalion for six months two years earlier.

January 8. *Breakfast* at Agnes Robinson's at high noon; had a fine night. *Hall says I ought to get a schooner, with all expenses paid by the captain for $1 per month. Dunlap says he can buy as cheap in Baltimore as New York or anywhere. Called on Miss Hibler with Dunlap.*

January 9. Gold at 221 to 235. *In New York. Procured transportation to Savannah. Goods (general merchandise) can be sent to Port Royal without any permit. CBF at Chesebrough.* [Illegible.]

**Comment:** Although Port Royal is located in South Carolina, it was under Union control at the time.

For unknown reasons, his brother Coddington Billings was visiting Charlie's old Camp Chesebrough outside Baltimore.

January 10. *Gold at 226-228 ½. Cotton 118. Went to Providence by steamer. CBF proposes to advance $5,000 for speculation at Savannah and in case it looks well, will send a vessel with a load. Check will be ready for me at Derry's Monday.* Called on HPL and though she was the same loving woman she always was, still the evening was not satisfying. The fact that I was going away seemed to destroy all feeling and we were both cold. Not even one long kiss was given or received and the pleasure of love so often enjoyed was far from the mind. And yet I feel she loves me the same as ever. But we could not rouse ourselves. The fact that so soon were we to separate was like a millstone. Both of us felt when we parted that an evening was lost.

**Comment:** Charlie's brother Billings had moved recently from New York to Providence and was obviously prospering as a businessman. His loan of $5,000 would be equivalent to about $150,000 today. Charlie used the funds initially to go into business as a general commission merchant in Savannah.

Charlie had been courting Harriet for nine months, yet he was still formally engaged to Georgia Parker. Now he was about to go south. It is no wonder that he and Harriet were in emotional turmoil, as he recorded in his code.

January 11. *Gold 218. Cotton 115.* How can I describe this evening so full of pain & anguish, still abounding with love? How sweet the dance when her form was in my arms. How dear each loop we walked up and enjoyed each other. She said "Charlie I shall never be true to any man but you. I must and will love you to the fullest extent."

January 12. *White Steamer Ball, splendid music. Opera cloak.* Spent the evening with HPW. HPL with Norton. Speaking of the evening and how she felt, she said "If I had had a pistol, I would almost have dared to have shot you; I wanted to."

January 13. *Party at Mary Williams'. "We will go out in a blaze of glory, won't we?" What a real pleasant time we had. We danced, talked, and ignored everyone.* And then the walk home and those moments ere we parted forever. What was life or anything? What raptures forever and ever each others'. "All was mine, dearest my darling; I die with rapture."

---

**Comment:** Charlie's parting memories of Harriet as he started south.

---

January 14. *Gold 217 ½ -220 ½. Started for Savannah, reached Meriden 8 p.m.*

---

**Comment:** Charlie went out of his way to Meriden to see Georgia; he could have caught a steamer or train directly from Norwich for New London and New York.

---

January 15. *Church twice.* Horace Wilcox made a proposal to Nellie to be married in June. The tour of the White Mountains in Canada goes with it. We had a long talk in the library, but would not listen to marrying for a better position. "I love you and will marry you." Fish told them that I was at the Meriden House with Dido. Sat up till one o'clock. Mr. Parker had an attack of bleeding.

---

**Comment:** In Meriden, Charlie seems to have tried to convince Georgia that someone else would make a better husband for her, but she would not be dissuaded.

---

January 16. *Left 8 a.m. for New York. Recd. check for $. Astor House. Wallachs.*

January 17. *Sailed in the Arago 5 p.m. for Hilton Head. Amongst the passengers whose acquaintance I formed en route were Mr. & Mrs. Snyder, Mrs. Arnesman, Mrs. & Gen. Danielson (2ⁿᵈ Mass.) & son, Dr. Willis, [illegible]. Noble. The nail cleaner etc.*

---

**Comment:** The voyage on the coastal steamer *Arago* from New York to Savannah, with a stop at Hilton Head, South Carolina, took four to seven days, depending on weather and tidal conditions.

---

January 18. *Mr. Willis of Savannah, President of Gas Works, is on board. He is well-acquainted there, and says that the city is barren of every thing and that there is little money there.*

January 19. *Judge Frazer of Florida is on board.*

January 21. *Arrived at 5 p.m. at dock of Hilton Head.*

January 22. *Called on Province Treasury Agent, a miserable puppy from Salem, Mass. Wrote to Mother, Georgia, and CBF.*

January 23. *Left Hilton Head Port Sherman for Savannah at 5 p.m. All night on board at anchor just off the Head. A cold, raw, miserable night.*

January 24. *Arrived 2 p.m. at Savannah's Pulaski House. Most miserable table, but good accommodations. Called on Gen. Geary.*

---

**Comment:** The original Pulaski House, located at 117 W. Charlton, has been rebuilt and now serves as an apartment building.

---

January 25. *204 ½ 207 ½. Saw Gen. Geary and obtained a permit to purchase rags, etc. in and about Savannah. Also to open a store as soon as my goods come.*

---

**Comment:** Savannah surrendered with hardly a shot fired in December 1864 after General Sherman had marched his army across Georgia. The city was now governed by a military commander, Major General J. W. Geary, and all businesses needed permits from him to operate. Charlie's note from President Lincoln undoubtedly convinced the general to issue him one.

"Rags" was the term for the type of cotton used in making paper. Charlie continued to follow the price of gold.

---

January 26. *Called on Mrs. and Col. Marcham at same Pulaski House.*

January 27. *Wrote CBF in regard to sending goods here and in relation to purchasing rags, etc.*

---

**Comment:** His brother Billings was acting as a buyer and shipper for Charlie, in addition to being his financier.

---

January 30. Obtained permission to purchase rags, etc. Also an order for a store.

February 1. *Rented store at 205 Bay Street for one year @ $800. Paid 1ˢᵗ quarter $200.*

---

**Comment:** Charlie's store, located on the street directly above the Savannah River, was later re-designated 205 E. Bay. A modern hotel now occupies the site.

---

February 3. *Maj. Marcy, Nichols came.*

---

**Comment:** Major George O. Marcy, Charlie's fellow officer in the First Connecticut Cavalry, resigned in November 1864 and now had come to Savannah.

---

February 5. *Church. Prayer book had rebel flag.*

---

**Comment:** It is hard to discern whether Charlie was surprised, annoyed, or both.

---

February 9. Noyes Billings is taxed on $8.233 income and William on $8.338.

**Comment:** These are Charlie's wealthy New London uncles, the brothers of his mother, the former Eunice W. Billings. To pay for Civil War expenses, Congress had enacted an income tax in 1861; it was repealed in 1872. Noyes and William Billings, who had prospered in whaling, shipping, and other businesses, were subject to high tax assessments.

February 10. Went to Camp 13ᵗʰ Conn (Inf.) to buy bounty checks. Price $8.

**Comment:** It appears that Charlie was running a check-cashing service for the Union soldiers who wanted cash for their re-enlistment bonus checks.

February 11. There. Three years ago tonight I became engaged to Georgia. Tonight I wrote her a letter. Rented a cellar for $5 per week.

**Comment:** Charlie's engagement to Georgia was made in February 1862, on the eve of his departure with the First Connecticut Cavalry from Meriden to Wheeling, Virginia, although at the time he did not record the event. By now, his ardor to marry her had cooled in the extreme.

February 12. *Wrote Georgia, Ned , Fred. Recd. letter from Atwater from Wheeler. States* [illegible] *sick. Ned.* Wrote HPL, sent to Fred.

**Comment:** Charlie was using his younger brother Fred to deliver letters to Harriet because it might have seemed improper, in the eyes of General and Mrs. Williams, for their boarder Harriet to be receiving correspondence from an engaged man.

February 19. *Church a.m. Christ Church p.m. Wrote CBF about Mother. Russell Dennison.*

**Comment:** Savannah's Christ Episcopal Church, founded in 1733, is considered the "Mother Church of Georgia" and is still in active use.

February 21. *Took room and board at Mrs. Cheves,' corner of Bull & Jones.*

*February 23. Recd. letter from Georgia of the 13th. Wrote Georgia about Ives. Fellis.*

*February 24. Wrote Mother a long letter in answer to her letter of the 17th.*

*February 25. Engaged all day superintending baling paper stock.* Col. Birle & Mrs. Kimball are flirting hugely.

*March 1. Gold $199 – 211.* HPL. Georgia. HPL full of love.
*Letters by Illinois mail from Fred & Georgia.*

---

**Comment:** The tone of his notations reflected a vast difference in his feelings toward Harriet and Georgia. One wonders if the visit by Fred and Georgia to Illinois had anything to do with the "Chicago affair" mentioned in earlier diary entries.

---

March 2. Gold 191 – 198. Answered HPL letter, sent to Fred. Made contact with Wrellis to buy iron on shares [illegible].

---

**Comment:** For propriety's sake, once again Charlie sent his love letter for Harriet via his brother Fred.

---

*March 3. Gold 198 – 199. Fulton's mail. Letter from Fred, CBF, & Atwater. Deafs for $240, sold to Ames. Wrote Georgia, & Billings for a pair of boots. Recd. letter of HPL of date 11 Feb. Answered it. To send by Arago mail.*

---

**Comment:** It is unknown what "deafs" were.

---

March 4. Gold 199 – 200. *Went to Hilton Head on Steamer Philadelphia. Left here 2 a.m., arrived at Hilton Head 12 p.m.* Played draw. Lost $40. *Ellis Warren bound to Morehead City with goods.*

*March 5. Doud, Nichols, Pierce all went to Charleston. Security.*

---

**Comment:** Charlie and the others could safely disembark at Charleston because its Confederate defenders had fled in February after being nearly cornered by General

Sherman's drive through central South Carolina. The city then was occupied mainly by black Union regiments, who managed to maintain order.[460]

---

**March 6.** *No boat for Savannah. Fulton detained four hours to take news of Sherman's fight. Dined 10 cents at Charleston.*

---

**Comment:** The steamship *Fulton* may have been delayed in order to receive news of the destruction of Columbia, South Carolina two weeks earlier (either by attacking Union, retreating Confederate, or rampaging criminal forces—or by all three) or word of General Sherman's subsequent march toward Goldsboro.[461]

---

**March 7.** *Left at 4 a.m. on the Wyoming. Capt. Bragg, the Judas that raised the flag in Sumter, is a humbug, as he was not there for two weeks after the capture. A most miserable little puppy. We ran aground and did not reach Savannah till the morning of the 8th.*

---

**Comment:** The Confederates had evacuated Fort Sumter in Charleston harbor on February 17, 1865, and the Union flag was raised on the twenty-second by a Captain Bragg of Major General Quincy A. Gillmore's staff. Gillmore had commanded an amphibious attack to retake the fort in September 1863, but had failed disastrously, eventually surrendering his entire landing party to the Confederate defenders. Nonetheless, without War Department authority, Gillmore issued medals to all involved.[462] Charlie thought it was disgraceful that a representative of this blundering expedition should conduct the flag-raising.

---

**March 8.** *Richmond rejoiced to see us.*

---

**Comment:** Reading this and the May 3 diary entry together, it appears that "Richmond" was Charlie's freedman servant in Savannah.

---

**March 12.** *Wrote a long letter to Georgia in answer to her letter of the 3rd. Sent letter by Ellis to New York, as the mail cleared before my letters were ready. Letter to CBF, $500 to Fred. And one to HPL, a long and truthful one.*

---

**Comment:** Charlie was finally confronting his tangled relations with two women.

---

March 21. *Major left for home. Sen. Foster here with wife and Miss Cannon. I left Cheves'. Went to Savage's.*

---

**Comment:** "Major" probably referred to George Marcy, a fellow officer of the First Connecticut Cavalry, who had also been looking for business opportunities in Savannah.

Charlie was honored by a visit from family friend and US senator Lafayette S. Foster, who within a month would become acting vice-president after Lincoln was assassinated and Andrew Johnson became president.

Changing his Savannah lodgings again, Charlie moved from the Cheveses' home to the Savage's. He had started in January at Pulaski House.

---

March 24. *A letter of p.m. from Norwich this day recd. Sent on the 2ⁿᵈ of April from HPL. Said to be* the last one to me.

---

**Comment:** Harriet was losing patience with Charlie's apparent indecision.

---

March 31. *Obtained permit to ship 5,000 hides, 400 bales paper stock, etc. on the Schooner W. B. Carlton.*

April 1. *Shipped today 167 bales, 22 crates paper stock. Cost here $28. Sold in Boston July 1865 for $1,400.*

---

**Comment:** As a general commission merchant, Charlie was shipping hides, paper, and cotton to the north—for huge profits, it seems.

---

April 2. *Dined with King at Mrs. Hayward's.*

April 3. *Mailed letter to Harriet, Fred, Mother. None from Georgia. Last HPL.*

---

**Comment:** Was this another ultimatum from Harriet?

---

April 8. *U. S. Grant to Hilton Head. Dr. Drew to clear. Carlton.*

April 9. *Hilton Head. Wiggins. Seward. Rodman.*

April 10. *Wellman could not clear.*

April 11. *Cleared the Carlton*

---

**Comment:** It is uncertain, but the last four entries seem to be noting whether certain passengers had been "cleared" by Union military authorities to proceed on their voyage.

---

April 12. *Left for Charleston. Ball at Gen.Gillmore's headquarters. There was anniversary of fall of Pulaski.*

---

**Comment:** Charlie's low opinion of General Gillmore did not prevent him from attending the general's celebration. Fort Pulaski, at the mouth of the Savannah River, had been taken by Union forces on April 10, 1862. The Union's blockade of the Savannah harbor had followed.

---

April 13. *In Charleston. News of Lee's surrender.*

---

**Comment:** General Lee had surrendered his army on April 9; it took four days for the news to reach Charleston.

---

April 14. *Raising of "Old Glory" at Sumter.*

---

**Comment:** Actually, this was the second flag-raising at the symbolic fort; the first took place on February 22.

---

April 15. *All day in Charleston. Dr. A lives here.*

April 16. *Home 10 a.m.*

April 17 *Wrote long letter to Mother.*

April 24. *Noyes Billings died 1:15 a.m. Howard to board.*

**Comment:** Noyes Billings, Charlie's uncle on his mother's side, was a prominent New London businessman.

---

April 25. *Wrote Mary & CBF in regard to money to buy cotton.*

---

**Comment:** Charlie was seeking an investment in his cotton brokerage from cousin Mary Meredith (and presumably from her husband Harry) as well as additional funds from his brother, Billings.

---

April 26. *N. B. Seward. N. L 3 p.m.*

April 29. *Engagement by Cyrus not kept.*

April 30. *Prayers for President of U.S. read for 1ˢᵗ time in Christ Church. Wildman short engagement not kept.*

---

**Comment:** Lincoln died from an assassin's bullet on April 15; it is odd that Charlie's first diary mention of the tragedy came two weeks later.

A man named Samuel Edgar Wildman, age twenty-six, became Charlie's business partner about this time. Known as Edgar (or Edward), he was from Danbury, Connecticut, the son of a prosperous farmer, and had personal wealth of about $3,000. There is no record of him serving in the Civil War.[463]

---

May 3. *Richmond went on Amagen to Augusta as a mate cook. $200*

May 4. Pery at store. 1ˢᵗ time.

---

**Comment:** Pery, or perhaps Perry, seems to have been a young woman Charlie had met in Savannah. He deemed it wise to encode their meetings, at his store and elsewhere, over the following weeks.

---

May 7. *At S's. Gay time. There goes Mc & H.* Pery that night 1ˢᵗ time. House. H came. Dressed in Mrs. Yaws' room. Went home.

May 14. All p.m. Pery.

May 18. *Marg. & Foster came in Chase. Harry* at Pery *until a note which was did at 2:30 a.m. that if such occurred again I was out.*

---

**Comment:** Connecticut Senator Foster and his wife arrived in Savannah by steamer. As president pro tem of the US Senate, Foster was now acting vice-president to President Andrew Johnson.

This was the fourth "Pery" entry in two weeks. Someone named Harry also seems to have been involved.

---

May 19. *Georgia* at stere. *Started for Augusta; left by the Jeff Davis. Paid Hayward $50.*

---

**Comment:** "At stere," in Latin, could be translated as "barren," suggesting that Charlie's engagement to Georgia would not bear fruit.

---

May 20. *Pery. Harry. River-sick.*

May 21. *Foster & self at Savannah. Myers, Merrill, etc.* Slept Pery.

---

**Comment:** Charlie made six "Pery" diary entries in seventeen days. He seemed to be enjoying himself at night, after accompanying Senator (and acting vice-president) Foster around Savannah by day.

---

May 22. *Left for Augusta at Station Savannah. 4 suits at Hayward.*

May 25. *Augusta with Mr. Leesburgh aground. King & Waddell. New York price cotton: Ordinary 46; Good 50; Mid 57; Good 59. Middling fair 62. Cotton can be bought here for 11 ½ to 20.*

---

**Comment:** The 300-400 percent mark-up for cotton was extremely favorable for a broker like Charlie. He was listed in the 1866 and 1867 Savannah city directories under "Farmsworth (sic) & Co., General Commission Merchants, 205 Bay Street." His was one of many such businesses, most of them long-established. We do not know whether he competed successfully or not after the war ended.

---

May 26. *Left 2 a.m. for Savannah. By 2 p.m. in Savannah. Made the trip in 20 running hours.*

---

**Comment:** Based on these figures, the downriver trip took twelve hours, and the upriver eight, which seems odd, unless the tide had been running in against the river current.

---

May 27. *Arrived 7 p.m. Savannah.* Pery ok.

May 28. *Spent p.m. at C's. Evening Capt. Horn came home. Seems up to S's.* Split on the C.S. Capt. *Well played.*

---

**Comment:** This was the first mention of "C," someone (presumably a woman) whom Charlie would turn to again. The rest of the entry is unintelligible.

---

May 29. *Took tea at S's. Called on Mrs. and Major Marcy. Sick.*

---

**Comment:** Charlie's fellow First Connecticut Cavalry officer Marcy had returned to Savannah with his wife.

---

May 30. *Left Station Savannah for Augusta.*

June 4. *St. Paul's Church a.m. Dull.*

---

**Comment:** A newer Episcopal church in Savannah, founded in 1852, it survives to this day.

---

June 5. *Capt. Perkins has order on Dunbar for $50 to collect leased property for one year.*

June 7. *Started press.*

---

**Comment:** This was probably the cotton "steam press" in Augusta that would be mentioned in the July 31 entry.

---

June 8. *Left for Savannah on the Comet. Tyler and family on board.*

June 9. [Illegible] *Robin. Jeff Davis.*

---

**Comment:** The *"Jeff Davis"* was a river steamer.

---

June 10. *Arrived Savannah. "I'm glad you have come."*

---

**Comment:** This time the run downriver from Augusta to Savannah took two days, rather than twelve hours.

Judging from the June 11 entry, he was probably quoting "C."

---

June 11. *Heavy rain. P.M. home. Evening T at S's: "How are you officers of the black regiment?" Frank Myers.* At C all night.

---

**Comment:** While Charlie was having tea at the Savageses' ("S's") house where he was boarding, a die-hard Confederate tried to goad Charlie about white officers commanding the black Union regiments that occupied Savannah.

---

June 17. *Left Savannah for New York.*

June 18. *Sailed 1 p.m. on Arago from Hilton Head on steamer Arago. Room with Col. Beebe, Tyler, Passon, Powell & others.*

June 21. *New York 5 p.m.*

---

**Comment:** The coastal steamer *Arago* took four days from Savannah to New York.

---

June 22. *Brook & Co. Ph.11. Boots 27. B&3B 40. L .5.*

June 23. *Norwich 2 a.m.*

June 25. *Dana Church evening. Ward. Walk. How funny. I don't* feel any different *than what I did* the last time. *What I did the* last time I sat *here. Wrote Georgia that I should be there Sunday.*

**Comment:** The encoded entry probably refers to his feelings toward Harriet. He was planning to see Georgia, to whom he was still engaged, a week later.

June 26. [Illegible] *returned to Slater's party. Stanton, Learned, Goulds, Etc. Went with L.A. and Miss A. Ward, Stanton, & self. Philopence.*

June 27. *Went to Boston 2 a.m. Sold cargo to Mr. Carlton. Home 7:30 p.m.*

**Comment:** The cargo may have been cotton which Charlie had bought in Augusta in late May.

June 28. *Left Norwich 10:30 a.m. for Washington. Wrote Georgia that the engagement had better be given up.*

**Comment:** Charlie apparently had lost his nerve about meeting personally with Georgia, and instead broke their engagement by letter. He then left for Washington.

June 29. *Washington.*

June 30. *Saw Schenck.*

July 1. *At Baltimore.*

July 2. *Left Baltimore 7:30 p.m.*

July 3. *From New York at 8 a.m. to Norwich 2 p.m. Evening walk at cemetery. "What did you mean Tuesday?"*

**Comment:** His engagement with Georgia Parker broken off, Charlie now felt freer to court Harriet and to record their conversations without encoding.

July 4. [Illegible] *and ladies. Bridge and supper. Home etc. Party at Harriet's. Saw Mother in between.*

**Comment:** Charlie sat down for a game of bridge with the ladies, checked in on his mother, and then partied with Harriet.

July 5. *Perkins party grave scene. Cauls on the flirt. Palmer stock above par. Mother wants to go to Hartford Monday.*

July 6. *Went to Providence.*

July 7. *From Providence to New York.*

July 8. *From New York to New Haven.*

July 9. *Spent day at Atwater's.*

July 10. *Left New Haven 3 p.m. Recd. letters from Fred that were sent here. Wrote a letter to GAP. Home in evening and called up HPL.*

**Comment:** "GAP" was Georgia Ann Parker. This may have been the final good-bye letter.

July 11. *Invited to Martha R. for the evening.*

**Comment:** Martha Ripley, Harriet's friend, gave another party.

July 12. *Party at Martha's last evening. Could not go as left for New York 9 p.m. to sail on steamer today. Steamer sails tomorrow.*

**Comment:** Charlie probably took one steamer from Norwich to New York and another from New York to Savannah.

July 13. *Steamer did not sail as per agreement yesterday. Left today at 5 p.m. Run into by a schooner off Highlands.*

**Comment:** Highlands, New Jersey, juts out into the Atlantic Ocean about twenty miles south of the Verrazano Straits, creating a navigational hazard.

July 14. *Splendid day.*

July 15. *Gale off Hatteras.*

July 16. *Arrived Hattaras.*

July 28. *On river for Augusta. Mrs. Ball, Mrs. Johnson.*

July 30. *Arrived at Augusta. Wildman, King, Dwight, Mrs. Johnson. Ball & mother.*

July 31. *Baldwin took possession of steam press.*

**Comment:** This quite likely was machinery for pressing cotton into bales.

August 1. *Settled with Govt., paying Gen. Grover $700.*

**Comment:** Sometime in the spring, General Cuvier Grover had replaced General Geary as military commander in Savannah. It seems likely that Charlie owed the military government of Georgia taxes on his business operations.

August 5. *Judge & Doc deal mentioned. Went to place. Seven people left without permission yesterday—ordered them discharged.*

**Comment:** Charlie was now farming rice, in partnership with Edgar (or Edward) Wildman, southwest of Savannah along the Ogeechee River, in addition to running his general merchandise store. He experienced some of the labor problems common at the time, as freedmen exercised their new rights. Conflict was particularly acute along the Ogeechee, where freedmen had been promised land of their own in January under General Sherman's Order No. 15, but the order had been revoked several months later.

August 11. *Paid tax on 36 bales of cotton.*

August 14. *Shipped per Helen 36 bales.*

August 15. *Helen grown did* [illegible] *7 bales. Rockin horse* [illegible] *above New York.*

August 16. *Went to Butler's.*

August 17. *Visited Gen. Harmon's place, South Carolina.*

August 18. *Recd. at Augusta by express from* [illegible] *a package of letters and papers* [illegible] *from New York embracing* [illegible] *from Wheeling, Va.to August 1865.*

August 19. *Destroyed the same.*

---

**Comment:** Although the August 18 entry is partially illegible, the thrust of these two entries is clear: Charlie destroyed a collection of letters that he had received from family and others during his military service and beyond. This had been his practice, which explains why almost no personal letters written to him have survived.

---

August 20. *Church with Judge Cady and Perkins.*

August 31. *Letter of the 22ⁿᵈ from HPL recd. in evening. Military Commission ordered for trial of Highs, Watkins and Doughty.*

---

**Comment:** Charlie was concerned with retribution from die-hard Confederates who were threatening violence to take back some of the lands still occupied by freedmen. Here he was following the "Heasley" case, in which three Confederate army veterans—High, Watkins, and Doughy—were charged before a Union military commission with the murder of a Freedmen's Bureau agent's assistant, Captain Alex Heasley, by shooting and stabbing him as he returned to his Augusta home on August 30. Only one of the defendants was convicted. He was condemned to hang, but the execution was never carried out. [464]

---

September 1. *Sale to Metcalf-Gold-$292.*

September 2. Testimony of Sarah [H]easley in the Heasley case.

**Comment:** The testimony, presumably of the decedent's wife, was taken as part of the pretrial investigative proceedings.

September 7. *HPL in letter of date speaks of my letter of Aug. 22 just recd.*
September 8. *Proposal from Wildman to open store near the rice fields.*

**Comment:** Charlie and Wildman were probably contemplating a company store that would cater to the freedmen working on their rice plantation.

September 9. *Waddell here. Left for Savannah. Volunteers left 7 a.m. Aug. 17 for Augusta. Perkins & Co. arrived Sep. 7 from Savannah, where they had been since 22ⁿᵈ of Aug. Invest. in case of murder closed.*

**Comment:** The Heasley murder investigation ended, and a trial of the three accused was ordered. Only one was convicted, but his death sentence was never carried out.

September 10. *Wrote RF, FWF, CBF, HPL.*

**Comment:** Letters to his father (Ralph F.), his younger brother (Fred Williams F.), his older brother (Coddington Billings F.), and Harriet.

September 11. *HPL should be at* [illegible].

September 12. *3 bales. ITI.*

September 13. *Colonel Wood of Indiana is on the Commission of Heasley.*

**Comment:** The Heasley murder trial before a military commission was beginning.

September 15. *Recd. letter from HPL*

September 26. *Arrived Savannah. Mr. Church's estimates on cotton made from* [illegible] *thought all the* [illegible] *to William. GPO KHH Ss.*

**Comment:** Charlie probably had returned from a trip upriver to Augusta, a cotton-growing area. The rest of the entry is unintelligible.

September 27. *In office all day. Wrote to Father, Mother, Hattie, CBF, and Claude.*

September 28. *In office all day. Called on Mary. Busy in back.*

October 9. *Went to Ogeechee with Wildman. Team run away.* [Illegible] *broke.*

**Comment:** It appears that their buggy harness broke on the road back to Savannah from the Ogeechee River rice farm.

October 12. *Made proposals for the Hujee & Chev place.*

**Comment:** Charlie was probably referring to the Ogeechee River property known as Prarie Plantation, owned by the Huger family (pronounced "Hujee") and the Cheves family.

October 13. *Bell and Self ran away with line broke.*

**Comment:** Another buggy breakdown.

Note: Charlie and Harriet were married November 1st in Norwich, but he made no diary entry of the event. The bride registered as twenty-four years old but was actually twenty-eight; the bridegroom was twenty-nine.[465] Officiating at the marriage was the Rev. Malcolm McGregor Dana, who eight years later would publish *The Norwich Memorial*, the most authoritative account of Norwich soldiers in the Civil War. The newlyweds stayed on in Norwich for several weeks, enjoying themselves and receiving gifts from family and friends. Someone gave them a flatware place-setting for twelve in the silver "medallion" style, the handles of the forks and spoons stamped with the image of Mars, the Roman god of war, which was an apt symbol for the groom.

November 18. *Old folks' concert. B. Hall. Stanton, H, Beige & Kibby back seat. Went up home with Mary Williams. Fun, fun, & frolic.*

---

**Comment:** Newlyweds Charlie and Harriet were making the rounds of parties.

---

*Savannah, Ga. Dec. 4 1865*

*My dear Brother,*

*Your letter of 25ᵗʰ ultimate and letter from Mother came duly by last evening's mail. We are sorry to hear of your illness, although do not fear for you from the line of letters, and suppose your M.D. will not send you back until you are well. I wrote you lately at New York. By the way, how about that letter & note paper for Hattie; send it out as soon as you can.*

*I am glad Bill is settled at the Mill and trust he will so manage as to keep it. He ought to make a good thing out of it. But the trouble is he will fly off with some of them and lose by the move. He cannot bear to have any one know what he does, and he will find in a firm that that style won't stand, and if he make a bad go he cannot keep it to himself for a year or more till he makes a lucky strike and then report OK. That may do with Mother & Co., but not with partners.*

*I bought Hattie a fair horse and buggy, one she drives herself, and she is much pleased. She needs it. She is not very strong, though ambition keeps her up at times when her strength is not quite up to it. She seems to like the place, and is making some acquaintances. I am new in rice buying. Whether we shall succeed in running a plantation next year or not, I don't know. We are disappointed in one, and may conclude to give it up.*

*I have a horse for Hattie to ride and as soon as she gets her skirt done will mount.*

> *Genl. Grant is here.*
> *Write me in full,*
> *With love, C*

---

**Comment:** From its tone, this letter seems addressed to his younger brother Fred, who was then studying medicine at Yale. The identity of "Bill" is unknown, but Charlie frequently offered practical advice like this to younger men, including Fred.

A month after their wedding, Charlie and Harriet had moved into a house in Savannah. "Hattie," as Charlie endearingly called her, was apparently feeling content, driving her buggy around town and meeting Savannahanians. Charlie wanted to acquire a horse that she could ride, in addition to her horse-drawn buggy.

Charlie was now growing rice, as well as brokering it through his store. He was disappointed in his first year of farming, but was determined to try again.

Grant was still general-in-chief of the army and probably was visiting Savannah as part of an inspection of the military occupation of Georgia.

---

January 6. *Came in from Ogeechee.*

---

**Comment:** While Charlie and Harriet were living in Savannah, Charlie was commuting to the Ogeechee River rice fields in Chatham County where he had begun farming. The Atlantic & Gulf Railroad served that area and Charlie probably rode it the approximately twenty miles from Savannah to Ways Station (near the present town of Richmond Hill) and then proceeded by horse to the plantation.[466]

---

January 7. *Home.*

January 8. *Went out to Ogeechee.*

January 9. *Went over to Prarie & Robbins mill.*

---

**Comment:** "Prarie" was the name of the rice plantation on the Chatham County side of the Ogeechee River that Charlie would lease two days later. Robbins was the rice mill near the Prarie tract that he used later to thresh and grind the harvested rice.

---

January 10. *Fireman's Hall dance.*

January 11. *Executed lease of Prarie for $2,000 currency, $2,089 gold per year for three years.*

---

**Comment:** Charlie leased the Prarie plantation for three years, at a rent of $4,089 per year; the lessors were probably the Huger and Cheves families. (See diary entry October 12, 1865.) The plantation had about one hundred acres planted in rice.[467]

---

January 12. *Hattie went to ride Gray.*

January 13. *Getting in rice for Savannah.*

**Comment:** Rice was typically harvested in August, not mid-winter, so Charlie may have been buying or selling from a storehouse.

*Strathy Hall*
*Mar 12ᵗʰ 1866*

*My dear Fred-*

*I wrote you 10 days back. Since then we have had but one mail, a letter from Mother to Hattie, as full of love as hers always are. We are hard at work, and doing finely as far as we have gone. Of course the end is only when harvest comes, when if reap our 30 or 60-fold we are all right. If all goes in as it has so far since we commenced we shall make a good crop of it.*

*Most of your letters, unless important, are destroyed when answered so I cannot give you dates of many late ones. Hattie is quite well now, much better than when in Savannah, and I think is well pleased to live out here, even though we see no one from one week to the other. I wish you could come down and stay a while. You could have lots of fun, outdoors, shooting, fishing, and the like. Besides, when Hattie comes to go home, taking her along. We have just engaged an M.D. on our plantation for our people at $600. He has two others at the same price and one at $200, making a practice of $2000, and not much to worry ever about his reputation if a patient goes off.*

*We have 110 negroes now and we are putting off work fast. I tell you they do well for now, but new brooms — we shall see how they will do the last part of the season. I wrote you I did not see Capt. Johnston, as no doubt I was out here when he was in Savannah. I am in hopes to hear soon of the shipment of the boat. I need it; am now using a scow but it does, and Hattie takes her regular boat rides with her faithful contraband for oarsman.*

*All send love,*
*Charlie*

**Comment:** Charlie and Harriet were now living a remote plantation life at Strathy Hall on the Bryan County side of the Ogeechee River, about five miles south of the present town of Richmond Hill. Their Prarie rice plantation lay just across the river, on the Chatham County side. Charlie was operating the rice plantation with freedmen laborers. While 110 seems like a large work force, Strathy Hall had 271 slaves before the war.

The Strathy house had been built in the late eighteenth century by sea captain James Mackay, who named it after his ancestral home of Strathnaver, Scotland. It was sold to the McAllister family in about 1800. They ran the plantation until 1864 when the head of the household, Major Joseph Longworth McAllister, went off to fight for the Confederacy and was soon killed at Trevillian's Station, Virginia, in the largest cavalry battle of the Civil War. His mother and two sisters abandoned the property and fled to northern Georgia as General Sherman's forces stormed across the state in December 1864. The home was one of only two along the Ogeechee that was not burned by Federal troops, who probably occupied Strathy for much of 1865. In late 1865, Charlie and Harriet moved in, apparently rent-free. The home, which currently bears the address of 51 Strathy Hall Road, Richmond Hill, is listed on the National Register of Historic Places.[468]

---

May 4. *Hattie over in place p.m. until dark. Rainy. Came home. 7:30 taken suddenly ill and quite seriously until 12 p.m.*

---

**Comment:** Hattie had apparently spent the day, and into the rainy night, at the Prarie fields with Charlie. It is unclear whether they crossed the Ogeechee by boat or rode a buggy north to a bridge and back down the Chatham side to the fields and back. It is also unclear who got sick, but the phrasing indicates that it was Harriet.

---

May 7. *Dr. Kollock came out. Everything straight and safe.*

---

**Comment:** Dr. Phineas M. Kollock, MD, a professor at Savannah Medical College, was under contract to treat the plantation's field hands, and undoubtedly the owners themselves.

---

June 2. *Hattie left for home with Fred, Chapin, Mrs. Beige & family.*

---

**Comment:** Sometime between March 12 and June 2, Fred had accepted Charlie's invitation to visit Strathy. After staying about a month, he accompanied Harriet, who wanted to escape Ogeechee's unhealthy summer heat, on the return trip to Norwich by coastal steamer. What Fred did at Strathy, and whether he enjoyed his visit, is unknown.

---

June 3. *A very rainy day. Was at home (Savages) with Brown most of the day. Met Ford in the evening.*

**Comment:** After Harriet and Fred sailed from Savannah for Norwich, Charlie spent the day in Savannah at the Savage home where he had once resided. The Savages were a very prominent Savannah family who also owned a plantation near Strathy Hall.

June 4. *Came out to the hall. Wildman met me at depot.*

**Comment:** Charlie took the twenty-mile train ride on the Atlantic & Gulf Railroad to Way's Station where his partner, Edward Wildman, probably picked him up in a buggy for the four-mile ride to Strathy Hall.

June 9. *Walter Farnsworth died. Pacis. Brain fever.*

**Comment:** Walter was his cousin, dead at age 22. Charlie had been critical of him for traveling to Europe while the Civil War was raging. Charlie meant "paces," plural for the Latin *pax*, i.e., peace.

June 21. *Wildman sailed in Barnes.*

**Comment:** Charlie's partner was sailing north on a coastal steamer, perhaps to visit his family in Danbury, Connecticut.

June 24. *Belfast. Wrote Hattie.*

**Comment:** Belfast is about six miles southwest of Strathy Hall, located on the Belfast River, a tidal area without the freshwater flow necessary for growing rice. Cotton and "provision crops," such as peas, sweet potatoes, and corn prospered there. Charlie was now farming in Belfast, on property known as Republican Hall, as well as at the Prarie Plantation. A large section of Republican had been owned for many years by Confederate major Jacob Motte Middleton. Charlie may have leased a portion in 1866 from Middleton, a transaction that could demonstrate both how the area welcomed northern investment and how Charlie was getting along with his former enemies. After a freedmen's labor revolt in late 1868 to acquire land that had been promised them by General Sherman, Major Middleton was among the plantation owners who suppressed the uprising and later testified against its leaders. One hundred seventeen freedmen were tried in May 1869 for the uprising, but only six were convicted, and they were promptly pardoned by Republican Governor Rufus Bullock.[469]

June 25. *Recd. a letter from Hattie.*

June 26. *Home.*

June 27. *Commenced to put water in old rice squares 1, 3, 5, 7, 9, 12, 13, 15. Taken very sick and had to return home. Harness broke and buggy overturned.*

---

**Comment:** Charlie was flooding Prarie with Ogeechee River fresh water during a high tide to promote the growth of seeds that were planted in the spring.
   Yet another buggy accident.

---

June 28. *Belfast. Very sick with a bilious attack. Commenced salt bank.*

---

**Comment:** The "bilious attack" probably was a stomach flu or some other intestinal infection.
   Embankments were needed at the Belfast property to keep the tidal flow of saltwater from the nearby Belfast River out of the fields of provision crops.

---

June 29. *Home very sick. People working on break, getting up dirt.*

---

**Comment:** Charlie was sick at home while work continued on the Belfast/Republican Hall field. It took five days to fix the leak in the embankment; it took a week for Charlie to get well.

---

An undated entry here by his wife Harriet reads: *"My poor darling. I never knew how sick he was."*

---

**Comment:** This note by Harriet shows that she read Charlie's diary at some later date. There is no indication, however, that she understood the code he used for his amorous entries.

---

June 30. *Sick at home. People working on break, making up bank, and setting trunk.*

July 1. *Sick home. People turned out and closed up the break. .*

*July 2. Sick at home. Mr. P drove blacks up to place. People working on bank, making up margin and bank.*

*July 3. Sick. Belfast. Wrote Harriet. People finished break today.*

*July 4. Drove to Prarie, killed the biggest rattlesnake I ever saw near the Church — 12 feet long, 12 inches around body, 19 rattles.*

---

**Comment:** Even if Charlie is exaggerating, this was clearly a huge snake.

Instead of crossing the Ogeechee River in a boat to get from Strathy Hall to Prarie, Charlie apparently drove north to a bridge and then back south on the Chatham County side of the river—a trip of about ten miles.

---

*July 5. Belfast all day fishing.*

*July 6. Drove to station. Dr. M went to Prarie. No one at work; had a regular row.*

---

**Comment:** This is probably Way's Station, about four miles north of Strathy, which served the Atlantic & Gulf Railroad on its run to Savannah.

Maintaining a disciplined workforce in the post-war years was a difficult task.[470]

"Dr. M." may be the former major Middleton, Charlie's Republican plantation partner who later took over Prarie.

---

*July 7. At Prarie. All at work. Replaced bridge. Put water on squares 6 & 8. Hold out squares 10 & 12.*

*July 8. Belfast all day. Wrote wife and Wildman.*

*July 9. Recd. letters of June 21 and July 1 from Hattie. Wrote her "if she remembered a year ago today."*

---

**Comment:** A year earlier Charlie had broken his engagement with Georgia, perhaps becoming engaged to Harriet on the same day; here he shared the memory with his wife.

---

July 10. *Wrote Father in regard to funds invested in New York. Letter at station from Hattie.*

July 11. *Went to plantation with Dr. M. Walked around. Men at work on break. Women in field.*

July 12. *Went up to place; repairing breaks.*

July 13. *Went to station. Made tax return. In horse and buggy, came to place. Bank broke again a short distance from last break. Heavy rain.*

July 14. *Went to place. Ordered peas planted Monday and checked bank repaired. Pouring in on left side of canal. Very poor work indeed.*

July 15. *At Belfast. Very quiet. Wrote Hattie.*

July 16. *Went up to place & rode all around it, mending check bank which will shut out salt. Planting peas in two lower squares N. range 36 & 37.*

July 17. *Went up to place & to depot. Recd. letter from wife of 9th & 11th, also from Wildman of 8th. Wife goes to Albany today under escort of Gov. Buckingham & family.*

---

**Comment:** Harriet was traveling in prominent company; she may have been going to visit her mother, who lived in Albany.

---

July 18. *Up to place. Everything doing well.*

July 19. *Up to place. Making Buckland, went Savannah, stopped Savage in evening. Called on Mrs. Lapham's; found C from Florida [at] home.*

---

**Comment:** Buckland was an area between Belfast and Strathy Hall that was later incorporated into the town of Richmond Hill. Charlie had been a friend of the Savage family since he lodged with them soon after arriving in Savannah in early 1865.

This was the first time during his marriage that Charlie recorded a visit to "C from Florida," whom he had first mentioned in his May 28, 1865 entry. He would mention her again.

---

July 20. *Collected two months' rent. [Illegible.] Nothing new in [illegible]. Steamer San Salvador quarantined with cholera, Mrs. Chipman on board. Mr. Chipman went down today to join her. Must stay until she comes off. Called on Mrs. Wilson and on C from Florida.*

**Comment:** This is the first indication that Charlie was sub-leasing a portion of his plantation to freedmen, presumably as sharecroppers, which may have been necessary to keep labor peace.

July 21. *Home per A & G. Sick with biles — did not stop at place.*

July 22. *Sick at Belfast.*

**Comment:** The Ogeechee area was not a healthy place to be in the summer.

July 23. *Home Belfast. Mr. P & L drove bay up. Caught in rain and soaked through.*

July 24. *Home. Everybody home. Recd. letters from Hattie of dates 15 and 16ᵗʰ. Mrs. HPF at Poughkeepsie.*

**Comment:** "Mrs. HPF" is Harriet/Hattie. Charlie's sardonic tone about his wife socializing in New York, while he tended the fields, is obvious.

July 25. *Home. All home.*

July 26. *Home Belfast. P & L went up to place.*

July 28. *Went to place, then depot. Left horse at Hall. Savannah evening. Savage's. C.*

**Comment:** Charlie took the train to Savannah to visit the Savage family again, and to see "C." This was at least the fifth time since mid-1865 that Charlie had called upon the mysterious "C from Florida."

July 29. *Church a.m. Brown. Home evening.*

July 30. *Savannah. Nothing important.*

July 31. *Came home. Betty at place. Everything OK.*

August 1. *Went to Stares Creek.*

August 2. *Went up with Mrs. P and went all over the place.*

August 3. *Judge and Doct went up. All the rest of us home.*

August 11. *Smooth as glass all the way from Frying Pan Shoals to New York.*

---

**Comment:** Charlie decided that he too needed a break from the oppressive Ogeechee summer. He caught a steamer north to New York, and another on to Norwich. Curiously, Hattie, accompanied by her Aunt Harriet, left for Savannah just two days after Charlie arrived in Norwich.

---

August 12. *Arrived New York.*

August 13. *Home at 8:30 a.m. Tea at Aunt Harriet's. G. there.*

---

**Comment:** Aunt Harriet was probably the sister of Harriet's mother. It seems odd that Charlie's former fiancée Georgia, if that is who "G" is, was invited to the tea.

---

August 15. *Hattie and aunt went to Savannah.*

---

**Comment:** Hattie and her aunt would return to Norwich in mid-September. It is not known whether they went out to Strathy during their time in Savannah.

---

August 16. *Went to Stonington via New London, arrived 6 p.m. Tea at Aunt Ann's. Night at the farm. Drive with Aunt Lewisa to Pequot.*

**Comment:** Charlie was visiting his mother's family (the Billingses and the Williamses) in southeastern Connecticut. Pequot was the original name for New London; the term was later given to an area about three miles south of the town.

August 17. *7 a.m. went to Williams grave yard.*

**Comment:** Charlie paid his respects to his mother's Williams grandparents, probably buried in Stonington, where both the Williams and Billings families had settled and prospered.

August 18. *Home via New London.*

August 19. *Church. Raining.*

August 20. *Home all day. Called on Nortons in evening. Goddard & Lesters.*

**Comment:** Henry P. Goddard was a childhood friend. The Lesters were probably Harriet's cousins.

August 21. *New London. Called on Humphries & son, Bond.*

August 22. *Wrote Wildman to send papers to Rich. Home in evening.*

**Comment:** "Rich" was probably Richmond, Charlie's personal assistant in Savannah.

September 8. *Ball match plain! Fred sick — we sat up all night with him.*

**Comment:** Charlie was watching a baseball game, a sport that had been played in the eastern states since at least 1846.

September 9. *At home. Church all day. Fred sick at home in p.m.*

September 10. *Went out shooting with William & Harry. 7 quail.* [illegible.]

September 11. *At home. Barker & Rickurse & Judson, Nortons and Lib R here to tea.*

---

**Comment:** Charlie attached here a clipping of two preacher jokes.

---

September 12. *Went to New York.*

September 13. [Illegible] *change — Benedict H. Bacon.*

September 14. *Raritan* [illegible], *worked well.*

---

**Comment:** Charlie paid a visit to the yachting town of Raritan, New Jersey, just across Lower New York Bay from Coney Island.

---

September 15. *Left Raritan p.m. New York. Home boat, train. Allan Phillips.*

> War Department (Room 52)
> Washington
> Sept 15, 1866

*Charles Farnsworth enrolled Nov 26th 1861 at Meriden and mustered into service as Captain Co. B. 1st Conn. Cav. Dec. 17th 1861 to serve 3 yrs. to date from Nov. 2nd 1861. Strength of Co. when mustered in: Total enlisted men 76, one 1st and 2nd Lieutenant and himself as Captain. Aggregate 79.*

*Mustered into service as Major March 30th 1863. Strength of Battln. for March 1863: Total enlisted 333, 1 Lieut. Col., himself as Major, 4 Capts., 4 1st & 4 2nd Lieutenants. Aggregate 347. Mustered out as Major April 28th 1863 to date back to March 30th 1863. Remustered as Capt. Co. B May 2nd 1863 to date from Nov. 26th 1861. Said muster in roll states: This officer was mustered as Major from March 30, 1863 to fill vacancy of Major Wm. Fish, promoted. (Wm. S. Fish enrolled and mustered as Lt. Col. Oct. 5th 1863.) By order of the War Department he was mustered out to fall on his original position.*

*Enrolled as Major Oct. 5th 1863 and mustered into service April 30th 1864 to date from April 30th 1864 by S. O. dated Army General Order March 31st and April 18th 1864. (E. B. 841 v.g. & E. B. 479 v.g.) Strength of Regt. for Oct. 1863: 480 enlisted & 18 commissioned officers, exclusive of field & staff for which there are no records covering dates on file.*

*Mustered out as Major April 30th 1864 to date January 19th 1864. Strength of Regt. for April 30th 1864: 915 enlisted men, 28 commissioned officers, and field & staff consisting of 1 Col., 1 Lieut. Col. (C. Farnsworth), 2 Maj,, 1 Surgeon & assistant, 1 Quarter Master, & 1 Commissary.*

*Enrolled January 20th 1864 and mustered into service as Lieut. Col. April 30th 1864 to date January 20th 1864 by S.O. dated March 31st 1864 and April 18th 1864, vice Lt. Col. Wm. S. Fish, promoted. (William S. Fish enrolled & mustered into service as Col. January 21st 1864.) Army General Order (E. B. 841 v.g. & E.B. 479 v.g.) Strength of Regiment for January 1864: total commissioned 33, enlisted 1,073. Rolls of field and staff for May & June 1864 report him "Discharged on tender of his resignation May 17th 1864. Signature appears to be genuine.*

H. H.

*When was Farnsworth mustered out as Capt. and when was his successor mustered in as Capt.?*

**Comment:** In response to a petition that Charlie had filed, a formal review of his promotional history was undertaken by the War Department, which concluded here that Charlie was not entitled to the rank of either lieutenant colonel or major.

**September 16.** *To Church three times. Eddy and Ludlow in evening.*

**Comment:** A remarkable display by Charlie of religious devotion.

**September 17.** *Called eve [illegible].*

**September 18.** *New London. Dined WWB. Drive.*

**Comment:** Charlie dined at the home of his uncle, William Williams Billings, a former whaling merchant and brother of his mother.

**September 25.** *Left for Providence via New London. Called on Major Thomas W. Reached CBF at 4 p.m.*

**Comment:** As he socialized, Charlie also conducted business, and seemed to be in no hurry to return to Savannah. "CBF" is his older brother Billings, a businessman now located in Providence, who had been lending funds for Charlie's Savannah enterprises. "Major Thomas W." was his great uncle and head of New London's largest whaling firm, best known as Williams & Haven.

September 26. *Rained all day. Drove around place in P.M.*

September 27. *Providence. Drove in and around with Claude p.m. Pleasant time.*

September 30. *Mrs. Fields.*

October 2. *Called on Meach and Hakes. Also on Louisa Meach and Mrs. Con Lanman. Out shooting with Sam. 12 quails. Dog seeked finely.*

**Comment:** Back in Norwich, Charlie went to see his close friend Dwight Hakes, with whom he had been imprisoned at Libby.

October 3. *Took tea at Martha Ripley's. Leit. Helston, Elgin, Perkins, Nailans in party on board Sabine. New London. To French office. Fred went down with party.*

**Comment:** The *Sabine* was a United States frigate, a warship.

October 4. *Morning at Jennings, shopping. Dinner at Aunt's. H, Mother, & Fred. Ball match. Eve. at home. Fred left for New York.*

**Comment:** Harriet probably had returned to Norwich a few weeks earlier, but it seems odd that Charlie did not mention exactly when. They watched another baseball game.

October 5. *Took tea at Governor Buckingham's. Spent the morning shopping with H.*

**Comment:** Harriet presumably accompanied Charlie to the governor's home for tea, but Charlie did not make that clear. The couple seems to have been purchasing furnishings for their Strathy Hall home in Georgia.

October 6. *At Martha Ripley's in morning. Took tea at Louisa's.*

October 7. *Church all day. Sent telegram to Mrs. Lester.*

**Comment:** Charlie and Harriet sent a telegram to her mother, Mary Elizabeth Lester (née Carpenter), who was living in Albany, N.Y.

October 8. *At home packing.*

October 9. *At home packing.*

**Comment:** After living at Strathy Hall for nearly a year, Charlie and Harriet were shipping some finer furnishings for their home there.

October 10. *Left at 4 p.m. for New London. Spent evening with WWB. Left by steamboat E for New York.*

**Comment:** Charlie and Harriet dined with his uncle William Williams Billings in New London before departing for Savannah, taking their new household furnishings with them.

October 11. *In New York. Called on Mrs. Days. Dined. On steamer at 3 p.m.; anchored all night at Staten Island.*

October 12. *Went to sea at 10 a.m. Very rough. Blowing hard.*

October 13. *Sea going down, some motion. Cape Hatteras at 8 p.m.*

October 14. *Weather fine. Ship making a good run.*

October 15. *Steamer Jeff Davis arrived Savannah 3 a.m. Waited until tide 12 p.m., reached city. Marshall. Brown.*

---

**Comment:** The port of Savannah is twelve miles up the Savannah River from the Atlantic, so ships must await high tide to dock.

Once again, the New York to Savannah run took four days. It is odd that a steamer from New York was still named for the defeated Confederate president.

---

October 16. *Came out to Bryan County. All well at Republican Hall.*

October 17. *Went to Prarie.*

October 18. *Went to Prarie.*

---

**Comment:** After an absence of more than two months, Charlie promptly checked up on his two properties.

---

Special Orders                          WAR DEPARTMENT
No. 522                        ADJUTANT GENERAL'S OFFICE
                               Washington, October 20th, 1866
                                                   (Extract)


      \*       \*       \*       \*


5. The musters into service of *Charles Farnsworth* as Major and Lieutenant-Colonel, 1st Connecticut Cavalry, as made April 30th, 1864, to date, respectively, October 5th, 1863, and January 20th, 1864, are hereby revoked, the authority for the same having been given under a misapprehension of the facts of his case, he having rendered no service in those grades, and being at the time said musters were made a paroled prisoner of war and also physically disqualified for field service.

By order of the Secretary of War:
E. D. Townsend,
Assistant Adjutant General

**Comment:** Notice of the War Department's revocation of Charlie's ranks of lieutenant colonel and major must have landed hard, whenever it was received, but Charlie made no diary entry about it. His wife Harriet would spend several decades seeking a reversal of Special Order No. 522.

October 28. *At home. Ride with Mrs. L. Called on Mrs. McGiffen.*

October 29. *Rained night and day. A perfect torrent. Wrote Mrs. Theo. Dunnell.*

October 31. *Mrs. Betty went to town.*

**Comment:** Charlie's diary, which he had kept since July 1863, abruptly ended here. Nor have any further letters from him been found.

## 1867

### *Examining Surgeon's Certificate*

*Norwich February 11th, 1867*

*I hereby certify, That I have carefully examined Charles Farnsworth, late a Lt. Col. in the 1st Regiment Connecticut Cavalry, in the service of the United States, who was discharged at Washington D.C. on the 17th day of May, 1864, and is an applicant for an invalid pension, by reason of alleged disability resulting Gunshot Wound.*

*In my opinion, the said Charles Farnsworth is entirely incapacitated for obtaining his subsistence by manual labor form the cause above stated.*

*Judging from his present condition, and from the evidence before me, it is my belief that the said disability was incurred in the service aforesaid in the line of duty.*

*The disability is probably permanent.*

*A more particular description of the applicant's condition is subjoined:*

*The applicant was wounded April 3rd 1862, near Moorfield, Va. The ball struck the 5th rib in left side, ¼ of distance from sternum to spine, and came out 1 ½ inch from spine. The rib was fractured, and he lost between 1 and 2 qts. of blood. After he recovered sufficiently to join his regiment, he was in several engagements, but always suffered from hard riding, usually causing hemorbage from lungs. He might have fully recovered, but his confinement for 9 months in Libby prison broke his constitution. He is now entirely incapacitated for obtaining his subsistence by manual labor. He also received a ball through his left arm, which has diminished a good deal of its strength. He has delayed his application this long in hope of entire recovery, but is disappointed.*

*Examining Surgeon*

---

**Comment:** Having lost his earlier promotion appeal, Charlie decided that he was at least entitled to an invalid's pension, and obtained a report in early 1867 certifying that he was permanently and "entirely incapacitated for obtaining his subsistence by manual labor" because of his war wounds. He submitted the doctor's certificate in support of the petition to the commissioner of pensions, Department of Interior, who did not immediately respond, but the eventual ruling would lead to another extended bureaucratic battle.

---

*Ogeechee*
*April 15ᵗʰ 1867*

My dear Mrs. Farnsworth,

This morning your son & Mr. Wildman left in a small boat for their plantation. The wind high & river rough, & the boat was too small for two. When they were part way across the river, their boat was almost unmanageable, as we understand it, & Mr. Wildman jumped out & swam no more than two feet before he sunk, never to rise again. Col. Farnsworth remained in the boat, which drifted down a short distance & then capsized, and it is supposed he immediately sunk. Their coats and hats were found & brought here. But no one on this side of the river knew anything about it until three hours after. The men in a flat who saw it could not manage their flat for a long time to bring it to launch, & when they did they landed on the other side & had to run some two miles for a boat to cross over here.

Mrs. Farnsworth is very much crushed, it came so suddenly upon her. We trust she will have the strength given her from God to bear up under the dreadful affliction. We hope she will consent to return home with us. Another would try to be a mother to her, in this sad hour of trial. They are trying to find the bodies, & so hope they will succeed. Your daughter does not feel equal to writing so I offered to write for her. You will receive a telegraph before receiving this. I am sorry to be the communicator of such sad, sad tiding, but I can truly sympathize.

Yours very sincerely,
Cornelia Talbot

---

**Comment:** To travel to his Prarie Plantation from Strathy Hall, Charlie had two choices: he could ride four miles north to a bridge, cross over the Ogeechee River, and ride four miles back down the east side to the fields; or he could row across the river, which was six hundred to a thousand feet wide near his home, using a small duck boat that he owned. He probably opted for the river crossing most often.

On the morning of April 15, Charlie and his farming partner Edward Wildman were rowing across the river from Strathy Hall to their Prarie fields. In the spring, the river runs swift with "freshets" and winds can make the current choppy as well as fast. A duck boat lies low in the water and can be easily swamped, especially a small one carrying two grown men. In his March 12, 1866 letter to his brother Fred, he wrote of taking Harriet rowing in a "scow," which probably was his droll term for the duck boat. He added then that he was trying to acquire a better boat.

The letter-writer here, Mary Cornelia Talbot, had been visiting her parents, the Richard James Arnolds, on the nearby White Hall/Cherry Hill plantation, when she got news of the accident. Although she was a Georgian by birth, Cornelia's parents were northerners who had come south as adults in the 1830s to manage a plantation given to them at their marriage. The Arnolds fled back north when Georgia seceded, returning only when the war ended in April 1865. It is quite conceivable that Cornelia and Harriet became acquainted during 1866-67 in the small Ogeechee rice farming community, given their geographical and political affinities. In fact, their two plantations—White Hall and Strathy—had been developed in the late 1700s by the same man, Captain James MacKay.[471]

---

The next day, the local newspaper reported:

> **DROWNED.**—Yesterday morning while Mr. Edward Wildman and Col. Chas. Farnsworth were crossing the Ogeechee river in a small duck boat, from their residence to a rice plantation directly opposite, the heavy wind prevailing at the time swamped the boat and both were drowned. The loss of these estimable gentlemen will be deeply regretted by all who knew them, as they were men of great integrity and honesty. They had been in this country but a short time.[472]

A follow-up story appeared a day later:

> **A PARTY,** consisting of the friends of the late Messrs. Farnsworth and Wildman, who were drowned in the Ogeechee river on Monday, left this city yesterday, provided with grappling irons, and other appliances for raising the bodies of the unfortunate men.[473]

The tragedy was covered in more detail by the Norwich newspapers:

### DEATH OF COL. CHARLES FARNSWORTH

> A brief telegraph dispatch received from Savannah, Ga., Monday night, announced the death by drowning near that city, of Col. Chas. Farnsworth, son of Dr. Ralph Farnsworth of this city. No particulars were received, except that a gentleman named Wilder—who was with him in a sail boat at the time—was also drowned. Nor do we learn whether the body was recovered.

Col. Farnsworth was born in this city, and at the time of his death was in the 31st year of his age. At the breaking out of the war he was in the West, and having been accustomed there to an adventurous life, on the frontiers in the saddle, and in the camp and field, he hastened home and offered his services to the Governor, in the first regiment of cavalry raised by the state. His offer was accepted, and he was commissioned as Adjutant of the First Connecticut Cavalry. Holding this position but a short time, he was promoted to a Captaincy, and thence to be Major and Lieut. Colonel, which office he held at the time of his discharge. While in West Virginia, in the Moorfield Valley, in the Spring of 1862, he was shot by bushwhackers, the ball entering his body and inflicting a serious wound, from which he did not recover for several weeks. On the 14th of July, 1863, while in command of a scouting party near Bolivar Heights, he with his party, was surrounded and taken prisoners. For months afterwards he was confined in rebel prisons in various parts of the South. His promotion to the Lieut. Colonelcy was received while he was still in prison. He was released early in 1864, and shortly afterwards resigned his commission on account of ill health. Just before the close of the war, he engaged in business in Georgia, and has resided there ever since. He was married in this city in November 1865, and returned with his wife immediately to his home in Georgia, where they have since remained, with the exception of a short visit home in the summer of 1866.

Col. Farnsworth was a brave and gallant officer, an earnest patriot, an upright citizen and honest man. He will be deeply lamented and sincerely mourned by all who knew him, and his family will received the sympathies of the whole community in their deep affliction.[474]

---

**Comment:** The newspaper erroneously called Charlie's companion "Wilder," and erred in describing the duck boat as a "sail boat"; it was a row boat. Charlie's family was probably the source for the background material, which was more or less accurate.

---

## Arrivals at the Hotels[475]

...

# MARSHALL HOUSE

...

Dr. R. Farnsworth, Conn.
T. Farnsworth, Conn.

---

**Comment:** This newspaper item shows that Charlie's father, Dr. Ralph, had arrived within five days to take Charlie's body back to Norwich. "T" Farnsworth was probably a misprint for younger brother Fred.

---

## LIST OF LETTERS [476]

Remaining in Savannah Post Office April 29, 1867. Persons calling for these letters will please say "Advertised," and bring with them the necessary change.

Ladies' List.

...

Farnsworth, Mrs. Chas.

---

**Comment:** Some letters to Harriet remained, uncalled for, at the Savannah Post Office, according to the newspaper. This suggests that she had already gone north with Dr. Ralph and Fred, accompanying Charlie's body.

---

The inscription on Charlie's headstone at Yantic Cemetery, Norwich reads:

**Charles Farnsworth**
**Born**
**Jan 30th , 1836**
**Drowned**
**Near Savannah, Ga.**
**April 15th, 1867**

**The Lord hath his way**
**In the whirlwind and in the storm.**

**Comment:** The family buried Charlie on April 26 at Yantic Cemetery in Norwich. A decade or so later, his parents were buried in front of him. Six siblings who died before age six were later transferred from an earlier cemetery and reburied at Yantic behind Charlie and their parents. His brother Billings and wife Carrie died later and are buried to one side. Only his younger brother, Fred, was buried elsewhere—in New London.

Charlie was soon eulogized at least twice by his comrades-in-arms:

*Mrs. Chas. Farnsworth*
*Madam,*
*I have the honor to herewith transmit you a copy of the Resolutions adopted at a meeting of the members of the 1ˢᵗ Connecticut Volunteer Cavalry on Friday April 26ᵗʰ 1867.*

> *Respectfully yours,*
> *Joab B. Rogers*
> *Chairman*

*At a Meeting of the members of the 1ˢᵗ Connecticut Cavalry, comrades in arms with the late Col. Charles Farnsworth, the following resolutions were adopted:*

*Resolved, That as it has pleased Almighty God to remove from us our late Colonel, we, as a body sincerely mourn his death;*
*Resolved, That in the death of this esteemed soldier, who served his country in time of need, gaining friends and leaving a glorious record to history, we sympathize deeply with afflicted family;*
*Resolved, That as a token of respect to his memory we will as a body attend his funeral on Friday the 26ᵗʰ instant;*
*Resolved, That a copy of these resolutions be transmitted to the family.*

| | |
|---|---|
| *Joab B. Rogers* | *J. Hammond Kane* |
| *John H. Hough* | *Henry P. Phillips* |
| *John Irish* | *Charles J. Barston* |
| *George A. Chapman* | *Thomas D. Phillips* |
| *William A. Gates* | *Chas. F. Smith* |

*Norwich, April 27ᵗʰ 1867*

**Comment:** Joab Rogers, of Norwich, had been a lieutenant in Charlie's Company B. The others were enlisted men in various companies of the First Connecticut Cavalry.[477]

---

*At a Re-union of the officers of the late 1ˢᵗ Conn. Cavalry at New Haven August 15, 1867, it was unanimously resolved:*

*"That we here express the profound sorrow which we feel upon learning this day the circumstances pertaining to the death of <u>Lieut. Col. Charles Farnsworth</u> by drowning in the Ogeechee River in the State of Georgia on the 15ᵗʰ of April last.*

*"We shall ever cherish his memory as a noble & generous friend and a brave and gallant officer.*

*"Our Earnest sympathy is extended to the bereaved widow whom we can only commend, prayerfully, to Him who has promised to be a friend to the widow & the fatherless."*

> *Theodore J. Holmes*
> *Secretary*

*Norwich April 26ᵗʰ 1867*

---

**Comment:** Theodore J. Holmes, of East Hartford, was the chaplain for the First Connecticut Cavalry.[478]

---

> ***Treasury Department***
> Second Auditor's Office
> April 20ᵗʰ, 1867

Sir:

*Your return of ordnance and ordnance stores appertaining to B Co., 1ˢᵗ Connecticut Cavalry, for the following quarters: 4/1861, 1-2-3/1862 consolidated, 4/1862, has been received, examined, and found correct, and closed except in 4ᵗʰ quarter 1862. Voucher required for 1 Colt's Revolver and 3 Lariats said to have been lost and destroyed.*

*Captain Charles Farnsworth*
*B Co., 1ˢᵗ Conn. Cavalry*

> *Respectfully,*
> *Your obedient servant*
> *E. B. French, Second Auditor*

*Return this letter.*

**Comment:** In late April, two years after the war ended, and obviously unaware of Charlie's death, the Treasury Department sent this and the following letter demanding that Charlie account for certain weapons, clothing, and equipment issued to his former Company B. The first letter arrived in Norwich about the time of Charlie's funeral, and probably did not sit well with the family. We do not know how the family responded, but we can guess that any reply by Charlie would not have been cordial, had he lived.

***Treasury Department***
*Second Auditor's Office,*
April 30th, 1867

*Sir:*

*Your return of Clothing, Camp, and G. Equipage appertaining to Company B, 1ˢᵗ Conn. Cavalry for the following quarter, viz., 4ᵗʰ Quarter 1862, has been received, examined, and found correct, except as follows.*

*Each signature on the Receipt Rolls should be witnessed separately, and by some officer other than the one accountable for the clothing.*

*An affidavit should be furnished to verify the issues to those who have not signed the Receipt Rolls.*

*Property said to have been lost, worn out, abandoned, or destroyed should be accounted for by an affidavit giving the circumstances.*

*Stores remaining on hand, to be accounted for.*

*Respectfully,*
*Your obedient servant,*
*E. B. French,*
*Second Auditor*

*To Capt. Chas. Farnsworth*
*Co. B, 1ˢᵗ Conn. Cavalry*
*Please return these letters with answer.*

**Comment:** Another untimely message from the government which no doubt irritated the family.

# Later Years

Washington D. C.
July 6<sup>th</sup>, 1870

Sir:

Under a recent decision of the Department you are entitled to a considerable amount for the use and risk of your horse while an officer in the service of the U. S., and I shall be pleased to collect the same for you. The necessary papers to collect the same will be forwarded upon reply to this being received.

Yours Respy.
L. C. Tallmadge
Box 430

---

**Comment:** This War Department letter, and the several that follow, were found in Charlie's military file at the National Archives. When the first one was written, the War Department was apparently unaware that he had died in 1867.

---

Washington
Feb 8, 1871

L. C. Tallmadge
Relating to Capt. Chas. Farnsworth, July 6, 1870

Respectfully referred to Doct. Farnsworth. All that can be obtained is 40 cents per day from the 26<sup>th</sup> Nov 1861, the day of enlistment, to the 1<sup>st</sup> of Jan 1862. Only 35 days @ 40 cents, $14. To look up the necessary proof and collect the amount would be more perplexity & trouble than it is worth.

W. A. Buckingham

---

**Comment:** Buckingham, now a US senator, somehow got involved and suggested to Charlie's father, Dr. Ralph, that applying for benefits for the one month that Charlie used his own horse was not worth the effort.

---

1<sup>st</sup> Conn. Cav. / Office Muster-in, March 25, 1886

Charles Farnsworth, Major, 1<sup>st</sup> Reg't Conn. Cav. Mustered in as Major from October 1, 1863. Record is amended, under the provisions of the act of Congress approved June 3, 1884, to muster into the service of the United States Charles Farnsworth as a Major in the 1$^{st}$ Conn. Cav. Vols., to take effect the 1$^{st}$ day of October 1863.

Parten,

Copyist

---

**Comment:** Charlie had been promoted from captain to major to lieutenant colonel in 1863 but then was reduced back to captain in October 1866 on the grounds that he had never been "mustered" into his regiment at those higher ranks because he had been imprisoned when the promotions were made. Nineteen years after his death, the War Department reinstated Charlie as a major. The effective date seems wrong, however. Charlie had served in action as major since March 1863, and he was being held at Libby in October of that year, unable to muster. It is likely that Harriet's lobbying of the War Department about Charlie's proper rank prompted this review.

---

# DECISIONS of THE DEPARTMENT OF THE INTERIOR

## Cases Relating to Pension Claims
## 1891

### SECONDARY DEATH CAUSES

### HARRIET C., WIDOW OF CHARLES FARNSWORTH

Secondary causes of death, in order to be the proper basis for pension, must be so established by the laws of evidence as to appear both logically and pathologically related to the pensioned or the pensionable causes; and, therefore, the pension system is averse to such a deduction of sequences as would lead to the acceptance of causations entirely too remote from the original cause of pensionable disability to be in harmony with any reasonable theory as to the intent or purpose of the law.

### Assistant Secretary Bussey to the Commissioner of Pensions, Sept. 22, 1890.

Herewith are returned the papers in the case of Harriet C., widow of Charles Farnsworth, late captain, Company B, First Connecticut Cavalry, which accompanied your report upon the appeal (special) from the action of your Bureau in rejecting the claim (No. 392,765) for widow's pension.

Colonel Charles Farnsworth has a record as a soldier from December 17, 1861, when he was mustered as captain until May 17, 1864, when he was discharged as lieutenant-colonel. October 15, 1866, he filed claim for an invalid pension. About April 15, 1867, he was accidentally drowned. His claim for pension was, however, prosecuted to an issue, and, in 1882, his pension was granted for "gunshot wound of left arm and left side" at the rate of $20, from date of discharge until date of death.

April 10, 1889, the appellant in this case, the widow of the soldier, filed a claim for widow's pension, alleging that the soldier's death was due to the disabilities resulting from wounds received in the service and from his general impairment of health due to these causes and to confinement in Libby prison for some months. Her claim is based upon the assumption that, but for this alleged enfeebled condition of health, the soldier would not have been drowned; and she argues, accordingly, that she is entitled to pension because the death was "by reason" of causes which would have entitled the soldier if living.

From your rejection of this claim it is presented on appeal.

---

I have most carefully examined every detail of the evidence in this case and given it earnest consideration. There is a voluminous mass of testimony on file, but the larger part of it is simply cumulative and corroborative of the fact of wounding of the soldier in the service and of resulting disability. The claim of the soldier having been allowed, this part of the evidence could have no value, except in so far as it might aid in the determination of the cause of death. It is conceded that the soldier was injured and incurred disabilities from gunshot wounds and from imprisonment of about nine months while in service. The only medical examination had in his case, held February 11, 1867, reported him "entirely unable to obtain his subsistence by manual labor," and that his disability was probably permanent. Coming to the vital question of the cause of death, the evidence seems to establish these facts: On April 15, 1867, Colonel Farnsworth, in company with Mr. Wildman, with whom he was associated in the management of a rice plantation in Georgia, attempted to cross the Ogeechee River in a small duck boat. Before reaching the eastern bank of the river, *both men* were drowned. A strong wind was blowing and the river was evidently very rough. There have been produced no witnesses who saw the drowning. The details and circumstances are supplied by the affidavits of several gentlemen, who repeat what is alleged to have been described to them by several negroes who claimed to have witnessed the drowning, and by copies of telegraphic dispatches sent to the newspapers at the former home of the soldier in Connecticut, at or about the date of the accident. The river was about 600 feet wide, and it appears that Mr. Wildman, either through fright, or under the conviction that, in such a wind, this small boat could not reach shore, jumped overboard and, in attempting to swim ashore, was drowned. After he left the boat Colonel Farnsworth remained in it until the wind caused high waves to fill the boat, and he was either washed out or jumped out. In attempting to swim ashore he was drowned. The newspaper dispatches report that some men in a flat boat witnessed the drowning, but had themselves so much difficulty in crossing the river that they could not render any assistance, nor get the news to Mrs. Farnsworth for several hours. It is alleged that the point at which Colonel Farnsworth was drowned was not over 40 feet from the shore. Some testimony is offered to prove that he was a good swimmer.

The attorney for the appellant has filed an extended argument covering over eighty pages, with a view to convincing your Bureau of the merits of this claim. With great zeal and ingenuity he discusses the law of evidence and the origin and theory of the laws governing the pension system, in an effort to bring the facts and the evidence in the case within such a rule of interpretation and construction of the words "by reason of" in section 4702, R.S., as will admit this claim.

The soldier having been drowned, and the fact, that his general health and strength had been impaired by reason of his wounds, being in evidence, the argument is that, but for this condition of health the drowning and death would not have occurred, and, hence, the death was "by reason" of the said *wounds* and disability. Several witnesses file affidavits of their *opinion* that death was due to the existence of the alleged disabilities. Two physicians, as expert witnesses, testify upon hypothetical cases admitted, that, upon the assumptions therein stated, their belief is that "death from accidental drowning was due to debility of the heart, weakness of the lungs, and pain in the region of the wounds." These hypothetical cases, however, are stated certainly *most favorably* to the claimant's theory in every detail, and take very little consideration of the main and real cause of the accident—*the storm upon the river.* This testimony is of little weight in view of the actual facts, accepting them even from the secondary evidence available.

The fact that Colonel Farnsworth's companion was drowned is a strong factor in *rebuttal* of the claimant's theory, strengthening, as it does, the conviction that this soldier's death was not "by reason" of the wounds, but due entirely to the independent cause, namely, the swamping of his boat in a squall of rough weather upon the river. The evidence of the difficulty in the management of the flat boat and its inability to render aid, gives additional weight to the theory of very severe weather.

The attorney makes the point that the soldier was engaged in his usual business and daily practice, to avoid the charge of contributory negligence. But if his health, physical strength, and bodily sufferings were equal to the representations made, it would not seem the part of prudence or discretion to brave the dangers of that storm in a small duck boat. The reported width of the stream—600 feet—leaves no room to conclude that the storm overtook them after starting. The fact that he had been a good swimmer, while decreasing the probability of drowning under favorable circumstances, can not be relied upon to counteract the force of the wind and tide, as shown by the constantly-occurring accidents to the most expert swimmers. The provision of law governing this claim, as incorporated in section 4702, R.S., recites that, when any soldier dies by reason of any wound, injury, or disease which would have entitled him to an invalid pension had he been disabled, his widow or, if there be no widow, his child or children under sixteen years, shall be entitled to the same pension as the husband or father would have been entitled to had he been totally disabled.

Suppose, instead of having been drowned, this soldier had contracted a severe cold as the result of the exposure and struggle in the water—a cold which had resulted in pneumonia or in permanent pulmonary disease—could it be held by any sort of argument or reasoning that the disability resulting therefrom would have entitled him to a pension? Can it be held that it would be a reasonable interpretation of this statute, to accept as a conclusion that, because *possibly* a strong, hearty man might not incur pneumonia or consumption from exposure in the water in an April day, therefore, this soldier, being disabled and somewhat debilitated as the result of gunshot wound and imprisonment in the service, would not have contracted cold, or pneumonia and consumption, but for these disabilities, and would, therefore, be entitled to a pension for the pneumonia or consumption, as having resulted from wounds, injury or disease incurred in the service and line of duty?

Such a deduction of sequences would lead to the acceptance of causations entirely too remote to be in harmony with any accepted or reasonable theory as to the intent or purpose of the law, and is utterly untenable.

Unless, then, the death was "by reason" of such wound, injury or disease, there is no basis for the widow's claim. A careful consideration of this case does not warrant the acceptance of the death as by reason of the disabilities which resulted from the service; and, however much of sympathy may be felt for the widow of this gallant soldier, there seems no proper construction of the law which will justify the admission of the claim. The action of your Bureau in rejecting the same is, therefore, affirmed.[479]

**Comment:** In 1889, some twenty-two years after Charlie's death and seven years after Harriet successfully had appealed his claim for an "invalid" pension (for which she received twenty dollars a month for three years), Harriet had applied for a widow's pension on the theory that Charlie's service-incurred disability had caused his drowning death. In 1890 the Department of Interior denied the petition. The ruling was made after a review of affidavits based on what the only eye-witnesses—several freedmen on the far shore—had said they had seen. The department estimated that the river was six hundred feet wide where Charlie and Wildman attempted to cross, although a modern map shows the Ogeechee to be about one thousand feet wide at its narrowest point near Strathy. The ruling concluded that after Wildman panicked and jumped out of their small rowboat, Charlie got within forty feet of the far side when either the boat became swamped or he jumped out, and then drowned, despite being "a good swimmer." The department ruled that Charlie and Wildman were at fault for setting off during stormy weather. Moreover, Harriet's claim that Charlie had drowned "by reason" of his war wounds was rejected, primarily on the grounds that Wildman too had drowned, even though not disabled.

Assistant Secretary Bussey's denial of Harriet's appeal from the initial ruling was based on a dubious analysis of the evidence. First, he said that because Wildman also drowned, Charlie's disability couldn't have been the cause of his drowning. It was simply the storm. But there was no evidence that Wildman knew how to swim. Charlie, on the other hand, had been a good swimmer before his war wounds. Second, Bussey rejected Harriet's medical experts' testimony as to the cause of drowning as "hypothetical." In fact, it was relevant expert opinion testimony based on the known facts of Charlie's injuries and should have been given as much consideration as the hearsay affidavits. Third, Bussey's labored analogy to a case of pneumonia as forming the basis for a disability claim is bizarre; Charlie had *already* been adjudged disabled. The question was whether that disability reduced his capacity to swim, causing him to drown; there was no persuasive evidence to the contrary.

In addition to his flawed reasoning, there were some odd *factual* statements in Bussey's opinion. He said the drownings occurred only forty feet from the far shore, while Cornelia Talbot wrote that they occurred "part way" across. Bussey estimated the river's width at 600 feet; from modern maps it measures nearly twice that. The boat, according to Bussey, got swamped by the high waves; Talbot wrote that it capsized. For the first time, the eyewitnesses to the drowning were identified as "several negroes," but apparently they did not provide affidavits at the time. Charlie being a good swimmer, even if disabled, the incident becomes all the more curious if it occured a mere forty feet from shore.

Colorado Springs, Colo.
11 West Dale Street
July 18, 1901

Dear Great Grandchildren,

This Grandmother has been asked to write you a letter giving you a little idea of her life in its western surroundings. It seems rather a ghostly thing to do — this writing to generations yet unborn, may be not my own dear descendents! Even my dear grandchildren, Alice five years old, Edith three will not be living, when this letter is opened and read. But I hope there will be some of their children who will be interested in the few details I shall put on this paper. It seems weird that the paper will outlive us all and bear witness that we have lived. When I was a girl in old Connecticut I little thought that I would spend the latter years of my life in this Great West, a part of which was on our maps as the "American Desert." A desert which certainly "bloomed and blossomed like the rose."

My home in Norwich, Conn. was a very happy one, and I had a happy girlhood. I married your [great] grandfather at the close of the Civil War, November 1st 1865. That terrible war between brothers, which has given you a great, undivided country. My husband was Lt. Col. of the 1st Conn. Cavalry, suffered in prison and from wounds, and knew the terrible sorrows of the North and South. He was drowned in the Ogeechee River, Georgia, eighteen months after our marriage, and two months before my son was born.

It means much to have lived thru these days of bloodshed, days which I suppose are almost a myth to you, but great men were ready and stood up, strong to help and to save. The greatest, Abraham Lincoln, to whose name the years will only add a glory and all time yield an undying homage. Just here, my dears, let me say, never be ashamed of enthusiasm. Any appreciation of greatness in others helps you to imitate them, and to follow, sometimes not far off. It is one of the most valued memories of my life, that I met Lincoln one quiet morning (if any morning could be called quiet in those days), the second year of the war. That he bore the sorrows and burdens of a great nation showed in every line of his face, though it was lighted now and then by a glint of humour, which must have helped him and brightened some moments, until his work for the nation and world was done.

Perhaps you will like to hear how I happened to come to this part of our country. Your grandfather, my son, was not well, and at the close of his term at Harvard Law School, we went abroad to Switzerland and Algeria in pursuit of health which we did not obtain, and then were advised to try California. We stopped here for a few days, and it helped my boy so much that we have lived here since, each of us building a house and making a home. Firm health has not come to your grandfather, but he

391

has been better, and enjoyed much after the fearful anxieties of those years of his ill health. I cannot write. God has ever been better to me than my fears.

Perhaps you are wondering what my surroundings are, so I will try to give you a picture of this Sunday afternoon, July 28, 1901. My little home has a wonderful view of Cheyenne Mt. & Pike's Peak, and as I look out of the door of my little den, the wondrous beauty of the mountains appeals to me so much that I should like you to see it, _just_ as I see it. Now and then a bird's note is heard but a Sunday quiet, a New England Sunday quiet, is over it all, and the peace of Nature's grand silence is felt. The "everlasting hills" will be the same to you which is a pleasant thought. This week is full of festivities in a public way, and I give on Friday a very informal breakfast for General and Mrs. Wheaton, who are guests of Mrs. Goddard. Gen. Wheaton was a very brave officer in the Civil War.

Sunday August 4th: Today, the Century Chest closed and I add a few words as I close this letter. We think the world goes at a rapid pace now, but what break-neck race yours must be. I trust you will not have advanced so far as to forget the truth and steadfastness of purpose of our New England ancestors.

This town is very cosmopolitan and the sanitary properties of the air have brought an infinite variety of people here. It is busy in its social life, and in its business life as well. The rich mines of Cripple Creek giving out their golden treasure to some, withholding from others. Withal, there is a very sad undercurrent, which must come to the surface at times, and the voice of pleasure is hushed for a little, but hearts here are full of sympathy & kindness and I feel sure that your hearts will be as sympathetic and your hands as helpful. I enclose a photograph of myself, and of my grandchildren, Alice and Edith. I must tell you an anecdote of Alice. When she was four years old, we were out in the yard one afternoon when she asked me to come in and have some tea, Cambric tea. Then looking at the colored coachman, with a [illegible] air, she said, "You come too, Thomas, you're white enough!!" As I close, let me put in a little plea for some observance of the Sabbath and one word of advice, no matter as to creeds or no creeds, let God's Day be a day of rest and peace to you. The advice is a quotation from Shakespeare which I heard today in a sermon: "Treat others not according to their deserts but according to your own dignity and honor."

> Your very loving
> [Great] Grandmother
> Harriet Peck Farnsworth

---

**Comment:** This letter by Charlie's widow Harriet was part of a "century vault" in Colorado Springs that was opened in 2001. A moving tribute to the Union cause, the letter also reveals that Harriet met President Lincoln in 1862, although the occasion for the meeting is not described. She may have been in the company of General and

Mrs. William Williams, with whom she then lodged, as a single woman. The letter is also noteworthy for its complete lack of fond memories of Ogeechee.

Harriet lived until 1916, forty-nine years beyond her husband Charlie's death, and never remarried.

---

1st Cav. Conn. / NOTATION
Washington March 10, 1904

Under the provisions of the act of Congress, approved February 24, 1897, this officer is held and considered by this Department to have been mustered into the service of the United States in the grade of major, 1st Reg't Conn. Cav. Vols., to take effect from March 21, 1863, *vice* Wm. S. Fish, promoted.

So much of para. 2, Gen. Order 282, hdqrs of the Army, Army Gen. Order Dec. 9, 1885, as recognizes this officer as of this grade & organ.from Oct. 1, 1863, is cancelled.

W. W. Gibson, Copyist

---

**Comment:** Eighteen years after the War Department reinstated Charlie as a major, effective October 1, 1863, the record was corrected to show his rank as dating from March 21 of that year.

---

**Department of the Interior**
Bureau of Pensions
Washington
Act of April 19, 1908
Oct. 16, 1908

Hon. W. A. Haggott, N. R.
My dear Mr. Haggott,

It gives me pleasure to inform you that the original claim for pension of Harriet P. Farnsworth, widow of Charles Farnsworth, late Capt., Company B, 1st Regiment, Conn. Vol. Cav., whose address is Colorado Springs, Colo., has been allowed under certificate No. 662361 at the rate of $12 per month from June 2, 1908, and that the certificate will soon be forwarded to the pension agent at Topeka for transmittal to the beneficiary with voucher for payment.

Very truly yours,
V. Warner,
Commissioner

**Comment:** Although her petition for a widow's pension was denied on appeal in 1890, Harriet revived the issue, again through attorneys, and finally prevailed (but without either opinion or retroactivity) eighteen years later!

W. A. Redmond
Attorney at Law
McGill Building
Washington, D.C.
Oct. 11th 1910

Mrs. Harriet P. Farnsworth
Colorado Springs, Colo.

Dear Madam:

I inclose a letter from the Auditor calling for an affidavit of a brother officer of Col. Farnsworth that he employed <u>two</u> private servants from March 21st 1863 to May 17th 1864.

This item will amount to a goodly sum and I would urge of you to try to find an officer who can make this affidavit. If it is impossible to secure the affidavit, kindly write me to that effect.

Also please sign and return the inclosed certificate of signature, which is desired to avoid error in forwarding check in payment of claim.

Very truly yours,
W. A. Redmond
Dic't. D/3 Incls.

**Comment:** Having been approved for the widow's pension, Harriet may have cast about for other military benefits. Here, her lawyer in Washington suggested that compensation would be paid if Charlie had employed two private servants within a specified period. Charlie was imprisoned during most of the time, however, and at other times had at most one servant—a "contraband" named Denny.

**Treasury Department**

## OFFICE OF AUDITOR FOR THE WAR DEPARTMENT

*Washington,* Oct. 6, 1910

William A. Redmond
Washington, D. C.

Sir:

The claim of Charles Farnsworth, Major, 1$^{st}$ Conn. Cav., is suspended for the execution and return of the inclosed blank form 3002.

If servant's pay and allowances, allowed by law, are claimed, it will be necessary to furnish the affidavit of the officer, or in case of his death, the affidavits of two disinterested persons cognizant of the facts, showing that he employed two private servants from March 21, 1863 to May 17, 1864 and whether the servants so employed were enlisted men or civilians.

> Respectfully,
> B. F. Harper
> Auditor

**Treasury Department**

## OFFICE OF AUDITOR FOR THE WAR DEPARTMENT

*Washington,* Dec. 22, 1910

Wm. A. Redmond
Wash. D. C.

Sir:

The claim of Charles Farnsworth, Lt. Col., 1$^{st}$ Conn. Cav., is suspended. Claimant is requested to furnish all papers in her possession relating to officer's service.

> Respectfully,
> B. F. Harper
> Auditor

---

**Comment:** It seems that Harriet had lost interest in applying for further benefits, undoubtedly because she realized that Charlie would have been ineligible for them.

---

# THE ADJUTANT GENERAL'S OFFICE
**War Department**
Washington, December 2, 1910

Under the provisions of the act of Congress, approved February 24, 1887, Charles Farnsworth, 1ˢᵗ Reg't Conn. Cav., is held and considered by this Department to have been mustered into the service of the United States in the grade of lieutenant colonel, to take effect from January 20, 1864, *vice* William S. Fish, mustered out.

W. W. Gibson, Copyist

---

**Comment:** Harriet's ultimate triumph came forty-three years after Charlie's death, when the War Department reinstated him as a lieutenant colonel, retroactive to January 20, 1864. That was the date when Colonel Fish had been mustered out because of court-martial charges against him, making Charlie the regiment's highest-ranking officer, even though he was confined at Libby Prison. Harriet now could take pride in winning her long battle for justice for her husband. Although she had always referred to Charlie as a lieutenant colonel, she and the family could do so now with official approval. She must have felt a great sense of satisfaction in her victory over the War Department. She died in Colorado Springs six years later, in 1916.

# Acknowledgements

Many have aided this project, and I want to acknowledge some who have helped the most. From the outset, my cousins Frannie and Erik Taylor provided the letters and diaries of Lieutenant Colonel "Charlie" Farnsworth for me to work on, initially in the comfort of their Denver home. Erik brilliantly broke the code Charlie had used for his most secretive diary entries. Robert Angelovich of Gettysburg, Pennsylvania, who is completing a history of Charlie's First Connecticut Cavalry, explained its early battles and sent me many useful documents. Dale Plummer, the city historian of Norwich, Connecticut, has been essential in digging into the Farnsworth family's history, tracking down people we had only initials or first names for, and guiding me through a brief history of 19th-century Norwich. I would have been lost without him. David Oat of Preston, Connecticut, researched the Farnsworth section of Norwich's Yantic Cemetery. The Otis Library in Norwich provided a rich trove of local newspapers and histories of Charlie's period. The Danbury Library found details about Charlie's business partner on the Ogeechee rice farm.

Buddy Sullivan, a historian of Bryan County, Georgia, helped orient me to the terrain where Charlie would try to make a living during Reconstruction. Alex Lee of Sylvania, Georgia, saved me from a grave misunderstanding of where "Ogeechee" was located. Carolyn Swiggart of Westport, Connecticut, helped explain the history of Strathy Hall, her ancestral home on the Ogeechee River, where Charlie and his wife Harriet lived and farmed in 1866-67. David and Katherine Slagel, the current residents of Strathy Hall, have maintained its historic appearance. Grove Ely of South Norwalk, Connecticut, generously gave me a copy of his file on his ancestor, General William G. Ely, a close friend of Charlie's. Faith Jennings of Norwich, and Matt Isenburg, of Hadlyme, Connecticut, provided useful photographs of Norwich in the 1860s.

My sister Susan, of Washington, D.C., made several field and library trips with me and for me. My wife Elizabeth helped with research and editing. Many friends and family members read early drafts and provided helpful criticism. And many have lent their financial support and encouragement for my efforts. I am deeply grateful to all for their help, but stand solely culpable for any mistakes or shortcomings.

# Notes

[1] Bill Stanley, *The 9-Mile Square*, Norwich, CT.: The Norwich Historical Society 2005, 72, 299.

[2] Frances Manwaring Caulkins, *History of Norwich, Connecticut*, 1874, 652-653.

[3] Albert E. Van Dusen, *Connecticut*, New York: Random House, 1961, 219-224; Matthew Warshauer, *Connecticut in the American Civil War*, Middletown, CT.: Wesleyan University Press 2011, 43-45.

[4] United States Sanitary Commission, *Narrative of Privation and Sufferings of United States Officers and Soldiers While Prisoners of War in the Hands of the Rebel Authorities*, Washington, DC 1864; Grove Ely, Essex, CT., Private Collection of Papers of William G. Ely.

[5] *John Gager & Co., Chicago City Directory*, 1856; *Zinkerson and Co., Chicago City Directory*, 1857; *D. B. Cooke & Co., City Directory for Chicago*, 1858.

[6] Charles Farnsworth, Diary, letters, and documents. Personal collection of the author. Diary, December 27, 1864.

[7] Charlie to Fred, February 28, 1860.

[8] Charlie to Fred, February 28, 1860; Charlie to mother, April 1, 1860.

[9] Charlie to mother , April 1, 1860.

[10] E. K. Abbott to Charlie, June 6, 1861.

[11] Governor Buckingham to Governors of Massachusetts and Rhode Island, September 4, 1861.

[12] Samuel A. Green, 1901. *Three Military Diaries*, Groton, Massachusetts 1901; first published in Proceedings of Massachusetts Historical Society 1898, 83-91.

[13] Benjamin Tinkham Marshall, *A Modern History of New London County, Connecticut*, Vol. 2 (New York: Lewis Historical Publishing Co. 1922) 91-92.

[14] *Norwich Courier* January 16, 1845.

[15] *Norwich Courier* January 28, 1845.

[16] *Jewett, Thomas & Co., Commercial Advertiser Directory, City of Buffalo*, 1849-50, 1850-51.

[17] W. A. Croffut and John M. Morris. 1869. *The Military and Civil History of Connecticut during the War of 1861-65* ( New York: Ledyard Bill 1869) 243.

[18] *Norwich Morning Bulletin* May 10, 1914.

[19] *Norwich Morning Bulletin* January 18, 1865; Bureau of the Census, Norwich, CT. 1870.

[20] Bureau of the Census, Norwich, CT. 1840, 1850, 1860.

[21] *The Day of New London* March 4, 1907.

[22] Charles Farnsworth, Diary, letters, and documents. Personal collection of the author. Letters by Eunice to her father, 1818-19.

[23] *Norwich Bulletin* May 31, 1935.

[24] Richard B. Wall, "Old St. James Rectory Was Built in 1792," *The Day of New London*, March 13, 1919.

[25] Mystic Seaport Curatorial Research Collection, Noyes and William Williams Billings Collection, No. 233, box 5, folder 4; Norwich City Recorders Office.

[26] Thomas Jewett & Co., *Commercial Advertiser Directory, City of Buffalo* 1849, 169; 1850-51, 42, 51.

[27] Mystic Seaport Curatorial Research Collection, Noyes and William Williams Billings Collection, No. 233, box 5, folder 4.

[28] Smithsonian American History Collection, ID No. DL65.0876.

[29] Kanisorn Wongsrichanalai, "The Burden of Their Class: College-Educated New Englanders and Leadership in the Civil War Era," (PhD diss., University of Virginia, 2010) 6-11; available on-line through ProQuest.

[30] Charlie to brother Fred, February 28, 1860; Charlie to mother, April 1, 1860; Bureau of Census, Norwich, CT. 1860.

[31] Buckingham to Charlie, October 19, 1861; Adjutant General to Charlie, October 21, 1861.

[32] Matthew H. LaConti, "William Buckingham: Leading Connecticut and the Republican Party through the Civil War," (Master's thesis, Southern Connecticut State University, 2009) 2, 7-8, 12, 17, 41; available on line through ProQuest.

[33] LaConti, p. 71.

[34] Charlie to Uncle Walter, October 27, 1861, October 31, 1861.

[35] Adjutant General to Charlie, November 26, 1861.

[36] Adjutant General to Charlie, December 4, 1861.

[37] LaConti, "William Buckingham," 56.

[38] LaConti, "William Buckingham," 47-55.

[39] Erastus Blakeslee, *Official History of the Connecticut Cavalry Volunteers in the War of the Rebellion, 1861-1865, with Addenda* (Hartford, CT.: Press of the Case, Lockwood & Brainard Company 1889).

[40] Maj. Gen. Benjamin F. Butler, order February 12, 1862.

[41] Blakeslee, *Official History*.

[42] Masonic certificate February 17, 1862. Personal collection of the author.

[43] Blakeslee, *Official History*.

[44] Starr, Stephen Z. Starr, 1979. *The Union Cavalry in the Civil War, Vols. 1-III* (Baton Rouge and London: Louisiana State University Press 1979), vol.1, 43.

[45] Charles M. Coit to his family April 26, 1862, Gilder Lehrman Collection.

[46] Bureau of Census, Norwich, CT. 1860; *150 Years of Meriden*, (Meriden Sesquicentennial Committee 1956) 95; *Meriden Daily Journal* , March 5, 1892; *Columbian Register of New Haven* March 10, 1860; Charles Henry Stanley Davis,

*History of Wallingford, Connecticut, including Meriden and Cheshire* (Printed by the author 1870) 600-601.

[47] *Hartford Evening Press* April 28, 1862.

[48] Private George N. Chapman, undated letter; Charlie to his mother, approx. April 1, 1862; Master Sergeant Weston Ferris to *New Haven Daily Palladium*, April 28, 1862; Croffut and Morris, *The Military and Civil History of Connecticut*, 208-9.

[49] Charlie to his mother, April 16, 1862.

[50] *Norwich Morning Bulletin*, April 10, 1862.

[51] Examining surgeon's certificate, February 11, 1867. Personal collection of the author.

[52] Buckingham to Secretary of War Stanton, General Banks , April 9, 1862.

[53] Special Order by Assistant Adjutant General, April 19, 1862.

[54] Charlie to his mother, April 16, 1862.

[55] Michael G. Mahon, ed., *Winchester Divided* (Mechanicsburg, PA.: Stackpole Books 2002); James McPherson, *Battle Cry of Freedom* (New York: Oxford University Press 2003) 777.

[56] Blakeslee, *Official History*.

[57] *New Haven Daily Palladium*, April 28, 1862.

[58] McPherson, *Battle Cry of Freedom*, 303.

[59] John Fabian Witt, *Lincoln's Code* (Free Press: New York 2012) 385.

[60] Witt, *Lincoln's Code*, 189-90.

[61] Charlie to his mother, May 31, 1862.

[62] Buckingham to Major Lyon May 29, 1862; Charlie to his mother June 10, 1862; *Norwich Morning Bulletin*, May 27, 1862.

[63] Charlie to father, June 6, 1862.

[64] Witt, *Lincoln's Code*, 202-3.

[65] *Hartford Daily Courant*, May 24, 1862; *Norwich Morning Bulletin*, May 27, 1862.

[66] McPherson, *Battle Cry of Freedom*, 501.

[67] *New Haven Daily Palladium*, June 21, 1862.

[68] Charlie to his mother, June 10, 1862.

[69] Jonathon A. Noyalas, *Stonewall Jackson's 1862 Valley Campaign* (Charleston: The History Press 2010) 118; McPherson, *Battle Cry of Freedom*, 460; Shelby Foote, *Civil War from Fort Sumter to Perryville* (New York: Vintage Press 1986).

[70] General Schenck, special order, June 22, 1862.

[71] Charlie to his father July 1, 1862; Charlie to his mother, July 2,1862.

[72] McPherson, *Battle Cry of Freedom*, 501; Witt, *Lincoln's Code*, 380, 385.

[73] Mahon, *Winchester Divided*, 46; Charlie to his mother, June 22, 1862.

[74] Charlie to his mother, June 22, 1862.

[75] Charlie to his father, July 14, 1862, July 20, 1862.

[76] Blakeslee, *Official History*; Charlie to his mother, July 2, 1862; Charlie to brother Fred, July 4, 1862.

[77] Charlie to his mother, August 3, 1862, September 28, 1862; note by Charlie's mother, late 1862.

[78] Charlie to his father, July 11, 1862, July 14, 1862, July 20, 1862.

[79] Charlie to his father, July 11, 1862.

[80] Starr, *The Union Cavalry, Vol. 1*, 144.

[81] Charlie to his father, July 28, 1862.

[82] Charlie to his father, August 5, 1862.

[83] Charlie to his mother, August 3,1862, August 15, 1862; Charlie to his father, August 5 1862, August 8, 1862, August 16, 1862; Charlie to his brother Fred, August 6, 1862.

[84] Bureau of Census 1860, Woodstock, CT., 1870, Putnam, CT.; Clarence W. Bowen, *The History of Woodstock, Connecticut* ( Norwood, Mass: The Plimpton Press 1926) 362, 460; *Columbian Register of New Haven*, October 20, 1855; *New Haven Register*, September 23, 1880; *New Haven Evening Register* June 23, 1887.

[85] Charlie to his father, July 29, 1862.

[86] Charlie to his father, 8 August 8, 1862, 14 August 1862.

[87] McPherson, *Battle Cry of Freedom*, 532.

[88] Blakeslee, *Official History*.

[89] McPherson, *Battle Cry of Freedom*, 638; Charlie to his father, September 3,1862.

[90] Charlie to his father, September 3, 1862.

[91] Charlie to his mother, September 28, 1862; Charlie to his father, September 3, 1862.

[92] Charlie to a brother, September 4, 1862; Charlie to his father, September 22, 1862.

[93] Charlie to his father, September 1, 1862.

[94] *Norwich Morning Bulletin*, March 9, 1862.

[95] Charlie to his father, September 18, 1862.

[96] Charlie to his father, September 7, 1862.

[97] Charlie to his father, September 7, 1862; Charlie to his mother, September 9, 1862, September 13, 1862; Blakeslee, *Official History*.

[98] Charlie to his father, September 18, 1862; Blakeslee, *Official History*; Charlie to his mother, September 22, 1862.

[99] McPherson, *Battle Cry of Freedom*, 544-545.

[100] Charlie to his mother, September 22, 1862.

[101] Charlie to his mother, November 10, 1862.

[102] Charlie to his mother, October 31, 1862.

[103] Charlie to his brother Billings, October 15, 1862; Charlie to his father, October 20, 1862; Charlie to his mother, October 31, 1862, November 3, 1862.

[104] Blakeslee, *Official History*; McPherson, *Battle Cry of Freedom*, 528.

[105] Charlie to his mother, October 31, 1862, November 3, 1862, November 10, 1862, November 20, 1862, November 21, 1862, December 1, 1862; Charlie to his brother Billings, September 30, 1862.

[106] Charlie to his mother, November 18, 1862.

[107] Charlie to his mother, December 18, 1862; McPherson, *Battle Cry of Freedom*, 572.

[108] Charlie to his father, Christmas 1862.

[109] Charlie to his father, Christmas 1862; Sergeant "Hal" to Charlie's brother Fred 26 February 26, 1863. Private collection of the author.

[110] Charlie to his mother, December 18, 1862.

[111] McPherson, *Battle Cry of Freedom*, 572.

[112] Charlie to his brother Billings, January 3, 1863; Charlie to his mother, January 3, 1863; Charlie to his brother Fred, January 6, 1863; Blakeslee, *Official History.*

[113] Charlie to his brother Billings, January 3, 1863; Charlie to his father, January 6, 1863; Blakeslee, *Official History.*

[114] Charlie to his brother Billings, January 3, 1863; Charlie to his mother January 3, 1863.

[115] Charlie to his brother Billings, January 3, 1863.

[116] Charlie to his mother, January 3, 1863.

[117] McPherson, *Battle Cry of Freedom,* 565-6.

[118] Charlie to his father, January 6, 1863.

[119] Charlie to his brother Fred, January 6, 1863.

[120] Charlie to his father, January 6, 1863.

[121] Charlie to his mother, February 3, 1863.

[122] Charlie to his father, January 6, 1863.

[123] *Wikipedia,* s.v. "Franz Sigel."

[124] Charlie to his mother, July 2, 1862.

[125] Charlie to his mother, February 11, 1863.

[126] Charlie to his mother, May 4, 1863.

[127] Charlie to his brother Fred, January 6, 1863.

[128] McPherson, *Battle Cry of Freedom,* 289; National Archives, Military Record of Charles Farnsworth, Gen. Ord. No. 1, January 13, 1863.

[129] Charlie to his mother, February 1, 1863.

[130] Scott S. Sheads and Daniel Carroll Toomey, *Baltimore during the Civil War* (Linthicum, MD.: Toomey Press 2008), 192.

[131] Mount Clare Museum House website.

[132] National Archives, Military Record of Charles Farnsworth, Gen. Ord. No. 2, January 25, 1863.

[133] Sheads and Toomey, *Baltimore during the Civil War,* 40, 54, 60, 61; Maryland Historical Society, Baltimore, Exhibit 2012.

[134] Sheads and Toomey, *Baltimore during the Civil War,* 64.

[135] Mark E. Néely, Jr., *The Fate of Liberty, Abraham Lincoln and Civil Liberties* (New York: Barnes & Noble 2007), 99-102.

[136] Sheads and Toomey, *Baltimore during the Civil War,* 111.

[137] Sheads and Toomey, *Baltimore during the Civil War,* 60-62.

[138] Sheads and Toomey, *Baltimore during the Civil War,* 27.

[139] Maryland Historical Society, Baltimore, "Divided Voices: Maryland in the Civil War," Exhibit, 2012.

[140] Mark E. Néely, Jr., *The Fate of Liberty, Abraham Lincoln and Civil Liberties* (New York: Barnes and Noble 2007), 4-8; Adam Goodheart, *1861, The Civil War Awakening* (New York: Knopf 2011), 124-5, 273; Sheads and Toomey, *Baltimore During the Civil War,* 59.

[141] Charlie to his mother, January 29, 1863.

[142] Blakeslee, *Official History.*

[143] Charlie to his mother, January 29, 1863, February 1, 1863.

[144] Charlie to his brother Fred, November 20, 1862.

[145] Charles Farnsworth, Diary, letters and documents, General Orders Nos. 6, 7, 9, personal collection of the author.

[146] National Archives, personal file of Charles Farnsworth, Quartermaster receipts, April 27, 1863, May 1, 1863.

[147] Charlie to his mother, January 26, 1863, January 29, 1863, February 3, 1863; Charlie to his brother Fred, February 3, 1863.

[148] Charlie to his mother, January 29, 1863, February 11, 1863, May 4, 1863, May 8, 1863; Charlie to his brother Fred, February 3, 1863; Charlie to his father, March 10, 1863; *Farnsworth Memorial II*, p. 255; document in personal collection of the author.

[149] Maryland Historical Society, Baltimore, Exhibit, 2012, Diary of Rebecca Davis.

[150] Charlie to his brother Fred, February 3, 1863.

[151] Charlie to his mother, February 11, 1863.

[152] Charlie to his brother Fred, February 3, 1863.

[153] Charlie to his father, March 6, 1863.

[154] Charles Farnsworth, Diary, letters, and documents, General Order No. 8.

[155] National Archives, personal file of Charles Farnsworth.

[156] Charlie to his father, March 16, 1863; Charlie to his mother, April 16, 1863, May 4, 1863, May 8, 1863.

[157] Charlie to his mother, May 4, 1863, May 8, 1863.

[158] LaConti, "William Buckingham," 62.

[159] Charlie to Lt. Col. Chesebrough, March 27,1863.

[160] Charlie to his mother, April 16, 1863; Laconti, "William Buckingham," 63.

[161] Charlie to his father, March 16, 1863.

[162] Charlie to his mother, May 8, 1863.

[163] Charlie to his father, June 21, 1863.

[164] Charlie to his mother, May 26, 1863.

[165] Charlie to his mother, June 10, 1863.

[166] Charlie to his father, June 24, 1863.

[167] Sheads and Toomey, *Baltimore during the Civil War*, 132.

[168] Charlie to his father, June 30, 1863

[169] McPherson, *Battle Cry of Freedom*, 597; Néely, *The Fate of Liberty*, 65-68; Charlie to his father, June 28, 1863.

[170] Charlie to his father, June 28, 1863.

[171] Charlie to his father, July 5, 1863; Charles Farnsworth diary, July 5, 1863, July 7, 1863.

[172] Diary July 9-12, 1863; McPherson, *Battle Cry of Freedom*, 666.

[173] Diary, July 13, 1863.

[174] Charlie to his father , July 14, 1863; Starr, *Union Cavalry in the Civil War, Vol. III*, 591-2.

[175] Charlie to his father, July 14, 1863; David Gilbert, *A Walker's Guide to Harpers Ferry* (Harpers Ferry Historical Association, 1995), 42; National Archives, personal file of Charles Farnsworth, Spec. Ord. No. 10, July 14, 1863.

[176] Diary, July 14, 1863; Charlie to his mother, July 30, 1863.

[177] *Norwich Morning Bulletin* , July 29, 1863; *Hartford Daily Courant,* July 31, 1863; Blakeslee, *Official History.*

[178] US Army Military History Institute Archives, Carlisle Barracks, Pennsylvania, Northwest Corner Civil War Round Table Collection, Weston Ferris Papers.

[179] Chester G. Hearn, *Six Years of Hell, Harpers Ferry During the Civil War* (Baton Rouge: Louisiana State University Press 1996), 224-6; McPherson, *Battle Cry of Freedom,* 324.

[180] Hearn, *Six Years of Hell,* 226.

[181] Diary, July 15, 1863, July 19, 1863, August 27, 1863.

[182] Charlie to his mother, July 30, 1863; Diary, November 6, 1863, November 10, 1863.

[183] Diary July 15, 1863, July 19, 1863, July 21, 1863; Major Pope to Major Bridgeford, July 17, 1863, Adjutant Stringfellow to officers, July 17, 1863, both personal collection of the author.

[184] Diary, July 22, 1863.

[185] Diary, July 23, 1863, July 24, 1863, July 25, 1863, July 26, 1863, July 27, 1863.

[186] Angela M. Zombek, "Libby Prison," in *Encyclopedia Virginia,* published by Virginia Historical Society, 2010; Richmond Civil War Centennial Committee, "Libby Prison," Richmond, Virginia,official publication #12, 1961-65.

[187] Charlie to his father (undated), September 1863, November 19, 1863.

[188] Diary, July 28, 1863, 29 July 29, 1863; Special Order 25, September 25, 1863, personal collection of the author.

[189] Charlie to his mother, March 6, 1864.

[190] Diary, January 29, 1864; Charlie to his mother, October 16, 1863; *Encyclopedia Virginia,* "Libby Prison."

[191] Charlie to his father (undated), September 1863.

[192] Diary December 23, 1863, December 24, 1863.

[193] Charlie to his father (undated), September 1863.

[194] Charlie to his father (undated), September 1863; *Encyclopedia Virginia,* "Libby Prison"; McPherson, *Battle Cry of Freedom,* 434, 442.

[195] Diary, September 20, 1863, November 23, 1863.

[196] Diary July 28, 1863, July 29, 1863, July 30, 1863; Civil War Richmond, "The Libby Chronicle," September 11, 1863; Colonel Streight to Confederate Secretary of War James A. Seddon, available on-line at www.mdgorman.com; McPherson, *Battle Cry of Freedom,* 303; Charlie to his father (undated), September 1863.

[197] Charlie to his father (undated), September 1863; Charlie to his mother, October 16, 1863; Roger Long, "Johnson's Island Prison," *Blue and Grey Magazine,* 1986-87.

[198] Charlie to his mother, October 16, 1863.

[199] LaConti, "William Buckingham," 57.

[200] Diary, November 25, 1863, January 23, 1864.

[201] Charlie to his mother 6 September 1863; Brig. Gen. Meredith to Charlie's mother, December 21, 1863.

[202] Charlie to his mother, October 16, 1863, November 10, 1863, November 28, 1863, December 9, 1863; Charlie to his father, November 16, 1863; Diary, November 8, 1863, November 27, 1863.

[203] Charlie to his mother, December 16, 1863.

[204] McPherson, *Battle Cry of Freedom*, 550-1; Charlie to his mother, January 20, 1864, January 22, 1864; February 28, 1864; Diary, January 16, 1864, January 21, 1864.

[205] Diary, December 11,1863.

[206] Charlie to his father (undated), September 1863; William Fish to Charlie's father, September 25, 1863; Diary, September 25, 1863.

[207] Charlie to mother, January 22, 1864, February 28, 1864; Diary, January 23, 1864.

[208] Charlie to his mother, March 6, 1864.

[209] Charlie to his father, November 2, 1863; Diary, November 2, 1863; Cavada to Charlie's father, March 10, 1864.

[210] Diary, December 18, 1863.

[211] Charlie to his mother, December 22, 1863.

[212] Charlie to his mother, January 4, 1864.

[213] Charlie to his mother, January 4, 1864, January 28, 1864.

[214] Diary, December 2, 1863, December 6, 1863; Charlie to his mother, January 4, 1864; Charlie to Billings, January 3, 1864.

[215] Charlie to a brother, January13, 1864; Charlie to his mother , January 22, 1864.

[216] Charlie to his mother, October 16, 1863; Diary, January 12, 1864, January 23, 1864.

[217] *Wikipedia*, "Belle Isle,Virginia."

[218] Diary, October 27, 1863, January 12, 1864; James M. Sanderson, *My Record in Rebeldom* (New York: Sibell Publishing, 1865), available on line.

[219] Diary, November 5, 1863, November 9, 1863.

[220] Diary, January 27, 1864; Charlie to his mother, January 28, 1864; Blakeslee, *Official History*.

[221] Charlie to his father, November 19, 1863; Commission of Inquiry of the United States Sanitary Commission, *Narrative of Privations and Sufferings of United States Officers and Soldiers while Prisoners of War in the Hands of the Rebel Authorities* (King & Baird Pubs., 1864), 159.

[222] Malcolm McG. Dana, *The Annals of Norwich, New London County, Connecticut, in the Great Rebellion of 1861-65* (Norwich, CT: J. H. Jewett and Company, 1873) 268-9.

[223] Diary, October 31, 1863.

[224] Charlie to his mother, February 21, 1864, February 28, 1864; McPherson, *Battle Cry of Freedom*, 796-7.

[225] McPherson, *Battle Cry of Freedom*, 681; Diary, November 28, 1863, December 8, 1863, December 9, 1863, December 10, 1863; William J. Cooper, *Jefferson Davis, American* (New York: Alfred A. Knopf, 2000), 466; William C. Davis, *Jefferson Davis, The Man and His Hour* (Baton Rouge: Louisiana State University, 1991), 529.

[226] Charlie to his mother, December 19, 1863, December 26, 1863; Diary, December 31, 1863, January 14, 1864; Charlie to a brother, January 13, 1864.

[227] Charlie to his father, November 19, 1863.

[228] Charlie to his father, January 6, 1864.

[229] Charlie to his father (undated), September 1863; Diary, November 6, 1863.

[230] Diary, December 30, 1863.

[231] Diary, December 31, 1863.

232 Diary, January 4, 1864.

233 Charlie to his father, January 6, 1864.

234 Buckingham to Charlie's father, January 25, 1864.

235 Diary, January 20, 1863; Blakeslee, *Official History*.

236 Charlie to his mother, January 22, 1864.

237 Charlie to his mother, September 6, 1863.

238 Diary, October 23, 1863, October 26, 1863.

239 Charlie to his mother, February 3, 1863.

240 Charlie to his mother, January 20, 1864.

241 Charlie to his brother Fred, January 23, 1864.

242 Diary, September 20, 1863, October 10, 1863, October 20, 1863, November 1, 1863, November 21,1863, December 17, 1863, December 21, 1863; December 27, 1863.

243 Diary, November 9, 1863, November 10, 1863, November 11, 1863, November 16, 1863, November 18, 1863, January 17, 1864; Charlie to his mother, November 10, 1863.

244 Diary, December 25, 1863; Charlie to his mother, December 26, 1863.

245 Dana, *Annals of Norwich*, 276; Diary, December 19, 1863, January 22, 1864.

246 Diary, November 24, 1863.

247 Diary, November 25, 1863, November 26, 1863, October 25, 1863, October 27, 1863, December 12, 1863, December 13, 1863, December 17, 1863.

248 Diary, January 15, 1864, January 29, 1864, January 30, 1864, February 1, 1864.

249 Diary, February 9, 1864, February 10, 1864; James M. Wells, "Tunneling out of Libby Prison," *McClure's Magazine*, January 1904; Zombek, *Encyclopedia Virginia*.

250 Charlie to his mother, March 6, 1864.

251 Commission of Inquiry of the United States Sanitary Commission, 160.

252 McPherson, *Battle Cry of Freedom*, 791-2; Charlie to his father (undated), September 1863.

253 John and David Eicher, *Civil War High Commands* (Stanford: Stanford University Press, 2002); Charlie to his mother, September 23, 1863, October 4, 1863; Diary, January 13, 1864.

254 Diary, December 7, 1863.

255 Diary, December 15, 1863.

256 Charlie to his mother, December 16, 1863.

257 Diary, September 22, 1863, October 27, 1863, October 31, 1863, December 7, 1863; Charlie to his mother, October 4, 1863, October 22, 1863; McPherson, *Battle Cry of Freedom*, 792.

258 Diary, December 26, 1863.

259 Charlie to his brother Billings, November 14, 1863; Diary, December 5, 1863.

260 Diary, December 29, 1863.

261 Diary, January 1, 1864.

262 Diary, January 6, 1864.

263 Charlie to his brother Fred,December 16, 1863.

264 Charlie (in "invisible" ink) to his mother, January 20, 1864.

[265] Charlie to his mother, January 22, 1864.

[266] Diary, October 28, 1863, October 29, 1863, November 3, 1863, November 6,1863, November 13, 1863, November 14, 1863, November 16, 1863.

[267] Captain W. H. Swift to Charlie's mother, March 9, 1864; National Archives, personal file of Charles Farnsworth, memo September 15, 1866 by Adjutant General, War Department.

[268] Charlie to his mother, November 20, 1863.

[269] Charlie to his father, January 24, 1864; Charlie to his mother, November 20, 1863.

[270] McPherson, *Battle Cry of Freedom*, 799.

[271] *Wikipedia*, 2010, s.v. "Robert C. Schenck"; Sheads and Toomey, *Baltimore during the Civil War*,54.

[272] Charlie to Schenck, January 25, 1864.

[273] Foster to Charlie's mother, February 3, 1864, February 24, 1864.

[274] Charlie to his mother, February14, 1864, February 21, 1864.

[275] War Department to Buckingham, December 28, 1863, personal collection of Grosvenor Ely.

[276] Captain Swift to Charlie's mother, March 9, 1864.

[277] Diary, February 21, 1864, March 6,1864, March 7, 1864.

[278] National Archives, personal file of Charles Farnsworth, Memorandum from Prisoner of War Records, March 14, 1864; Swift to Charlie's mother, March 9, 1864.

[279] Diary, March 18-21, 1864.

[280] *Norwich Morning Bulletin*, March 17, 1864, March 25, 1864.

[281] Diary, March 22, 1864.

[282] Diary, March 22, 1864.

[283] Private collection of Grosvenor Ely.

[284] Diary, April 18, 1864, April 28, 1864.

[285] Blakeslee, *Official History*; Charlie to his mother, September 6, 1863, February 3, 1863.

[286] National Archives, personal file of Charles Farnsworth, Charlie to Colonel A. R. Root, May 6, 1864; Surgeon F. H. Gross medical certificate May 6, 1864.

[287] Diary, May 12, 1864, May 14, 1864; National Archives, personal file of Charles Farnsworth, Charlie to Colonel E. Townsend, Assistant Adjutant General, War Department, May 14, 1864.

[288] National Archives, personal file of Charles Farnsworth, War Department Special Order No. 179, May 17, 1864.

[289] Charlie to his father, July 20, 1862

[290] Blakeslee, *Official History*.

[291] Diary, May 15, 1864, May 17, 1864.

[292] *Norwich Morning Bulletin*, May 21, 1864.

[293] Diary, August 8, 1864.

[294] Diary, May 18, 1864, June 11, 1864.

[295] Report of a Commission of Inquiry, Appointed by the United States Sanitary Commision, *Narrative of Privations and Sufferings of United States Officers and Soldiers*

*While Prisoners of War in the Hands of the Rebel Authorities,* 1864, affidavits subscribed June 30, 1864, July 18, 1864.

296 Report of a Commission of Inquiry, supra.

297 Starr, *The Union Cavalry in the Civil War, Vol. II*, 383.

298 Diary, May 18, 1864, June 18, 1864.

299 New London County Marriages and Death Records from Newspapers, 1864, Vol. 5, p. 827; Hale Cemetery Inscriptions, Town of Stonington, New London County, Connecticut, April-June 1933, Vol. 1, 240; G. W. Blunt White Library, Mystic Seaport, *Overview of Mallory Family Collection.*

300 Diary, July 26, 1864.

301 Frances Manwaring Caulkins, *History of Norwich,* 1873 ed., 351, 565; Mary E. Perkins, *Genealogical Notes, Box 97,* Otis Library, Norwich, Connecticut.

302 Debra F. Wilmes, *Barbour Collection of Connecticut Town Vital Records,* Norwich 1847-1851, p. 199; Perkins, *Genealogical Notes, Box 97.*

303 Norwich Probate District Records, Town of Norwich, 1853, Harriet P. Lester estate, No. 6945; Norwich Probate District Records Town of Norwich 1894, Elizabeth Lester estate; Bureau of Census 1860, Norwich.

304 Stedman's City Directory, Norwich, 1861.

305 Caulkins, *History of Norwich,* 642.)

306 The Public Records of the State of Connecticut from May 1816 through October 1817, Volume XVIII, page 19; Caulkins, *History of Norwich,* 697.

307 Stephen W. Williams, *The Genealogy and History of the Williams Family in America* (Greenfield, Massachusetts: Merriam & Mirick 1847), 210-215; Caulkins, *History of Norwich,* 697-8; *Wikipedia,* s.v. "Norwich, Connecticut;" *Norwich Morning Bulletin,* January 28, 1865.

308 *Norwich Bulletin,* October 29, 1870.

309 Norwich Probate District Records, Town of Norwich, 1880, Mrs. William Willams estate, No. 11595.

310 E. K. Abbott to Charlie, June 8, 1861; Diary March 22, 1864; Charlie to his mother, December 9, 1863; Stedman's City Directory, Norwich, 1861; Calvin Goddard Zon, *The Good Fight That Didn't End: Henry P. Goddard's Accounts of the Civil War and Peace* (Columbia: The University of South Carolina Press 2008) , 227; Caulkins, *History of Norwich,* 665.

311 Diary, November 7, 1864.

312 Diary, November 20, 1864.

313 Diary, December 5, 1864.

314 Diary, December 6, 1864.

315 Diary, December 9, 1864.

316 Diary, December 14, 1864.

317 Diary [undated, but probably between 14 and 22 December] 1864.

318 Diary, December 22, 1864.

319 Personal collection of the author.

320 Diary December 16, 1864.

321 Diary December 27, 1864.

[322] Diary December 28, 1864.

[323] Sheads and Toomey, *Baltimore during the Civil War,* 62-63.

[324] Charlie to his father, September 28, 1862.

[325] Diary, June 15, 1864, January 1, 1865.

[326] Diary, January 4, 1865, January 5, 1865.

[327] Richard N. Current, "Northernizing the South," *Journal of American Studies* (1983)18:3, 68; McPherson, *Battle Cry of Freedom,* 825.

[328] Diary, January 6, 1865.

[329] Diary, January 7, 1865, January 10, 1865.

[330] Diary, January 10, 1865.

[331] Diary, January 13, 1865.

[332] Diary, January 15, 1865.

[333] Diary, January 17, 1865, January 18, 1865, January 19, 1865.

[334] C. Mildred Thompson, *Reconstruction in Georgia* (Savannah: Beehive Press, 1972), 308.

[335] Diary, January 18, 1865; Thompson, *Reconstruction in Georgia,* 89, 98, 114-115.

[336] Diary, February 3, 1865; *Norwich Morning Bulletin,* October 23, 1865.

[337] Diary, January 25, 1865, January 30, 1865, February 1, 1865, February 11, 1865.

[338] *New Georgia Encyclopedia,* s.v. "Reconstruction in Georgia," Alan Conway, *The Reconstruction of Georgia* (Minneapolis: University of Minnesota Press, 1966), 27.

[339] Diary, April 1, 1865, March 31, 1865.

[340] Diary, February 10, 1865; Cincinnati Civil War Round Table, January 1965, William C. Moffat, Jr., "Soldiers Pay."

[341] Diary, March 12, 1865, May 18, 1865, May 21, 1865.

[342] Diary, February 11, 1865, February 12, 1865, March 1, 1865, March 2, 1865, March 12, 1865, March 24, 1865, April 3, 1865, May 1, 1865, May 9, 1865, May 28, 1865.

[343] Diary April 13, 1865, April 14, 1865, April 30, 1865.

[344] Diary June 22, 1865, June 25, 1865, June 28, 1865, July 3-5, 1865, July 10, 1865, July 12, 1865.

[345] *Rigg's Meriden Literary Recorder,* December 27, 1873; Sheldon B. Thorpe, *The History of the Fifteenth Connecticut Volunteers* (New Haven: Price, Lee & Adkins Co., 1893) 191-197; Bureau of Census, 1920, Brooklyn, N.Y.

[346] Bureau of Census, 1860, Danbury, Ct.; National Archives letter to author , September 21, 2012.

[347] Diary, October 12, 1865, January 11, 1866; Carolyn Clay Swiggart, *Shades of Gray,* (Darian, CT.: Two Bytes Publishing, Ltd.,, 1999), map inside back cover.

[348] Buddy Sullivan, *From Beautiful Zion to Red Bird Creek, A History of Bryan County, Georgia.* (Bryan County Board of Commissioners, 2000), 105-6; Karen B. Bell, "Narratives of Freedom: Communities of Resistance in Low Country Georgia, 1798-1897" (PhD diss., Howard University, 2008), 144; Blanton E. Black, "The Rise and Decline of Plantation Agriculture in Coastal Georgia" (master's diss.,University of Chicago, 1937), 64-65.

[349] Sullivan, *From Beautiful Zion to Red Bird Creek,* 117; Black, "The Rise and Decline of Plantation Agriculture,"10, 24-25, 65.

[350] Black, "The Rise and Decline of Plantation Agriculture," 52-54.

[351] Black, "The Rise and Decline of Plantation Agriculture," 56; Charlie to his brother Fred, March 12, 1866; Smith, *Slavery and Rice Culture in Low Country Georgia,* 45-50.

[352] Diary, August 5, 1865; Charlie to his brother Fred, March 12, 1866; Black, "The Rise and Decline of Plantation Agriculture," 40, 58, 69.

[353] Eric Foner, *Reconstruction* (New York: Harper & Row 1988), 70, 104, 163; Bell, "Narratives of Freedom,"101.

[354] Bell, "Narratives of Freedom," 104; Paul A. Cimbala, *Under the Guardianship of the Nation* (Athens: University of Georgia Press, 1997), 190; Julia Floyd Smith, *Slavery and Rice Culture in Low Country Georgia 1750-1860* (Knoxville: University of Tennessee Press, 1985), 217.

[355] *Savannah Daily New & Herald,* December 19, 1866.

[356] Diary, August 5, 1865, July 6, 1866, July 20, 1866; Black, "The Rise and Decline of Plantation Agriculture," 66-68.

[357] Cimbala, *Under the Guardianship of the Nation,* 75, fn. 146; Diary, August 31, 1865, September 2,1865; September 9, 1865, September 13, 1865.

[358] Efraim S. Rosenbaum, 2011. "Incendiary Negro: The Life and Times of the Honorable Jefferson Franklin Long," *Georgia Historical Quarterly,* 2011 (Winter issue).

[359] Norwich Marriage Records, Book 12, page 33.

[360] Charlie to his brother Fred, December 4, 1865; Diary, January 6-9, 1865.

[361] Roger S. Durham, *Guardian of Savannah* (Columbia: The University of South Carolina Press, 2008), 1-5.

[362] Swiggart, *Shades of Gray,* 74.

[363] Durham, *Guardian of Savannah,* 135, 140; Sullivan, *From Beautiful Zion to Red Bird Creek,* 80, 194; Swiggart, *Shades of Gray,* 25-27.

[364] Charlie to his brother Fred, March 12, 1866; Diary, July 5, 1866.

[365] Diary, June 28, 1866, May 4-8, 1866, July 21, 1866; Smith, *Slavery and Rice Culture,* 208.

[366] Charlie to his brother Fred, March 12, 1866; Diary, June 2, 1866.

[367] Bell, "Narratives of Freedom," 70; Black, "The Rise and Decline of Plantation Agriculture," 33; Cimbala, *Under the Guardianship of the Nation,* 181; Diary, July 4, 1866.

[368] Diary, March 21, 1866, June 3, 1866, July 14, 1866, July 17, 1866, July 19, 1866; Swiggart, *Shades of Gray,* 16.

[369] Diary, July 19-20, 1866, July 28, 1866.

[370] Diary, August 15, 1866, October 4-9, 1866; October 15, 1866.

[371] National Archives, personal file of Charles Farnsworth, Memo, September 15, 1866; War Department, Adjutant General's Office, Special Order No. 522, October 20, 1866.

[372] Examining surgeon's certificate, February 11, 1867, personal collection of the author.

[373] *Savannah Daily News & Herald,* April 16, 1867; Interior Department. Commissioner

of Pensions. *Secondary Death Causes, Harriet C.* (sic) *Widow of Charles Farnsworth*, decision by Assistant Secretary Bussey, Sept. 22, 1890, 1891.

[374] Cornelia Talbot to Charlie's mother, April 15, 1867; US Geological Survey, 1979. Map of Burroughs, Georgia.

[375] Cornelia Talbot to Charlie's mother, April 15, 1867.

[376] Frederick Law Olmstead Collection, Papers of Mary Cornelia Talbot, box 2, American University Library, Washington, DC; Smith, *Slavery and Rice Culture in Low Country Georgia*, 222.

[377] *Savannah Daily News & Herald*, April 17, 1867.

[378] *Savannah Daily News and Herald*, "Arrivals at Hotels," April 20, 1867, "List of Letters Remaining at Post Office," April 30, 1867.

[379] *Norwich Aurora*, April 17, 1867, citing *The Norwich Bulletin*; Joab Rogers to Charlie's mother, April 27, 1867; resolution signed by Theodore J. Holmes, August 26, 1867, personal collection of the author; *Savannah Daily News & Herald*, April 16, 1867.

[380] *Danbury Times*, April 18, 1867; *New York Herald Tribune*, April 20, 1867, p. 5.

[381] Karen B. Bell, "The Ogeechee Troubles: Federal Land Restoration and the 'Lived Realities' of Temporary Proprietors, 1865-68," *Georgia Historical Quarterly*, Fall 2001, 384-389; Smith, *Slavery and Rice Culture in Low Country Georgia*, 222; Sullivan, *From Beautiful Zion to Red Bird Creek*, 204; Cimbala, *Under the Guardianship of the Nation*, 190, 339.

[382] Sullivan, *From Beautiful Zion to Red Bird Creek*, 204-5; Cimbala, *Under the Guardianship of the Nation*, 191; Bell, "The Ogeechee Troubles," 392-3.

[383] Bliss Perry, *Life and Letters of Henry Lee Higginson* (Boston: Atlantic Monthly Press, 1921), 3, 266; Tony Horwitz, *Midnight Rising* (New York: Henry Holt, 2011), 74-76.

[384] Bell, "The Ogeechee Troubles," 385; Perry, *Life and Letters of Henry Lee Higginson*, 266; Swiggart, *Shades of Gray*, 34.

[385] War Department to Charlie, July 6, 1870; Buckingham to War Department, February 8, 1871.

[386] Interior Department, *Decisions in Cases Relating to Pension Claims*, 203-206.

[387] Interior Department to W. A. Haggott, attorney, October 16, 1908, personal collection of the author.

[388] Treasury Department to W. A. Redmond, attorney, October 6, 1910, December 22, 1910; Redmond to Harriet, October 11, 1910, personal collection of the author.

[389] Treasury Department to Charlie, April 20, 1867, April 30, 1867, personal collection of the author.

[390] National Archives personal file of Charles Farnsworth, War Department order March 25, 1886, order March 10, 1904, order December 2, 1910.

[391] K. Stephen Prince, "Stories of the South: The Cultural Retreat from Reconstruction," (PhD diss., Yale University, 2010), 63-68.

[392] Bureau of the Census, 1870, 1880, Norwich.

[393] Harriet to her great-grandchildren, July 18, 1901, personal collection of the author.

[394] *Chicago Tribune*, December 23, 1897, p. 10.

[395] Bureau of the Census, 1870, Norwich.

[396] *Springfield Republican,* May 8, 1897; *The Day of New London,* May 8, 1897, May 10, 1897; Norwich Town Clerk, "Will, Etc.," Vol. I, 17 May 1897; Norwich Probate Court, June 23, 1897, p. 543.

[397] *Norwich Morning Bulletin,* May 6, 1897; *Springfield Republican,* May 8, 1897; David Hochfelder, "Where the Common People Could Speculate," *Journal of American History,* September 2006, Vol. 93, 335-45.

[398] *Norwich Morning Bulletin,* August 30, 1909, February 24, 1914, March 18, 1914.

[399] Robert L. Brown, *The Great Pikes Peak Gold Rush* (Caldwell, Idaho:Caxton Press 1985); Stephen M. Voynick, *Colorado Gold, From the Pike's Peak Rush to the Present* (Missoula, Montana: Mountain Press Publishing 1992).

[400] McPherson, pp. 144, 457.

[401] R. Glen Nye, *Farnsworth Memorial II,* 1974 edition, 254.

[402] Shelby Foote, *The Civil War, Fort Sumter to Perryville* (New York: Vintage Books, 1986) , 463; McPherson, *Battle Cry of Freedom,* 303, 458.; Blakeslee, *Official History of the Connecticut Cavalry Volunteers with Addenda,* 1861-1865.

[403] *Encyclopedia Virginia,* available on line.

[404] Blakeslee, *Official History.*

[405] McPherson, *Battle Cry of Freedom,* 463-5.

[406] McPherson, *Battle Cry of Freedom,* 501.

[407] McPherson, *Battle Cry of Freedom,* 526.

[408] Foote, *The Civil War,* 599-602; McPherson, *Battle Cry of Freedom,* 526.

[409] Foote, *The Civil War,* 599-602.

[410] McPherson, *Battle Cry of Freedom,* 464.

[411] McPherson, *Battle Cry of Freedom,* 532.

[412] McPherson, *Battle Cry of Freedom,* 533-4.

[413] McPherson, *Battle Cry of Freedom,* 724.

[414] Blakeslee, *Official History.*

[415] McPherson, *Battle Cry of Freedom,* 470, 541.

[416] Blakeslee, *Official History.*

[417] McPherson, *Battle Cry of Freedom,* 572.

[418] McPherson, *Battle Cry of Freedom,* 624.

[419] McPherson, *Battle Cry of Freedom,* 641-2.

[420] Blakeslee, *Official History.*

[421] McPherson, *Battle Cry of Freedom,* 584.

[422] *Farnsworth Memorial II,* p. 255.

[423] Croffut and Morris, *The Military and Civil History of Connecticut,* 490.

[424] Croffut and Morris, *The Military and Civil History of Connecticut,* 491.

[425] McPherson, *Battle Cry of Freedom,* 642.

[426] McPherson, *Battle Cry of Freedom,* 649.

[427] McPherson, *Battle Cry of Freedom,* 600.

[428] McPherson, *Battle Cry of Freedom,* 653.

[429] *Norwich Morning Bulletin,* June 26, 1863.

[430] McPherson, *Battle Cry of Freedom,* 597; Néely, *The Fate of Liberty,* 65-68.

[431] Gilbert, *A Walker's Guide,* 42.

[432] Blakeslee, *Official History.*

[433] US Army Military History Institute Archives, Carlisle Barracks, Pa., Northwest Corner Civil War Round Table Collection, Weston Ferris Papers.

[434] National Park Service, *18th Connecticut Regimental Roster.*

[435] Wiatt, Jr., *Richmond Civil War Centennial Committee*, 1961-65; *Encyclopedia Virginia* 2010, s. v. "Libby Prison."

[436] Civil War Richmond, on-line at www.mdgorman.com., Col. A. D. Streight letter to Confederate Secretary of War James A. Seddon, August 31, 1863, in "The Libby Chronicle," September 11, 1863, published by the prisoners.

[437] McPherson,, *Battle Cry of Freedom,* 303, 432-434, 442, 551, 796-802; *Virginia Encyclopedia, s.v.* "Libby Prison."

[438] McPherson, *Battle Cry of Freedom,* 792.

[439] John and David Eicher, *Civil War High Commands* (Stanford: Stanford University Press, 2002)

[440] Roger Long, "Johnson's Island Prison," *Blue and Grey Magazine,* 1986-87.

[441] Blakeslee, *Official History.*

[442] McPherson, *Battle Cry of Freedom,* 792.

[443] Wiatt, Jr., "Libby Prison."

[444] McPherson, *Battle Cry of Freedom,* 618.

[445] McPherson, *Battle Cry of Freedom,* 792.

[446] McPherson, *Battle Cry of Freedom,* 666-688.

[447] McPherson, *Battle Cry of Freedom,* 681.

[448] McPherson, *Battle Cry of Freedom,* 672-678.

[449] William J. Cooper, Jr., *Jefferson Davis, American* (New York: Knopf, 2000), 466; William C. Davis, *Jefferson Davis, The Man and His Hour* (Baton Rouge: Louisiana State University, 1991) , 528.

[450] Cooper, *Jefferson Davis,* 468.

[451] Davis, *Jefferson Davis,* 529.

[452] McPherson, *Battle Cry of Freedom,* 792.

[453] McPherson, *Battle Cry of Freedom,* 536; Sheads & Toomey, *Baltimore during the Civil War,* 134; Blakeslee, *Official History.*

[454] James M. Sanderson, *My Record in Rebeldom* (New York: W. E. Sibell Stationer and Printer, 1865).

[455] McPherson, *Battle Cry of Freedom,* 800.

[456] McPherson, *Battle Cry of Freedom,* 799.

[457] Blakeslee, *Official History.*

[458] Blakeslee, *Official History.*

[459] McPherson, *Battle Cry of Freedom,* 722.

[460] McPherson, *Battle Cry of Freedom,* 828-830.

[461] McPherson, *Battle Cry of Freedom,* 829.

[462] *Wikipedia, s.v.* "Fort Sumter," "Gillmore Medal."

[463] Bureau of Census 1860, Danbury, Connecticut; National Archives September 21, 2012 letter to author.

[464] Cimbala, *Under the Guardianship of the Nation,* 75, fn. 146.

[465] *Norwich Marriage Records*, Book 12, page 33.

[466] Sullivan, *From Beautiful Zion to Red Bird Creek*, 212.

[467] Swiggart, *Shades of Gray*, map on back fly-leaf.

[468] Bureau of Census 1860, Bryan County, Georgia; Sullivan, *From Beautiful Zion to Red Bird Creek*, 78; Swiggart, *Shades of Gray*, 74.

[469] Bell, "The Ogeechee Troubles," 375-393.

[470] Foner, *Reconstruction*, 103.

[471] *Frederick Law Olmstead Collection*, papers of Mary Cornelia Talbot.

[472] *Savannah Daily News & Herald*, April 16, 1867.

[473] *Savannah Daily News & Herald*, April 17, 1867.

[474] *Norwich Aurora*, April 17, 1867, citing *The Norwich Bulletin*.

[475] *Savannah Daily News and Herald*, April 20, 1867.

[476] *Savannah Daily News and Herald*, April 30, 1867.

[477] Blakeslee, *Official History*.

[478] Blakeslee, *Official History*.

[479] Interior Department. 1891. *Decisions in Cases Relating to Pension Claims*, Vol. IV. (Washington: Government Printing Office, 1891) , 203-206.

# Bibliography

Bell, Karen B. "Narratives of Freedom: Communities of Resistance in Low Country Georgia 1798-1897." PhD diss., Howard University, 2008.

Billings, Noyes and William Williams. *Letters and papers.* Norwich, CT: Mystic Seaport Curatorial Research Collection, Norwich City Recorders Office.

Black, Blanton E. "The Rise and Decline of Plantation Agriculture in Coastal Georgia." Master's diss., University of Chicago, 1937.

Blakeslee, Erastus. *Official History of the Connecticut Cavalry Volunteers in the War of the Rebellion, 1861-65, with Addenda.* Hartford, CT: Press of the Case, Lockwood & Brainard Company, 1889.

*Blue and Grey Magazine.* 1986-87.

Bowen, Clarence W. *The History of Woodstock, Connecticut.* Norwood, Mass: The Plimpton Press, 1926.

Brown, Robert L. *The Great Pikes Peak Gold Rush.* Caldwell Idaho: Caxton Press, 1985.

Caulkins, Frances Manwaring. *History of Norwich.* New London, 1873.

*Chicago City Directory.* John Gager & Co., 1856.

*Chicago City Directory.* Zinkerson & Co., 1857.

*Chicago Tribune,* 1897.

Cimbala, Paul A. 1997. *Under the Guardianship of the Nation.* Athens, Georgia: University of Georgia Press.

*Cincinnati Civil War Round Table 1965,* s.v. "Soldiers' Pay."

*City Directory for Chicago.* D. B. Cooke & Co., 1858.

*City of Buffalo Commercial Advertiser Directory.* Thomas Jewett & Co., 1849-50, 1850-51.

Civil War Richmond, "Libby Prison," on line at www.mdgorman.com.

Coit, Charles M. *Letters to his family.* Gilder Lehrman Collection.

*Columbian Register of New Haven,* 1855.

Connecticut State Public Records, 1816-1817.

Conway, Alan. *The Reconstruction of Georgia*. Minneapolis: University of Minnesota Press, 1966.

Cooper, William J. *Jefferson Davis, American*. New York: Alfred A. Knopf, 2000.

Croffut, W. A. and John M. Morris. *The Military and Civil History of Connecticut during the War of 1861-65*. New York: Ledyard Bill, 1869.

Dana, Malcolm McG. *The Annals of Norwich, New London County, Connecticut in the Great Rebellion of 1861-65*. Norwich: J. H. Jewett and Company, 1873.

*Danbury Times*, 1867.

Davis, Charles Henry Stanley. *History of Wallingford, including Meriden and Cheshire*. Printed by the author, 1870.

Davis, William C. *Jefferson Davis, The Man and His Hour*. Baton Rouge: Louisiana State University, 1991.

*Day of New London*, 1897, 1907, 1919.

Durham, Roger S. *Guardian of Savannah*. Columbia: The University of South Carolina Press, 2008.

Eicher, John and David Eicher. *Civil War High Commands*. Stanford: Stanford University Press, 2002.

Ely, Grove. *Papers of William G. Ely*. Private collection. Essex, CT.

*Encyclopedia Virginia*, s.v. "Libby Prison," Virginia Historical Society, publisher.

Farnsworth, Charles. Diary, letters, and documents. Personal collection of the author and attached as appendix.

Foner, Eric. *Reconstruction*. New York: Harper & Row, 1988.

Foote, Shelby. *Civil War from Sumter to Perryville*. New York: Vintage Press, 1986.

*Georgia Historical Quarterly*, 2001, 2011.

Gilbert, David. *A Walker's Guide to Harpers Ferry*. Harpers Ferry Historical Association, 1995.

Goodheart, Adam. *1861, The Civil War Awakening*. New York: Knopf, 2011.

Green, Samuel A. 1901. *Three Military Diaries*. Groton, MA, first published in Proceedings of Massachusetts Historical Society, 1898.

*Hartford Daily Currant*, 1862.

*Hartford Evening Press*, 1862.

Hearn, Chester G. *Six Years of Hell, Harpers Ferry during the Civil War*. Baton Rouge: Louisiana State University Press, 1996.

Horwitz, Tony. *Midnight Rising*. New York: Henry Holt and Company, 2011.

*Journal of American History*, 2006.

*Journal of American Studies*, 1983.

LaConti, Matthew H., "William Buckingham: Leading Connecticut and the Republican Party through the Civil War." Master's thesis, Southern Connecticut State University, 2009, available on line through ProQuest.

Mahon, Michael G., ed. *Winchester Divided*. Mechanicsburg, PA: Stackpole Books, 2002.

Marshall, Benjamin Tinkham. *A Modern History of New London County, Connecticut.* New York: Lewis Historical Publishing Company, 1922.

Maryland Historical Society, Baltimore, "Divided Voices: Maryland in the Civil War," exhibit, 2012.

*McClure's Magazine*, 1904.

McPherson, James. *Battle Cry of Freedom*. New York: Oxford University Press, 2003.

*Meriden Daily Journal*, 1892.

Meriden Sesquicentennial Committee. *150 Years of Meriden*, 1956.

Mount Clare Museum House website. 2012.

National Archives, Military Record of Charles Farnsworth, First Connecticut Cavalry Volunteers.

National Park Service, *18th Connecticut Regiment Roster.*

Néely, Mark E. *The Fate of Liberty, Abraham Lincoln and Civil Liberties.* New York: Barnes & Noble, 2007.

*New Georgia Encyclopedia*, s.v. "Reconstruction in Georgia."

*New Haven Daily Palladium*, 1862.

*New Haven Evening Registe,r* 1887.

*New Haven Register,* 1880.

*New York Herald Tribune*, 1867.

*Norwich Aurora*, 1867.

*Norwich Courie,r* 1845.

Norwich District Marriage Records, 1865.

Norwich District Probate Records, 1853, 1880, 1894, 1897.

*Norwich Morning Bulletin*, 1865, 1897, 1909, 1914, 1935.

Norwich Town Clerk, "Wills," 1897.

Noyalas, Jonathon A. *Stonewall Jackson's 1862 Valley Campaign*. Charleston: The History Press, 2010.

Nye, R. Glen. *Farnsworth Memorial II*, 1974.

Olmstead, Frederick Law Collection, "Papers of Mary Cornelia Talbot," American University Library, Washington, DC.

Perkins, Mary E. *Genealogical Notes*. Otis Library, Norwich.

Perry, Bliss. *Life and Letters of Henry Lee Higginson*. Boston: The Atlantic Monthly Press, 1921.

Prince, K. Stephen. "Stories of the South: The Cultural Retreat from Reconstruction." PhD diss., Yale University 2010.

Richmond Civil War Centennial Committee. *Libby Prison*. Richmond, VA., 1961-65.

Sanderson, James M. *My Record in Rebeldom*. New York: Sibell Publishing, 1865.

*Savannah Daily News & Herald*, 1866, 1867.

Sheads, Scott S. and Daniel Carroll Toomey. *Baltimore during the Civil War*. Linthicum, MD: Toomey Press, 2008.

Smith, Julia Floyd. 1985. *Slavery and Rice Culture in Low Country Georgia 1750-1860*. Knoxville, Tennessee: University of Tennessee Press.

Smithsonian American History Collection. Washington, D.C.

*Springfield Republican* 1897.

Stanley, Bill. *The 9-Mile Square*. Norwich, CT: The Norwich Historical Society, 2005.

Starr, Stephen Z. *The Union Cavalry in the Civil War*, vols. I-III. Baton Rouge and London: Louisiana State University Press, 1979.

*Stedman's City Directory, Norwich*, 1861.

Sullivan, Buddy. *From Beautiful Zion to Red Bird Creek, A History of Bryan County, Georgia*. Bryan County Board of Supervisors, 2000.

Swiggart, Carolyn Clay. *Shades of Gray*. Darian, CT: Two Bytes Publishing, Ltd., 1999.

Thompson, C. Mildred. *Reconstruction in Georgia*. Savannah: Beehive Press, 1972.

US Army Military History Institute Archives. "Northwest Corner Civil War Round Table Collection," Carlisle Barracks, PA.

US Bureau of Census. *Norwich, CT*: 1840, 1850, 1860, 1870; *Danbury, CT*: 1860; *Woodstock, CT*: 1860; *Putnam, CT*: 1870; *Bryan County, GA*: 1860.

US Geological Survey, Burroughs, GA., 1979.

US Interior Department, Commissioner of Pensions. 1891.

US Sanitary Commission. *Narrative of Privation and Sufferings of United*

*States Officers and Soldiers While Prisoners of War in the Hands of the Rebel Authorities.*Washington, DC: King & Baird Publishers, 1864.

Van Dusen, Albert E. *Connecticut.* New York: Random House, 1961.

Voynick, Stephen M. *Colorado Gold, From the Pike's Peak Rush to the Present.* Missoula, MT: Mountain Press, 1992.

Warshauer, Matthew. *Connecticut in the American Civil War.* Middletown, CT: Wesleyan University Press, 2011.

*Wikipedia,* s.v. "Franz Sigel;" "Belle Isle, Virginia;" "Robert C. Schenck;" "Norwich, Connecticut;" "Fort Sumter;" "Gillmore Medal."

Williams, Stephen W. *The Genealogy and History of the Williams Family in America.* Greenfield, MA: Merriam & Mirick, 1847.

Witt, John Fabian. *Lincoln's Code.* New York: Free Press, 2012.

Wongsrichanalai, Kanisorn, "The Burden of Their Class: College-Educated New Englanders and Leadership in the Civil War Era." PhD diss., University of Virginia, 2010, available on line through ProQuest.

Zon, Calvin Goddard, ed. *The Good Fight That Didn't End Henry P. Goddard's Accounts of the Civil War and Peace.* Columbia: The University of South Carolina Press, 2008.

# Index to Text and Comments

# Open Book Editions
## A Berrett-Koehler Partner

Open Book Editions is a joint venture between Berrett-Koehler Publishers and Author Solutions, the market leader in self-publishing. There are many more aspiring authors who share Berrett-Koehler's mission than we can sustainably publish. To serve these authors, Open Book Editions offers a comprehensive self-publishing opportunity.

## A Shared Mission

Open Book Editions welcomes authors who share the Berrett-Koehler mission—Creating a World That Works for All. We believe that to truly create a better world, action is needed at all levels—individual, organizational, and societal. At the individual level, our publications help people align their lives with their values and with their aspirations for a better world. At the organizational level, we promote progressive leadership and management practices, socially responsible approaches to business, and humane and effective organizations. At the societal level, we publish content that advances social and economic justice, shared prosperity, sustainability, and new solutions to national and global issues.

Open Book Editions represents a new way to further the BK mission and expand our community. We look forward to helping more authors challenge conventional thinking, introduce new ideas, and foster positive change.

For more information, see the Open Book Editions website:
http://www.iuniverse.com/Packages/OpenBookEditions.aspx

Join the BK Community! See exclusive author videos, join discussion groups, find out about upcoming events, read author blogs, and much more!
http://bkcommunity.com/

CPSIA information can be obtained at www.ICGtesting.com
Printed in the USA
BVOW05s1556240314

348583BV00004B/12/P

9 781491 719633